Praise for *Power Shift*

Deeply researched and filled with stories and historical details that will surprise and inform even the most experienced observers, *Power Shift* is the definitive account of the rise of Latino politics in Los Angeles and California. Neatly weaving between timelines and personalities, Ayón and Pla never shy away from the conflicts and tensions that characterized this evolution — but they also note that the "Latino century" is open to all comers. This is a compelling and important read that both captures the past and provides a blueprint to a more inclusive future.

— **Manuel Pastor**, Professor of Sociology and American Studies & Ethnicity
at the University of Southern California and author of
*State of Resistance: What California's Dizzying Descent and Remarkable
Resurgence Mean for America's Future*

The rising prominence of the Latino community in California politics is quite possibly the most important driver of California's transformation from a red to blue state. And yet, until now the story has not been told with the insight and detail that it deserves. Ayón and Pla have done a masterful job of weaving the story together in an entertaining and insightful way.

— **Bruce E. Cain**, Charles Louis Ducommun Professor in Humanities
and Sciences at Stanford University and author of
Democracy More or Less: America's Political Reform Quandary

Through engaging, deeply researched profiles of key figures in Latino politics, Ayón and Pla tell the critical story of California politics in the twenty-first century — the rise of Latino power at the ballot box and in the halls of government. *Power Shift* is both an important piece of historical research and a great read. It's the story of a transformation that has already changed politics in America's largest state and that will soon change the nation.

— **Lisa García Bedolla**, Director, Institute of Governmental Studies at the
University of California, Berkeley and author of *Latino Politics*

MUST READ: Masterfully written, *Power Shift* shows how Latinos in California, in their quest for the American dream, developed the political and economic might to transform politics in what is now the world's fifth-largest economy. Pla and Ayón's remarkable historical account is designed to educate and engage a new generation facing one of the greatest challenges to our democracy in the devastating aftermath of Trump's election. This is a much-needed book.

— **Maxine Waters**, U.S. Repr̶e̶s̶e̶n̶t̶a̶t̶i̶v̶e̶ ̶ 's
ct

California Latinos are transforming the nation — politically and culturally. *Power Shift* is essential reading for anyone who wants to understand how Latinos used electoral politics to challenge the status quo and amplify the voice of Latinos across the state. Ayón and Pla trace power through 10 figures who went on to not only change California but whose impact can be felt throughout the United States. Ultimately, this book reframes the influence of Latinos in electoral politics by mapping out key moments that render power visible and provide a roadmap for future leaders.

— **Mireya Loza**, Curator, National Museum of American History and author of
*Defiant Braceros: How Migrant Workers Fought for Racial, Sexual,
and Political Freedom*

California is different, and Ayón and Pla illustrate why. Latino politics are at the basis of what makes California work: a combination of tolerance, social justice, and pioneering progressive politics mixed with realism. Ayón and Pla show how progressive politics function successfully in the real world. They identify the grassroots political organizations with the power and the vision to work with corporations to lead California not only to social, ecological, and economic reform, but also to prosperity. If we need a model of how to make American politics and society work in a challenging future, this book shows that Latinos have already designed it.

— **Jacob Soll**, Professor of Philosophy and History at the
University of Southern California and author of
The Reckoning: Financial Accountability and the Rise and Fall of Nations

Here's the real story of how Latinos turned big numbers into real power. California is, in many ways, an experiment. Latino leaders are flexing California's newfound political muscle as the state has become a symbol of the resistance to Trump. Cesar Chavez was right when he said, "We've looked into the future and the future is ours." This inspiring and insightful book explains how we got here and why America will look more and more like California — and more like us.

— **Jorge Ramos**, News Anchor, Univision and author of
Stranger: The Challenge of a Latino Immigrant in the Trump Era

Power Shift takes you inside an epic story of our times, capturing what George Pla calls "California's Latino political genius," a force for progress in America that could only have arisen in Los Angeles. I know because I was there and had the privilege of both seeing and being part of some of the transformations that Latino leadership based in LA contributed to — expanding Civil Rights, empowering LA's Eastside, and integrating labor and Democratic Party politics. The "progressive Latino political tradition" shaped through the efforts of leaders portrayed in this book is working today to defend and advance American democracy, even at this difficult time in our nation's history.

— **Mickey Kantor**, former Secretary of Commerce and
U.S. Trade Representative

POWER SHIFT:
How Latinos in California Transformed Politics in America

POWER SHIFT:
How Latinos in California Transformed Politics in America

David R. Ayón and George L. Pla

Berkeley Public Policy Press
Institute of Governmental Studies
University of California, Berkeley
2018

Library of Congress Cataloging-in-Publication Data

Names: Ayón, David R., author. | Pla, George L., author.
Title: Power shift : how Latinos in California transformed politics in America / David R.
  Ayón and George L. Pla.
Description: Berkeley : Berkeley Public Policy Press, [2018] | Includes bibliographical
  references and index.
Identifiers: LCCN 2018010110 | ISBN 9780877724568 (pbk.) | ISBN 9780877724575
  (hardback)
Subjects: LCSH: Hispanic Americans--California--Los Angeles--Politics and government.
  | Hispanic Americans--California--Los Angeles--Social conditions. | Power (Social
  sciences)--California--Los Angeles. | California--Politics and government. | Los An-
  geles (Calif.)--Politics and government. | United States--Politics and government.
Classification: LCC F869.L89 A237 2018 | DDC 979.4/9400468--dc23
LC record available at https://lccn.loc.gov/2018010110

We dedicate this work to our living "principals" —
Esteban Torres, Richard Alatorre, Art Torres, Gloria Molina,
Richard Polanco, Maria Elena Durazo, Gilbert Cedillo, and
Antonio Villaraigosa — and to the memory of
Edward Roybal and Miguel Contreras,
heroes all.

Contents

Foreword

By Leon E. Panetta

Power Shift is part of the great American story of the struggle for equality in our democracy, a rich and layered account that resonates with moments in my own life. Many familiar with my service in the Clinton and Obama administrations may not know I was born to immigrant parents in Depression-era California, that I was a first-generation college student, or that I served in Congress for years alongside fellow Representatives Edward Roybal and Esteban Torres of Southern California. The rise of Latino leaders such as these former colleagues of mine and others are captured in this book by my old friend George Pla and his co-author David Ayón. Together they have woven a rare and sensitively human narrative on the shaping and exercise of leadership, and on these leaders' contributions to advancing democracy and access to the American Dream — advances I witnessed, experienced, and devoted much of my career to as well.

Like these and other leaders whose "origin stories" are told between these covers, as a child, my bilingual Catholic family was my world. Reading how Esteban Torres's father was deported to Mexico in the 1930s, I could not help but recall my Nono, as Italian children call their grandpa. He was visiting us in Monterey when World War II broke out in Europe and kept him from returning home to Italy. With my parents working hard every day, Nono became my constant companion. But my world changed when the attack on Pearl Harbor brought the war to America. I had not turned four when Nono became one of some ten thousand Italian "enemy aliens" ordered to relocate further inland.

Italian Americans were largely spared the mass repatriation that Mexican Americans experienced during the Depression — not to mention the wholesale internment of Japanese Americans in camps during WWII — yet my grandfather's forced separation from our family was also a shameful instance of treatment, not as an individual based on his merits but as a category based on background. Nevertheless, it pleases me, as a former Secretary of Defense, to be able to say that Esteban Torres, Ed Roybal, and I all went on from our California childhoods to serve our country in the US Army, an essential step on our respective paths to careers in politics.

My first job after the military took me to Washington, as an aide to California Senator Tom Kuchel, a centrist Republican and a champion of civil rights. I, too, was a Republican in those days, when the Civil Rights and Voting Rights Acts passed with strong bipartisan backing. The senator put me to work on civil rights, budget, and environmental issues. Working with other staff, I helped coordinate support for the Fair Housing Act in the fateful year of 1968. When Martin Luther King, Jr. was assassinated, we saw Washington and other cities burn.

Targeted by the far-right, Sen. Kuchel got "primaried" that year. We watched the returns together in Los Angeles and learned that his political career was ending — and then the shocking news that Sen. Robert Kennedy had been shot. That fall, in spite of mental reservations, I accepted an invitation to join a transition team for the Department of Health, Education, and Welfare of the incoming Nixon administration, and then some months later the offer to head HEW's Office of Civil Rights. My legal duty was to compel the desegregation of public schools, district by district, and I expanded our focus to address segregation and discriminatory treatment of Mexican-American students in the Southwest. Nixon's men came to see me as a "bloodthirsty integrationist," and the president had me fired. I wrote a book about the administration's retreat from civil-rights enforcement and left the Republican Party, which was also moving away from its historic support for civil rights.

Ed Roybal's family was at one time Republican as well, but he, too, changed parties out of substantive policy differences. When I got to Congress in 1977, Roybal was starting his eighth term as the only Latino representative from California. But as *Power Shift* vividly recounts, Ed was in the forefront of policy reforms for educational equity, voting rights, and the coming 1980 census. In the years that followed, I came to know George, who was in Governor Jerry Brown's cabinet back in California. His range of experience, from the grassroots level in East LA to state government in Sacramento to managing Esteban Torres's campaign for Congress in 1982, and much more in the ensuing years, uniquely prepared George to join forces with scholar David Ayón to write this deeply researched and elegantly written account of the long Latino quest for inclusion.

Each generation has had to fight to prove the pledge of our forefathers that we are all "created equal." As the son of Italian immigrants, I was able to live the American dream. But as this book shows, that dream is not a gift, it is a struggle. *Power Shift* presents the journey of 10 groundbreaking Latino leaders who made that struggle, transformed politics, and gave their people a chance to live the American dream.

* * *

Leon E. Panetta served as Secretary of Defense and CIA Director under President Barack Obama, experiences he recounts (with Jim Newton) in *Worthy Fights: A Memoir of Leadership in War and Peace*. He directed the Office of Civil Rights of the Department of Health, Education, and Welfare from 1969–70, which formed the basis of his book (with Peter Gall), *Bring Us Together: The Nixon Team and the Civil Rights Retreat*, and was nine times elected to Congress from 1976–92. He left Congress in 1993 to direct the Office of Management and Budget, and then served as Chief of Staff to President Bill Clinton.

Introduction

Prelude

November 8, 2016
The Trump Shock and the Heart of the Resistance

It was the best of elections — and the worst. By the end of the day, more than 14 million Californians had cast ballots, with over four million Latino voters showing greater unity than ever. In marked contrast to the racial turmoil and polarization of two decades before — over immigration, language, and affirmative action — the results also showed Latinos to be strikingly close to most other voters. Californians loudly affirmed the values of solidarity and progress this day, taking major strides in both politics and policy, but few would sleep well that night.[1]

For the first time in history, Southern Californians headed both houses of the state legislature at the same time. Not coincidentally, both leaders were from the Los Angeles area and particularly successful members of the state's influential Latino Legislative Caucus, founded by their predecessors some 44 years earlier. More importantly, both Speaker of the Assembly Anthony Rendon and President pro Tempore of the Senate Kevin de León led their fellow Democrats this day in winning two-thirds "supermajorities" in their respective chambers — what the *Los Angeles Times* called a "rare and almost-magical status" — although they would not be sure of this for weeks, until all votes were counted.[2] Once they were, California's first-ever Latino Secretary of State Alex Padilla certified the results.[3]

Beyond this political achievement, the election marked a number of further advances for these and other Latino leaders, their communities, and the governing coalition they were a critical part of — in metropolitan Los Angeles, the state, and the country. Latinos had become the state's largest ethnic group only a couple of years before, surpassing non-Hispanic whites, and were now voting in record numbers. This time, in a genuine electoral landslide, their votes restored bilingual education and overturned two decades of mandatory English-only instruction. They also approved additional gun-safety and environmental measures, as well as further funding for schools, for healthcare, and to complete the massive Los Angeles Metro system. These choices meant more taxes for both the wealthy and for all residents, and they indicated forthright support for an activist vision of government, however unfashionable that may be in other quarters.[4] A record dozen Latinas and Latinos were sent to represent the country's largest state in Congress, helping raise total Latino representation there to a new national high.[5]

The day, however, did not have a unified Latino narrative, but two divergent ones. This best of elections had another, radically different side: Donald Trump — bitterly opposed by an overwhelming majority of Latinos — won the Electoral College and thus the forty-fifth presidency of the United States. An abundantly shared expectation of continuity in national administrations, from Obama to Clinton II, was shockingly dispelled, and a Latino exodus from the executive branch soon began. By January, Latino representation in the presidential cabinet fell to zero for the first time in decades, and established Latino policy gains at every level were set to be severely challenged.[6]

In time, it became clear that Hillary Clinton won the popular vote nationwide by nearly three million, while winning California alone by over four million. Just the number of Latinos in California who voted for Clinton exceeded her national margin over Trump. Nearly nine million California voters, some three and a half million of them Latinos — far more than in any other state — would have to come to terms with the political shock of their lives. It would be up to their elected representatives to find fitting words and a way forward.

The next morning, California's legislative leaders, the Assembly Speaker and the Senate "pro Tem," sitting atop an integrated complex of institutional and Latino political power built laboriously over decades, exercising influence on the country and increasingly in the world, declared in a joint statement in English and Spanish: "Today, we woke up feeling like strangers in a foreign land, because yesterday Americans expressed their views on a pluralistic and democratic society that are clearly inconsistent with the values of the people of California."[7] Such was American Latino leaders' opening response to the Trump shock of 2016.

A war of words erupted. Trump charged that he only lost the national popular vote due to millions of illegal voters in this very state. California's top elections official, its Latino secretary of state, repeatedly went on national television to repudiate the baseless allegation. Battle lines emerged. The legislative leaders and the governor developed aggressive plans of resistance to the incoming Trump regime and announced them to the world, as did the mayor of Los Angeles. The wise and crafty septuagenarian governor showed his ability to deliver for the constituency most challenged by Trump. Jerry Brown nominated Xavier Becerra — a veteran Democratic leader in Congress representing Los Angeles — to be the first Latino attorney general in the history of the state.[8] Becerra was charged with defending California's inclusive, activist-government policies and exceedingly diverse population against the designs of the new administration in Washington.

The legislators made national headlines the next day by hiring the immediate former US attorney general, Eric Holder, to assist in fortifying California's laws and policies against the power of his former Justice Department, now coming under Trump's control. LA's mayor, Eric Garcetti, himself the Spanish-speaking grandson of Mexican immigrants, helped fashion the "Los Angeles Justice Fund" for immigrant legal defense, with contributions from the city, the county, and foundations, and began working with city council to fashion laws to protect immigrants from federal repatriation pressures.⁹ The battle — many battles — would soon begin.

***

IN THE SPAN OF A SHORT LIFETIME, LESS THAN 70 YEARS, LATINOS IN CALIFORNIA had gone from having no significant representation, to holding leadership and power at the highest levels of state and metropolitan government, as well as being substantially involved in national policymaking. At the beginning of this story, in the mid-twentieth century, Latinos were "disposable people" living in "expendable neighborhoods."¹⁰ They were not only unrepresented and unconsulted, they were subject to racialized treatment in education, employment, housing, health, law enforcement, land use, and urban renewal, as well as in the siting of dumps, freeways, and other public works. Movie theaters and public swimming pools were segregated. But now the old threat of a new administration hostile to immigrants generally, and to Mexican immigrants in particular, could be met with the strength of a politically awakened community and leaders armed with institutional authority and clout. These leaders could speak not only for their Latino constituents but on behalf of the most populous state in the country and, as they were fond of pointing out, the sixth largest economy in the world.

That Latino public officials in California were now so empowered to openly resist a newly elected and unusually aggressive president on the national stage was a revelation to many, and one that marked the most recent and perilous height of a dramatic journey. This was the culmination of a hard-fought, epochal shift in political power in a state so large and dynamic that it weighed heavily on the shape and direction of the country. *Power Shift* traces this journey through 10 key figures who paved the way and laid the foundation for California's resistance to Trump today.

These women and men, all based in Los Angeles, had to not only overcome their community's historic marginalization and subordination, but they also had to weather periodic waves of social and political reaction to the progress they were able to effect. They knew well that their community's progress was a complex and cumulative, not linear, quest. The split-level narrative of the 2016 elections in California and the nation was hardly new to them: major setbacks on lofty electoral levels had repeatedly come after, were paired with, or were soon followed by solid advances on the ground. Latino empowerment and even simply the increased presence of Latinos fostered a recurring backlash to the community's rise and the social and political changes that came with it. The leaders of the journey of Latino empowerment, the inventors and engineers of professional, progressive Latino politics in the crucible of urban Southern California, repeatedly had to withstand and overcome these periods of adversity.

That leadership lineage began with Ed Roybal, the stern pioneer of collective Latino political action and the first Hispanic officeholder of twentieth-century

California. Elected to the Los Angeles City Council in 1949, Roybal — who experienced segregation, police abuse, and housing discrimination, and took them on — went on to become the state's first Latino member of Congress, where in his 30 years of service he founded the Congressional Hispanic Caucus, reformed voting rights, and changed how the country counts its people. Known for decades as *El Viejo,* "the Old Man" of Eastside politics, Roybal was the onetime youthful political pioneer who lived and saw it all.

Just within his adult life as a political leader, this latest drama of 2016 would have reminded Roybal of the experiences of 1952, which marked the end of the New Deal that shaped him. The country moved decidedly to the right in the elections of that year and brought down the curtain on the extended Roosevelt era. Decades of activist government — grappling with economic depression, war, and the rebuilding of the world — had indelibly shaped the outlook of the earliest Latino political pioneers, but they had scant ability to resist the rightward tide that changed control of Congress and swept a genial former general into the presidency by a landslide — accompanied by a young and ambitiously red-baiting running mate from Southern California.

Twenty years earlier, Franklin Roosevelt had taken office in the midst of the Great Depression, when local authorities — set in motion by the outgoing Hoover administration's Department of Labor — were arranging and pressing for the repatriation of hundreds of thousands of Mexican immigrants and their US-born children. That campaign, which was particularly intense in Los Angeles, came to an end the following year, and the Roosevelt administration would declare a "Good Neighbor Policy" toward Mexico and Latin America. But in the wake of the country's swing to the right in 1952–53, the new Eisenhower administration soon launched "Operation Wetback," to even more forcefully apprehend and deport hundreds of thousands of undocumented Mexican migrant workers. At that time, Ed Roybal was the only Latino elected official holding significant public office in all of California, as a second-term city council member from the Eastside of Los Angeles. He would take a stand against discrimination in employment and housing, against the destruction of neighborhoods without consultation, against police abuse and red-baiting, but most often found himself the lone vote on these issues in the council.

The shocking setback combined with advances of 2016 was also reminiscent of 1980, when politically active Latinos were similarly stunned by an unforeseen, radical change in national administration, an upset that set off its own exodus from Washington. The election of Ronald Reagan sent key Latinos back to LA, including Esteban Torres and Gloria Molina, who had been serving in the Jimmy Carter administration. But the overturning of the White House coincided with far-reaching policy advances that would not be undone, such as the revised US Census for that year, which for the first time mandated a "complete count" of all Hispanics in the country. And in California, this was the year that an audacious coup in the Assembly marked a historic breakthrough for both African-American and Latino political power, in the form of Willie Brown's speakership in league with Richard Alatorre. The numbers provided by the new census and Alatorre's new position in the state Assembly made possible a redrawing of electoral districts that favored Latinos in both the short and long term. By the very next election, Latino representation in Congress of LA's Greater Eastside would triple, most notably including the election of Esteban Torres, while Gloria Molina would win an Assembly race to become the first Latina ever to serve in that body. The onset of the Reagan era had not halted the march of Latino political empowerment, nor had Nixon before him or Pete Wilson and Newt Gingrich afterwards.

In fact, the political empowerment of Latinas on the Eastside that began in this era continued, with Molina becoming the first to be elected to the LA City Council in 1987. Lucille Roybal-Allard, Ed Roybal's daughter, succeeded Molina in the state Assembly and then became the first Mexican-American woman elected to Congress in 1992, the "Year of the Woman" in American politics. Latina representation in the Assembly tripled that year, with the election of Martha Escutia, Hilda Solis, and Diane Martinez, all from the Greater Eastside.

Then there was 1994 — dubbed the "Year of the Angry White Man" — when control of the US House of Representatives changed hands for the first time in 40 years. Following that election, the new Republican Speaker proceeded to try to dismantle the ethnic caucuses of the House, including the Congressional Hispanic Caucus that Ed Roybal founded in the 1970s.[11] Meanwhile, in California that year the sitting governor and a majority of voters pushed back against the rise of the Latino population by passing a draconian package of anti-immigrant measures, and the Latinos' preferred party, the Democrats, lost control of the California Assembly.[12] These setbacks resulted from the familiar backlash to advances Latinos had been making over the previous two decades, which included signal achievements of state legislators such as Richard Alatorre, Art Torres, and Richard Polanco, who between them had founded and grown the California Chicano/Latino Legislative Caucus, helped make possible the long, historic speakership of Willie Brown, and redrawn the electoral map of the state.

Governor Pete Wilson's anti-immigrant campaign in 1994 fostered the first organized, mass resistance to repatriation pressures in American history, focused in Los Angeles, in which California's premier political champion of immigrant rights, Gilbert Cedillo, and Molina, by then on the county board of supervisors, played leading roles. Two years later the Assembly was retaken and resurgent Latino political muscle, led by Polanco, engineered the first Latino speakership in the chamber's history. A series of Latino Assembly Speakers would follow, and Latino legislative strength would grow to the point that it could dismantle all anti-immigrant state legislation and proceed to lead the nation in establishing immigrant-friendly policies. LA as well would transform into an immigrant-friendly town, with an officially mandated "living wage," and ultimately its first Latino mayor since the 1800s, Antonio Villaraigosa, who would lead advances in education, transportation, public safety, healthcare, and the environment. These achievements were largely a result of the accelerated organization and empowerment of the burgeoning immigrant component of the Los Angeles Latino community, led by labor leaders Maria Elena Durazo and Miguel Contreras, who would be dubbed, "The unlikely power couple that remade L.A. politics."[13]

The dual narrative continues. In spite of leading the country, and in many ways the world, in combining growth with increasingly aggressive environmental measures, and in having overcome severe social divisions and even unrest, California's ability to address the very real challenges that remain — of poverty, inequality, housing, and homelessness — is further challenged by a political offensive directed from Washington that seeks to roll back advances already won. But the historic creators of Latino empowerment who continue to lead in the key positions they currently hold or are pursuing, and the new generation of Latino leaders now serving in Sacramento, bring to the fight and to the continuing journey a proven ability to act, to innovate, to legislate, and to resist. Together they continue a modern tradition of and commitment to sustained progress that is stronger than the designs of those who seek to dismantle, withdraw, enclose, banish, bespoil, and suppress.

Introducing *Los Diez* — The Ten

FROM ED ROYBAL'S FIRST LOSING CAMPAIGN IN THE 1940s, to Antonio Villaraigosa's breakthrough mayoral win in the 2000s, these 10 key leaders effected a historic shift in power, reshaping politics in California and building a base in Los Angeles from which to change America. They were sometimes rivals, partners, allies, and adversaries — and in one case even lovers, after also having been other things to each other. All descended from settlers and immigrants who ventured north from Mexico, and all ended up one way or another in Los Angeles. Educated in American schools, there came a time, or several, when they caught the eye of influential people looking for potential leaders, whether for their underrepresented community or fellow workers. Sometimes they were tapped, chosen, urged onto paths of leadership, sometimes they struck out on their own, or with another. In every case their journeys intersected, sometimes collided, and put them at the forefront of efforts by Latinos to change the country and their place in it.

***

EDWARD ROSS ROYBAL and ESTEBAN EDWARD TORRES landed as children with their families in polyglot Boyle Heights in the 1920s and '30s. Although from starkly different New Mexico and Arizona backgrounds, they were similarly brought to Los Angeles, the biggest city to the west, by parents escaping hard times. Each having launched innovative efforts as young men to organize and uplift their adopted communities, they pursued divergent paths until decades later they wound up serving in Congress together as allies.

Congressional Hispanic Caucus on US Capitol steps, circa 1985. Edward Roybal was principal founder of the CHC in 1976. Esteban Torres joined him in Congress in 1983. They, along with the other California member at the time, Matthew "Marty" Martinez, are front-row right. Others in front, from left, are Representatives Henry B. González of Texas, and Manuel Luján, Jr. and Bill Richardson of New Mexico. Behind them from left to right are Jaime B. Fuster, Resident Commissioner of Puerto Rico, nonvoting member; Robert Garcia of New York; Tony Coelho of California, of Portuguese descent; and Ron de Lugo, Territorial Delegate of the US Virgin Islands, also a nonvoting member. (The first Latina, Ileana Ros-Lehtinen of Florida, was not elected to Congress until 1989.)

Like hundreds of thousands of other Latinos, Roybal was drafted and served during World War II. When he left the army, he pursued a professional career as a health educator combating the perennial scourge of tuberculosis. His role in public outreach gave him a professional profile and got him noticed. Just over a year out of uniform, with a wife and a growing family to support, Roybal was summoned by community leaders, successful suits in business and law, who he had organized into a committee to advise and support his countywide work. They wanted him to run for city council. No Hispanic had been elected to any significant office in all of California since the 1800s. Roybal objected at first, but they pressed and he relented. Roybal ran and promptly lost but did not stop running. Instead of turning back, he figured out how to win on a second try. Just two years later, in 1949, on the ballot again facing the same incumbent, Roybal won in a blowout, and served at city hall for 13 years, before moving on to Congress for another 30, where he would make his mark on the country.

Esteban Torres, November 2015, a decade after Roybal had passed away; photographed at home for a Los Angeles Times story on the mass-deportation plan Donald Trump had proposed in a forum with Republican presidential candidates that month. When Torres was a child in an Arizona mining town, his Mexican-immigrant father was deported and never heard from again. (Photo by Barbara Davidson. © 2015, Los Angeles Times. *Reprinted with permission.)**

Esteban Torres also served in the army, in Europe at the start of the Cold War, then took advantage of the GI Bill to study art and education. He was a talented artist, but marriage and family led him to a job as a welder on the assembly line at the Chrysler plant near Maywood. There, leftwing Jewish activists in the United Automobile Workers, Communist Party members and sympathizers, noticed him. The Jewish lefties were shunned at the plant and in the union they had helped to build, and themselves were barred from union posts. They urged Torres to stand for shop steward, which he did. Soon he was offered a staff job as a regional organizer. Five years later, the great Walter Reuther himself, the United Auto Workers head who purged the union of communists, heard Torres speak during a summer training seminar and offered him a position directing the UAW's growing presence in Latin America. Eventually, Torres would be the first of our 10 power shift leaders to rise through the ranks of the labor movement and attain elected office — but not the last. He would revitalize East LA, return to Europe as a US ambassador, serve in Congress, and play an unexpected role in reinventing US relations with Mexico — and he never stopped practicing his art.

***

RICHARD ALATORRE and ARTHUR "ART" TORRES burst on the California political scene in the early 1970s, jarring the staid state Capitol like an aftershock of the tumultuous late 1960s. With their hair, smart suits, and swagger, Alatorre and Torres marked the arrival of the hip, new *Chicano* generation, urban Mexican Americans

---

* Kate Linthicum, "The Dark, Complex History of Trump's Model for His Mass Deportation Plan," *Los Angeles Times*, November 13, 2015.

born and raised on LA's Eastside. They stood out not only from the vast majority of the 80-member state Assembly, historically dominated by rural, white Californians, but also from the few older and decidedly unflashy Mexican-American legislators from suburban districts. And they stood together, pushing an assertive Chicano agenda and supporting the even flashier African-American San Francisco Assemblyman Willie Brown in his first, premature bid to become Speaker. Their combined impact led the Sacramento crowd to senselessly dub Alatorre and Torres "the Bobbsey Twins" of the legislature, missing their deep differences.

The dark, gruff, often foul-mouthed Alatorre cut a curious figure in his lean, three-piece suits, while the quick-witted and smooth-talking Torres confounded with an intimidating verbal facility never before seen in a "Mexican." The streetwise Alatorre set basketball records at Garfield High in unincorporated East LA, and hung with the few black students at the then overwhelmingly white Cal State LA. Working on a last term paper as graduation approached, Alatorre was sent downtown by his genteel Mexican-American professor to interview a real activist Chicano leader, head of the benign-sounding Foundation for Mexican American Studies. Phil Montez strode in late, oblivious to his scheduled appointment, and came upon this college kid waiting to see him. Montez reflexively spat, "Who the f*** are *you,* and what the f*** do you want?"

Montez's style, and its contrast with that of Alatorre's proper college professor, appeared like a fork in the road to a graduating senior with no plan or direction. The conversation went on long beyond the appointed time, for the rest of the day. Alatorre left the organization's office with his first gig as an education policy analyst. He had been yanked into the fast-emerging and often fierce 1960s world of Latino policy and politics that would become his life. Elected to the state Assembly in the 1970s, Alatorre founded the California Chicano Legislative Caucus — as it was then called — and co-authored the state's historic charter of farmworker rights, the California Agricultural Labor Relations Act. At the dawn of the 1980s, as head of the Assembly's Elections and Reapportionment Committee, Alatorre set in motion the sustained and far-reaching growth in Latino representation in California, but to do so took audacity without parallel in state politics — enough to pull off a palace coup.

Though it began in Boyle Heights as well, the route Art Torres took into politics was quite different. His progress, from leading Bible study to running for class president and winning awards at statewide speech and debate tournaments, seemed destined for the moment when he would score a ticket out of the Eastside. Opportunity knocked when Torres was student body president of East Los Angeles College. The dean of students called him in to meet the chancellor of the new University of California, Santa Cruz, the cutting-edge experimental school up north; they urged Torres to transfer and finish college in the company of freethinkers and towering redwoods. At UC Santa Cruz, Torres founded student government at Stevenson College and became its first president. He developed life-long relationships, and on regular weekends in San Francisco with his well-

California State Assemblymembers Art Torres and Richard Alatorre shown backing up United Farm Workers union president Cesar Chavez around 1975, when they supported the UFW's farm labor reform bill against Governor Jerry Brown's version.

born roommate, got to know leading political families with names like Moscone, McCarthy, and Pelosi. The articulate young man, who made a deep impression everywhere he went, was said to be destined to become the first Mexican-American governor of California in the twentieth century. Torres served 20 years in the legislature, founded the Senate Toxics Committee, authored pioneering environmental legislation, and reformed the state's healthcare system. As head of the California Democratic Party for 13 years, from 1996 to 2009, Torres presided over the state's emergence as the national leader in Latino political empowerment. Together, the duo of Alatorre and Torres were key to helping turn California from historically red to thoroughly blue, and advancing Latinos on a journey from the sidelines to the political center.

* * *

Originally from unincorporated East Los Angeles, RICHARD GARCIA POLANCO and JESUS GLORIA MOLINA were activists who wound up serving on the Alatorre and Torres state Assembly staffs, and succeeded them in office in the 1980s. But unlike their predecessors, the so-called "twins" of the legislature, Polanco and Molina collided dramatically in their first run for the seat Art Torres left open in 1982. The repercussions of their rivalry lasted past the turn of the century to Villaraigosa's mayoral bid in the 2000s, shaping many other political contests along the way.

Molina got politicized at East LA College, and even walked out in solidarity with the Eastside high school students in 1968, although it cost her an exam she had scheduled that day. She went on to volunteer in the Robert Kennedy primary campaign that spring, working into the night on Election Day. Police turned her and her friends away from the Ambassador Hotel victory party without explanation. They learned of the assassination on the drive home. Polanco's political epiphany happened in a parking lot on the border between Boyle Heights and East LA. Out one morning with his young son, he stepped in to help with the United Farm Workers grape boycott. He hustled leaflets and made his pitch to

*Gloria Molina, backed by Mayor Tom Bradley, at her 1987 swearing-in, when she became the first Latina to serve on the Los Angeles City Council. (*Los Angeles Times *Photographic Archives. Collection 1429. UCLA Library Special Collections, Charles E. Young Research Library, UCLA.)*

the supermarket patrons around the lot, asking them to support Cesar Chavez and shop elsewhere. By noon, only the employees' cars were left. In shutting down the grocery store for the farmworkers, Polanco learned what he would call "the power of one."

As their youthful activism led to their own governmental careers and electoral campaigns, Polanco and Molina added to the rising foundations of Eastside Latino political power, but their eventual rivalry introduced a new pattern to numerous races in which they backed opposing candidates. Throughout the '70s Molina had developed her own base of support, a force of Chicanas who had always helped men get elected. They pressed Molina, who had been Art Torres's chief deputy in LA, to run to succeed him in the Assembly — against Richard Polanco. Molina won her maiden race, becoming the first Latina ever elected to the California Assembly. There she stood up to the governor and the Speaker of her own legislative chamber to stop the construction of a state prison in her district. She moved on to become the first Latina on the Los Angeles City Council, where she blocked the likely dismantling of LA's core Central American neighborhood and topped her career as the first Latina on the county board of supervisors, where she shifted the basic balance of power after 10 years of conservative domination.

Polanco developed into "the architect" of Latino power in Sacramento, leading the California Latino Legislative Caucus for a dozen years, and growing it into the third and often second most powerful grouping in the Capitol after the Democratic Party. He cultivated Latino electoral mobilization up and down the state, recruiting and helping elect candidates in numerous districts and planting the seeds of local Latino empowerment. In 1996, Polanco scored a political "hat trick" by making critical contributions to regaining Democratic control of the Assembly, and doubling LA County Latino representation in it, which in turn enabled him to

*Richard Polanco celebrates his election to the California State Assembly in 1986. (*Los Angeles Times *Photographic Archives. Collection 1429. UCLA Library Special Collections, Charles E. Young Research Library, UCLA.)*

engineer the first Latino speakership in state history. Cruz Bustamante of Fresno, in the Central Valley, would be followed by a series of Latino Speakers from Eastside LA, largely made possible by the strength of the caucus. But Polanco was not done. He then authored the California Voting Rights Act, fostering the creation of single-member districts in local government, where Latinos could run and win.

Richard Polanco's legacies include his efforts to recruit and elect a new wave of Latinas to public office, especially Martha Escutia — first woman to head the Latino Legislative Caucus — Deborah Ortiz, Nell Soto, Liz Figueroa, and numerous others who followed him in the state legislature.[14] As much as the two-man team of Alatorre and Art Torres before him, Polanco, in taking Latino collective political action to a new level, played a signal role in turning once-red California blue. Molina and Polanco each advanced the power shift in their own way, with their competition drawing in more fellow Eastsiders and supporters from all over, raising the profile of Latino politics throughout California and the country.

* * *

Maria Elena Durazo and Miguel Contreras, activists from migrant farmworker families who came to Los Angeles as adults, clashed the second time they met in the late 1980s. But the results of their collision were radically different from that of Polanco and Molina and would have transformative consequences for the city, labor, and Latino empowerment. Durazo got to LA in the late 1970s, having journeyed from a childhood working in the fields, through college and marriage, to starting over as a single mom. She found her way to a job as a union organizer, but the idea of helping immigrant families as a lawyer beckoned and drew her, along with Antonio Villaraigosa and others, to the activist-oriented Peoples College of Law, tucked into the MacArthur Park area just west of downtown. Her legal training led to a position at a labor law firm, which in turn introduced her to another union that lured her back into organizing — except that this union, she would discover, was not really committed to organizing, and especially not

Maria Elena Durazo and Miguel Contreras at 1997 protest march, backed by Los Angeles City Councilmember Richard Alatorre. Congressman Esteban Torres on left. (Photo by Lori Shepler. © 2014, Los Angeles Times. Reprinted with permission.)

Latina immigrant workers, people like her family. Her questioning and criticism of the union local's leadership got her fired. Pushed into taking action, Durazo decided to challenge the leaders of Local 11 of the Hotel and Restaurant Employees Union, known as HERE, in the next union election, six months away.

The success of Durazo's insurgent campaign provoked claims of election irregularities and led national union leaders to place the local under trusteeship. Miguel Contreras, an experienced union fixer formed by years with the United Farm Workers, was sent by HERE from San Francisco as one of three trustees. Arriving in Los Angeles, he found Durazo had organized a picket line to protest the trusteeship and demand recognition of her slate's election win. "She was a firebrand of a woman giving this passionate speech about workers' rights," Contreras told a reporter. "She denounced me individually. I knew then that if I was to be successful here in LA, I had to get her on my side." Working together and soon married, Contreras and Durazo inaugurated a new era of organizing, growth, and political activism at Local 11.

Within a couple of years, Durazo would win a new election and take charge of the revived local, setting a dramatic example for other heavily immigrant unions. In the 1990s, Contreras became political director of the immense but sluggish Los Angeles County Federation of Labor, and soon thereafter took the top leadership post. By the end of the decade, Contreras transformed "the Fed" into the most powerful force in LA politics and became the recognized leader of a Latino-immigrant turn in the American labor movement. Durazo and Contreras had to work together to resolve the crisis in the union that had fired Maria Elena, and in so doing they put LA at the head of an overhaul of American labor. Maria Elena Durazo and Miguel Contreras assumed the leadership of organized labor in LA County, elected a new generation of Latino officeholders, and won the "living wage" for urban workers. Along the way, they also fell in love, married, and became the city's premier turn-of-the-century Latino power couple — until Miguel's sudden death, days before their close friend Antonio was elected mayor in 2005.

***

ANTONIO RAMÓN VILLARAIGOSA and GILBERT ANTHONY CEDILLO, raised in English-speaking homes, "homies" since high school in Boyle Heights, fashioned careers in labor and politics that forged major influences old and new that had been driving Latino empowerment in Los Angeles. They were drawn into the Chicano student movement at UCLA, then into a Mexican nationalist movement that stressed solidarity with undocumented immigrants, followed by further studies at People's College of Law, along with Maria Elena Durazo, and years of union organizing. In the 1990s, support from LA's resurgent labor movement increasingly led by Durazo and Miguel Contreras allowed them to join the Eastside tradition of entering politics through election to the state Assembly.

Villaraigosa might not have made it. Involved in many fights, expelled from a Catholic high school, he simply stopped going to Roosevelt, the public school in Boyle Heights. His mother cried one morning, seeing he had come home bloodied and bearing a second tattoo. She insisted to him that he had a destiny. Having failed all his classes the previous spring when he stopped attending, he went back to school in September. A guidance counselor helped him get back on track by going to class every day and four nights a week, driving him to the SAT exam, and paying the fee. Villaraigosa managed to graduate on time and went immediately into community college. After another year of intense effort, he transferred to UCLA, fulfilling his mother's long-held dream. Villaraigosa would consider his admission to UCLA as his greatest turning point, the break that got him out of the Eastside and "opened up a whole world" to him. Relations he started developing with LA's Westside would figure critically in his political career, most of all in his campaigns for mayor.

Cedillo benefited from a more protected life, one that propelled him from an early age on a character-shaping path that culminated with performing before thousands all over the Eastside as starting quarterback at Roosevelt High. But an even more transformative experience was a youth program, a bridge to his future college years that took him across town to that whole other world of UCLA on the weekends and over the summer. After UCLA and Peoples College of Law, Cedillo became an organizer for a huge union local representing county workers, while Villaraigosa went to the unionized office of the Equal Employment Opportunity Commission, where he became shop steward among professionals, and then to the teachers' union as an organizer. Cedillo moved up from organizer to the legal department to general manager of his local, the Service Employees International Union 660. By 1994, Cedillo would be in a position to display the emerging power of Latino-led labor in LA, putting the muscle of his union behind Villaraigosa's

Los Angeles City Councilmember Gilbert Cedillo being sworn into office. (Photo by Sandoval Media/Hector Cruz Sandoval.)

run for state Assembly in the spring and, in the fall, behind the unprecedented mass protest against the anti-immigrant Proposition 187.

In 1997, after having left his union but with the all-out support of LA labor now formally led by Miguel Contreras, Cedillo followed Villaraigosa into the Assembly, where he would make immigrants' rights the cause of his career. The next year, Villaraigosa became the second Latino Speaker of the Assembly, but in so doing added substantially to his predecessor's breakthrough. Now the Latino Speaker, second only to the governor as the most powerful leader of the state, was a genuine progressive and organizer from LA's Eastside, a movement leader, not a self-described centrist from the Central Valley. When term limits made him return from Sacramento, Villaraigosa set his sights on running for mayor of Los Angeles. On the election night of his first run in 2001, Gov. Gray Davis proclaimed to the crestfallen crowd, "Antonio Villaraigosa is the future of Los Angeles" — and four years later would be proven right.[15] Villaraigosa came back in 2005 and was not only elected the first Mexican-American mayor of Los Angeles since the 1800s, but he went on to serve two terms, registering major advances in transportation, school reform, and the environment. Yet, his biggest race and challenge would still lie ahead.

Back in Sacramento, Cedillo had moved up to the state Senate until limits made him return to the Assembly for a final term. Never wavering in his commitment to win back access to driver's licenses for the undocumented, he introduced the evolving bill nine times, got it passed repeatedly, had it vetoed twice, and even got it signed into law, only for it to be repealed when the political winds shifted. Cedillo was tagged with the nickname "One Bill Gil" for his efforts in the state capital, and then joined the trek back to Los Angeles. A decade after his bill was

first signed by one governor, when Cedillo had already moved on to the LA City Council, a different governor signed the last version, which was finally allowed to go into effect. The Stanford Immigration Policy Lab later found that the issuing of 600,000 driver's licenses to the undocumented in the first year alone significantly reduced hit-and-run accidents statewide.[16] When the number of new licenses reached over a million, Cedillo adopted a new nickname: "One Mil Gil."[17]

Both men made critical contributions to consolidating the Latino power shift in California and Los Angeles. In the early 2000s, these oldest of friends and comrades diverged and remained estranged for years. But early on a cool Saturday morning in the winter of 2017, when Cedillo faced in his last reelection an unexpectedly spirited challenge from a young opponent endorsed by the *Los Angeles Times*, Villaraigosa showed up at his campaign office to give a pep talk and join the volunteers about to go out walking precincts.[18] Villaraigosa spoke to the gathering about the years Cedillo had devoted to winning back the right of all Californians to a driver's license without discrimination based on their federal immigration status, about the fresh terror immigrant families were experiencing under the new administration's intensified deportation campaign, and of the community's continuing need for leadership like Cedillo's on the city council.[19]

In this strip-mall campaign office at the corner of Daly and Main in Lincoln Heights, up the street from the old plaza and pueblo of Los Angeles, the unbroken arc of the Latino quest for empowerment in LA and California, and the progressive political tradition that is its legacy, were reaffirmed. That morning, a biblical lifetime of precisely 70 years after Edward Roybal first ran for LA City Council in 1947, these two graduates of Roosevelt High in nearby Boyle Heights, as was Roybal, were once again a team. With Cedillo's landslide reelection later that spring, the quest and the tradition would go on into the next decade, for at least another term on the council. Villaraigosa would uphold that tradition and take the quest to the highest possible level within the state, with his new campaign, which, if successful in 2018, would bring to office the first Latino governor in the history of California.

Antonio Villaraigosa and family lead procession from Cathedral of our Lady of the Angels to his 2005 mayoral inauguration at Los Angeles City Hall. (Photo by Gary Friedman. © 2018, Los Angeles Times. *Reprinted with permission.)*

* * *

PEOPLE, INSTITUTIONS, AND SOCIAL TRENDS combined to transform Los Angeles, the state, and the country since Roybal was first elected in 1949. By that time, major contours of twentieth-century California were set or settling into place: the country's largest agricultural sector, with its requisite migrant labor force; LA's water supply, which vastly enlarged the city's expanse; the movie and television industries, with their hegemonic and ethnocentric standards of beauty; the "hospitality" industry and its labor needs; the state's university system, with limited access; the incipient freeway system, which would divide and destroy particular urban neighborhoods in a particular way; the political, economic, and social elites who controlled government, business, and cultural institutions.

For most of the twentieth century, the state's Latino population mainly provided cheap and disposable — that is, deportable — labor, and sometimes expendable neighborhoods, all needed to build and sustain California's infrastructure, industries, and institutions. In the second half of the century, and into the twenty-first, California's Latinos undertook a long march of empowerment, gaining representation in government, challenging segregated and unequal public schools, entering into its universities in greater numbers, reforming working conditions and wages, redirecting public investment, combating abusive policing, and democratizing the culture. In presidential and statewide elections, California morphed from predominantly red to thoroughly and consistently blue.

Twenty-first-century Los Angeles, after a 60-year building drought, would see the dedication of one new high school after another, bearing names like Roybal, Torres, Contreras, Chavez, Mendez, Sotomayor, Cortines, and Rivera. Latinos would lead the country's second largest school district and its largest sheriff's department. LA became known for the first time in its history as an immigrant-friendly town, a labor town with a mandated "living wage," and increasingly a "rail town," with metro lines extending from the beach to far eastern and southern reaches of the county. There have been high-profile cultural consequences of Latino empowerment in LA as well. In the course of Antonio Villaraigosa's terms as mayor, a bishop born in Mexico became the first Latino to head the largest archdiocese in the country and preside over its modern, downtown cathedral complex, and a young South-American conductor would lead the city's symphony to become what the *New York Times* called "America's Most Important Orchestra. Period."[20]

There were many participants in this shift in cultural, economic, and political power. Tracing the rise of the 10 leaders in this book, and their contributions to the shift, offers a human way of understanding its origins, nature, and implications. These were the head engineers of the shift in power that we see in the form of California's determined resistance today, led by a new generation of Latinos — a second dawn of what one of the state's top analysts dubbed, perhaps prematurely, California's "Latino Century."[21] The forerunners overcame both a condition of powerlessness that dated back to the 1800s and repeated waves of reaction to the progress they were able to achieve. Their experience makes comprehensible the unhesitating commitment of today's leaders, what they are defending and fighting for, the tradition they are upholding, and the clout they bring to the fight — a contest between the greatest backlash Latinos have ever seen and the most formidable power they have ever had to wield.

Notes

1. Final official results from California Secretary of State; characterization of volume of California Latino vote derived from National Election Pool (NEP) exit poll estimates for the state; characterization of Latino voter solidarity based on Latino Decisions 2016 Election Eve Poll, http://www.latinovote2016.com/app/. Closeness to non-Latino vote based on official results.

2. The President pro Tempore (or simply "the pro Tem") of the California Senate is majority leader and functional equivalent of the Speaker of the Assembly. Although formally the Senate's "president," the lieutenant governor plays no substantive role in the California Senate except for being authorized to vote to break a tie. See California State Legislature, "Leadership," at www.legislature.cav.gov/the_state_legislature/leadership_and_caucuses/

leadership.html. On supermajorities, see "California's Legislature Should Use Its Super-majority Power Judiciously," *Los Angeles Times*, December 5, 2016, http://www.latimes.com/opinion/editorials/la-ed-democrats-supermajority-20161130-story.html.

3. Anthony Rendon was elected to the California State Assembly (District 63) in 2012 and became Speaker in March 2016; Kevin de León represents California Senate District 24 and became Senate president pro tempore in October 2014, serving until March 2018. Alex Padilla was elected secretary of state of California in 2014.

4. Proposition 58, developed by Sen. Ricardo Lara as Senate Bill 1174, established the "California Non-English Languages Allowed in Public Education Act," repealing major provisions of the 1998 Proposition 227 "English in Public Schools." Proposition 63 mandated background checks for the purchase of ammunition; Proposition 67 banned plastic single-use carryout bags; Proposition 51 authorized $9 billion in state bonds for schools and education; Proposition 52 secured continuing hospital-fee funding for the state's Medicaid program; Proposition 55 extended personal income-tax increases on incomes over $250,000, funding public schools, community colleges, and California Medicaid (Medi-Cal); Proposition 56 increased tobacco taxes, providing additional revenue for health-related programs; Los Angeles County Measure M extended and increased sales taxes, increasing revenue for the Metropolitan Transportation Authority. See Ballotpedia.org for all.

5. On increased Latino representation in Congress, see NALEO Educational Fund, "Election 2016: Races to Watch," https://d3n8a8pro7vhmx.cloudfront.net/naleo/pages/680/attachments/original/1476779831/RTW-2016-5.pdf.

6. After reported pressure and efforts to include a Latino in the new cabinet failed during the transition, an unexpected opportunity emerged when Trump's original nominee for secretary of labor was withdrawn in mid-February and replaced by Alexander Acosta, son of Cuban immigrants and a law-school dean in Miami.

7. "Joint Statement from California Legislative Leaders on Result of Presidential Election," November 9, 2016, Press Release, sd24.senate.ca.gov.

8. California's attorney general, Kamala Harris, was elected to the US Senate to succeed the retiring Barbara Boxer; this left her office to be filled by the governor, subject to confirmation by the state Senate.

9. Dakota Smith and Cindy Carcamo, "Responding to Trump, L.A. Proposes $10-Million Legal Defense Fund for Immigrants Facing Deportation," December 19, 2016, http://www.latimes.com/local/lanow/la-me-ln-lafund-20161219-story.html.

10. Sanchez, "Disposable People, Expendable Neighborhoods."

11. Representative Newt Gingrich led the Republican takeover of the House of Representatives in the 1994 midterm elections with a national platform called the "Contract with America." Once in power the following year, the new Republican majority eliminated funding for Legislative Support Organizations including the Congressional Hispanic, Black, and Women's Caucuses. In 1996, the same Congress passed the "Personal Responsibility and Work Opportunity Reconciliation Act" that denied federal welfare and health benefits to recent legal immigrants.

12. Governor Pete Wilson embraced Proposition 187 as the main platform of his re-election campaign in 1994. Dubbed the "Save Our State" initiative, this ballot measure

required proof of citizenship or legal immigration status for all public services beyond emergency medical attention. Wilson won and the proposition passed by substantial margins, although the latter was later ruled unconstitutional in federal court.

13. Harold Meyerson, "The Unlikely Power Couple That Remade L.A. Politics," *Los Angeles Times*, November 8, 2014, http://www.latimes.com/opinion/op-ed/la-oe-meyerson-durazo-contreras-20141109-story.html.

14. Including Diane Martinez, Denise Moreno Ducheny, Eloise Gómez Reyes, Blanca Rubio, and Sarah Reyes.

15. James Rainey, "Hahn Coasts to Victory: Latino Turnout Can't Carry Villaraigosa," *Los Angeles Times*, June 6, 2001, http://articles.latimes.com/2001/jun/06/news/mn-31987/2.

16. Lueders et al., "Providing Driver's Licenses," 4114.

17. See Tatiana Sanchez, "California surpasses one million driver's licenses for undocumented immigrants," *East Bay Times*, April 4, 2018, https://www.eastbaytimes.com/2018/04/04/california-issues-1-millionth-drivers-license-to-undocumented-immigrants/.

18. In the first-round city election on March 7, 2017, Cedillo was forced into a runoff held on May 16, which he won by a landslide with approximately 70 percent of the vote. Between the two elections, his opponent, Joe Bray-Ali, lost several of his endorsements, including that of the *Times*, when offensive statements he had made on "a provocative website" came to light, to which he responded with a videotaped "litany of admissions." A voter-approved change in the city election schedule meant that Cedillo and other incumbents who won reelection in 2017 would serve extended, five-and-a-half-year terms, through the end of 2022. See Dakota Smith, et al., "L.A. City Council: Cedillo Wins Reelection," *Los Angeles Times*, May 17, 2017, http://www.latimes.com/local/lanow/la-me-ln-city-council-races-20170516-story.html.

19. An informal video recording of the campaign gathering was posted on Villaraigosa's Facebook page later that day, February 25, 2017.

20. Zachary Woolfe, "Los Angeles Has America's Most Important Orchestra. Period," *The New York Times*, April 18, 2017, https://www.nytimes.com/2017/04/18/arts/music/los-angeles-has-americas-most-important-orchestra-period.html.

21. Phrase coined by Mark Baldassare in *A California State of Mind*; his sixth chapter is titled "The Latino Century Begins." A former professor of sociology at the University of California, Irvine, Baldassare was then director of polling and other programs of the Public Policy Institute of California, of which he subsequently became president and CEO.

Part I

Boyle Heights and East Los Angeles: A New Hope

PART I

Boyle Heights and East Los Angeles: A New Hope

Dream with me of a Los Angeles that is the leading economic and cultural center in the world. As Venice was in the fifteenth century, as London was in the nineteenth century, Los Angeles can be the great global city of our century.
—Mayor Antonio Villaraigosa Inaugural Address
Los Angeles City Hall Steps
July 1, 2005

FROM THE COMING OF THE RAILROADS TO THE 1950S, waves of Midwesterners swept Southern California, many lured by boosters with a fevered dream: to realize the promise of a land that could lead the nation and the world. But the vision of Los Angeles as the premier city on the coast was invented neither by Anglo-American entrepreneurs nor by the Spanish missionaries and soldiers who, a century earlier, colonized what came to be known as the Golden State. That vision was original to Southern Californians, who took the colonial pueblo they inherited and officially raised Los Angeles to city status, making it the capital of the nineteenth-century Mexican territory of Alta California. But they were soon overwhelmed in the American-era makeover of the Southland.

In 2005, Los Angeles elected its first Mexican-American mayor since that earlier transformation. More than most of the 28 men who held the office since the last of the Mexican mayors was defeated for reelection in 1872, Antonio Villaraigosa campaigned on the promise of fully realizing the city's potential and that of its extraordinary diversity. His opportunity to act on this deeply embedded vision required a dramatic journey — for him personally, as well as for his community — from the physical, political, and cultural margins to which they had been relegated, back to the center, where power resided in the modern downtown, separated by a roaring freeway from the remains of the old pueblo.

That journey required pioneers, the first two of whom came to Southern California from lands also once part of Mexico, just to the east. They made their place where they could, on the fringe of the increasingly vast metropolis: the Eastside. There they would be shaped and infused with the mission to raise their community up and make possible a new and expanded sense of belonging; there, they would seize the opportunity to renew the old vision of a great city that would lead a great country toward a new century.

CHAPTER 1

Go West

LATINO POLITICS SNUCK INTO CONGRESS IN THE TUMULT OF THE LATE 1960s, years before anyone recognized it. In pushing legislation that established bilingual education, Hispanic Heritage Week, and a presidential cabinet committee on Hispanic issues, Edward Roybal took the first steps to develop a Latino agenda on the national stage. He advanced values and concerns rooted in centuries of his forebears' experience in New Mexico — as well as his own, starting in first grade in Los Angeles. To understand what Roybal and the other nine of our principal figures set out to do in LA, DC, and Sacramento; the impetus they gave to the quest for Latino empowerment; and the political tradition they forged over the decades, we need to capture the arc of their development, from origins to legacies, as best we can.

Before it became a volatile ingredient of the state's politics and its ongoing Latino transformation, immigration from Mexico fueled the development of twentieth-century California. But the political rise of Latinos also owes much to the attractive power of Los Angeles on Mexican Americans throughout the Southwest — not immigrants but migrants — from other states, like Ed Roybal and Esteban Torres in the 1920s and '30s, as well as from small towns in California, like Maria Elena Durazo and Miguel Contreras in the 1970s and '80s. They were drawn into what became the urban crucible of Latino social and political invention and innovation: Los Angeles.

The Roybals of New Mexico

GENERATIONS BEFORE LA WAS FOUNDED, the first Roybal — a Spanish soldier from Galicia who rose to captain in far-off New Mexico — helped restore control of that rebellious land for the Spanish crown. Ignacio de Roybal y Torrado was among the few of his compatriots on a seventeenth-century expedition who chose to stay, marrying into an already well-established Hispanic family. Over the centuries, their descendants saw control of the territory pass from Spain to newly independent Mexico to an expanding United States. Over four hundred years later, the home Don Ignacio built still stands in a village north of Santa Fe.[1]

Eduardo Roybal, later to become Edward and known as Eddie, was born in Barelas, the oldest neighborhood of Albuquerque, in the winter of 1916. Founded as a river-crossing settlement in the Spanish colonial era, more than a century before US independence, Barelas predated Albuquerque. It was later enveloped by the growing city after the railroads arrived. After decades of determined effort, New Mexico and neighboring Arizona became US states in 1912, mere territories no more. Not coincidentally, this goal was achieved the year after the US Census found that New Mexico was no longer majority Hispanic. During the long, frustrating statehood struggle, New Mexicans insisted that its Hispanic community was not really "Mexican" but rather descended from Spanish colonizers and settlers from centuries before, and that they should be referred to as *Hispanos*.

In the 1970s, an acrimonious debate emerged between Anglo and Chicano historians over whether the newly restive and assertive Mexican Americans of the late twentieth century could claim any continuity between their community and the experience of the population that had been annexed by the United States in the nineteenth century, along with the vast territory won from Mexico by war. After all, most Mexican Americans descended from later immigrants. But for the Roybals, this was a matter of family and neighborhood history. Decades later, Congressman Roybal would tell interviewers that his family could not trace their background to any place other than New Mexico.[2]

Roybal's mother Eloisa Tafoya was indeed from another family that dated to seventeenth-century colonial times, a lineage that, combined with his father's, made Ed "an aristocrat, an Hispanic Knickerbocker," according to the late dean of modern California historians, Kevin Starr.[3] But Ed's father Baudilio, like many Hispanic New Mexicans, as well as Mexican immigrants, worked for the railroad that bore the Santa Fe brand. The Atchinson, Topeka, and Santa Fe had repair shops and a roundhouse right in Barelas. By the time little Eduardo came to awareness, as the United States was emerging from World War I, Barelas was a poor barrio wedged between the rail yard, downtown, and the Rio Grande. One of the neighborhood's main streets would later be designated part of the original Route 66, twentieth-century America's fabled "mother road," directly connecting the old barrio with modern Los Angeles on maps and in the imagination.

That modest neighborhood had been home for some years to the family of future Congressman and US Senator Dionisio "Dennis" Chavez, a distant relative on Ed's mother's side who would become his greatest hero. Chavez, too, was the son of a railroad worker. Barelas would later also become home to a key predecessor of Chavez's, Octaviano Larrazolo, who served as both governor and the first Latino US senator. Both politicians established reputations as champions of New Mexico's Hispanic community. Chavez, in particular, managed to set an extraordinary example for Roybal to follow in his political career, breaking with his family's Republicanism to become a fervent New Deal Democrat and dogged advocate for Hispanic needs and interests. Ultimately a sort of historic poetry would play itself out, when Roybal won election to Congress in 1962, just days before Senator Chavez passed away. Roybal's first speech on the floor of the House was a eulogy to his hero.[4] This passing of a mantle of leadership itself seemed to foreshadow Roybal's own passing within months of Antonio Villaraigosa's election as mayor of Los Angeles.

When a nationwide railroad strike threw him out of work in 1922, Baudilio moved the family some 800 miles west to Los Angeles, to join Eloisa's, already living and working there. More than a half century later, Roybal the congressman would explain that his father chose moving to California over crossing a picket line, an account that served him well in speaking to labor audiences. But the actual circumstances of this decision were likely complex, as most of the railroad unions at the time did not admit either black or "Mexican" members — however supposedly aristocratic their lineage or whatever they liked to call themselves.

Welcome to LA

Los Angeles was the great boom city of America's Roaring Twenties. That decade, when the Roybals arrived, LA doubled in size, soaring to well over a million inhabitants, while its Mexican-American population officially tripled, registering a massive comeback from its late-nineteenth-century eclipse. San Antonio had been home to the United States' largest population of Mexican origin since its acquisition of the vast Southwest from a defeated Mexico. But by 1930, Los Angeles had pushed ahead, with the census counting nearly 100,000 Mexican-American residents in the city and 167,000 in the county. Estimates place the Mexican population of the city alone considerably higher, between 100,000–200,000 in 1930, a far larger community but a lesser proportion of the total than in much smaller San Antonio.[5]

As Los Angeles was a Mexican town before California became part of the United States, its Mexican population had traditionally concentrated around and centered on the old village square, the Los Angeles Plaza, later known as "La Placita." But the flood of midwestern Anglo-American migration, released by the completion of transcontinental railroad lines that ran directly to the Southland, reshaped the region, including its center. Pío Pico, the last Mexican governor of Mexican California, opened a lavish hotel on the Plaza, within view of the new railroad station. An old West-style entertainment district developed in the immediate vicinity, which included a number of stage theaters. The Mexican proportion of the city's population shrank rapidly, falling to less than five percent by the turn of the century. The violence of the Mexican Revolution of 1910–1920, however, was among several spurs to migration that contributed to somewhat re-Mexicanizing the population in the area and the region; with that growth, the plaza district experienced a cultural resurgence.

By the 1920s, the Main Street theater district by the Plaza was once again distinctly Mexican, offering traveling theatrical performances from Mexico, increasingly accompanied by movies, both Hollywood productions starring "Latin" actors and early expressions of the incipient Mexican movie industry. The Southland's Mexican population grew beyond the central plaza district, especially

Forerunner Duo: José Antonio Carrillo and Pío Pico

Pico House looms beside the old Plaza of Los Angeles, just northeast of the modern civic center and downtown, a monument to the vision and commitment to the city of the "Californios." José Antonio Carrillo was three times mayor of Los Angeles in the Mexican period. As Alta California's sole delegate to Mexico's  *Congress, Carrillo secured the elevation of the Pueblo of Los Angeles to city status, and its designation as capital of the territory. Carrillo married the sister of a future governor of Alta California, Pío Pico, and built a grand home facing the Plaza, complete with a ballroom, where he frequently entertained. His brother-in-law, Pico, was married in the home and purchased it when Carrillo died. Pico had become one of the wealthiest of the land-owning Californios and served as the Mexican territory's last governor. He fled Alta California during the US-Mexico War, but returned after Californio forces accepted their defeat and Mexico relinquished its claims to what had been the northern half of its territory. After California became a US state, Pico, holding fast to a belief in the future of Los Angeles, razed the sprawling Carrillo compound and built the most luxurious hotel in the Southland. He would soon lose his lands and all his wealth, but Pico House still stands, in mute testimony to Pío Pico's and José Antonio Carrillo's vision for the future metropolis.*

eastward, just across the Los Angeles River, but the attractions of the old city center would continue to draw Mexican audiences back. The Roybals, and all their friends and neighbors in Los Angeles, experienced a much more robust, urban Mexican culture than they had ever seen in New Mexico.[6]

The Roybals landed in the storied LA neighborhood of Boyle Heights, on the east bank of the river from the rising, modern city center — another community that would have one of its major avenues designated part of Route 66. They had, in a sense, moved down the street across three states, and they would long retain a sense of connection. Big-city life stirred nostalgia in many. Other Mexican Americans who had similarly migrated to Los Angeles from the Southwest formed a New Mexico-Arizona Club, with offices and a ballroom in the plaza area. Nonetheless, the Roybals also developed an attachment to Los Angeles, their new home and new lives.

Eloisa's father trained Baudilio in carpentry and fashioned the railroad hand into a cabinetmaker. Eduardo, thoroughly a little Hispanic son of old New Mexico who spoke only Spanish, started first grade in 1922 in a Prohibition-era city dominated by Anglo Midwesterners; there he became Eddie. But Boyle Heights was different from the rest of Los Angeles, as was much of the near Eastside. The area's diversity was becoming legendary, especially its activist, working-class Jewish component.

The Jewish community dominated Boyle Heights from the twenties through the forties. It nostalgically centered on Brooklyn Avenue, the neighborhood's main thoroughfare, so named before the turn of the century to attract New Yorkers to LA.[7] With delis, bookstores, and busy offices of secular Jewish organizations and publications, the avenue is said to have hummed with Yiddish and arguments about the Russian Revolution. But over the course of these decades, the area also featured the serenity and song of dozens of synagogues — about 10 at the same time in the early 1930s — including the Breed Street Shul, which boasted the largest Jewish congregation west of Chicago.[8] These were not the affluent German Jews of the Westside or the Hollywood Jews who were fashioning an "empire of their own" in the movie industry.[9] These were radical activists of the Workmen's Circle, the Communist and Socialist Parties, and leftist labor unions. This progressive, "hyperactive" political atmosphere would await Ed Roybal's plunge into public life in the 1940s.

Back when Eddie was making his way through grade school, a future Jewish activist legend from Chicago was spending high-school summers in his neighborhood. Saul Alinsky's divorced father had moved to Los Angeles in the 1920s and set his son up in his own Boyle Heights apartment during his extended visits.[10] Alinsky's familiarity and interest in LA would play a critical role in Roybal's life and career some 20 years later. It was perhaps meaningful that America's "mother road," which sliced through the Albuquerque neighborhood of Ed's birth, stretched from Los Angeles to Chicago. That road beckoned from either end, especially in hard times. When Roybal's father, Baudilio, could not find work in Los Angeles in the early 1920s, he moved the family back to New Mexico for several years. But once back in LA, the Roybals built their own house in Boyle Heights, and it appears that not even when Baudilio lost his job again during the Depression would they be driven back. They temporarily moved in with relatives and rented the house, so as not to lose it.[11]

First Person: Education of Eddie Roybal

When I went to Soto Street School I didn't speak a word of English. I went into the first grade and, of course, I could not communicate with the teachers and the teachers could not communicate with me.

It was quite difficult, and I suppose that is why I became the author of the Bilingual Education Act. If we had had bilingual education at that time, I think the progress that I and others would have made would have been much greater.

Being the son of a carpenter, a cabinet maker, I was taught by my father to add, to use a ruler, and I happened to be a little bit better than others. In those grades, we were adding three and two, and four and seven, and so forth. One day the teacher caught me mumbling and she wanted to know what I was saying. When I tried to tell her, she tried to force me to say it in English. Well that was an impossibility. The result was that, instead of being the first in the class, because of the fact that I was prohibited from using Spanish, I was the last.

We could not use Spanish on the playground nor in the classroom. This idea of forcing the youngster to speak only English is probably about the biggest mistake that this country has ever made.*

* *Roybal, "Interview no. 184," 3.*

The Urban Crucible

IN 1928, A LIFETIME BEFORE THE CENTERS FOR DISEASE CONTROL named its main campus in Atlanta for then-retired Congressman Roybal, Ed's family returned to Los Angeles for good.[12] While the Roybals were gone, many changes — good and bad — had occurred or were underway in the booming city. In 1923, Theodore Roosevelt High opened, eventually becoming a key community institution that would play a role in shaping prominent future Latino leaders for decades. But in the fall of 1924, an outbreak of pneumonic plague in Mexican neighborhoods provoked official quarantines and claimed 30 lives. One of those neighborhoods was just across the LA River from Boyle Heights, on the downtown side, blocks away from the old Los Angeles Plaza. The other quarantined neighborhood was east of Boyle Heights, in unincorporated East LA. The newspapers and public officials referred matter-of-factly to the plague as a "Mexican disease."[13]

Roybal's youth unfolded in Los Angeles in the intensely nativist post-World War I era. Nationally, the 1920s opened in the midst of the first "Red Scare" that precipitated the Palmer Raids, named for Attorney General A. Mitchell Palmer, to apprehend and deport suspect immigrant radicals. Prohibition, which shut down industries dominated by immigrants, discriminatory national-origin quotas on immigration from eastern and southern Europe, and an outright ban on immigration from Asia soon followed. This atmosphere prepared the way for a racialized response by Los Angeles authorities to the plague.

Both the Spanish flu pandemic and the plague outbreak blended into a cultural cityscape in which one disease in particular, tuberculosis, which many Anglo Americans had sought the arid climate of Southern California to treat, seemed to loom all around. Not only had the Southland attracted those with the disease, immigrants especially were considered carriers of it. Growing up in this period, and having lost two siblings to the Spanish flu, Roybal deeply internalized a combination of concerns and commitments that years later would move him to change plans suddenly and become a health educator.[14] That consequential career move would lead directly to another — a life in politics, where a concern with public health would become an enduring hallmark of Ed Roybal's service. In the course of that long second career, he would rise to take a place on the powerful House Appropriations Committee. In that capacity, Roybal would be able to secure the first funding for AIDS research and programs at the Centers for Disease Control and every new CDC facility for over a decade, culminating with the Edward R. Roybal Laboratory Building, dedicated some eight years after his retirement.

The way in which representation was structured in city government had also changed in the Roybals' absence. In 1925, LA returned to electing its city council by district, instead of at large. Now Boyle Heights had a specific representative on the council, and residents on the Eastside would become increasingly aware over the years of how district lines were drawn for legislative bodies, how they could be used to divide and disempower communities. For those living within the city limits, the dedication of LA's towering new city hall, the very year the Roybals returned, made city government more salient in every way.

How Latinos learned about government, themselves, and the world was also in transition. A new Spanish-language daily, *La Opinión*, appeared on the streets of LA on Mexico's Independence Day, 1926. *El Heraldo de México* had held unchallenged sway in this market, but it scaled down to a weekly in 1929, not long after the Roybals got back from New Mexico. The launch of *La Opinión* in LA — which went on to become the country's biggest daily in Spanish — by the publisher of San Antonio's prestigious *La Prensa*, marked a turning point that was already apparent in the city's burgeoning population of Mexican origin in the 1920s: San Antonio was being displaced from its long dominant role as capital of the Mexican-American Southwest.[15]

The following year, the Southland's first daily Spanish-language radio program, known by the name of its featured musical group "*Los Madrugadores*,"

Forerunner Duo: Don Ignacio Lozano and Frank Fouce

Lozano was the publisher of La Pren-sa, *the country's largest Spanish-language daily in San Antonio, when he founded a second paper,* La Opinión, *in the booming Los Angeles of the 1920s, and located its offices on Main Street near the old Plaza. In the same decade, Francisco "Frank" Fouce became manager of the most prominent entertainment venue of Mexican LA, the Teatro Hidalgo, also nearby on Main Street. In 1927, the region's first Spanish-language radio program began transmitting from the theater early every morning.*

Fouce went on to become the country's leading Spanish-language movie and entertainment theater impresario, owning and operating multiple screens and stages in Los Angeles and with them bolstering the "golden age" of the Mexican movie industry.

In parallel fashion, La Opinión *became the country's leading Spanish-language daily. Each in their own way, Lozano's and Fouce's businesses stitched together the Greater Eastside and the fragmented, far-flung Latino population of the larger Southland.*

Fouce went further, pushing Edward Roybal to run for Los Angeles City Council in the late 1940s and backing the creation of a national network of Spanish-language television stations. Decades later, La Opinión *and* Univision, *reaching millions through every means of communication, would come to play critical roles in the political empowerment of the Latino community, in Los Angeles and across the country.*

---

debuted live from downtown, near the old Los Angeles Plaza. Between the new daily paper and its accompanying bookstore; the radio show; dance clubs; and the growing number of theaters staging a mix of plays, concerts, variety shows, and films in Spanish, Mexican cultural life was on the upside of a boom — what historian George Sanchez calls a "Mexican cultural renaissance" in LA.[16] The city's Spanish-language theater culture was in the early years of transition, from live performances to movies. The great rise of the Mexican movie industry and Latino movie going would become factors in Ed Roybal's professional life in the 1940s and prepare his segue into politics.

The real world of Latino, predominantly Mexican, LA was becoming more apparent every year of the 1920s, simultaneous with the vertiginous ascent of Los Angeles as a top-tier big city. The US Census first placed LA among the country's 10 largest in 1920, and by 1930 the city's population would double and place it at number five.[17] The lure of gold had powered Northern California's growth in the nineteenth century, but in many ways population growth itself was the Southland's gold mine — and it aroused deep ambivalence.[18] The midwestern Protestant white majority abhorred the image it had of big cities back East, with their corrupt machine politics and dense mix of ethnic groups packed into dark, concrete canyons.[19]

Boosterism and the promotion of Los Angeles, especially, required the projection of a different kind of city and urban life. But the rise of the area's urban Mexican-American population could not be ignored and was a cause of concern that threatened the majority's idealized picture of the state — the California of their imaginations that had brought them out west. The crusading lawyer and journalist Carey McWilliams, who single-handedly invented California and Southwestern social history, found over 50 articles on the subject of "the Mexican Problem" published in the 1920s, and a "mountainous collection of masters' theses" that "'proved' conclusively that Spanish-speaking children were 'retarded.'"[20] Such racialized stigmatization of "Mexicans" — regardless of citizenship — handily complemented segregated and inferior schooling, hidden *colonias* without services for the needed manual labor, and mass repatriation and deportation when that need sagged.[21]

In that decade, mainstream English-speaking Los Angeles determinedly undertook to adopt and elaborate a "fantasy heritage" of old Spanish California through architecture, literature, the staging of historical pageants, and, in an alley extending from the old plaza, an amusement-park-like recreation of a village street market. Both public buildings and private homes — and in nearby Santa Barbara, the entire town — were designed following what was first called "Mission Revival," then "Authentic Spanish" and "Spanish Colonial Revival," finally seeming to settle on "California Spanish." The style, according to the architectural writer Wade Graham, fostered an illusion and satisfied a longing: the illusion of "standing apart in space and time," and the longing "to not live in a modern city at all, to have nothing to do with what the city stands for — work, toil, struggle, urgency and other people, especially undesirable ones."[22]

A substantial faction, seeking yet greater distance from the here and now, took the endless promotion of the state's "Mediterranean climate" further, to promote Italian and classical revival styles, as well as vaguely biblical, oasis-like landscapes with the introduction of over a thousand nonnative species of palms, where there had once been only one. But Spanish Revival architecture would win out, becoming quasi-official in public buildings and especially pervasive in domestic architecture.[23] The tension between the contemporary big-city reality of increasingly Mexican Los Angeles and a deepening mainstream preference for an imaginary Spanish ideal would soon become uncontainable, with the onset of the Great Depression, followed by a heavily racialized world war.

***

IN TRADITIONALLY HISPANIC NEW MEXICO, DISCRIMINATION AND SEGREGA-
TION were usually relatively subtle and rare — at least compared with elsewhere in the Southwest, such as Texas and Arizona, and especially in the small towns, including in California. But the Roybals did in fact encounter discrimination in the modern big city of Los Angeles as well. There was the barbershop in Boyle Heights that "wouldn't cut a Mexican's hair."[24] Ed and his youngest sister, Elsie, would also remember the separate sections in movie theaters and the one day a week that Mexicans were allowed to swim in city pools. A year after Ed's death, Elsie recalled how her teenage brother took his first plunge into politics by speaking to the Los Angeles City Council on the practice of swimming-pool segregation, which resulted in a policy change.[25]

Conditions in small towns and rural areas beyond the city were considerably more severe. The region's "citrus belt" stretched north and south of LA, and especially to the east, across the fertile San Gabriel Valley. Mexican "*colonias*" emerged throughout, largely out of sight of main roads and incorporated areas, supplying the seasonal labor that made the picturesque "citrus suburbs" and their evident wealth possible. The isolation of these settlements and the lack of major urban centers in the vicinity made it "most convenient" in Carey McWilliams' words, "to establish separate schools and to minimize civic conveniences in the satellite *colonia*."[26]

The overarching authority of county government, headquartered in downtown Los Angeles, brought together the realities of the San Gabriel Valley "*colonia* complex" and of the urban barrios of LA's Eastside. As the financial panic of 1929 turned into the Great Depression, with soaring unemployment, LA County government in particular vigorously executed the Hoover administration's call to repatriate "illegal aliens" en masse.[27] From Roybal's last year in middle school to his junior year at Roosevelt High (1931–34), the County of Los Angeles spent hundreds of thousands of dollars on special repatriation trains, shipping thousands of immigrant Angelenos — along with their US-born children — to Mexico.[28]

Finding a Political Identity

THE ROYBALS HAD BEEN REPUBLICANS IN NEW MEXICO, like most of the state's Hispanics as well as its Anglos; this had been characteristic of the territory since the Civil War and was reinforced by the long struggle for statehood.[29] But the Great Depression hit the Roybals just over a year after they returned to Los Angeles to stay. Ed's four years at (Theodore) Roosevelt High were divided between the end of the Herbert Hoover administration and the start of Franklin Roosevelt's.

During Roybal's first fall term in high school, his distant relative Dennis Chavez ran for Congress in New Mexico. Chavez had worked for the city of Albuquerque at an early age and found himself drawn to a more activist, Democratic Party view of government than the limited-government orthodoxy upheld by the Republican Party. He wound up working as a Spanish interpreter for a successful Senate candidate who then offered him a staff job in Washington. While there he managed to study law and graduate from the Georgetown law school before returning to Albuquerque.

In 1930, little New Mexico had a single representative in Congress and Chavez, a driven man, won the statewide seat, putting him electorally on par with the state's two senators. His cousin Ed Roybal, in high school across the continent, separated from the colonial New Mexico neighborhood they had in common, avidly followed Chavez's congressional career.[30]

By Roybal's junior year, when FDR came into office, his father was out of work and the Roybals were on the verge of losing their home. He would later recall in an interview that his father was able to get a job with the Works Progress Administration, and that Roosevelt's Home Owners' Loan Corporation saved their house from foreclosure. "I remember the suffering under the Hoover administration," Roybal said, adding that the New Deal "turned the situation completely. I became more interested in the political process as a result."[31] Chavez, reelected in the wave that brought Roosevelt to power in 1932, strongly supported the New Deal and its programs, such as the Civilian Conservation Corps that brought tens of thousands of jobs to New Mexico. Instead of seeking a second reelection to the House, the growing strength of the Democrats and Roosevelt's support led Chavez to challenge New Mexico's incumbent Republican senator in 1934.[32]

Roybal, like Chavez, was a translator. His biographer notes that the language he was prohibited from speaking in grade school became an asset in high school. Roybal's senior yearbook featured a full-page group portrait of the Roosevelt High Spanish Club, complete with its motto *"¡Adelante! ¡Siempre Adelante!"* Prominently positioned beneath the motto is recognition of "Edward Roybal, W'34 *President*." In the photograph, Roybal is in the first, seated row, just off center, wearing a big smile and a necktie.

Roybal's biographer tells of how Eddie, as a child, first took to the idea of becoming a professional, a man who wears a suit and tie. His father worked exhausting 10-hour days, coming home so tired and dusty he would lay on the floor to take a short nap. Ed's view of life and his own future were altered when a man in a suit came to the house to deliver a watch to his father. Apparently, it was the necktie that got Eddie's attention most of all. He asked his mother about it and learned that it takes an education to become a professional, to do the sort of work that goes with dressing up. He was good at arithmetic, which he learned could make him an accountant.[33] Ed's father got him a tie. Wearing it got him teased and into fights. He learned to box, discovered he liked to fight, and years later at Roosevelt, Ed would make the boxing team — when high schools still had boxing teams. He soon left boxing behind, but in almost every available photograph from his childhood to retirement, Roybal appears wearing a tie.

In the context of the Spanish Club, Roybal had his identity affirmed at Roosevelt and rose to leadership. Outside of it, however, he experienced discrimination. Decades later, as a member of Congress, he would recall that the teachers there were not encouraging, and "not really interested in having a Spanish-speaking person become an A student."[34] He participated in sports, and considered himself the best runner on the track team, yet he recalled receiving no encouragement or even coaching from his coach. But his most vivid and humiliating experiences of discrimination were yet to come, at the hands of LA police.

The lasting effects of the New Deal on Roybal's politics may have been sealed when he was unable to find a job for months after graduation — until he got work with the Civilian Conservation Corps that fall. In New Mexico, meanwhile, Dennis Chavez narrowly lost his audacious bid to knock off a popular senator, a progressive Republican widely thought to be a potential challenger to Roosevelt for the presidency in 1936. Chavez gave up his statewide seat in Congress only to just miss what could have been his best shot at higher office. But history took another turn. In May 1935, the reelected incumbent was killed when the plane he was flying back to Washington got lost over Missouri and crash-landed in dense fog. New Mexico's governor chose to appoint Chavez to the suddenly empty seat, since he had come so close to winning the election just six months before. This made Chavez the second Hispanic senator in history and the only one to serve between 1929 and 1964. However much Chavez may have been seen as an outsider in the halls of Congress, he could hardly have loomed any larger to Roybal.

Having worked for a senator and then served two terms in Congress, Chavez certainly knew his way around the Capitol, but the Senate was dominated by monolingual WASPs from the East, South, and Midwest. This Hispanic Catholic newcomer was from a distant, romanticized, and vaguely exotic part of the old frontier. When Roybal's turn to serve in Washington would come around, he would certainly be seen differently, as a representative of a minority group with big-city issues.

Fraught relations between the Mexican-American community and Los Angeles police were another lasting influence on Roybal's political outlook, making him into a leading critic of cop misconduct and an advocate of reform. According to historians, long before the term "stop-and-frisk" gained currency and became a national issue, the LAPD pioneered this tactic as an urban policing strategy.[35] Roybal would recall in later interviews the issue of policemen groping Mexican-American women under the pretext of searching for guns or drugs, and his parents telling his sisters that in the event of trouble, they should not ask a cop for assistance.[36] He, in turn, would instruct his own children never to get into a police car, no matter the pretext officers gave them.[37]

Roybal came to tell several versions of a particular incident in which a police-man deliberately humiliated him when he was out on a date with his bride-to-be, Lucille Beserra. In one telling, he described being frisked; the cop thrust his hands in Ed's pockets and made racial slurs.[38] In another, he described the cop taking cards out of his wallet, dropping them on the sidewalk, and telling him to pick them up.[39] On a separate occasion, at an outdoor stand at Fourth and Soto Streets in Boyle Heights, a cop dumped the couple's dinner of chili beans and crackers on the sidewalk. "That kind of stuff was happening all the time," he told *Los Angeles Times*.[40] But far worse abuses were yet to come.

By the time of that police incident, in mid-1940, Ed Roybal was six years out of high school, where he met Lucille, and had worked multiple jobs while taking classes whenever he could, mainly in business administration, across town at UCLA extension. Since childhood he had dreamed of first becoming an accoun-tant, and then also a lawyer, to focus on "tax problems . . . things that I felt at that time were important."[41] He took rides with a milkman to get to UCLA, but had to stop doing the commute to make more money for his family instead. Already working as an accountant, he went back to taking classes, but at Southwestern Law School, which was considerably closer and particularly dedicated to provid-ing opportunities for women and minority students. Roybal would not complete a degree at either institution. As his biographer tells it, a paper he wrote for one class in the 1930s would have lasting significance, a plan to politically organize and empower low-income communities. But Roybal would put that idea aside for a good 10 years.[42] Social work, combined with the war, would be the stepping stones to yet another career and life, in politics.

* * *

ED ROYBAL HAD A BUSY LIFE AS US INVOLVEMENT IN WWII INTENSIFIED. He and Lucille were married and had their first baby in 1941, just six months before Pearl Harbor. He then learned of and applied for a job that would train him for a new career in three months, directing health education for the California Tuberculosis Association. He began working as a health educator in 1942. His two younger brothers went off to the Pacific to serve in the navy. A second baby arrived in April 1943 and Roybal's mother, Eloisa, although still in her forties, died that September following surgery.[43]

In those early war years, Roybal attended a social-worker convention, where he met Saul Alinsky. Alinsky had imbibed innovative urban and social theory at the University of Chicago; he forged his own approaches to juvenile delinquency and criminology on the city's streets and over several years conducting research and working at Joliet State Prison. But his biographer points out that what most set Alinsky on his life's course as the author and apostle of urban community or-ganizing was the revolution in labor led by John L. Lewis, who organized millions of workers into the Congress of Industrial Organizations (CIO) in the span of two years during the Great Depression. Alinsky's mission would be to revolutionize urban America in a similar way. His first great achievement was organizing Chicago's biggest slum, known as the Back of the Yards. He went on to form the Industrial Areas Foundation (IAF), a vehicle for exporting his methods to other cities, which would outlive him. [44]

Roybal had thought deeply about how to organize communities like his own for that term paper he wrote in the 1930s, but was suspicious of Alinsky's leftism. He got over his suspicions through a conversation with the convention's keynote speaker, Archbishop Robert E. Lucey of San Antonio, who introduced the two men.[45] Roybal was moving into politics and won a place on the Los Angeles Central Committee of the Democratic Party in 1944. The following two years he used his vacations to learn Alinksy's strategies and doctrines at the IAF's community-organizing school in Chicago.[46]

As the final year of the war opened, Roybal lost another family member, his brother Robert, who died in service in the Pacific.[47] Just months later, Roybal finally got called up himself by the army, but following boot camp was assigned a stateside office job, utilizing his accounting skills at nearby Fort MacArthur. Without seeing or coming anywhere near combat, he nevertheless returned to his civilian job by the end of the year as a veteran — a key credential for a postwar political career.

Notes

1. See Chávez, "La Conquistadora is a Paisana," 302–03; Berumen, *Edward R. Roybal*, 28–29; Baxter, "The Ignacio de Roybal House."

2. Roybal, "Interview no. 184."

3. Starr, *Golden Dreams*, 443.

4. Berumen, *Edward R. Roybal*, 198.

5. See Starr, *Material Dreams*, 147–48; and Nicolaides, *Survey LA*, 7.

6. See Kanellos, *A History of Hispanic Theater in the United States*, chapter 2; Agrasánchez, *Mexican Movies in the United States*, chapter 2; Gunckel, "The War of the Accents"; Gunckel, *Mexico on Main Street*; Sanchez, "The 'Golden Age' of Spanish-Language Theaters in Los Angeles"; and Carmen Tse, "Golden Age Latin American Films Return to Downtown L.A. for Screening Series," *LAist*, September 22, 2017, http://laist.com/2017/09/22/cine_de_espanol.php.

7. David Margolick, "Brooklyn Expatriates in Los Angeles Mourn Fading Reminders of the Past," *New York Times*, April 3, 1994, http://www.nytimes.com/1994/04/03/us/brooklyn-expatriates-in-los-angeles-mourn-fading-reminders-of-the-past.html?pagewanted=all&mcubz=1.

8. Starr, *Material Dreams*, 144–45; Los Angeles Conservancy, "Breed Street Shul," https://www.laconservancy.org/locations/breed-street-shul.

9. Gabler, *An Empire of Their Own*.

10. Horwitt, *Let Them Call Me Rebel*.

11. See Berumen, *Edward R. Roybal*, 33, 36.

12. "CDC Dedicates Campus to Edward R. Roybal," Centers for Disease Control and Prevention, Press Release, July 9, 1999, https://www.cdc.gov/media/pressrel/r990709.htm.

13. Deverell, *The Whitewashed Adobe*, chapter 5.

14. Not quite three years after Ed Roybal was born and his family was still in New Mexico, the Great Pandemic of Spanish flu swept across the country. At one point all four of the Roybal children at that time fell ill, and the two youngest died within days of each other. They were buried in Albuquerque. The next two Roybal children were born in Boyle Heights.

15. See Kanellos, *Hispanic Periodicals in the United States*, 39–44, 102; di Stefano, "'Venimos a luchar'"; Medeiros, "*La Opinión*"; Rivas-Rodriquez, "The Mexican Exile Publisher Who Conquered San Antonio and Los Angeles"; and the symposium of seven articles and reflections on *La Prensa* in *The Americas Review* 17, nos. 3–4 (Winter 1989): 121–68.

16. Sanchez, *Becoming Mexican American*, 180. "Los Madrugadores" means "the early risers," referring to the broadcast's original 4:00–6:00 AM time slot. See Fowler and Crawford, *Border Radio*, 277–79, and chapter 8, generally.

17. Campbell Gibson, "Population of the 100 Largest Cities and Other Urban Places in the United States: 1790 to 1990," US Census Bureau, June 1998, https://www.census.gov/population/www/documentation/twps0027/twps0027.html.

18. As Robert Fishman put it, "The Los Angeles elite very early realized that their real business was growth itself," in his foreword to the reissued classic by Robert M. Fogelson, *The Fragmented Metropolis*, xvi.

19. The tension between the city's addiction to sustained, massive growth and homeowners' abhorrence of urban life, only partially resolved by the endless horizontal expanse of a metropolis of suburbs, is the main theme of the more recent classic by William B. Fulton, *The Reluctant Metropolis*.

20. McWilliams, *North from Mexico*, chapter 11. The late Kevin Starr, definitive historian of California and for a decade the state librarian, pronounced McWilliams to be "the single finest nonfiction writer on California — ever," in the sixth volume of his "Americans and the California Dream" series, *Embattled Dreams*, 103; for a careful and detailed assessment of McWilliams's work, see Richardson, *American Prophet*.

21. See Thompson, *America's Social Arsonist*, 66–67.

22. The classic statement of California's old Spanish "fantasy heritage" is from McWilliams, *North from Mexico*, chapter 2. See also Starr, *Material Dreams*, chapter 8, and especially Graham, *Dream Cities*, chapter 1.

23. Holliday, *American Arcadia*, 31; Starr, *Material Dreams*; and Graham, *Dream Cities*.

24. Roybal, "Interview no. 184," 10–11.

25. Berumen, *Edward R. Roybal*, 56.

26. McWilliams, *North from Mexico*, 197–201. See also Garcia, *A World of its Own*; and Lewthwaite, *Race, Place, and Reform in Mexican Los Angeles*, chapter 6.

27. For an overview of the repatriation and deportation efforts of the Hoover administration, as well as detail on local efforts in California, see Guerin-Gonzalez, *Mexican Workers and the American Dream*, 77–87. Writers sympathetic to Hoover, as well as other academics, argue that while this president may have failed to restrain his secretary of labor, who directed repatriation efforts from Washington, Hoover did not personally order mass deportations; see Spencer Howard, "Hoover on Immigration," The National Archives, *Hoover Heads: The Blog of the Herbert Hoover Library and Museum*, August 4, 2016, https://hoover.blogs.archives.gov/2016/08/04/hoover-on-immigration/.

28. Sanchez provides a vivid account of specific repatriation measures and expenditures by LA County, and also interprets the repatriation case in conjunction with other coerced movements of residents of Boyle Heights, including the internment of Japanese Americans and the clearing of sections of the neighborhood for public works, all of which took place within a span of 12 years; see "Disposable People, Expendable Neighborhoods."

29. New Mexico was admitted as a state in 1912 during the Republican administration of William H. Taft. It appears that in Washington, Republicans were more supportive of New Mexico statehood, and in the territory the more ardent supporters of statehood were Republican as well; see Tom Sharpe, "1910's Enabling Act: Where New Mexico's March to Statehood Begins," *The New Mexican,* November 27, 2010. From the Civil War through 1930, the great majority of Hispanics who represented New Mexico in Congress, whether as "delegates" in the territorial period, or representatives since statehood, were Republicans. See "Hispanic-American Representatives, Senators, Delegates, and Resident Commissioners by Congress, 1822-Present," *History, Art & Archives, U.S. House of Representatives*, accessed October 9, 2017, http://history.house.gov/Exhibitions-and-Publications/HAIC/Historical-Data/Hispanic-American-Representatives,-Senators,-Delegates,-and-Resident-Commissioners-by-Congress/.

30. Roybal, "Interview no. 184," 12.

31. Ibid.

32. See "Chavez, Dennis: 1888–1962," *History, Art & Archives, U.S. House of Representatives*, accessed October 9, 2017, http://history.house.gov/People/Listing/C/CHAVEZ,-Dennis-(C000338)/.

33. Berumen, *Edward R. Roybal*, 32–33; Roybal, "Interview no. 184," 6.

34. Roybal, "Interview no. 184," 5–6.

35. Alex Elkins, "The Origins of Stop-and-Frisk," *Jacobin*, May 9, 2015, https://www.jacobinmag.com/2015/05/stop-and-frisk-dragnet-ferguson-baltimore/.

36. Escobar, *Race, Police, and the Making of a Political Identity*, 173.

37. Roybal told the *Los Angeles Times* that he lost sleep worrying that the police were capable of abducting his children, and that he warned them "to never get into a squad car, 'even if the guy said I'd been taken to the hospital and that he would take them to my bedside,'" Antonio Olivo, "Grandfather of Latino Politics Faults New Leaders," *Los Angeles Times*, July 27, 1999, http://articles.latimes.com/1999/jul/27/local/me-59994.

38. Escobar, *Race, Police, and the Making of a Political Identity*, 174.

39. Berumen, *Edward R. Roybal*, 62.

40. George Ramos, "Pioneer in Latino Politics in Los Angeles: Edward R. Roybal 1916–2005," *Los Angeles Times*, October 26, 2005, http://articles.latimes.com/2005/oct/26/local/me-roybal26.

41. Roybal, "Interview no. 184," 6–7

42. Berumen, *Edward R. Roybal*, 58–59.

43. Ibid.

44. Horwitt, *Let Them Call Me Rebel.*

45. Ibid., 228.

46. Burt, *The Search for a Civic Voice*, 54.

47. Berumen, *Edward R. Roybal*, 32.

CHAPTER 2

Making It

FLASH FORWARD — EARLY IN 1983, TWO YEARS INTO THE REAGAN ERA, ESTEBAN TORRES, in Washington as a freshman in Congress, gathered his new staff together and reflected on his life's journey to that point. A trained artist and student of art history, he could have reminisced about Paris, where with the rank of ambassador he represented the United States before UNESCO, the cultural arm of the United Nations. His wife, Arcy, would recall those years as the best of their lives. Or he could have shared what it was like more recently to serve in the White House as President Jimmy Carter's top advisor on Hispanic affairs, or related the shock of Carter's 1980 loss to Ronald Reagan, which had sent Torres and many other Latino appointees back to California.[1]

Torres talked instead about his birth in a tent in a mining camp in Arizona, at the dawn of the Great Depression; about his father's deportation back to Mexico when Esteban was only five, and about his patched-up family's move to Los Angeles a year later. He grew up wanting to be a scientist. Fellow students in grade school called him "the professor." But eventually, he told his staff, when he was not allowed to take an aeronautics class in which students actually learned to fly, he lost interest and stopped going to high school in unincorporated East LA. The teacher, who had the same name as Esteban but in English, Mr. Towers, spotted Torres hanging around nearby with his friends. Towers approached Torres and talked him into coming back to school to take his class.

The teacher had an agenda. He needed illustrations for a textbook he was writing on the science of aeronautics, and Torres was known for his artistic ability. From Towers he learned to fly and made drawings for him of weather processes, like the condensation of moisture in clouds that is "released as rain," as he described it. He graduated from Garfield High, enlisted in the army, and never again heard of his teacher or the book; but in 1983, his story propelled a young staffer on a search at the vast Library of Congress, the mandatory repository of all books published in the country. And there it had sat on a shelf for decades, an old tome with the new congressman's illustrations from 35 years before, from when he had dropped out but then returned to Garfield in East Los Angeles, 2,700 miles away. Taking in his hands for the first time the book he had illustrated but never saw as a teenager, Torres found that Mr. Towers acknowledged the support of his principal, experts, other colleagues, friends, and family. The artwork went uncredited.

Life without Father

TORRES'S FATHER, ESTEBAN T. TORRES, CAME TO ARIZONA from the once-wealthy silver mining town of El Rosario, in the western Mexican state of Sinaloa. He ventured north to work in the copper mines of what was then the newest state of the union, where he met and married a young Mexican-American woman from Clifton, Rina Gomez. They settled in the mining town of Miami, called "Miama" by locals, over a hundred miles further west. Miami had started out as a mining camp in Arizona's territorial days and grew quickly as demand for copper boomed. The industry at that time maintained a dual wage system for Anglos and "Mexicans," whether immigrant or US-born, distinguishing between "Anglo work" and "Mexican work." The town's schools, churches, and theaters were segregated, and the YMCA maintained separate buildings for Mexicans and Anglos.[2] Esteban *Eduardo* Torres — later to become Esteban Edward — was born in late January of 1930, three months after the stock market crash that set off the Great Depression. On his state-issued birth certificate, which indicated the "color or race" of the parents, Torres's Mexico-born father and his US-born mother were both designated simply as Mexican.

As the Depression deepened, copper prices collapsed, and one mine after another cut back and ultimately ceased operation; the copper companies and the county arranged for the repatriation to Mexico of hundreds of families in 1931–32, many with US-born children. The Torres family was able to hang on in Miami through the repatriations, into the mid-1930s. But as mining companies began preparing to resume operations, Esteban's father was identified as an activist involved in efforts to introduce the radical International Union of Mine, Mill and Smelter Workers to the Miami area. He was arrested and deported to Mexico in 1935.[3] Unable to support herself without her husband, Rina and her five-year-old son moved back to her mother's home in Clifton. Believing herself to be permanently cut off from her husband, Rina remarried. She and her new husband moved to Los Angeles, leaving Esteban temporarily in Arizona with his grandmother.

* * *

TORRES'S INTRODUCTION TO LIFE IN BOYLE HEIGHTS WAS A REVELATION. He had never seen indoor plumbing or readily available hot water. These comforts were "like a dream." He encountered the prohibition on speaking Spanish when he started school, but had the advantage of being bilingual, like his mother and grandmother. Rina was also an avid reader, and Torres took quickly to books. His teacher asked him to lead a reading circle, to help his fellow students learn words in English, which led them to start calling him "the professor."

His stepfather had trained as an engineer, which drew Torres to science. His mother equipped him with a child's microscope, telescope, and chemistry set. Though he wanted to become a scientist, he also developed an ability to draw,

Parallel Life: Romana Acosta Bañuelos

Bañuelos signature on the dollar bill.

The Acostas of Miami, Arizona were one of the many Mexican-American victims of the collapse of copper prices and production in the early 1930s. Assured that they would be able to return when the economy recovered, the family accepted repatriation to Mexico in 1933. But the experience was a shock for eight-year-old, Miami-born Romana, who was taken out of grade school. A decade later, during WWII, Romana and an aunt returned to the United States and made their way to Los Angeles.

After starting as a dishwasher, and then working as a waitress, Romana found a job at a defense plant and was able to save enough money to start a tiny tortilla-making business in downtown LA with her aunt. In league with her new husband, Alejandro Bañuelos, Romana's startup grew into the multimillion-dollar Ramona's Food Products, Inc. In the early 1960s she helped found and lead what was the oldest Latino-owned bank in California, Pan American Bank of East Los Angeles, until it merged with another bank in 2016. Romana Acosta Bañuelos's success came to the attention of President Richard Nixon, who in September 1971 appointed her as the first Hispanic Treasurer of the United States.*

---

* *Richard Nixon, "Statement Announcing Nomination of Romana A. Bañuelos as Treasurer of the United States," September 20, 1971, posted by Gerhard Peter and John T. Woolley,* The American Presidency Project, *http://www.presidency.ucsb.edu/ws/?pid=3148; Christine Marín, "Romana Acosta Bañuelos: United States Treasurer,"* Latino Perspectives Magazine *(April 2009).*

like the naturalists of old. Torres was close to his stepfather but was troubled by the loss of his biological father, repeatedly asking his mother about it. He came to understand that his father had been deported for his union activism, a reason that would stick with him. His family moved from Boyle Heights to the neighborhood of Maravilla in unincorporated East Los Angeles, which was distinctly more Mexican. Torres had never been to Mexico and knew of no family there other than his father, who he never saw or heard from again.

The heightened racial tensions of the World War II home-front experience, as viewed from the eastern fringe of Los Angeles, also marked Torres's adolescence. He had no memory of the period of mass repatriations of the 1930s, but knew that his father had been among those deported. Within months of entering the war, US authorities "interned" in army-run camps all West Coast residents of Japanese descent. After the initial incarceration of thousands of Japanese-American community leaders in the immediate aftermath of Pearl Harbor, soldiers arrived in Eastside neighborhoods in the spring of 1942 to order the remaining family members out of their homes.[4]

As the war in the Pacific intensified and domestic mobilization went into high gear, sustained and heightened racial tensions generated new fears, dangers, and opportunities. According to Carey McWilliams, "Within a few days after the last Japanese had left, the Los Angeles newspapers, led by the Hearst press, began to play up 'Mexican' crime and 'Mexican' juvenile delinquency."[5] In early June of the following year, mobs of white servicemen, joined by civilians and even some police, roamed for several days through downtown Los Angeles attacking Mexicans, Filipinos, and blacks, beating and stripping them of their clothing.[6] Policemen generally looked on without intervening. LA's "Zoot Suit Riots" were seen as sparking others across the country that summer of 1943.[7]

Living east of city limits, in territory patrolled by the county sheriff's department instead of the LAPD, the drama and violence that unfolded in those years, mainly in LA proper, were impossible to ignore but not directly threatening to Torres or his family, friends, and neighbors. The war ended just weeks before Torres started high school, but the wartime stress on practical training continued. That fall, East Los Angeles Junior College was launched on the campus of Garfield High, just as Torres began his classes there. Earlier that year, a prominent Eastside Latino leader who happened to originally be from New Mexico, like the Roybals, ran for LA City Council on the platform of getting a junior college opened on the Eastside. That leader, Eduardo Quevedo, would lose and soon abandon politics altogether, but within a couple of years, East Los Angeles College — famously known as ELAC — would open its own new campus in the unincorporated community of East LA.

In various ways, East LA seemed both part of and not part of the city of Los Angeles. Garfield High, like Roosevelt, was in the LA City School District, as was ELAC. Later, when the community colleges separated from the school district, ELAC, like LA City College, would be part of the Los Angeles Community College District. But unlike neighboring Boyle Heights, East Los Angeles was not part of the city, did not vote in city elections, was not represented on city council, and its law enforcement was provided by the sheriff, not LAPD.

Torres's high-school counselors, learning of his artistic abilities, tried to steer him into print shop and, in promoting vocational skills in general, urged him into electrical shop, which he actually enjoyed. But it took his quiet act of rebellion, and a teacher who wanted to make use of his talents, to get Torres into the class he most longed to take. Mr. Towers's class on aeronautics and aerodynamics included regular use of the flight simulator of the era, known as a Link Trainer, and weekly flights at Vail Field in Montebello, an airfield that no longer exists. Although the students never piloted a plane themselves, they planned the flights, and Torres was assigned the role of the field's weatherman.

Wedging himself into the lingering martial spirit of the late 1940s appeared to have an effect: Torres enlisted in the US Army upon graduation and was sent to Europe — just as the contest with the Soviet Union over the future of Europe increasingly became a test of military strength and will, and as the newly mobilized Mexican-American community in Boyle Heights, in coalition with Jews and others, was catapulting Ed Roybal onto the LA City Council.

Casting a Command Performance

LOS ANGELES, FALL 1946 — FRANK FOUCE WAS A PLAYER — nationally and beyond — and Ed Roybal had him on his team. But Fouce had his own agenda — one that would set in motion a series of ultimately transformative political advances. When he returned to his health-educator job after a brief local stint in the army, Torres ramped up his community outreach and penetration, assembling advisory committees of business leaders and professionals to support and guide his work for the Tuberculosis Association. Fouce was an ideal "get" to chair Roybal's main committee, supporting the fight against TB and venereal disease in the Latino community. He owned and operated all the successful theaters showing Mexican movies in the Los Angeles area — most of all in the concentrated theater district by the old plaza downtown. He advised Hollywood studios on the portrayal and casting of Latinos and had worked closely with Nelson Rockefeller and his Office of the Coordinator of Inter-American Affairs, helping manage the WWII US partnership with the Mexican movie industry, part of the wartime effort to combat German influence in Latin America.[8]

In Fouce's world, the movie business and the war effort blended together and transcended borders, as did the Mexican population and the movies made in Spanish in both countries for this growing transnational audience. The war had the fundamental home-front political dimension of securing popular support for the government, meaning the US government and its allies. This orientation carried over directly into electoral politics and continued beyond the war's end. In 1946, Fouce played a leading role in organizing the transnationally dubbed "Latin American Division" of the California Democratic Party, to mobilize Latino support in that year's midterm congressional elections. Fouce excelled at drawing

Spanish-speaking crowds to his theaters. This year he also drew them to a campaign rally in the cavernous Shrine Auditorium near downtown LA.[9]

It was in this political context that Fouce and his circle also turned their attention to Los Angeles City Council elections, which take place in the first half of odd-numbered years. At that time, the council was entirely white, male, and Christian. The city was less than 10 percent Hispanic, but the ninth council district, which had been redistricted in the 1940s to include Boyle Heights, was nearing one-third Latino.[10]

The Ninth District was represented by the most liberal member on the council, a midwestern political warhorse in his late seventies, said to be an alcoholic. In 1945, Eduardo Quevedo, perhaps the most prominent Mexican-American political activist in the state, challenged this longtime Anglo incumbent and lost. But many among the politically inclined believed that the councilman would not run again in 1947, which would open up a special opportunity for the first Hispanic anywhere in California to achieve a significant public office in the twentieth century. Quevedo, however, was eliminated in the first round of voting in '45 and had since withdrawn from politics upon the death of his wife.[11] The community needed a new and better candidate in 1947 for the first city council election of the postwar era, and with the primary coming up in March, time was fast running out.

Fouce's support had been critical for the Tuberculosis Association and Roybal's work in particular. The movie-theater impresario had film-production capability and had produced health-education shorts in Spanish featuring Roybal, which he ran at his theaters in Los Angeles and beyond. "I became a success because of that," Roybal would recall, "and he knew it."[12] Nevertheless, Fouce and his allies were looking around for their new candidate when a community leader they interviewed told them, "Eddie Roybal is your man." Fouce is said to have exclaimed, "Oh my God, he's been right under my nose and I forgot him."[13] Roybal, the educated, socially minded professional, an army veteran and bilingual communicator who was regularly projected onto numerous movie screens, seemed to be the perfect candidate. Surely he would agree. He appeared to be preparing for such a move, having been active in FDR's reelection in 1944 and himself elected to the Los Angeles Democratic Party Central Committee, where he was the only Mexican American.[14]

As an entrepreneur, Fouce was always looking for the next big thing. Fouce, the wannabe political kingmaker, pictured the 30-year-old Roybal as a winning candidate, a city councilman, and then who knows what more. Roybal was summoned to a meeting at a downtown law firm, where he found Fouce and other community notables gathered to propose that he run in what would likely be an open race, though he might have to take on the old incumbent if necessary. They had $250 to spare from their efforts in the congressional midterms and a campaign manager ready to go. All they needed was to get him started. But Roybal said no, that he was not a politician.

Fouce's movie-mogul forcefulness took over. As Roybal would later recount, "He told me in no uncertain terms that if I didn't run I could just forget about showing any of my 'propaganda' in any of his motion picture houses. He called my boss in San Francisco and told him that. My boss immediately called me."[15] The man was used to having his way, wielding his "You'll never work in this town again" clout over entertainers. The next thing Roybal knew, he had another summons, from his boss at the California Tuberculosis Association, to go before the association's board and request a leave of absence to run for city council. Fouce had effectively cast Roybal in a local, Latino version of *Mr. Smith Goes to Washington*, only in this case to first do battle against an incumbent, so that he could then go up against the goyish, lily-white city council.[16]

* * *

EVEN IF ED ROYBAL NEVER LEFT BOYLE HEIGHTS, he would have been steeped in many social issues that affected him, his family, and his community. He would never forget being judged less capable as a kid for speaking only Spanish, or his exhausted and work-dirty father napping on the bare floor. He wanted to know how you got to work in a coat and tie. He and his friends were turned away from the city pool.

There were the high-school teachers and coaches who showed no interest in his development, the local barbershop that would not cut "Mexican hair," the cop who humiliated him in front of his future wife, the neighbors taken away to internment camps. He had two brothers in the navy when mobs of white servicemen went on a rampage against Mexican Americans for over a week, forcing the governor to create a "Special Committee on the Los Angeles Emergency."[17]

But Roybal also saw his father open his eyes and get off the floor, saying, "I gotta go vote," and went with him to the polling place. He wore the tie his father gave him whenever he could. He learned his family would have lost their home if not for a New Deal program. He got the swimming-pool policy changed. After months of looking after high school, he finally found a job with another government program, which took him out of LA for several months. He began hitching rides across town to attend classes at UCLA — and for one of them wrote a paper on registering low-income community voters, decades before a professor at USC came up with the term "empowerment."[18] He got a health-educator job that sent him around the county and parts of the state, and talked with local leaders everywhere he went. As his biographer put it, "He crosscut various communities, seeing similarities and distinctions, real differences and perceived ones."[19]

By 1944, still in his twenties, Roybal had become known for pitching free TB examinations in Spanish on movie screens. He ran to be on the LA Democratic Party Central Committee and was asked to endorse a Franklin Roosevelt reelection campaign event.[20] This "Good Neighbor Rally" — named for Roosevelt's signature policy toward Latin America — was headlined by Roybal's longtime hero, US Senator Dennis Chavez of New Mexico. Roybal was not drafted until 1945, the peak year of US military mobilization, when over 11 million Americans were in the armed forces. His youngest brother had died on an island in the Pacific. Roybal served briefly and nearby, but lived the full experience of wartime mobilization on the home front, the nation's jubilation over victory, and the millions of returning servicemen and women. From his army base in San Pedro, by the LA harbor, he saw the prominent community activist Quevedo, originally from New Mexico like his own family, run for city council in a wartime election and lose. Roybal spent his next two vacations in Alinsky's community-organizing school in Chicago.

Now it was 1946. Rumblings in the "Citrus Belt" surrounding Los Angeles broke out into the open when a federal district court in downtown LA declared unconstitutional the segregation of Mexican-American schoolchildren by the Westminster Schools of Orange County.[21] An independent, crusading Mexican-American journalist in Pomona and an innovative community organizer from LA were mobilizing the *colonias* behind the "orange curtain," and even winning some local elections.[22] Veterans, from Nixon in nearby Whittier to JFK in Massachusetts, were running for Congress under the banner of fresh leadership for the new postwar world. Roybal was asked to succeed a 77-year-old incumbent on city council. If he agreed, he would have a ready-made platform and profile for at least some strategic segments of voters. Did he really have to be pressured to say yes?

Rumor had it that the elderly incumbent, Ninth District City Councilman Parley Christensen, would not run again, which attracted a large field of contenders. But New Year's Day 1947 brought the news that he changed his mind and decided to run. In this, LA's first postwar city election, Roybal found himself not the only veteran among the challengers. A Jewish candidate and a woman were also bidding to break the white, Christian, male lock on the council in their own ways. The unions mainly stuck with the incumbent. Mexican-American voter registration was low. Roybal placed a distant third in the primary, eliminating him from the runoff. Christensen cruised to reelection.

Perhaps the first glimmer of a restless world looking ahead came in the form of a curt telegram from Saul Alinsky the next day, asking, "What are you going to do next?"[23] Two weeks later, the Ninth Circuit Court of Appeals in San Francisco upheld the district court's ruling against the segregation of Mexican-American students in Westminster, Orange County. Roybal met with his campaign group at a restaurant in Boyle Heights to discuss what to do. They decided to stay together, converting the campaign into an ongoing group to be called the Community Political Organization and planning a fundraising dance in June. City council terms were only two years at that time, meaning they would have another shot in 1949.[24]

Alinsky came out to Los Angeles that June and on entirely separate tracks met with Roybal and with Fred Ross, the roving activist who had thrown himself into organizing in the Citrus Belt. A historic convergence was approaching. Ross had discovered what was for him a whole new world of marginalized and largely hidden Mexican-American neighborhoods all over Southern California. He developed a new approach to organizing in these communities, working his way up the scale to larger, more urban concentrations.[25] Alinsky wanted to hire him, but Ross would only agree if he could focus next specifically on Mexican Americans in Boyle Heights. While in Los Angeles, Alinsky quickly raised the modest funds needed to get Ross started and then returned to Chicago.

Ross decided the best way to start organizing Mexican Americans in Boyle Heights was to work with the group around Roybal. It took him weeks to win their trust and have them accept him as their full-time paid organizer, courtesy of Alinsky's Industrial Areas Foundation. The group strategically changed its name to Community *Service* Organization (CSO), dropping the "political," but nevertheless made its top priority registering Mexican-American voters — which it did with extraordinary results.

Contrary to widely held beliefs, CSO and Ross did not employ the basic approach Alinsky used in Chicago, nor did Alinsky teach Ross organizing or even guide his work in Los Angeles. Ross had developed a method, or better put, a method had *emerged* organically from the work Ross did together with residents of the Mexican *colonias* in the Citrus Belt. In Chicago, Alinsky built the Back of the Yards Neighborhood Council by convening existing, primarily black community organizations and parishes. Ross explained to Alinsky that the Mexican colonias lacked similar organizations to convene, and most of the churches they attended would not lend themselves at that time to community organizing. Instead, a new organization would have to be built from the ground up. The method for doing so was the house meeting, which would carefully tap into existing networks among relatives, neighbors, and friends. Those who agreed to come to a house meeting were asked to bring along one or two others. At each gathering, participants were asked to host their own, and so on.[26]

In Boyle Heights, Ross started out by pairing every night with one of the Roybal campaign volunteers, and together they visited the home of someone the volunteer knew. At each such visit Ross would try to get the new contact to arrange another meeting with someone they knew. Very soon the whole core group of Roybal campaign veterans was visiting homes every night and growing the meetings into small gatherings, like those Ross had undertaken in the Citrus Belt colonias. This process went on for almost two years. Along the way, general neighborhood meetings were convened that formalized the organization and its leadership, and developed a committee structure. "We had to set up committees on health, employment, civil rights, housing, education — wherever there was discrimination," Ross recalled to Saul Alinsky's biographer.[27] With a basic leadership structure in place, the organization could develop ties with the Church, labor, and government officials.

In less than two years CSO grew into a neighborhood assembly, with Ed Roybal as chairman, that drew hundreds of members to weekly meetings, deputized hundreds of door-to-door voter registrars, and registered approximately

*Ed Roybal is sworn in as the first Mexican-American Councilmember for the city of Los Angeles. (*Los Angeles Daily News *Negatives. Department of Special Collections, Charles E. Young Research Library, University of California at Los Angeles.)*

17,000 new voters before the next city council election. CSO formed numerous committees working on a range of issues. The organization succeeded in getting the LAPD to accept a number of reforms of its policing practices and training, and it got the captain in charge of the station in Boyle Heights replaced.

In January 1949, Roybal transitioned from CSO chairman to, once again, candidate for city council. Christensen also chose to run again for reelection. In this rematch, Roybal made it past the other challengers in the primary to face the incumbent one-on-one in the runoff. Christensen's campaign went negative, with both racialized and red-baiting messages, but Roybal won by a landslide. He was the first Mexican American elected to the Los Angeles City Council since 1881.[28]

Cold War Soldier

TO BE IN HIGH SCHOOL ABOUT TO GRADUATE AND JOIN THE ARMY IN 1949 was like getting strapped to a rocket being readied on a launch pad. Torres's blast-off was getting airlifted 6,000 miles to divided and occupied Germany. The jubilation that had broken out when the war ended the summer before high school was but a fading memory, as the alliance with the Soviet Union turned into a Cold War. All Torres's senior year, the United States and the Soviets were enmeshed in a constant and harrowing confrontation right where the war with Nazi Germany ended, at the new divide between East and West in the heart of Europe, as well as on a massive scale in the sky over Soviet-controlled territory. The Russians were trying to blockade Berlin and the West into submission, while the United States and its allies undertook hundreds of thousands of flights, a hundred miles behind Soviet lines, to supply the isolated city with thousands of tons of provisions a day.

The Berlin Blockade was lifted shortly before Torres graduated from Garfield High, but not before the formation of the new Western military alliance that would bring many thousands more American troops back to Europe, soon including Torres. He rocketed from East LA to what was at that moment the center ring and flashpoint of world history, to serve in engineering units assessing the terrain; their task was to determine the most likely routes a potential Soviet onslaught would take and what could be done, if anything, to slow it down. The United States had quickly demobilized the millions of men it had under arms at the end of the war and slashed military spending, but the Russians had not.

In the midst of dizzying changes of scene, a constant that became a recurring theme in Torres's life was that his artistic talent caught the eyes of colleagues and superiors, who took note and would find a way to employ it. He liked to draw cartoon depictions of goings on around him. In Germany, in addition to his regular duties, Torres was put to illustrating training materials about the Russian adversary for the army intelligence school. "My art was really taking me places," he recalled later, "I always had a good position somewhere because I could draw." He would rise to the position of sergeant first class, in command of his own reconnaissance team, giving Torres his first managerial experience.

While Torres and his comrades spent years meticulously reconnoitering the militarized frontier inside Germany, the Russians tested their first atomic bomb, the United States tested its first hydrogen bomb, communists took power in China, the USSR and "Red China" forged a military alliance, and North Korea invaded the South. While Torres, who had never even been to Mexico, served on the German front of the deepening Cold War, the United States partially remobilized and entered into a new hot war on the other side of the world. China reacted by plunging into the Korean conflict with armies totaling over half a million men. American and allied troops fought Chinese forces on the ground while American and Soviet jet fighter pilots dueled in the air.

When Torres joined the US occupation force, the new government, called the Federal Republic of Germany, and the new military alliance, called the North Atlantic Treaty Organization, existed mainly on paper. But at the end of the next year, the liberator of Europe, the German American who led the D-Day invasion and defeated the Nazis on the western front, General Dwight Eisenhower, returned to assume the title of Supreme Commander Allied Forces Europe, military head of NATO. The unretired general was back in uniform to get things moving, and he demanded a fast pace. The alliance and posture of the West quickly took on a new look. By the time Torres got back to East LA in 1953, Eisenhower, his former top commander in Europe, was already installed as the new president of the United States.

In the midst of a Red Scare that had taken the form of McCarthyism, and as a worldwide Cold War turned into a military stalemate in Korea, the Republican Party turned to Eisenhower to bring an end to two decades of New Deal coalition control of the White House and Congress, electing him president in November of 1952. Ed Roybal, who had been shaped politically by the New Deal, was in his second term on the Los Angeles City Council. Esteban Torres was by then an army short-timer, completing his tour of duty in Germany, along the East-West divide. After four years in Europe, Torres returned to East LA in 1953 wanting to make a career out of his artistic talent. The GI Bill offered him the chance to study art and become an art historian, which he pursued in classes at the LA Art Center, ELAC, and Cal State LA, but plans for marriage, with the intention of starting a family, took precedence and led him to take on full-time industrial work. Torres continued taking art classes in the 1950s, but they eventually got squeezed out.

Eisenhower was no radical right-winger and would not attempt a wholesale rollback of the New Deal. But just over a year into his term, there was a return to a policy thrust not seen since the Hoover administration — a national campaign of mass deportations and repatriation pressures, officially named "Operation Wetback," specifically and insultingly targeting Mexican migrants.[29] This could not but hit close to home for Torres, whose broken and patched-up family had come to LA during the Depression as a result of his father's deportation, reportedly triggered by his union activism in Arizona. It is with the Eisenhower administration's Operation Wetback underway, as well as with his plans for a family, that Torres changed his life's course. Practical necessity may have dictated his taking a factory job, but at the same time Torres could not shake the thought that his father had been persecuted and banished for being a union man. He felt drawn to taking a stand in life, the same stand as his father's. The assembly-line welder job at the Chrysler Maywood plant would make of Torres a union man, a member of the United Auto Workers, Local 230.[30]

His evident interest in the union deepened Torres's contact with fellow workers knowledgeable about the UAW, which in turn opened a special new world to him — that of the Jewish left. LA's Eastside boasted the largest Jewish population in the West, especially concentrated in Boyle Heights from the 1920s through the 1940s, but it went into decline after WWII when Jews started moving to the Westside. The more political, left-wing Jews, many of them committed to unions and working-class solidarity, tried to hang on in the 1950s. They were a presence in many LA industrial unions when the "Second Red Scare" erupted in the late 1940s, morphing into the McCarthy Era in the 1950s.[31]

By the time Torres got there, radical Jewish labor activists at the Chrysler plant were shut out of any formal role in the union. UAW President Walter Reuther had systematically purged the communist faction within the union in the latter half of the 1940s.[32] But these were friendly lefties, whom Torres and his wife Arcy took to socializing with. They noticed Torres's artistic talent and encouraged him to draw cartoons for the union newspaper, and then to run for shop steward, which he did and won. By the time he was elected chief steward, in 1958, Torres's life was once more set on a new course, now working for the union, not the auto plant, which in a few years would take him out of East LA again.

Taking on LA

ROYBAL DID NOT IMMEDIATELY PUT COMMUNITY ORGANIZING BEHIND HIM after being sworn into office on July 1, 1949. He went to a real estate office in East Los Angeles that refused to sell to "Mexicans," although it advertised specifically to military veterans. He tried to put a down payment on a house but was sheepishly rebuffed by the agent, who said he could not sell to him. Roybal gave the man his LA City Council card and strode off to his car. The agent looked at the card and scrambled after Roybal to apologize, telling him that he could buy the house if he said he was Spanish or Italian instead of Mexican. Roybal drove off and made a speech about his experience the next day at the city council. CSO swung into action, putting a picket line outside the real estate office. Between the protest and the extensive bad publicity over refusing to sell a house to a veteran, the realty company agreed to negotiate with CSO and change its policies. The organization went on to successfully address housing discrimination in other Eastside communities.[33]

Roybal's election to the Los Angeles City Council in 1949 gave his district a new and energetic representative, but more importantly it gave Mexican Americans and the multiracial coalition that elected him an authoritative voice. As an activist councilman, he delivered for his district the basic services that those residents newly organized and registered by CSO needed: paved streets, stop signs, street lights, and the like.[34] But there were big issues to contend with as well in the charged atmosphere of the Cold War and intensifying domestic Red Scare, growing agitation on civil rights, and all the challenges of LA's renewed, rapid growth.

Roybal moved quickly to act on the first plank that his predecessor city-council candidate Eduardo Quevedo ran on in 1945 — a fair employment practices commission (FEPC) to combat job-related discrimination in the city.[35] The issue touched an especially sensitive nerve in LA, which had been the target of congressional hearings of the House Un-American Activities Committee less than two years before, and where employment blacklists had been instituted as a result. As final debate approached on Roybal's proposal, the *Los Angeles Times* charged that "Communists" (capital C) were pushing for the ordinance. The council session attracted a crowd of 600 people and went on for six hours before Roybal's measure was voted down eight to six.[36] The following year an ordinance came before the council requiring that communists register with the police department. The final debate and vote attracted an overflow crowd again, but this time Roybal found himself alone, 13 to one, and assaulted by a chorus of boos.[37]

Roybal went on to propose a civilian review board to combat police abuse, an increase in the minimum wage, and continuation of rent controls that dated to the war — all without success. He fought the eviction of residents to make way for the Interstate 5 freeway through his district, and for the redevelopment of the Bunker Hill area downtown, and for the clearance of Chavez Ravine to build Dodger Stadium — again striking out each time. Nevertheless, Roybal won reelection in

*City Councilmember Ed Roybal, in suit at center, meets with the last evicted residents of Chavez Ravine, May 1959. (*Los Angeles Times *Photographic Archives. Collection 1429. UCLA Library Special Collections, Charles E. Young Research Library, UCLA.)*

1951, 1953, and, when terms lengthened from two to four years, in 1957 — with increasing landslide margins, capturing over 70 percent of the vote. At that point, after eight years in office, Roybal was able to post a win at the intersection of two of his constant concerns: discrimination and redevelopment. Roybal's proposed ordinance prohibiting discrimination in the rental of redeveloped property passed the council unanimously.[38]

His evident popularity among his LA constituents encouraged Roybal to seek higher office; he ran statewide for lieutenant governor in 1954 and for county supervisor in 1958. Although he won the Democratic nomination for the first of these posts, he felt that the party failed to support his bid in the general election. In the supervisorial contest, Roybal was initially declared the winner, but then wound up losing when additional ballots were discovered in three recounts of the vote. In the 1958 election, a friend and colleague of Roybal's, Henry P. Lopez, was also on the ballot, as the Democratic candidate for California Secretary of State. In this case as well, the Mexican-American candidate and his supporters felt that the party failed to invest in the race, which Lopez lost. Dissatisfaction with the Democratic Party led Roybal, Lopez, and others to create an independent organization, the Mexican American Political Association (MAPA), to mobilize the support and resources necessary to win higher office in the state. It is this restiveness and momentum that California Latino political activists would pour into the Viva Kennedy campaign in 1960, only to find themselves disappointed yet again with the results.[39]

To the New Latino Frontier

JOHN F. KENNEDY LANDED IN LA ON NOVEMBER 1, 1960, in his opponent Vice President Richard Nixon's home state, to start the last seven days of the presidential campaign — incidentally pushing Latino political mobilization to a historic climax. By the end of the day, speaking to a vast crowd in East Los Angeles, JFK's efforts would help forge a critical link between the past and future of Latino empowerment, between all Edward Roybal and his movement had done and was doing, and what his eventual successor — then a skinny local high-school kid named Richard Alatorre — would do to advance Latinos in the state, including reclaiming Roybal's seat on the LA City Council a quarter century later. Alatorre's father took him to the JFK rally at East Los Angeles College stadium, the big venue in the area, days before the massive 1960 surge in Latino voting. The experience would have wide-ranging and lasting effects.

After City Councilman Ed Roybal presided over the creation of MAPA at the statewide convention back in the spring, chapters promptly started forming up and down the state. In July, the Democratic National Convention, meeting for first time in LA, nominated Kennedy, who gave his televised acceptance speech before a record crowd at Los Angeles Memorial Coliseum. Shortly afterward, the Kennedy campaign directed its first Latino staff member to organize "Viva Kennedy," an unprecedented national Latino voter mobilization effort. Roybal was the obvious choice to chair the Latino campaign in California and convert the state's new MAPA chapters into Viva Kennedy Clubs. In the opening of the first-ever presidential debate, with Nixon on national television in September, Kennedy explicitly affirmed his commitment to advancing the rights of Latinos, at the urging of his Mexican-American aide. His wife Jacqueline filmed a TV appeal in Spanish. And now JFK was in LA a week from Election Day, to cap his Latino outreach under stadium lights in East Los Angeles.[40]

Later in the 1960s, Esteban Torres's United Auto Workers union would play a major role in Robert Kennedy's presidential campaign, but his brother John was not liberal enough for the UAW's taste in the 1960 primaries. After eight years of Eisenhower, many in labor, starting with UAW head Walter Reuther, were hankering to bring back the New Deal and they favored Senator Hubert Humphrey. Others remained loyal to Adlai Stevenson from the last two contests; and there were those who supported Kennedy. The split would not be resolved until the Democratic Convention in LA, when Reuther directed the UAW delegates to put Kennedy over the top, while hoping to get Humphrey onto the ticket as his running mate.[41]

Esteban Torres, shown with Cesar Chavez at the picket line in the fields of the state's Central Valley, would return from Washington, DC in 1968 to an East LA and California in social and political upheaval.

Indecision on labor's part made relatively more middle-class Mexican-American efforts seem more important. In this cycle, Roybal and Viva Kennedy were able to propel Latino politics into a new era, as they sought and were granted full autonomy from the party and the campaign organization. But Roybal would soon be disappointed with the meager rewards the new administration offered for his efforts, just as he was already disappointed with the California Democratic Party's failure to support Latino candidates in the 1950s. He was convinced Latinos needed to unite and fight to advance their agenda in every arena and at every level.

* * *

ESTEBAN TORRES WENT ON FROM CHIEF SHOP STEWARD OF HIS LOCAL to become a United Auto Workers regional organizer, an executive position that made him responsible for the western states. His ascent up the union ranks reached a lofty high in 1963 when Walter Reuther himself asked Torres to join him back East at "the international." Torres was named director of the union's Inter-American Bureau for Caribbean and Latin American Affairs, based in Washington, DC — for a Latino, a historically rare instance in which "speaking Spanish paid off."

Now, in the mid-1960s, Torres's domain stretched from Mexico to Puerto Rico to Argentina, at a time when revolutionary ferment, encouraged by the Castro regime in Cuba, was in the air. As the 1960s unfolded, however, the UAW, and Torres personally, grew increasingly interested and concerned with domestic developments, not least of all in California. A combination of factors would lead the union to send a willing Esteban Torres back to East LA, where, when he arrived, he found that, there too, something akin to revolutionary ferment seemed to be in the air.

Notes

1. Much of this chapter is based primarily on multiple, original interviews with Esteban Torres (see references), and other sources as noted.

2. Marín, "Always a Struggle."

3. We are deeply indebted to Dr. Christine Marín for her uniquely valuable scholarship and generosity in sharing her knowledge, documents, notes from interviews, and a range of other sources, affording us a level of understanding of the history of Miami and the experience of Esteban Torres's family that we would not have otherwise reached.

4. Sanchez discusses the experience of Japanese-American relocation from Boyle Heights in "Disposable People, Expendable Neighborhoods," 141–44. The full LA experience and context is examined in Leonard, *The Battle for Los Angeles*, especially chapter 2.

5. McWilliams, *North from Mexico*, 206.

6. Escobar, *Race, Police and the Making of a Political Identity*, especially chapter 11.

7. McWilliams, *North from Mexico*, 230.

8. Fein, "Myths of Cultural Imperialism and Nationalism in Golden Age Mexican Cinema." This son of Spanish immigrants who came to specialize in Mexican movies tiered his theaters for every level of the market. Born in Hawaii, he had been drawn to show business on the mainland and discovered the opportunity provided by the blossoming of Mexican-immigrant communities all over the country. He struck out on his own, touring and showing Mexican silent movies in pop-up locations, wherever concentrations of Mexicans could be found. But by the mid-1920s, it was clear that Los Angeles was the place to focus his efforts. Innovative and forceful, Fouce was also politically wired, active, and public minded. With Rockefeller and his team, Fouce helped make possible Mexico's "Golden Age" of film. World War II controls could have shut the rising industry down but instead they allowed it to flourish, modernize, and best its rival, Argentina, in Latin America and the US Spanish-language market.

9. Burt, *The Search for a Civic Voice*, 53–54.

10. The 1950 US Census put the city's Hispanic population at eight percent, the ninth city council district at 34 percent, and the Boyle Heights neighborhood at 43 percent. Cited in Underwood, "Pioneering Minority Representation," 402–03.

11. Ibid., 404; Burt, *The Search for a Civic Voice*, 50–55.

12. Dependent, as was all the movie business, on constantly drawing crowds to his theaters, Fouce had a stake in public health, starting with universal TB examinations. Roybal had mobile units and could make the pitch to the public in Spanish; Fouce had money and film-production capability. Soon Roybal was regularly seen on Fouce's screens, selling Mexican moviegoers on getting checked for TB.

13. Underwood, "Pioneering Minority Representation," 405.

14. Burt, *The Search for a Civic Voice*, 54.

15. Roybal, "Interview no. 184," 13.

16. In addition to the sources cited both in this chapter and the previous one, the preceding discussion of Fouce is based on our interviews with Ignacio Lozano, Jr.

17. Burt, *The Search for a Civic Voice*, 44–45.

18. See Julian Rappaport's historic address to the 1980 meeting of the American Psychological Association (Rappaport, "In Praise of Paradox," 15).

19. Berumen, *Edward R. Roybal*, 76–77.

20. Burt, *The Search for a Civic Voice*, 54.

21. Strum, *Mendez v. Westminster*.

22. Garcia, *A World of Its Own;* Thompson, *America's Social Arsonist.*

23. Horwitt, *Let Them Call Me Rebel*, 228.

24. Berumen, *Edward R. Roybal*, 77; Burt, *The Search for a Civic Voice*, 59.

25. Thompson, *America's Social Arsonist.*

26. Ibid, 72–73.

27. Horwitt, *Let Them Call Me Rebel*, 231–32.

28. Berumen, *Edward R. Roybal*; Burt, *The Search for a Civic Voice.*

29. The standard, book-length study of this program remains Juan Ramon García's, *Operation Wetback.* The *Los Angeles Times* has usefully looked back at its coverage of the program; see Kate Linthicum, "The Dark, Complex History of Trump's Model for his Mass Deportation Plan," November 13, 2015, http://www.latimes.com/nation/la-na-trump-deportation-20151113-story.html; and Matt Ballinger, "From the Archives: How the Times Covered Mass Deportations in the Eisenhower Era," accessed October 10, 2017, http://documents.latimes.com/eisenhower-era-deportations/.

30. For some history of this local and the broader context of labor in LA, see Laslett, *Sunshine Was Never Enough*, 138–41, 186–87.

31. See Wilson, *Jews in the Los Angeles Mosaic*; and Kenneth C. Burt, "Yiddish Los Angeles and the Birth of Latino Politics: The Polyglot Ferment of Boyle Heights," *Jewish Currents* (May-June 2008).

32. See Boyle, *The UAW and the Heyday of American Liberalism*, 31–34.

33. Roybal, "Interview no. 184"; Sanchez, "Edward R. Roybal and the Politics of Multiracialism."

34. Berumen, *Edward R. Roybal*, 106.

35. Ibid., 107–08; Burt, *The Search for a Civic Voice*, 50.

36. Berumen, *Edward R. Roybal*, 107.

37. Ibid., 112–13; Edward Ross Roybal, "Justification for Vote against the Communist Registration Ordinance," September 13, 1950, Online Archive of California, http://www.oac.cdlib.org/view?docId=hb4z09p124&brand=oac4&doc.view=entire_text.

38. Berumen, *Edward R. Roybal*, 106–54.

39. Ibid., 161–63; Burt, *The Search for a Civic Voice*, chapters 7–8.

40. Burt, *The Search for a Civic Voice*, 179–94; Leal, *Paving the Road to the White House or to La Panamericana?*; García, *Viva Kennedy*; "1960 Jackie Kennedy Spanish Ad," uploaded by PoliticalHistory on June 30, 2008, https://www.youtube.com/watch?v=x-WnsJmBsvHU.

41. Boyle, *The UAW and the Heyday of American Liberalism, 1945–1968*, 139–47; Barnard, *American Vanguard*, 379–80; Conway interview by Hackman, 38.

CHAPTER 3

Born in East LA

IT COULD HAVE GONE OH SO BADLY. Art Torres was a standout, brainy junior-college student soon to jet off to a new, lily-white UC in Northern California, leaving his suburban SoCal Mexican-American identity behind. Richard Alatorre was a dark, gruff-sounding East LA graduate of Cal State, now working for the so-called "radical" head of an aggressive Chicano-movement organization. The year was 1965, remembered for momentous events like the "Bloody Sunday" civil rights march in Selma, Alabama; the explosion of rioting in nearby Watts; the launch of the Delano grape strike that gave birth to the United Farm Workers — and the first encounter between Richard Alatorre and Art Torres. They were dating the same girl, unbeknownst to each other, when they met at her doorstep.[1]

That Alatorre and Torres would laugh off their dangerously awkward first encounter and instantly become friends was telling. They were two young men born in Boyle Heights, whose families, like so many others, moved further east, past city limits, not far but in different directions. Both developed a strut — but very different struts. Despite the huge gap in style between them — the exemplary, overactive, student-body-president type, favorite of teachers and deans, and the streetwise, sharply dressed basketball player who got girls to do his homework — they immediately began comparing notes about the larger world they were entering and the notable people in it who caught their eye. Each was confident in his own way and quick to recognize that the other, however different, was also going places. They could help each other, use each other. They could, and would, become politicians and acquire real power. They shook each other's hand that day. Together, they would shake up the state.

Alatorre and Torres were on starkly different paths that first crossed by chance, diverged, and then came back together, allowing them to form a political team, on the Eastside and in Sacramento. As a team, they played a key role in setting California politics on a new track. But what drew them to lives of professional, party politics — or even made their careers possible? What brought them back together? Most of all, what accounted for the surprising impact they were able to have on the biggest state and its biggest city?

Becoming Richard Alatorre

SON OF A STERN, STENTORIAN MEXICAN-IMMIGRANT FATHER who, to avoid discrimination, rarely took his family out of East LA, Richard Alatorre would become a statewide power, a distinctly *Chicano* politician of legendary chutzpah, a shrewd and fearless backroom operator in a slim-fit three-piece suit.[2] But getting there was not easy. He was born in the midst of World War II, on the eve of the Zoot Suit Riots, in Boyle Heights, where Richard's tiny family would live during his earliest years. His father dropped out of junior high in East LA, had a stable job for decades at classic LA stove manufacturer O'Keefe and Merritt, but hated his work as an appliance inspector and repairman. Adamant that Richard and his older sister Cecilia do better by completing their education, Jose Alatorre and his wife Maria stopped at just the two children, believing they could not properly provide for any more. The family's financial stability, and living in their own two-bedroom house, shielded Richard from any thought that they were poor, but Jose was not satisfied. Across the street stood the Bravo Medical Clinic, a symbol of Mexican-American professional success. Dr. Francisco Bravo was a graduate of Stanford Medical School and a political activist committed to advancing Mexican Americans and the Eastside. Unfortunately, Jose would not live to see his son reach heights of influence that neither he nor Dr. Bravo could have imagined.

Jose was an avid newspaper reader, in both English and Spanish. Richard would pick up the habit himself at a young age, graduating from *My Weekly Reader* to the "throw-away" community weeklies that provided local coverage. Although "not a joiner of any organization, an observer," Jose was acutely aware of politics — and resentful.[3] He especially resented how district lines were drawn to split up the Eastside Mexican-American vote, making it seem impossible to elect Latino representatives. He must have been animated when, with the war still raging, the best-known community leader at the time, Eduardo Quevedo, ran in 1945 to represent Boyle Heights on the LA City Council. Quevedo ran on a platform of fighting job discrimination and bringing a junior college to the district. Jose may have also been enthused when Ed Roybal ran for the same seat in 1947. But in those years neither Quevedo nor Roybal so much as made the runoff election. Before the next time Roybal ran and won in 1949, Jose had moved his family across city limits, back to his old neighborhood in unincorporated East LA, across the street from the junior high he had dropped out of.

Experience taught Jose to avoid venturing out of the Eastside. Richard remembered hearing the story of his father's humiliation when, while working at a construction site deeper in Los Angeles, he attempted to buy lunch one day and was told he would not be served. Protesting the discrimination got him arrested, and fired. Nevertheless, he enjoyed the Eastside's own diversity and taking the family to Canter's Deli, on Brooklyn Avenue, in the immigrant refuge that was Boyle Heights.

Richard would retain at least a few fond memories of that eclectic neighborhood from before his family moved to Belvedere. Alatorre made friends with his new immediate neighbor kids; they were a little older, taught him to play sports, and looked out for him. Alatorre then developed another small set of friends when he started grade school, but just walking the few blocks to school or to catechism exposed him to much older boys, bullies, in gangs. To protect themselves, he and his new classmate friends started calling themselves a gang, too. Alatorre took to playing basketball in the gym of the junior high across the street with some older guys, which became for him a "safe haven." His peewee gang of classmates was made up of just four grade-school boys banding together out of friendship and to survive. But just before starting junior high, one of them, also named Richard, went to a party back in Alatorre's old neighborhood of Boyle Heights, got into a fight, and was stabbed to death. Alatorre would later write that this violent killing of his friend shook him deeply. Once in junior high school, Richard began distancing himself from his remaining gang mates.[4]

Though a good athlete, Alatorre did not follow in his father's footsteps when it came to working with his hands, something that Jose repeatedly berated him for. But Jose always added the leavening lesson: Richard would have to get an education and learn to use his brain. LA schools, however, even after WWII, had not developed such expectations of a boy like Alatorre, any more than they had for Ed Roybal a quarter century earlier. By the late 1940s, the Los Angeles City School District, which served numerous communities beyond city limits, including unincorporated East LA, had for decades been employing intelligence tests and assigning students to different educational "tracks." One consequence of these practices, attributable to some degree to testing only in English, was the overrepresentation of Mexican-American children in "slow learner" and fourth-tier "development" classrooms — when not relegated outright to separate "Mexican" and "foreign" schools. Eventually, the designation of "educable mentally retarded" (EMR) was established and used to assign students to "Special Ed."[5] These policies would be significantly revised following settlement of the landmark California court case *Diana v. State Board of Education* (1970), which resulted in a series of revisions to the California Education Code, followed by the issuance of the California Master Plan for Special Education (1974) and the federal Education for All Handicapped Children Act (EHA, 1975).[6]

As he would recall in his memoirs, when Alatorre started school at Belvedere Elementary, he had "a hard time speaking English" because he was nervous with the language and stuttered. Spanish continued to be as prohibited and punished in late-1940s LA schools as it was in Roybal's time, and would continue to be for many more years. Alatorre found himself assigned to EMR classes. Nevertheless, he started doing well enough that teachers singled him out to stand up and read aloud when parents visited the classroom, to demonstrate the good job the teachers claimed to be doing. Though Alatorre started grade school nervous, stuttering, at a disadvantage with language, and concerned about bullies, he did not end it that way. A teacher in sixth grade would tell the now rebellious, class clown Alatorre, who was often sent to the principal's office to be swatted, that he would never make it and would wind up in jail by the age of 16. His resentment of LA schools began early and would last long.[7]

* * *

RICHARD'S FATHER WAS ANXIOUS TO IMPROVE HIS FAMILY'S STATION IN LIFE. Not long after moving to Belvedere, Jose was again looking around at other homes. He took the family to see a house in a nearby neighborhood with better schools, but a sense of apprehension must have grown within him on the short drive over. He parked the car around the corner of the house and told the family to wait while he went to check on it. He soon returned to say they were going home. Alatorre later learned that his father had gone ahead to make sure the house could be sold to a Mexican, and he was told no. Jose had acted to spare his family and himself another humiliation.

Discrimination limited the options the Alatorres had, but Richard's parents were determined to prepare their children for a better future. Along with drawing the line at two children, unlike most Mexican families, in a further break with convention, Jose and Maria did not want Richard to work; they feared it would take the focus off his studies. But Richard had other ideas. When he was in high school, an uncle got him a nighttime summer job in a meat-packing plant. The pay from working in a bloody plant allowed Richard to indulge his taste for nice clothes and start dressing with distinction early in life. Richard and his father both had their aspirations, however different.

In addition to learning to play basketball well enough to eventually start on his high-school varsity team, Richard was learning to play the game at school. He became a good talker. He could get girls to do his homework, and by junior high he charmed his way into student government. Alatorre enjoyed acting audaciously and taking risks. On one occasion, he managed to distract an elderly teacher with conversation while deftly changing his grades on the gradesheet lying on the desk between them. By the time he was an upperclassman at Garfield, Alatorre was an athlete and a personality, and was elected student-body president his senior year. At the start of his semester as president, he used his opening school-assembly address to lay into the faculty. He had developed a swagger, and even wore a suit to school. His grades had lifted him onto the collegiate track, but more than a few teachers resented him, thought he was "a joke," and failed to inform him of the interviews being held to get into the honor society. Insistently advised to settle for junior college, Alatorre had to complain to the principal to get his transcript sent to Cal State LA. Alatorre would be one of only four students in his class to go directly into a four-year college or university.[8]

"Just a freeway removed from East LA and there weren't any Mexicans," Alatorre would say, recalling California State University, Los Angeles, when he got there in the spring of 1962. This was alien territory. Though he had no black friends prior to college, he was drawn to the few black students at Cal State. Among them, he found guys who played basketball and valued nice clothes like he did, and they listened to the same music. The friendships and alliances he began building with African Americans in college would become an abiding part of his life and career.

The demands of college-level work, however, were a shock and a challenge. Perhaps his teachers were right. Alatorre was a slow reader. By the end of the first week he felt defeated and ready to transfer to East LA College. The next morning, Alatorre told his father what he wanted to do. Jose thought for a moment before reacting caustically. His acid words hit their mark. Richard reconsidered and proceeded to make one life-changing decision after another. He resolved to stay at Cal State and, if necessary, put in three times the work as other students. He also got a job handling credit for a jeweler — work he needed because he also got married. He had been involved in big high-school activities, had already thought of a political career, but now could not have any kind of college life. He tried taking a reduced load one semester but could not stand the thought of dragging out his studies for years on end. Alatorre had found his capacity for discipline. His first son was born two years into his time at Cal State, on the same day that his father died. Alatorre still managed to finish college in four and a half years.

Against the odds, he not only got into college and made it there, he went into the field of education with a bit of a vengeance. In his first job fresh out of college, Alatorre became an aggressive Chicano-education policy advocate, dueling with the school district and the state superintendent of schools over the treatment of Mexican-American students and their culture. In an interlude between policy and politics, Alatorre also had a brief career as a college professor. From there, he embarked on a path to becoming a legislator. Once in office, he was able to vote on statutory revisions of the state education code governing the classification of students as "EMR" and their assignment to Special Education. And long before he was done, he would be in a position to strategically threaten to breakup the LA Unified School District — the second biggest in the country.[9]

* * *

RICHARD ALATORRE'S BRACING ENCOUNTER WITH PHIL MONTEZ — he of the f-bombs — at the Foundation for Mexican American Studies, toward the end of his years at Cal State in the spring of 1965, would prove fateful. Montez, in effect, brought Alatorre into his Chicano-education policy world as an apprentice and soon gave him the opportunity to create his own job. Not just any job, but a real challenge designing and running an academic program for at-risk Latino teens, hiring and directing hundreds of teachers — many twice his age — to serve them. The youths were already organized into a network of War on Poverty-funded "Teen Posts" — safe, alternative recreational and enrichment spaces in their own communities.[10] The area coordinator of the Chicano Teen Posts on the East-side was another young man with a mission, son of an Evangelical preacher, David Lizarraga.[11] A lasting and fruitful connection was forged. Alatorre's program would deliver educational human resources: tutors, coaches, whatever the Teen Post directors needed.

The goal of community empowerment emerged in myriad forms in this work. In developing the educational resource program that paid his salary, Alatorre met with the directors of all the Teen Posts to sound out their needs and ideas, but in his memoir, he mentioned only one by name, David Lizarraga. In fact, he quotes what he recalls Lizarraga asked for from the new program: "to teach kids how to participate in the political and community process — to learn how to speak up for themselves and their community."[12] Lizarraga considered himself a community organizer and student of Alinsky's *Rules for Radicals*.[13] What he wanted from Alatorre's program appears to have informed and shaped the program itself. Alatorre also noted in his memoir that African-American kids were more "vocal and self-assured" in exercising their rights; both he and Lizarraga wanted Latino kids to learn the same skills. His program took teens on a variety of field trips, to meetings of political bodies, government agencies, boards of directors, school boards, and conferences "so they [could] practice advocating for their interests in front of them."[14] Alatorre's program at the Teen Posts was evaluated "by the success of the teachers in . . . developing leadership skills among the students."

Eventually, Teen Post would sunset and Alatorre's program would lose its funding. But as a regional coordinator, Lizarraga put on a masterful display of organizing and management acumen. As the end neared, Lizarraga convened his individual directors to discuss what to do next with the skills they had acquired and networks they had developed. Together, they constituted a substantial cache of human capital and a valuable store of relationships. Lizarraga made a proposal. The Maravilla Housing Project in East LA had an empty lot in back that was used mainly for gang fights. The Department of Motor Vehicles had built a new location in nearby Montebello and designated their old 5,000-square-foot building for destruction. What if Lizarraga and company could get permission to develop the empty lot, buy the old DMV building, and arrange to move it to the Maravilla site? Utilizing his son-of-a-preacher-man skills and relationships, Lizarraga approached a slew of Evangelical congregations that funded missionary and charitable work in developing countries, and asked each of them to donate a staff slot to work on saving Mexican-American youth, "down the street" in East LA.

Lizarraga and his team succeeded in getting permission to take the empty lot, bought the DMV building for a dollar, and raised the money to have it cut into three pieces and moved. They mobilized squads of teens they had been working with and tackled preparing the ground and foundation. The churches came through with a dozen staff slots to hire Lizarraga and his directors and assign them to the new center at the housing project. Virtually from one day to the next, Casa Maravilla, true to its name, appeared on the old gang battleground.[15] Step by step, the Maravilla Housing Project would become a historic focal point and crucible for the emergence of a new approach to redevelopment in areas of Latino concentration in Greater Los Angeles.

* * *

ACKNOWLEDGED IN ALATORRE'S MEMOIR AS HIS FIRST MENTOR, Phil Montez brought Alatorre into much else that was going on among the education professionals who considered themselves part of the Chicano movement, trying to effect something like a cultural revolution in California. Montez had also founded and headed the Association of Mexican American Educators. In assisting Montez with its growth and maintenance, Alatorre became an organizer of a different sort — not of a local community, as Roybal did in Boyle Heights with CSO or Esteban Torres in East LA with TELACU, and more broadly with the Congress of Mexican American Unity — but of a strategic sector of Latino professionals on a statewide level. Montez also sent Alatorre to speak to a gathering of federal prison wardens, which led to several years of teaching night classes to both Latino and Latina inmates, while at the same time also teaching college students at either the University of California, Irvine, or Cal State Long Beach.

Many of the skills Alatorre developed while working with Montez in 1965–66, observing and representing him, served well to prepare him for a political career, much as Roybal's work as a roving health educator did for him in the 1940s. The knowledge and perspectives the young Alatorre acquired on a variety of dimensions of society would inform his later work as a policymaker, and the great array of relationships he accumulated would help him get there and be more effective.

Perhaps as importantly, Richard developed a public political identity through association with Montez and his organizations. He became a professional Chicano policy advocate, and he moved on in that capacity to work for the NAACP Legal Defense Fund — one of the premiere organizations of the Civil Rights Movement. Also in collaboration with Montez, Alatorre joined in forming an initiative called the Mexican American Action Committee — as he would later put it, "a handful of guys" who saw themselves as "the new breed of 1960s activists." He would stress the generational aspect of the group over ideological positions: their self-concept was less about militancy than the fact that "the established Latino political leaders are the old and we are the new."[16] As "an organization of college students and professional young men from East Los Angeles," this committee had anything but a radical appearance. Instead, it signaled its new, hip approach by working with a different group of more militant leanings to place an ad attacking Governor Ronald Reagan on the cover of the first issue of the legendary Chicano-movement newspaper *La Raza*.[17]

The Man Who Would Be Governor

BORN IN BOYLE HEIGHTS IN 1946, ART TORRES WAS THE FIRST BABY BOOMER that would become a principal Latino leader on the Eastside and on the state level. Though he had only two younger siblings, Torres began developing judicious political skills at home from an early age. He was the firstborn of a mixed marriage between a Catholic, Mexican-American father and a Baptist, Mexican-immigrant mother. Besides being condemned to two decades of entire Sundays spent doing sacred and social double duty, he was called upon to be the bridge and mediator between his parents' and their respective families' distinct religious sensibilities. "There was a major, constant confrontation between the Catholic side of the family and the Protestant side," he would recall a half century later. Years of Bible study and teaching in two languages fashioned him into an alarmingly quick, wide-ranging intellect and a disarmingly loquacious raconteur.

Torres's family and personal experience would also cover a breathtaking range. His father's family had been orange-picking farmworkers in the Ventura County Citrus Belt before settling in Boyle Heights. But then during WWII his father, who would later become a butcher, worked in the once-again booming Arizona copper mines. His grandfather was a baker at the fabled Brown Derby restaurant in Hollywood, before taking an industrial job at the American Can Company in Boyle Heights. His mother was born on Mexico's Pacific coast to a Baptist missionary, but from the age of two grew up in East LA. Their lives seemed marked by repeatedly navigating and traversing between worlds and settings, rural, urban, industrial, Mexico, California, Catholic, Evangelical. They saw many sides of life and of the state firsthand, and Torres would continue and see much more after striking out on his own.

When he finished third grade, Torres's family moved from LA to the then white suburb of Monterey Park. But he continued traversing in his younger years, often visiting his grandmother Rafaela back in Boyle Heights on Saturdays. In her world, he followed her rules. Rafaela made him speak only in Spanish and often took him on the bus *al cine*, to see Mexican movies at the grand theaters in downtown LA on Broadway. These were theaters with real stages, where the movies were accompanied by *variedades*, Mexican vaudeville, the live variety show that preceded or followed. Rafaela treated him as well to the occasional full concert by a Mexican musical star.[18] Living in a suburb had not cut the young Art Torres off from urban life and culture, as long as he kept shuttling back and forth.

* * *

HIS BAPTIST AFFILIATION ALSO AFFORDED TORRES A SPECIAL OPPORTUNITY to further transcend his immediate neighborhood's ethnic confines and connect in a useful and lasting way with African Americans. Down the street from his mother's church in East LA was a black Baptist congregation. The joyful noise emanating from that outpost of African-American culture drew Torres in, where he was welcomed. As a scholar once memorably put it, "The scriptures are a language and one either speaks it fluently or not at all."[19] Torres spoke Gospel, and appreciated the singing. He would credit this experience for making him familiar, at ease, and effective in working with African Americans in politics and moving in black circles. Many years later, the Rev. Jesse Jackson would tell Torres he had a double afterlife insurance policy.

When Torres was 13, he worked his first job at a store his aunt and uncle owned. With his savings from work he made a major purchase — a Smith-Corona typewriter. Torres was drawn to the romance of writing and composed his own stories on the keyboard. His work doubly connected him to his aunt and uncle's traumatic loss, when both their store and home were condemned for the construction of the Pomona Freeway. Art would later say that the experience destroyed their lives, that they tried to rebuild in the suburbs but could not make their business work there. The damage done to this part of his family stayed with him and contributed to Torres's opposition to the completion of another freeway on the Eastside, once he had become an elected official.

Art Torres's widely noted way with words was born in Bible study and teaching Sunday school from an early age at his Spanish-language Baptist church, which made him "perfect" his Spanish.[20] He honed his verbal skills over five years of interscholastic debate and speech competition and exercised them in a stellar career in student government, both beginning in junior high. Torres developed the ability to open doors with his voice. His talent took him from Lorena Street Elementary in Boyle Heights to Montebello High School to East Los Angeles College to UC Santa Cruz. His father had scoffed at the idea of Torres passing up USC and UCLA to leave home and attend a university nobody heard of, but the opportunity to leave to attend an elite out-of-town university was rare among Mexican-American Eastsiders of his generation. From Santa Cruz, he would go on to UC Davis School of Law, and later top his life in academia with a fellowship at Harvard's Kennedy School of Government.

* * *

IN HIS TWO YEARS AT UC SANTA CRUZ, ART DEFTLY NAVIGATED between advancing his long-developing political aspirations and relating to the 1960s counterculture swirling around him. He would also say that the woodsy setting, "in the middle of nature," where he saw a deer for the first time in his life on his first walk to the library, had "an incredible impact" on him.[21] Torres would have many occasions to contemplate the distinct qualities and merits of California's coastal-ridge forests and the gleaming port city of San Francisco, as he regularly traversed between the two.

Torres had been student-body president from junior high to junior college, but now found himself a pioneer at a new school that had an assertive faction of anarchists and no student government. Here, in miniature, was what Kevin Starr called "the golden dream by the sea" — the opportunity to reinvent oneself and start the world (or a little part of it) anew.[22] At Montebello High and at ELAC he had to honor traditions and stay within established lines. At Santa Cruz he would be a founder of the student association at his residential college, Stevenson, and become its first president.

As student president, Torres placated the hippie crowd by arranging to have the classic 1960s California band Jefferson Airplane perform on campus. The next year he had the challenge of landing a commencement speaker suitable for a graduation amidst the upheaval and generational conflict of 1968. His solution was to have two speakers. Torres wowed his classmates' parents by securing the legendary but politically opaque Alfred Hitchcock, who had a home nearby. He paired the movie director with another artist, Indian sitarist and Beatles mentor Ravi Shankar, who had famously performed just around the bay the year before at the historic 1967 Monterey International Pop Festival.[23]

The most consequential influence of Torres's late-'60s college experience was his close friendship with roommate David Haet and his well-connected San Francisco family. The Haets introduced Torres to "a whole new world." Since high school, or even junior high, he had aspired to become a lawyer and have a political career that would lead to the governorship of California. His roommate's father was a successful big-city attorney — cultured, cosmopolitan, and highly political — with a family home in posh Forest Hill.

Torres spent "every weekend" in San Francisco, staying at the Haets' beautiful home, where at an endless series of dinners he met a parade of rising politicians: county supervisors George Moscone and Leo McCarthy, one a future mayor, the other a future Speaker of the state Assembly and later lieutenant governor; Assemblymember, future Speaker, and Mayor Willie Brown; future member of Congress and Speaker of the House Nancy Pelosi and her family. Most of these political luminaries were close neighbors of the Haets.

Torres learned not only about California's politics and society from a guest perch in the great city and state's ruling class, but also about fine wine and cuisine at the Haets' table. He had visited San Francisco before with his family, but finding his place and his way through this scene, as well as Santa Cruz, made Torres feel much further away from LA's Eastside than ever before, not to mention the orange groves his family had once worked. Asked who or what he was at Santa Cruz and at the Haets' — a bright LA Chicano student? A Mexican friend? Or had he transcended ethnicity? "I transcended it," he replied.

* * *

As was his habit, Torres went directly from one school to another. Moving on from Santa Cruz, the opportunity to continue his studies while at the same time start fresh at another brand-new institution presented itself. He set his sights on the just-opened UC Davis School of Law, ushered into being by legendary governors Earl Warren and Pat Brown — and located in a suburb of the state capital, not 20 miles from the governor's desk.

While at Davis, Torres got his first professional job working for California Rural Legal Assistance, the fabled CRLA, a new state agency created during the Johnson administration's War on Poverty. His boss was Cruz Reynoso, a future justice of the California Supreme Court.[24] This work took him to lobby and testify in hearings at the Capitol on issues concerning the rural poor, and it introduced him to Dolores Huerta and Cesar Chavez of the United Farm Workers.

Torres soon bonded with Huerta while they worked together on legislation. A seed must have been planted, so to speak, or nourished by this contact. Perhaps it began in the glory of the Santa Cruz redwoods. Included in the campaigns the UFW had been developing in the late 1960s was a focus on the use of pesticides in agriculture and their effects on farmworkers (and consumers). In about five years Torres would actually go to work for the union and have a role in these efforts. He would later continue working on pesticides and related issues of toxics throughout his political career. Many writers consider the modern environmental justice movement, which has gained considerable influence in California, to have its origins here in the UFW's pesticides campaigns.[25] Art Torres was to become a pioneer in advancing policy responses to these issues.

After law school, as he began positioning himself for the goal of public office, Torres took the first of his jobs on the staffs of Los Angeles-area state senators, starting as field representative to newly elected Senator David Roberti. This job put Torres back in LA in the fall of 1971, working the same area where Richard Alatorre was running in a special election for Roberti's old Assembly seat. Torres reconnected with Alatorre, and naturally became part of his campaign. They were embarked on a test of the proposition that a Chicano with a professional approach could be elected to the state Assembly from LA, in Reagan's California and Nixon's America, in a diverse district, a couple of years after Tom Bradley was defeated in the mayoral race by negative, racialized scare tactics, and just a year after an antiwar protest in East LA devolved into rioting.

Into the Fire

ESTEBAN TORRES RETURNED TO EAST LOS ANGELES, his real hometown, in the midst of apparent revolutionary tumult — both there and around the world — in May 1968. He had served the United Auto Workers in Washington as its director of Inter-American Affairs since 1962, in support of labor organizing and politics in Latin America. His boss, Walter Reuther, who recruited Torres to work in the UAW International Affairs Department, wanted to implement a new idea for American organized labor: *community* unions to address urban poverty and related ills, and in the process, reinvigorate the labor movement. Torres came home to make it happen in East LA and, in a sense, there lead the revolution [26]

Greater LA was a car-making metropolis, and the union, with its big stake in the tinderbox of Detroit, was particularly sensitive to what was starting to look like a national urban crisis. The UAW had launched its first community-union organizing effort in the Watts district — just months before the riots of summer 1965. It wanted to start a second organizing effort in a Mexican-American area, but the Watts riot at once confirmed the union's view of a deepening urban crisis and complicated its ability to press ahead with its plans.

The East LA initiative would not get underway until 1968, and when it did, the launch came between Cesar Chavez's historic, weeks-long fast calling attention to the United Farm Workers' years-long strike in nearby Delano, plus the walkout of thousands of Mexican-American students from Eastside high schools in March, and the assassination of Robert Kennedy on the night of the hotly contested Democratic primary election in June. The UAW was in the middle of it all, supporting Chavez and the farmworkers as well as Kennedy. In fact, a key UAW officer, Paul Shrade, was literally so close to RFK that he was hit by one of the rounds fired by the senator's assassin.

Shrade had been coordinating not only the UAW's support of the Kennedy campaign and of Chavez, he had also been laying the organizational foundation for the community union that Torres had come back to East LA to run.[27] The board Shrade pulled together had just secured an office for the new operation when the Chicano walkouts swept from one school to another, shortly before the end of Chavez's fast in nearby Delano. Kennedy flew into LA to drive up to Delano for the breaking of the fast, and on this trip decided to enter the race for president. The tumult in Southern California seemed of a piece with a worsening national crisis, with Lyndon Johnson's surprise withdrawal from the election at the end of March, and the assassination of Dr. Martin Luther King in April, which set off riots in cities across the country.

* * *

Torres launched TELACU — The East Los Angeles Community Union — out of a strip-mall office near Garfield High, a few blocks south of Richard Polanco's neighborhood. In time, the organization would develop into a new hub of Eastside political power, independent of Ed Roybal and his Community Service Organization, though it did share intellectual roots with that earlier effort centered next door in Boyle Heights. As a general project, the "community union" initiative was the "brainchild" of top leaders of Torres's powerful and highly progressive union, the UAW, which provided his salary and modest funding, but the concept owed much to Saul Alinksy's invention of community organizing in Chicago.[28] This new East LA version of the idea would suffer setbacks, evolve, and ultimately prove to have much more staying power than CSO.

Walter Reuther developed his thinking about applying union-organizing methods to neighborhoods together with his top assistant, Jack Conway. Conway admired Alinsky, and like him studied sociology at the University of Chicago. In fact, as an undergraduate who stayed on for graduate study, Conway had a deeper and longer immersion in the "Chicago School" of urban sociology than Alinsky had, before going into organizing with the UAW. Thus Conway, a Detroit native, spent years in Chicago with Alinsky's old professors precisely when, at the end of the 1930s and start of 1940s, Alinsky was gaining notice for his remarkable success in organizing the city's tough Back of the Yards district.[29] As he was always on the lookout for talent, Alinsky inevitably learned of the promising student at his alma mater and followed his progress.

During WWII, Alinsky tried to lure the young Conway from the UAW to go organize a multiracial coalition in Los Angeles. Following the Zoot Suit Riots of 1943, Alinsky expressed his "grave concern over the Los Angeles situation, which is filled with dynamite," and his belief that after the war LA would be "hell" if racial tensions were not dealt with.[30] Conway considered Alinsky's proposal but decided against it. The year following the war, Walter Reuther rose to the presidency of the UAW and made Conway his top assistant. Conway went on to serve in the Kennedy campaign and administration, helped create the Department of Housing and Urban Development, and participated in the task force that developed Lyndon Johnson's "War on Poverty."[31]

LBJ famously called for this "war" in his first State of the Union Address, which he followed up two months later with a special message to Congress presenting its core legislation: the Economic Opportunity Act of 1964. The policies Johnson launched were so innovative that they were not assigned to any federal department; instead, the Economic Opportunity Act (EOA) created the Office of Economic Opportunity (OEO) as a direct extension of the Executive Office of the President (EOP). Johnson signed the act into law in August. A key provision of the law created what would be called the Community Action Program, or CAP, "a program which is developed, conducted and administered with the *maximum feasible participation* of residents of the areas and members of the groups served," and that, by all appearances, was conceived by Conway; he was subsequently named director of CAP in the OEO.[32] By then, Conway was a leader in the AFL-CIO, but remained close to Reuther and played a role in the UAW's decision to go forward with the idea of community unions, beginning in Los Angeles. The UAW planned to get neighborhood unions started in black and Mexican-American areas of the metropolis — much as Alinsky proposed to Conway two decades earlier. The first to get started was the Watts Labor Community Action Committee in 1965. The Watts riots later that year played a role in delaying the start of the planned counterpart community union in East LA until 1968.[33]

Following the Watts project model, the UAW, assisted by Conway at the AFL-CIO, prepared the way for TELACU, convening a variety of other trade unions and with them forming a board of directors, naming its first staffer, renting office space, and establishing it as a nonprofit. With Esteban Torres officially at the helm as executive director, TELACU went fully operational in May 1968 — a couple of months after the high school walkouts.[34] Torres, starting with a staff of one, plunged into developing an ambitious array of initiatives aimed at addressing the needs of East LA, from youth programs to economic development and political empowerment.

* * *

IN THE ENSUING HYPER-CHARGED YEARS, Torres also came to head a large coalition of community groups called the Congress of Mexican American Unity, a.k.a. "*El Congreso.*" Its formation in 1967 offered compelling evidence of accelerating levels of mobilization and organization among Mexican Americans on the Eastside and metropolitan LA. Twenty years back, Fred Ross had explained to Alinsky that they had to build a Mexican-American organization from scratch, rather than convene existing organizations and congregations, as Alinsky had done among blacks in Chicago and had become the practice of the Industrial Areas Foundation.[35] *El Congreso* was in fact formed by convening scores of organizations that signed up for the specific political objective of electing the first Mexican American to the board of the Los Angeles School District, which it succeeded in doing in 1967.[36] By the time Torres became head of the coalition in 1970, it had reportedly grown to an extraordinarily diverse collection of 300 organizations.[37]

Torres, an army veteran, led this coalition to support the Vietnam War protest movement known as the Chicano Moratorium.[38] The national antiwar movement was vast and militant, yet by all appearances almost entirely white-led and based among white youth. The Mexican-American community, which contained many highly decorated veterans, was seen as patriotic and conservative on military service. But Chicano activists and academics, anxious to encourage resistance to the draft in their community, increasingly called attention to the disproportionately high level of Mexican-American casualties in Vietnam. They felt that the white antiwar movement was not reaching the Mexican-American community, even if it occasionally included token Chicano speakers at its rallies.[39]

The moratorium committee staged a number of protests that culminated in a historic and surprisingly large march and rally in East LA on August 29, 1970. This protest spurred a massive mobilization of law enforcement from throughout the area and devolved into a violent clash, rioting, and three deaths, including of prominent journalist Ruben Salazar.[40] The events of that day, and the long, bitter controversy set off by the killing of Salazar, drew in and affected the majority of politically engaged Eastsiders who identified with the Chicano movement.[41] For many, including the young Richard Polanco, the moratorium was transformative. The heat of those years was such that a coalition that included numerous mainstream service and professional organizations, such as *El Congreso*, refused to endorse Edward Roybal's reelection in 1970, and chose to support a radical Chicano candidate against Democrat Richard Alatorre in the following year's special Assembly election.[42]

The protests and the violence that broke out added greatly to pressure to address the Eastside's social, economic, and political needs. TELACU, with Esteban Torres in command and leading the *Congreso* coalition as well, was uniquely positioned "to serve as the intermediary for all sides at this critical juncture," as historian John Chávez put it.[43] The Johnson administration's War on Poverty had set in motion a new flow of resources to distressed communities, infused with a new spirit of social reform. A continuing sense of urban crisis helped to extend some of these programs into the Nixon era, but to make something of scale happen, resources would have to be matched with capable local partners and a viable strategy of community engagement.

* * *

FROM THE POINT OF VIEW OF LA'S MEXICAN-AMERICAN COMMUNITY, the historical significance of the connection to the War on Poverty's Community Action Program lay in how its most famous and controversial provision — "maximum feasible participation" — departed from previous experience with government-backed redevelopment. The most notorious case of housing redevelopment gone wrong was Chavez Ravine, just northwest of downtown, where three Mexican-American neighborhoods comprising hundreds of homes were razed in the early 1950s, presumably to make way for public housing that would allow the evicted residents to move back. But after all but a handful of homes had been demolished, the city council killed the project, and years later provided the Ravine to the Dodgers for their new stadium. Residents had no voice in this civic debacle, but the memory of it and the lost neighborhoods more than lingered in the larger Mexican-American community for decades and was given a sharp, even radical edge by the Chicano movement.[44] On the Eastside itself, the community's experience with the use of eminent domain to build the core of LA's freeway network remained inescapably present in daily life, as the area was riven by five wide freeways and became the site of one of the largest and busiest interchange complexes in the world.[45]

TELACU only got started in the last year of the Johnson administration, did not apply for an OEO grant until 1969, and was not awarded OEO funding until 1971 — well into the Nixon years. Community engagement had been so central to the Johnson administration's approach that one legal scholar dubbed "maximum feasible participation" as "the first commandment of the War on Poverty."[46] By then, however, the ethos of community action had been widely discredited among policy elites, most of all by Harvard academic and recurrent policymaker Daniel Moynihan, who mockingly dubbed the policy "maximum feasible misunderstanding."[47]

By mid-1971, however, TELACU was driving toward its goal of comprehensively orchestrating the redevelopment of the Maravilla Housing Project, making full use of the community-action concept, even as it was also working to achieve a different official status, that of "CDC," a Community Development Corporation. With foundation support, supplemented by the OEO grant, TELACU focused on planning for "Nueva Maravilla," which required the relocation of the project's residents, complete demolition of the old structures, and the design and construction of the new housing complex. The delicacy of this grand endeavor was both TELACU's challenge and its source of clout: East LA was in dire need of redevelopment, but community buy-in would be essential and this young, unconventional operation claimed that it could pull off the job.

The County Housing Authority and federal funds would finance the replacement of the old projects with Nueva Maravilla, while an entirely new model of community engagement was deployed to make the transformation humanly possible in this section of East LA. Torres knew he had to get David Lizarraga and Casa Maravilla on board. Once convinced, Lizarraga and his top staffer Richard Polanco helped convene and win over residents of the old projects, but even more critically, they worked to bring the area's gangs together to make peace for the sake of new housing for the community. Out of this effort emerged the East LA Federation of Barrios Unidos.[48] The residents were then organized into a Tenants Advisory Board, which followed the planning process and implementation in detail.[49]

The Housing Authority also provided relocation assistance and hired George Pla, freshly graduated from Cal State LA with a degree in sociology, as a relocation advisor. His office was in the kitchen of one of the housing units in the projects. TELACU, for its part, conceived the projects' redevelopment to be the central piece of its larger revitalization plan for East LA. As the relocation of the projects' residents got started in the fall of 1972, TELACU threw itself vigorously into community action in the surrounding area, dividing the neighborhood into 14 sections, holding block meetings in each, and building up to weekly town hall meetings for all. A variety of jobs were negotiated for residents in the demolition, construction, and decoration involved in the redevelopment.

By the end of 1972, with the process of the tenants' relocation well underway and the demolition phase approaching in 1973, overlapping advances were being reached. A new model of redevelopment had been devised that departed radically from historical experience and was being successfully implemented in an Eastside Mexican-American barrio. Along the way, TELACU, as an experimental community organization, was acquiring strategic new capacities and credentials, and key relationships were being forged that would provide the foundation for a wide variety of new efforts in the years ahead.

TELACU's formal designation that November as a CDC by the federal Office of Economic Opportunity represented both an ongoing transformation and a level of consolidation of the empowerment project it was created to bring to unincorporated East LA.[50] Both the organization and the community saw this as a historic component of a larger social movement, but it was also something more. This was a case of a movement giving birth to an ongoing institution. At the very

David Lizarraga and Esteban Torres at White House with President Jimmy Carter in Fall 1977, when Lizarraga, by then CEO of TELACU, was appointed to the president's National Commission on Neighborhoods and Torres was named US Permanent Representative to UNESCO in Paris, France, with rank of ambassador.

same time, the early 1970s, a parallel process of formal political empowerment was unfolding on the LA city side of Indiana Street, a breakthrough election that would gain notice across town and up and down the state. The time was soon approaching when what was born in East LA would be able to join forces with newly elected political clout across the municipal divide, a critical step in overcoming the fragmentation of the Greater Eastside.

Notes

1. Torres interview by Edgington, 29.

2. This section draws from multiple original interviews conducted by the authors with Alatorre, Art Torres, and Lou Moret from 2012–2016; quotes come from these interviews unless otherwise noted. Other sources include Alatorre interview by Vásquez; Torres interview by Edgington; Alatorre with Grossman, *Change from the Inside*; *El Malcriado*, entire issue about Art Torres; "Art Torres" biographical entry, Institute of Politics, Kennedy School of Government, Harvard University, http://iop.harvard.edu/fellows/art-torres; and

"Art Torres" biographical page, Covered California, under "Board of Directors of the California Health Benefit Exchange," http://board.coveredca.com/member/torres/index.shtml

3. Alatorre with Grossman, *Change from the Inside*, 6.

4. Ibid., ix.

5. Valencia, *Chicano Students and the Courts*, 117–20.

6. Congress reauthorized and renamed the EHA as the Individuals with Disabilities Act (IDEA) in 1990. Colker, *Disabled Education*.

7. Alatorre with Grossman, *Change from the Inside*, 8.

8. Ibid., 23.

9. The Los Angeles City School District became the Los Angeles Unified School District in 1961.

10. According to James Diego Vigil, 135 Teen Posts were established in the LA metro area in the 1960s. Vigil, *Gang Redux*, 64, and *The Projects*, 177.

11. Martinez, *Rising Voices*, 40.

12. Alatorre with Grossman, *Change from the Inside*, 35.

13. Lizarraga interviews with authors.

14. Alatorre with Grossman, *Change from the Inside*, 35.

15. Lizarraga interviews with authors.

16. Alatorre with Grossman, *Change from the Inside*, 39.

17. The other group was known as "Young Chicanos for Community Action" at the time of the joint ad with the Mexican-American Action Committee, in volume 1, number 1 of *La Raza* on September 16, 1967. The YCCA would soon rename itself the Brown Berets, affecting a Black Panthers-style appearance of militancy. See Ides, *Cruising for Community*, 342, 365. *La Raza* would become a magazine by 1970. Ironically, its editor in 1971, Raul Ruiz, would oppose Alatorre in his first election, disparage him as having "gone the establishment route," and proclaim to have cost him the win, throwing the race to the Republican candidate. See García, *The Chicano Generation*, 129. In a sign of the changed times in LA, the Gene Autry Museum of the American West — a cowboy museum — staged a retrospective exhibit of the highly visual *La Raza* in 2017, 40 years after the newspaper/magazine ceased publication; see Richard Guzman, "See How the Newspaper *La Raza* Shaped Chicano History 40 Years Ago," *Los Angeles Daily News*, September 21, 2017, http://www.dailynews.com/2017/09/21/see-how-the-newspaper-la-raza-shaped-chicano-history-40-years-ago/.

18. On this cultural scene of legend, see Koegel, "Mexican Musical Theater and Movie Palaces in Downtown Los Angeles before 1950."

19. Akenson, *Surpassing Wonder*.

20. Torres interview by Edgington, 8.

21. Ibid., 9; Interview by Kara Guzman in "UC Santa Cruz Celebrates 50 Years," *Santa Cruz Sentinel*, January 1, 2015, http://www.santacruzsentinel.com/article/NE/20150101/NEWS/150109997.

22. Kevin Starr seems to have attributed Arnold Schwarzenegger's meteoric political career to his having become "an eloquent advocate" of "the golden dream by the sea that had empowered him to reinvent himself" (*California*, 350). Schwarzenegger used the

"golden dream" phrase in his 2003 inauguration speech; transcript at "Schwarzenegger's Inauguration Speech," CNN.com, November 17, 2003, http://edition.cnn.com/2003/ALL-POLITICS/11/17/arnold.speech/.

23. Torres returned to Stevenson College in 2012 to keynote its commencement exercises. His times as Stevenson student president were recalled in 2015 during UCSC's year-long celebration of its 50th anniversary; see Guzman, "UC Santa Cruz Celebrates 50 Years."

24. See Bennett and Reynoso, "California Rural Legal Assistance (CRLA)."

25. See Tracy Perkins, "The Environmental Justice Legacy of the United Farm Workers of America: Stories from the Birthplace of Industrial Agriculture," *Tales of Hope and Caution in Environmental Justice*, August 10, 2014, http://hfe-observatories.org/blog/2014/the-environmental-justice-legacy-of-the-united-farm-workers-of-america-stories-from-the-birthplace-of-industrial-agriculture/. Randy Shaw discusses the early role of the UFW in environmental justice and its complicated relations with the major environmental organizations in *Beyond the Fields*, 134–37 and generally chapter 5; Laura Pulido traces the roots of the UFW pesticide campaign several years earlier in *Environmentalism and Economic Justice*, 57–124.

26. This section draws on multiple original interviews with Esteban Torres in 2010–2011, as well as Chávez, *Eastside Landmark*, and other sources as noted.

27. Boyle, *The UAW and the Heyday of American Liberalism, 1945–1968*, 239, 244; Schrade interview by Connors.

28. Chávez, *Eastside Landmark*, 27.

29. Horwitt, *Let Them Call Me Rebel*, 127–29.

30. Horwitt questions Alinsky's sincerity and motives on this point (ibid., 128).

31. Gillette, *Launching the War on Poverty*, 100; "Jack Conway, 80, Leader in War on Poverty," *New York Times*, January 11, 1998, http://www.nytimes.com/1998/01/11/us/jack-conway-80-leader-in-war-on-poverty.html.

32. *Economic Opportunity Act of 1964*, Public Law 88–452 (August 20, 1964), Title II, Sec. 202 (a) (3), emphasis added. The "commanding general" of the War on Poverty under Johnson, former Peace Corps director Sargeant Shriver, was quoted by his top assistant as saying, "Jack Conway is the only man I know of who had the guts and the vision to put together the Community Action Program." See Gillette, *Launching the War on Poverty*, 100.

33. Chávez, *Eastside Landmark*, 33.

34. Ibid., 34–39.

35. Thompson, *America's Social Arsonist*, 80.

36. Dr. Julian Nava was endorsed by the founding convention of the Congress of Mexican American Unity in January and went on to defeat an incumbent on the LA School Board that year. According to Nava, 92 Mexican-American organizations participated in the convention. See his memoir *Julian Nava*, 71–73, and Chávez, *Eastside Landmark*, 57.

37. Chávez, *Eastside Landmark*, 70.

38. The antiwar movement in the United States had a "moratorium movement" phase in 1969, considered the largest protest in American history to that point, which culminated

with the National Moratorium against the War in November. See Bingham, *Witness to the Revolution*, 164–87.

39. See García, *The Chicano Generation*, 249–50; and Oropeza, *¡Raza Sí! ¡Guerra No!*, 67.

40. Chávez, *Eastside Landmark*, 57, 70–73. The August 1970 protest is very well documented, with different sources estimating the number of participants from over 20,000 to over 30,000. See Escobar, "The Dialectics of Repression," and Oropeza, *¡Raza Sí! ¡Guerra No!* for meticulous scholarly accounts that provide substantial context. The head organizer of the protest, Rosalio Muñoz, gives his first-person account of that day and all that led up to it in García, *The Chicano Generation*, 272–82.

41. The law-enforcement attack on the moratorium protestors and the death of Salazar in 1970 have been memorialized in many ways, much like other dramatic events of LA Mexican-American history, such as the Zoot Suit Riots, the destruction of the Chavez Ravine neighborhoods, the displacement on the Eastside caused by freeway construction, and unwanted sterilization of Mexican-American women at Los Angeles County Medical Center in the 1960s and 1970s. See the exceptional PBS documentary *Ruben Salazar: Man in the Middle*.

42. "ROYBAL, Edward R.: 1916–2005," *History, Art and Archives, US House of Representatives*, http://history.house.gov/People/Detail/20684?ret=True; Chávez, *Eastside Landmark*, 170.

43. Chávez, *Eastside Landmark*, 77.

44. Laslett, *Shameful Victory*, 40; Podair, *City of Dreams*, 197. The Latino theatrical trio Culture Clash revived the story of the demise of Chavez Ravine for new generations of Angelenos with their 2003 play of the same name, staged close to the site itself at downtown LA's Mark Taper Forum; see Garcia, "Remembering Chavez Ravine." The play was revived in a new version in 2015; see Deborah Vankin, "Culture Clash adds more bite in 'Chavez Ravine: An L.A. Revival,'" *Los Angeles Times*, January 29, 2015, http://www.latimes.com/entertainment/arts/la-et-cm-chavez-ravine-culture-clash-20150301-story.html.

45. Michael Ballard, "East Los Angeles Interchange Complex," *Southern California Regional Rocks and Roads*, http://socalregion.com/highways/la_highways/east_los_angeles_interchange/.

46. Sherman, "Maximum Feasible Participation."

47. Moynihan, *Maximum Feasible Misunderstanding*.

48. This discussion based primarily on Bauman, *Race and the War on Poverty*, and Chávez, *Eastside Landmark*, as well as the personal observations of George Pla and original interviews with Esteban Torres, David Lizarraga, and Richard Polanco.

49. Chávez, *Eastside Landmark*, 86.

50. Ibid., 87–92.

Part II

Rebranding and Power

PART II

Rebranding and Power

It comes down to this . . . there are good Mexicans and bad Mexicans. The good Mexicans are well spoken and presentable in majority society, adept at making a favorable impression in any crowd. My longtime compadre and ally Art Torres is a great example. . . . I'm always the bad Mexican. A lot of it is my fault, coming out with my flashy style of dress, my bravado and colorful language. I hold a master's degree in public administration from the University of Southern California, but you don't know it from how I act and talk.
—Richard Alatorre, *Change from the Inside:*
My Life, the Chicano Movement, and the Story of an Era (46)

IF THE 1960S ACCELERATED LATINO POLITICAL LIFE IN CALIFORNIA — as they quickened American life overall — the 1970s were a political roller coaster, with Richard Alatorre and Art Torres riding front car. Time seemed to have a different pace for Ed Roybal in Congress, where he kept busy quietly introducing dozens of bills and amendments. When Esteban Torres returned to East Los Angeles to start building a community union in 1968, he found himself in what seemed like a revolutionary situation. Roybal backed historic legislation in Washington that year, but it had no chance of satisfying the burgeoning Chicano movement. By the 1970s, pressure to bring new faces and forces into the political system reached a tipping point — and by the end of the decade, a transformation of California politics was underway. But at the same time, the Los Angeles City Council had gone without Latino representation since Roybal left, to say nothing of the county board of supervisors, which had not included a Hispanic member since 1876. The needle that gets threaded in the 1970s is Alatorre's breakthrough election to represent LA in Sacramento, and what in time he and Art Torres were able to pull off there. Basic elements of political engineering and reengineering were necessary for significant Latino empowerment to start falling into place.

CHAPTER 4

The Mexican Problem and the Chicano Threat

URBAN AMERICA WAS IN RACIAL CRISIS when President Richard Nixon, back in his native Southern California, revealed his worries about "the Mexican problem" and the threat of "violent revolution." The summer of '69 was midway between the massive Chicano student walkouts from Los Angeles high schools the year before and the anti-Vietnam War protest that cops would beat into a deadly riot in East LA a year later. In the aftermath of urban turmoil across the country, from Watts to Detroit to Newark and DC, LA had just gone through a bitter mayoral election in which incumbent Sam Yorty staved off an African-American challenger of regal bearing, City Councilman Tom Bradley, by warning that this cop-turned-politician would bring black radicals to power.[1]

Nixon had met with notoriously rightwing Cardinal James Francis McIntyre, archbishop of Los Angeles, a month after his election in 1968 and again in August 1969, both times at huge, elite dinners he addressed at the Century Plaza Hotel.[2] Thanks to Nixon's fateful practice of taping all presidential working meetings, we have a vivid recounting of some of the cleric's insights that Nixon shared with his Urban Affairs Council that gathered at the San Clemente "Western White House" that August. "McIntyre tells me the Mexican Americans are worse off than the Negroes," he told the group, which included cabinet members and advisors. "With the natural volatile temperament they are supposed to have, if they blow, it will make the Negro thing look mild. . . . Don't overlook the Mexican problem. I'd hate to have it blow up on us." Nixon added a concern about the particular restiveness of those who went to college: "I've never assumed that education is the sacred cow some believe it is. It is so goddamn ridiculous to assume everyone should go to college. . . . [I]n terms of violent frustration, far more than black, white, or potentially Mexican, the frustration of a man or woman with a college degree, having nothing he is prepared for, is the greatest. There is nothing for him or her to do but join the revolution."[3]

Conservative worries — not only about minority radicalism but the potential rise of minority political power — charged the atmosphere in urban areas across the country. It is in this climate that two years later, in 1971, Richard Alatorre would run in a special election for a seat representing downtown, Boyle Heights, and Northeast Los Angeles in the California State Assembly. Nixon's Committee to Reelect the President would appear to have taken note. A secret Nixon Committee operative, Donald Segretti, who knew Alatorre's campaign manager from their student years at USC, would be in touch with his old friend during the campaign at the same time he was organizing "dirty tricks" operations.[4] But the opportunity for Alatorre to run for an open seat in a special election in the first place was a late echo of a political earthquake that in the mid-1960s had suddenly transferred a huge load of political power and opportunity to urban California, and especially Greater Los Angeles.

Political Transitions

FLASHBACK — THE CALIFORNIA RICHARD NIXON WAS BORN AND RAISED IN, that millions of Americans moved to in the 1920s and '30s, including the families of Ed Roybal and Esteban Torres, was in a practical sense a one-party Republican state. It may seem paradoxical that California was also a bastion of Progressive Era politics and reform early in the twentieth century, but extended and sometimes disguised Republican hegemony resulted from many "progressive" changes to American electoral systems.

The great, stated objective of progressive political reform was to combat official corruption, weaken the hold of party machines on elections and government, and restore power to the citizenry. Progressives used direct primary elections to wrest control of candidate selection from party bosses by making local and judicial elections nonpartisan. Urban political machines that typically controlled cities in the Northeast were further blocked by a system of at-large elections and small legislative bodies, as opposed to the nefarious "ward system" of district elections. Nonpartisan local elections were separated on the calendar from partisan national and state contests. Thus, in Los Angeles, nonpartisan city elections were held some four months after presidential, congressional, and state elections.[5]

Combined, these measures depressed voter participation, reduced the salience of local government, and kept out machine politics associated with Democrats and urban ethnic groups, facilitating the purportedly depoliticized administration of local official functions. Formally nonpartisan — but de facto Republican — and some conservative Democratic local government became the order of the day. These reforms were augmented in the early 1920s by severely constricting what were seen as the feeding tubes of the Democratic machines: ongoing, large-scale immigration.[6]

Nonetheless, the partisan nature of those federal and state elections remained, as did the danger that the huge influx of new arrivals from states to the east might alter the historic Republican advantage in voter registration and domination of elected offices. More reform was needed. One was a mechanism of direct democracy via ballot initiative and the ability to recall elected officials. Another extended the *appearance* of nonpartisanship to state and federal legislative elections by allowing "cross-listing" or "cross-filing" in party primaries, meaning candidates could appear simultaneously on different party ballots, without making their own affiliation known. Instituted in 1913, the year Nixon was born in Southern California, this feature proved to be a boon to incumbents, who were predominantly Republican. As Quinn notes in *Carving Up California*, in 1928, before the Great Depression set new political forces in motion, 109 of the state's 120 legislators were Republican.[7]

Nixon himself benefited from cross-filing in his first reelection to Congress in 1948. Appearing on both the Republican and Democratic primary ballots as the incumbent, without his party affiliation listed, he won both primaries and thus had no opponent in the fall general election. Having similarly won nomination by both parties in the 1952 primaries, 26 of the 31 Assemblymembers representing Los Angeles County faced no opponent in the general election.[8]

One more election-system curiosity fortified Republican power in Sacramento for decades. Apportioning legislative districts by population meant that, given its explosive growth in the 1920s, Los Angeles city and county would acquire a bounty of new seats in the Assembly and state Senate by virtue of the redistricting that would follow the 1930 census. Northern and rural interests argued for a deal in which the Assembly would continue to be apportioned on the basis of the rapidly growing population, but that representation in the state Senate should be based on fixed geography, with no more than one senator assigned to each county. Passed in 1926, this "federal plan" system, in which California counties on the state level mimicked the representation of states in the US Senate, held until the 1960s, when the Supreme Court ruled that state legislatures were constitutionally obligated to distribute representation equally by population, which came to be known as the "one man, one vote" rule. As a result, Los Angeles County catapulted from having a single state senator to 14 (and part of a fifteenth Senate district) in the elections of 1966.

The impact of this sudden change was that with 13 additional state Senate seats assigned to the county at once, at least as many of its incumbent representatives in the state Assembly had new and presumably more prestigious positions to aspire to. Those ambitious Assemblymembers would, in turn, open up their seats for potential successors to fight over.

Coincidentally, that same election also marked the culmination of legendary Assembly Speaker Jesse Unruh's dogged efforts to "professionalize" California's legislature. Unruh had already succeeded in increasing the legislators' staffs. In 1966, he successfully promoted a ballot measure that, with a pay raise, larger budgets, and other provisions, was construed as turning the jobs of members of the state Assembly and Senate into full-time positions. This transformation alone would have major implications, some unforeseen.[9]

The elections of 1966 in California are best remembered for launching Ronald Reagan, who took the governorship as his entry-level position for a new career. But they also marked the start of a great infusion of new blood and dynamism in the state legislature and in the representation of Greater Los Angeles in Sacramento. That infusion, in combination with the professionalization of the legislature, would be a key step in the development of new generations of Latino political leadership, and make possible a qualitative leap in policy innovation in California.

When Richard Met Wally

WALTER KARABIAN WAS A DIFFERENT KIND OF ETHNIC STRIVER drawn to Los Angeles and a life in politics. An Armenian American from Fresno, he came to the big city for his higher education, became a lawyer, and was pulled into the local governmental and political scene of the 1960s. His background, both ethnically and geographically, gave him an outsider's oblique perspective on the workings of power and its interaction with California's diverse and changing society; his work would give him a roving vantage point to survey the landscape with an ability to zero in on particular places of interest. The path he took from Fresno to USC to the LA District Attorney's office, where he served as a very junior deputy DA, ultimately sent him to local courts all over the county, including East Los Angeles, in 1965.[10] His work as a "runner" deputy DA, a sort of substitute teacher for the more established prosecutors assigned to specific courts, made him familiar with the county's complex social geography, governmental structures, and political dynamics.

Wally, as he was known, had originally registered to vote as a Republican when he was at USC and got involved in student government, where he went from junior class president to student body president. He was already thinking of a political career when he graduated in 1960, in the midst of John Kennedy's presidential primary campaign. The Democratic National Convention in Los Angeles made Kennedy the party's candidate. JFK, who exuded a rare combination of idealism and glamour, in turn made Karabian into a Democrat, which led Wally to work in Lyndon Johnson's 1964 campaign.

When Los Angeles County gained an additional 13 state Senate seats in 1965, Karabian had something of a political epiphany. Everyone following politics knew that the county's representatives in the Assembly would run for the new Senate positions, which in turn would set up an unprecedented number of open successor races in their own districts. This was the opportunity of a lifetime for a politically ambitious young lawyer, especially one in a position to scrutinize a range of options. He looked for the best Assembly district he could "parachute" into and win. Wally settled on the 45th, where the East Los Angeles court he knew was located.

Karabian saw Mexican Americans as historically neglected and marginalized by the political system. This was evident in the Assembly district lines that split East Los Angeles six ways in the 1950s and '60s. Democratic leaders in charge of redistricting had seen these neighborhoods as "putty, to be shaped" to beat Republicans in general elections, not a community entitled to elect its own representatives.[11]

Karabian, if given the opportunity, could cultivate the Latino vote and combine that novel strategy with his ability to raise campaign funds through his ethnic Armenian, USC, and legal networks. But he needed to move into district AD45 and start working it. The Grade 1 deputy DA went through several layers of authority to approach his top boss, the district attorney, who planned to run for higher office himself, to make his case for being assigned to the East LA court. This promotion would lift Karabian over a number of more senior deputy DAs and allow him to acquire the credentials and relationships he would need for a campaign. That the district would elect a Democrat was a given. The Republican district attorney was impressed with his Democratic deputy's pledge of future loyalty from a seat in the Assembly.

The electoral system appeared increasingly transparent to Karabian as a complex tangle of three-dimensional chess-like moves; he was perfecting his ability to see several steps ahead and to persuasively explain some of what he could see to others. This would be the way to plot a fast-ascending political career, if he could figure out the steps others would, could, or should take; the additional opportunities certain steps would create; and the loyalties he could cultivate by providing timely counsel and support.

Once assigned to East LA, Karabian found himself occasionally discussing and in effect negotiating some cases with a young Richard Alatorre. At that time Alatorre was in another of his series of one-year jobs, now working for the NAACP Legal Defense Fund, and, although not a lawyer, lobbying prosecutors on behalf of minority community interests. Wally needed relationships with Mexican Americans on the Eastside and saw much potential in Richard. Alatorre would get a privileged, inside view of Karabian's maiden campaign and the particulars of organizing an ambitious rookie Assemblymember's operation. Two years later he would take a formal role in Karabian's first reelection effort, in the tumultuous year of 1968.

Mexican Americans were dramatically more visible in the first half of '68, especially in California, than they had been in decades. There was Cesar Chavez's fast calling attention to the United Farm Workers strike, greatly magnified by Robert Kennedy's support and the union's grape boycott; the Chicano students' mass walkout from LA high schools; the UFW's mobilization of Mexican-American voters for Kennedy in the June 5 California primary, and Kennedy's declaration of victory with the union's co-founder Dolores Huerta at his side — moments before being fatally shot.

In perhaps the greatest comeback in American political history, Nixon, a native Californian, would emerge from the tumult of that year as president. Within the state, Karabian won his first reelection, with Alatorre deeply involved in the campaign, but his party lost control of the Assembly. This result ended the historic speakership of Jesse Unruh, the leader who had remade the state's legislature into a full-time professional body. But with a bare, one-vote Republican majority, the Assembly would be largely deadlocked for the entire term, and Karabian's political ascent placed in a holding pattern until the 1970 midterm elections, which Democrats across the country had high hopes for.[12] The social and political turmoil that swept the United States in the 1960s, however, would continue unabated, largely fueled by mounting opposition to the Vietnam War and proliferating movements of historically marginalized groups.

There was now the sense of a sustained Chicano movement asserting itself in communities scattered across the Southwest. Twin vehicles for this diffusion were efforts in support of the UFW grape boycott and the rise of a Chicano student movement in high schools, colleges, and universities. The concerns Nixon expressed about "Mexicans" to his Urban Affairs Council in San Clemente in the summer of 1969 were echoed in the halls of Congress that fall. "The militants in our community are on our backs almost every moment of the day," Congressman Roybal declared in a House hearing. "The question that is being asked of me, members of Congress, and other elected officials is, 'Is it necessary for us to riot?'" Roybal stressed that representatives like him had "quite a problem" on their hands: "We do not want to see the violence of Watts erupt in East Los Angeles. . . . But the answers must be found."[13]

In January 1970, activists in South Texas took another step by forming a separatist Chicano political party, which proceeded to win a number of local elections in small Rio Grande Valley towns. At the end of the year before, an incipient Chicano antiwar organization had formed on LA's Eastside and begun staging demonstrations. On a rainy day in February, several thousand antiwar protestors marched in East LA, and the organizers planned for a national march to take place there later in the year, which would grow to historic proportions with the support of Esteban Torres and the Congress of Mexican American Unity that he headed.[14]

The UFW strike and grape boycott reached a climax that summer when growers relented and started signing contracts with the union. Antiwar protests reached their own climax in East LA on August 29, when clashes with police and rioting claimed three lives, including that of journalist Ruben Salazar. Liberal Democrats, caught between waves of protest on one hand and a Republican president and governor on the other, struggled to keep their brand of professional politics "relevant" to the times and issues. That fall, activists working with that Chicano political party known as *La Raza Unida* staged the first of three campaigns for the state legislature, starting with a challenge to Wally Karabian.[15]

* * *

FROM THE START OF THAT SAME MIDTERM ELECTION YEAR, KARABIAN HAD SEEN that a nearby congressional seat was opening up and that the race to fill it was drawing in a state senator halfway through his four-year term. He calculated that the senator would win, which would, in turn, require a special election in early 1971 to elect his replacement in the Senate. Karabian also saw that an Assembly colleague in one of his neighboring districts would run and win that special election, which would, in turn, necessitate another special election later in the year to fill the vacated Assembly seat. Now was the time to plan to position a candidate for the second hypothetical special election, an open race for the Assembly in a district adjoining Karabian's own. Wally called Richard Alatorre.

Karabian had come to believe that the best position for a prospective candidate for the Assembly — certainly the best position that he could arrange — would be as "administrative assistant" to an incumbent, but California's electoral rules required that candidates not hold such a public job for 90 days before filing to run in a state election. He would need a work-around, to which he applied his legal skills. By the end of the year, Karabian had again been reelected, and was positioned on the side of the next Speaker of the Assembly, the San Fernando Valley member of mixed Italian and Armenian parentage, Bob Moretti. In January, Speaker Moretti would make Karabian the youngest-ever majority leader of the Assembly. Karabian would now command considerably more power and money than before.

Karabian devised a way to hire Alatorre, to establish his credentials as administrative assistant to the majority leader, while paying him from a campaign account rather than the state payroll. This arrangement would comply with the rules for the required period preceding the filing deadline for the election Alatorre was being recruited to run in. Karabian would be able to assign Alatorre to start working the district that was expected to open up, help the assemblyman there become a senator, and position himself to run. All he needed was for Alatorre to say yes.

By this time, Alatorre was teaching at UC Irvine and living in nearby "Surf City" Huntington Beach. He had signed for another year at UCI and was reluctant to relocate again — especially to Sacramento. But not only was Karabian offering this particular opportunity, he had strategic plans for the big picture. Karabian was convincing on the double special-election scenario, had the clout and resources to sponsor Alatorre's campaign, and held out the prospect that Alatorre would join the Assembly in time to benefit from that year's obligatory round of redistricting. In the Assembly, Alatorre could participate in unifying more of the Latino Eastside into legislative districts that it would control. Karabian believed that the Democratic establishment knew that it needed a Chicano member of the Assembly, and at long last had to fashion a majority Hispanic district. Alatorre would thus be a strategic element — indeed the leader — of a concrete strategy of Latino political empowerment, redressing the situation that had angered his late father. He simply had to commit to first working the district effectively and then to campaigning relentlessly.

There would be challenges and setbacks to come, but once he agreed, Alatorre stuck to the route he had embarked upon. His campaign would innovate and break new ground, and Alatorre would indeed play a historic role — and not only in overcoming the debilitating effects of political fragmentation on the Latino community of Greater LA and California. Alatorre would do more than any other Latino leader to put state politics on a new course. What was unforeseeable was what elements of the California that would soon be left behind, in this case associated with Richard Nixon, would do to keep Alatorre out of office. Those right-wing machinations would succeed in delaying Alatorre's ascent to the state Assembly by a year, but in so doing also effectively end the political career of his unique mentor, Wally Karabian.

A Four-Way Fight

THE SPECIAL 1971 ELECTION TO FILL THE VACATED FORTY-EIGHTH DISTRICT ASSEMBLY SEAT, representing Boyle Heights, downtown, and Northeast Los Angeles, developed into an extraordinary contest involving distinct historical forces, political visions, intrigue, and an unusual amount of national attention. Unbeknownst to Karabian, Speaker Moretti, planning to run for governor in 1974, had his own designs on AD48. Moretti saw Congressman Ed Roybal as by far the most significant Mexican-American elected official in the state. It would serve Moretti's interests in a gubernatorial run to back an Assembly candidate pleasing to Roybal — and that was not Karabian's man Alatorre.

Karabian, however, was in too deep with his plans for Alatorre to yank him out of the race. The special primary would have to be a two-level test of strength. On one level, the test would pit the historic force that was Ed Roybal — in the form of the candidate he supported — against the potential of a new breed of Eastside leader ready to be born, a *Chicano* politician. On another, the primary was an unusual test of wills between the new Speaker of the Assembly and the member he had promoted to majority leader. On neither level would the contest be an even match.

Karabian was committed, knew his candidate and the territory, and was focused in a way Moretti could not be. He brought in his own campaign manager and devoted on the order of $100,000 to the Alatorre campaign, freeing Richard to concentrate on finding and motivating his voters. With its significantly greater preparation, this campaign had superior talent, organization, and the luxury of experimenting with a range of techniques and stratagems. They mailed potholders with a smiley face to the entire district. Precinct walkers were equipped with portable TVs that ran a short film on Alatorre. And Karabian came up with the idea of organizing "Italians for Alatorre," because he and Richard could secure endorsements from well-known Italian-American politicians, and "Alatorre" was itself an ambiguous-sounding name.

Nor was the primary anything like an even match between the candidates themselves. Pushed by his campaign manager, Alatorre walked the district at a rapid pace, covering as much as two precincts per day. The Moretti-Roybal candidate, an activist lawyer named Ralph Ochoa, was not capable of much physical exertion. And then there was a secret weapon: Alatorre's manager serendipitously discovered that a couple of the district's neighborhoods were home to surprisingly large numbers of gay voters. He developed contacts at a gay bar that was two doors down from the campaign office. With Alatorre's support, the campaign organized outreach to a substantial gay community that no candidate in Southern California had ever appealed to before. Lists of probable gay voters were culled from voter registration rolls and tailored mailings were sent to them. Alatorre and campaign volunteers went specifically to likely gay households with a similarly tailored message. Alatorre attended a service at a famous gay congregation, arranged for a candidate forum there, and came back to attend a same-sex wedding. He took to working gay bars on weekends.

In his time working for Karabian, Alatorre had shuttled back and forth between LA and Sacramento, learning about writing legislation and connecting with electeds and other staffers in the Capitol. Early on, Richard struck up a friendship with San Francisco Assemblyman Willie Brown that would, in time, become of great consequence. Brown was sponsor of the then-historic "consenting adults" bill. Alatorre knew this proposed legislation was a top priority for gay voters. He expressed his support for the bill in the campaign's outreach and reiterated it when he spoke last among the participants in the candidates' forum at Metropolitan Church. Alatorre won overwhelming support at the forum, a supportive letter to campaign with from the pastor, and the endorsement of the gay newspaper *The Advocate*.

Such measures, in combination, powered an Alatorre landslide among Democrats in the special October 19 primary.[16] Given the party registration of the district, he appeared sure to win the second round against his Republican opponent.[17] But hazards lurked on the road ahead. Among those not fully understood at the time were the lengths certain elements in the state Republican Party and the Nixon reelection effort were willing to go to in order to usher in "The Emerging Republican Majority," per the title of the seminal 1969 book by Nixon campaign operative Kevin Phillips.[18] Multiple efforts were being developed in 1971 to undermine Democratic candidates, including a wide-ranging campaign of espionage and sabotage sponsored by the Nixon reelection organization and coordinated by an undercover operative based in Los Angeles.

The following year, in the last month of the presidential election, the first reports would appear on the dozens of operatives who were "employed by the White House and the Committee for the Reelection of the President to spy on and disrupt the primary campaigns of the major Democratic presidential candidates."[19] The coordinator of this dirty-tricks operation was Donald Segretti, who, along with several Nixon White House aides, was a veteran of the notorious college-campus variety of similar tactics used in student elections at USC in the early 1960s. Although he had very different politics, Segretti was also a friend of fellow USC alum Kenny Katz, who was managing the Alatorre campaign. A USC connection was a common bond in these and other political circles in the LA area. Wally Karabian was also an alumnus, and Katz had managed several of his campaigns. Alatorre had worked in one of those campaigns in 1968 and had also gotten a graduate degree at USC.

Within a couple of years of the special election that brought Alatorre, Katz, and Karabian together, Segretti would have the distinction of working out a plea deal with the Watergate special prosecutor, and then served time in a federal correctional facility. Segretti's testimony helped convict Dwight Chapin, the college friend and White House aide who hired him, but this probably facilitated his own plea deal for relatively minor charges of distributing forged, defamatory campaign literature. Indeed, Nixon would still be president when Segretti was released in early 1974.[20] The revelation of the Nixon reelection dirty-tricks operation was something of a sideshow to the larger Watergate scandal, but it nevertheless had a particular effect on Democratic politicos: it made them revisit incidents in their own recent campaigns. Fraudulent mailings and disruptive behavior would in fact attend the fall 1971 Alatorre campaign — as well as a far worse and never satisfactorily explained incident virtually on the eve of Election Day. Suspicion that the Nixon operation may have tried out its dirty tricks in this special election, in advance of the 1972 presidential primaries, would persist among California Latino political circles into the next century.[21]

Another hazard was that the most prominent activist of the Raza Unida Party, Raul Ruiz, who became famous for his coverage of the protest in East LA at which Ruben Salazar was killed, would file as an Independent candidate a year later for the special election in AD48. The key question regarding the more radical Chicano organizing efforts by parties like Raza Unida that emerged in this period was precisely whether they could get traction with the greatest concentration of Mexican Americans in the country — in LA's Eastside. But strictly in the context of this election, the more specific and pertinent question was whether an Independent Chicano candidate could play the role of a spoiler, sufficiently splitting the Democratic vote so as to throw the result in a district like this to the Republican. Alatorre and Karabian had their futures riding on the answer.

*   *   *

Unusually high stakes brought statewide and national attention to the 1971 special election. There was the unheard of political duel between Assembly leaders Moretti and Karabian, who backed opposed candidates in the October 19 primary.[22] Furthermore, both major parties in Sacramento and in Washington saw every California Assembly seat as critical in the fight over that year's redistricting, which remained unresolved.[23] And to top things off, prospective challengers to Nixon's reelection the next year and other national figures — such as former Vice President Hubert Humphrey and senators Ed Muskie, Ted Kennedy, and Alan Cranston — made appearances for Alatorre in the weeks leading to the November 16 runoff. The spotlight would turn out to be both a blessing and a curse for Alatorre, as it also drew menacing Republican attention and made the special election, which usually had a low rate of voter participation, a target of protests and unconventional candidacies.

Redistricting had an important role due to a standoff between the Democrats in control of the legislature and Governor Reagan, who vetoed the plan they submitted to him. Democratic leaders reached an understanding with Reagan contingent on the outcome of the special election in AD48. If a Democrat won, the partisan balance in the Assembly would be restored to 43–37 in the Democrats' favor. The leaders in charge of redistricting intended to make AD48 more Latino, to secure it in the hands of Alatorre if he won. It was understood that Reagan, with little time left in the year to get redistricting done, would sign the next plan the Democrats brought to him — unless a Republican won in AD48. Assembly Republicans could break this deal if their candidate won the race outright in the primary, which would require passing the 50 percent threshold. Here was the opening for intrigue.

The Republican candidate would have a shot at winning in this majority Democratic district — first, precisely because it was a special, stand-alone election, which inevitably depresses turnout, especially of minorities and working-class voters. Second, if there were only one Republican candidate, while several Democrats and others split the more liberal vote, the Republican's chances would be enhanced further. And in fact, the first-round ballot featured a single Republican, a young millionaire named Bill Brophy, against seven Democrats, a third-party candidate (Peace and Freedom), and the Independent Raul Ruiz, who was active in the Raza Unida Party. Of these candidates, four were Latino. Sacramento Republicans leapt at the opportunity to help Brophy and possibly break the Democratic leaders' understanding with Reagan. Winning this special election would strengthen the Republicans' hand in redistricting and embolden other candidates to run in Democratic districts. Republican money flowed to Brophy, and activists from Sacramento descended on the district to lend a hand.[24]

What would not come out for nearly two years — until the Watergate hearings and investigations were in high gear — was that Republicans also secretly and illegally helped fund leftist parties and candidates in this as well other races in 1972.[25] California Secretary of State Jerry Brown — then a few years away from becoming governor for the first time — ordered an investigation that found illegal Republican payments made to Peace and Freedom Party campaigns in 13 different races in 1972.[26] Deputy Secretary of State Thomas Quinn, who was in charge of the investigation, added that this Republican funding operation began precisely with the 1971 special election, specifying that in this case funding went to the Raza Unida Party candidate who ran formally as an Independent.[27] Subsequently, Secretary Brown and Deputy Quinn expanded their investigation to determine if a large quantity of funds left over from the 1968 Nixon campaign had been transferred to California.[28]

Other elements of foul play surrounded the election. Fraudulent mailers attacking Alatorre were sent out.[29] La Raza Unida protested at a campaign appearance by Senator Edmund Muskie for Alatorre, pelting his motorcade with eggs. The final incident of the campaign, however, dramatically surpassed all that had transpired to that point. After midnight on the Sunday night before the Tuesday election, shots were fired into Brophy's house, while he and his administrative assistant were inside. News of the reported drive-by shooting of eight to ten rounds from a .22 rifle upended the final day of campaigning and the election-day field efforts, dominating the local news for the duration.[30]

When the *Los Angeles Times* reported Brophy's upset win two days later, it introduced a hint of skepticism in the front-page story's lead: "Republican Bill Brophy, who told police he had been shot at just before Tuesday's election, caught Democrats by surprise with an upset victory in the 48th Assembly District balloting."[31] The story went on to note, "The shooting at Brophy's home, complete with dramatic pictures, 'gave Brophy publicity and momentum we had never hoped to achieve,' a key Republican strategist said."[32] Years later, in a sworn deposition in a voting-rights lawsuit, Alatorre would charge that this election, at his expense, "was used as the training grounds for what ended up being the dirty tricks during the Nixon reelection campaign."[33]

The conclusions reached in the secretary of state's 1973 investigation plainly indicated that a broad operation to secretly fund splinter-group candidates had been adopted after the success of this tactic in the 1971 special election. At the time of the result, well before the illegal payments became known, the Raza Unida Party candidate boldly claimed responsibility for Alatorre's loss. Ruiz's vote tally did indeed exceed the margin by which Brophy bested Alatorre.[34]

Another source of suspicion was the Republican candidate himself. Brophy, by all accounts, came out of nowhere to run first in the special state Senate election the previous summer — the opportunity that opened the Assembly seat in District 48. After losing that race, he filed for AD48. As the regular 1972 electoral cycle followed soon after the start of the new year — which Richard Alatorre promptly filed for — Brophy was naturally expected to run for reelection, but he chose not to. Instead, he filed to run to challenge Ed Roybal in the Thirtieth Congressional District. But after winning the Republican primary, and his new wife's involvement in a fatal auto accident, Brophy quit his campaign and dropped out of politics.

The 1971 special-election result had a range of significant consequences. First of all, Wally Karabian's big bet on Alatorre cost him his position as majority leader of the Assembly. Alatorre went on to win in the regular 1972 election by a large margin and took his seat in the Assembly in January 1973, where he also became founding chair of the California Chicano Legislative Caucus. In perhaps a fitting bookend to the journey traversed over the previous four years of the Nixon era, Alatorre's team, led by his top aide, Lou Moret, organized a fundraising dinner of unprecedented scale in the fall of his first year in the Assembly.

Alatorre and Moret chose as their venue the swank Century Plaza Hotel, on Avenue of the Stars in Century City. In 1969, this hotel had been the site of the event at which Nixon and Cardinal McIntyre discussed "the Mexican problem." Since then, Nixon's party had funded a radical Chicano party for the purpose of damaging a progressive — but mainstream and professional — Chicano Democrat. That gambit had succeeded in 1971 in keeping Alatorre out of the California Legislature. But, of course, he came back promptly in 1972 and embarked on a new path of Latino empowerment. And by the fall of 1973 Alatorre was selling out the same hotel that Nixon used 1969. A year later, Alatorre's career would go on, while Richard Nixon would be forced to resign from the presidency, precisely for having fostered a culture of abuse of power, dirty tricks, illegality, and obstruction of justice.

Art Takes the Plunge

WHEN ALATORRE RAN AGAIN IN 1972, just months after his initial loss in the 1971 special election, Art Torres decided to pursue his own seat in the Assembly alongside Alatorre, but significantly, in his own way. He had put himself in a position similar to Alatorre's, as an aide to a state legislator, and like Richard had the year before, Torres was working an Eastside district that he could conceivably represent — but with an important caveat. In his maiden campaign, Alatorre ran for an open seat, and even in his second effort in '72, there was no incumbent holding the office. Torres would have to challenge a sitting officeholder, as there was no other open seat on the Eastside to run for. This meant Torres, combining conventional political aspirations with the revolutionary spirit of the times, was undertaking to "primary" an incumbent Latino Democrat, Assemblyman Alex Garcia, decades before the term was coined.[35]

For Torres to challenge Garcia, a former aide to Congressman Ed Roybal, who was in his second term in the state Assembly, was to break multiple unwritten political rules. His boss, David Roberti, was the first to turn against him and stand by his Senate colleague, Garcia. Torres could not have mounted a credible challenge without the strong, personal support of Cesar Chavez and the UFW. This campaign, even more than Alatorre's, was attempting to force the dawn of a new era in Eastside politics — a Chicano era that would effectively sweep aside, more than build upon or add to, a previous Mexican-American political achievement. Chavez, Huerta, and the United Farm Workers had delivered unheard of levels of Eastside votes for Robert Kennedy in the California primary four years before.[36] Now the question was, could they knock off a Mexican-American incumbent who failed to support their legislative agenda, by backing a young man less than a year out of law school.

Torres had the endorsement, moral fire, and field support of the UFW, who assigned workers to his campaign and devoted an entire issue of their newspaper to promoting his candidacy.[37] But the idealistically underfunded Torres lost; he had limited campaign contributions to $50. Following his defeat, Dolores Huerta prevailed upon Torres to come work for the union.[38] His father reacted with dismay. Why, instead of joining a major law firm, would he "go back" to the miserable agrarian world his family left behind decades before? Working for the UFW

In the 1980s, Art Torres and Richard Alatorre would assume the mantle of senior Latino political leaders, alongside pioneer Congressman Ed Roybal, and joined by breakthrough Latina politician Gloria Molina. Torres is seen here leading a 1988 press conference urging undocumented immigrants to apply for legal status, as provided by immigration reform that President Ronald Reagan signed into law in 1986. (Photo by Chris Gulker/ Herald-Examiner *Collection. Los Angeles Public Library.)*

entailed a vow of poverty. Nevertheless, Torres accepted and became "like a son" to Cesar Chavez. Two years later, Torres got another chance at the seat he had lost when Garcia left it open to run for the state Senate. But Torres did not want to run in 1974 with his UFW position defining his identity; he switched back to a Senate staff job, this time with Senator Mervyn Dymally. The UFW still supported Torres, but now he would rely more on Richard Alatorre, who helped financially, and Alatorre's administrative assistant (AA), Lou Moret, who managed Torres's campaign.

Elected to the Assembly in 1974 to represent East LA, Torres joined Alatorre in Sacramento and helped reinforce the perception that Chicano politics had graduated from protest to the state's corridors of institutional power. In the 1980s, a more heavily armed and seasoned Art Torres would go after Alex Garcia again, and again be up against his former boss, Roberti, who would stand by Garcia as before. This time, however, the UFW would switch sides on Torres, and strongly back Garcia. Besides, Roberti by then would be *president* of the state Senate, not a freshman member of that house. But also in that future time, Torres would have the power of the Speaker of his own house behind him, in the context of a new landscape of Latino political power in California that he, Alatorre, and Roybal had helped to shape.

Notes

1. See Sonenshein, *Politics in Black and White*, chapter 6. The PBS documentary by Lyn Goldfarb and Alison Sotomayor, *Bridging the Divide: Tom Bradley and the Politics of Race* (Our L.A., 2015), provides an extraordinary window on the 1969 and 1973 Los Angeles mayoral-election bouts between Bradley and Yorty and their context, expertly ad-

vised by over a dozen of the leading scholars on LA history, politics, and society; see www.
mayjortombradley.com. The film can be viewed online at the website of the Academy of
Television Arts and Sciences, www.emmys.com/video/la-2016-4468.

2. McIntyre hosted the charity dinner for 1,350 that Nixon keynoted on December 5, a
month to the day after his election; see John Kendall, "Nixon's Speech at LA Dinner Hints
at Post for Finch," *Los Angeles Times*, December 6, 1968. The *Times* provided extensive
coverage, across several editions, of the August 13, 1969 "dinner party of the decade, perhaps of the century," honoring the Apollo 11 astronauts, less than a month after their return
from the moon, attended by "a glittering array of 1,440 celebrity dinner guests," including
44 governors, the cardinal, and many others; Ted Thackrey, Jr. "Glittering Party for Astronauts," *Los Angeles Times*, August 14, 1969. See those editions for several other articles
and the complete guest list released by the White House. On McIntyre's dramatic collision
with Chicano activists later that year, see Chávez, *Eastside Landmark*, 69–70.

3. Reeves, *President Nixon*, 121–22.

4. See Nate Rawlings, "Donald Segretti and the Nixon Gang: Top Ten Dirty Political Tricks," *Time.com*, January 18, 2012, http://swampland.time.com/2012/01/19/top-10-
dirty-political-tricks-2/slide/donald-segretti-and-the-nixon-gang/.

5. This section draws upon Putnam, "The Progressive Legacy in California," and
Quinn, *Carving Up California*. See also Starr, *Inventing the Dream*, 254 and chapter 8
generally.

6. Mellow, "The Democratic Fit," 207.

7. Quinn, *Carving Up California*, chapter 1, page 2 (each chapter is separately numbered).

8. Quinn observes that if not for his cross-listed primary wins, Nixon would have
faced competition on the November ballot and might not have prevailed in this, his first
reelection, given that Harry Truman managed to carry California in his upset 1948 win over
Thomas Dewey that fall (*Carving Up California*, chapter 1: "Introduction," page 4). On the
Assembly races, see chapter 1, page 13.

9. Swatt, *Game Changers*, 143–64; Bill Boyarsky, *Big Daddy*, 163–72.

10. This section based on original interviews with Lou Moret, and jointly with Karabian and Moret, and "Biography," *Walter J. Karabian Papers*, Online Archive of California,
http://www.oac.cdlib.org/findaid/ark:/13030/kt5v19q8zd/admin/#a2.

11. Quinn, *Carving Up California*, chapter 1, page 8. By the time of the 1975 congressional hearings to consider extension of the Voting Rights Act, East Los Angeles was
"divided into seven state house districts, five senatorial districts, and four congressional
districts, so that the Mexican-American population did not exceed 20 percent in any of
them" (Berman, *Give Us the Ballot*, 108).

12. Richardson, *Willie Brown*, 163–78.

13. Quoted in Mora, *Making Hispanics*, 35.

14. See Chávez, *Eastside Landmark*, 71–75.

15. La Raza Unida Party did not qualify for the ballot, so its activists most often ran
as Independents.

16. California laws governing the special election at that time placed all candidates on a single ballot. If none gathered over 50 percent of the vote, the top finishers from each party and the top Independent candidate — not just the top two finishers overall, as is the case today — would go on a runoff ballot. Alatorre came in second overall in the primary, but well ahead of six other Democrats on the ballot, who were eliminated for the second round. The runoff featured Alatorre, the top Democrat, against the only candidates who ran as Republican, Peace and Freedom, and Independent. Richard Berholz, "Alatorre, Brophy Face Runoff for Seat in Assembly," *Los Angeles Times*, October 20, 1971.

17. The district was 65 percent registered Democrat. Robert Fairbanks, "Brophy Assembly Victory Aids GOP in Reapportionment Fight," *Los Angeles Times*, November 18, 1971.

18. Phillips, *The Emerging Republican Majority.* The contemporaneous *New York Times* review of the book called it "the talk of political Washington, where it is regarded, fairly or not, as the campaign agenda for the second Nixon coming." Warren Weaver, Jr., "The Emerging Republican Majority," *New York Times*, September 21, 1969, http://www.nytimes.com/packages/html/books/phillips-emerging.pdf?mcubz=1.

19. John M. Crewdson, "Out of Prison a Month, Segretti Tries to Pick Up the Pieces of His Old Carefree Life," *New York Times*, April 22, 1974, http://www.nytimes.com/1974/04/22/archives/out-of-prison-a-month-segretti-tries-to-pick-up-the-pieces-of-his.html?mcubz=1.

20. Ibid.

21. Burt, *The Search for a Civic Voice*, 292.

22. "Moretti's Image Rides on L.A. Vote," United Press International, *The Argus*, October 18, 1971.

23. Fairbanks, "Brophy Assembly Victory," *Los Angeles Times*, November 18, 1971; Alatorre, *Change from the Inside*, 109; Kousser, Colorblind Justice, 103.

24. Kousser, *Colorblind Justice.*

25. Steven V. Roberts, "Leftist Group Says G.O.P. Aide Aimed at Democrats," *New York Times*, July 2, 1973; Associated Press, "GOP Aide Says He Paid Left-Wing Candidates," *Long Beach Independent*, July 12, 1973.

26. Associated Press, "Brown Cites Use of Secret Funds," *Petaluma Argus-Courier*, July 19, 1973.

27. Associated Press, "GOP Aide Says."

28. Wallace Turner, "California Seeks Kalmbach's Data," *New York Times*, October 2, 1973, http://www.nytimes.com/1973/10/02/archives/california-seeks-kalmbachs-data-officials-ask-accounting-of-753000.html?mcubz=1.

29. Kousser, *Colorblind Justice*, 103.

30. John Kumbula, "Shots Fired into Candidate's Home," *Los Angeles Times*, November 16, 1971.

31. Richard Bergholz, "Brophy in Upset, Defeats Democrat," *Los Angeles Times*, November 17, 1971.

32. Ibid.

33. Quoted in Kousser, *Colorblind Justice*, 104.

34. Frank del Olmo, "Chicano Party Says it Defeated Alatorre in 48th District," *Los Angeles Times*, November 18, 1971. Brophy won with 16,346 or 46 percent of the vote; Alatorre polled 14,759 (42 percent); Ruiz 2,778 (7 percent); and Blaine (Peace and Freedom) at 1,108 (3 percent).

35. Primary challenges have acquired strong ideological and partisan dimensions, especially in congressional elections (both houses), as American politics have become more polarized in recent years. See Boatright, *Getting Primaried.*

36. Kennedy won over 90 percent of the vote in some Mexican-American Eastside precincts; see Burt, *The Search for a Civic Voice*, 270.

37. See *El Malcriado* 2 (June 6, 1972). The UFW devoted this entire issue of its newspaper to promoting Torres in the primary election, featuring eight pages crammed with stories and photographs; this and most other issues of the newspaper are available online at the UC San Diego Farmworker Movement Documentation Project, https://libraries.ucsd.edu/farmworkermovement/.

38. Torres interview by Edgington, 13.

CHAPTER 5

Rebranding in DC

FLASHBACK — GROWING LANDSLIDE WINS IN 1951, '53, AND '57, combined with the lengthening of city council terms to four years, practically invited Ed Roybal to seek higher office.[1] Though he lost campaigns for lieutenant governor and county supervisor in the '50s, he saw another chance with the reapportionment that followed the 1960 census, when booming California was awarded a bounty of eight new seats in Congress. Before the districts were drawn, Roybal complained at hearings in Los Angeles of the state Assembly Reapportionment Committee about the lack of Mexican-American representation in the California Legislature and in Washington, but according to his and other accounts, the committee ignored him.[2]

One of the new districts created the following year included Roybal's city council territory, but it was designed by the committee chair to suit another candidate, a white, Westside college professor. The chairman of the Reapportionment Committee that year was none other than California political legend Jesse Unruh, who was making deals to become the next Speaker of the Assembly. Before the 1962 race got underway, Unruh scored his speakership, which meant that if Roybal was to run, he would be opposing the Assembly Speaker's man in the congressional primary. Roybal nevertheless seized the opportunity to be the first announced candidate, taking advantage of a luncheon where he was set to introduce Governor Pat Brown and would be guaranteed headlines. Roybal went on to win his primary and general election contests by wide margins, becoming California's first Latino member of Congress since the 1800s.

Nearly a decade later, as the 1970 census was about to go into the field, Roybal again found himself at a hearing, this time of the state Senate's Reapportionment Committee and conducted right in the community, at East Los Angeles College. Times had certainly changed, as this committee was chaired by a black state senator, Mervyn Dymally, known as a champion of minority group coalitions and civil rights. The hearing's Eastside location reflected Chairman Dymally's intention to address Latino underrepresentation. On this occasion, however, Roybal questioned the legislature's ability to fashion predominantly Mexican-American districts even if it wanted to. According to his biographer, Roybal laid the blame directly on the Census Bureau. He argued that the legislature did "not know where Mexican Americans lived" because the census simply did not count them.[3]

By this time, years of increasing pressure on the bureau had yielded a modest concession, a new means of gathering data on Hispanics in the next decennial census. The bureau agreed to try, for the first time, a question that would allow people to identify themselves as Hispanic by choosing among the following categories of "origin or descent": Mexican; Puerto Rican; Cuban; Central or South American; Other Spanish; or "No, none of these."[4] Roybal's frustration was due to the fact that in finally accepting such a question, in the fall of 1969, the bureau insisted that it was too late to be included in the "short form" questionnaire to be sent to all households for the 1970 census. The bureau would instead introduce the question into one of its longer-form instruments, one of which would go to 15 percent of households, and the other, the longest, that only went to five percent. The bureau chose to add the new question to the longest questionnaire, which would go to just one out of 20 homes. Such a sample survey would not yield data on Latinos at a very local level and would be virtually useless in the precision work of setting district lines.

After the 1970 census was in, Roybal was not inclined to wait another decade for the government to start comprehensively collecting data on the "social, health, and economic condition of Americans of Spanish origin or descent." He fashioned a bill calling for an immediate "government-wide program for the collection, analysis, and publication" of such data, with specific directives for the Departments of Commerce, Labor, Health Education and Welfare, and Agriculture, as well as for the Office of Management and Budget and "other data-gathering federal agencies." Public Law 94–311, which came to be known as "the Roybal Act," ends with three sections that read like a volley of righteous artillery fire aimed at the Census Bureau. Section 4 directs the Department of Commerce, in cooperation with other agencies at every level, as well as with nongovernmental groups and experts, to immediately undertake a study to *project* the undercount of Hispanics in *future* censuses, given the limitations of established practices. Section 5 calls for Spanish-language questionnaires and bilingual enumerators, and Section 6 directs the Department of Commerce to implement an affirmative action program specifically for the employment of Hispanics by the Census Bureau, and to report progress to Congress within a year.[5]

Politics of Passage

RICHARD NIXON LEFT THE WHITE HOUSE IN DISGRACE IN AUGUST 1974, not two years after his landslide reelection, to return to ever-changing Southern California. Three months later, Democrats picked up 49 seats to claim a two-thirds supermajority in the House of Representatives. From coast to coast, the country was in political upheaval and transition. Ed Roybal introduced his bold Hispanic-counting bill in January 1975, the first month of the post-Watergate 94th Congress. In California, both Nixon and Governor Reagan had adamantly opposed the United Farm Workers since the 1960s, but that same January, Jerry Brown — son of the man who beat Nixon in 1962 — succeeded Reagan as governor.[6] Brown pointedly called for equal rights for farmworkers in his inaugural address and made his first legislative proposal a nationally unprecedented bill regulating labor relations in agriculture. The new governor had to call a special session to pass California's Agricultural Labor Relations Act, which he signed into law in June.[7]

In Washington, Roybal's measure went on to pass the House that fall. But the bill would not come up for a Senate vote until spring — by then amidst the 1976 presidential primaries — when, once amended, it passed in May. Its fate would ultimately rest with President Gerald Ford, who for over a decade had been Roybal's House colleague across the partisan aisle. California's sole Hispanic congressman had multiple reasons to expect the replacement Republican president to go along with this big data-generating step. As law, the Roybal Act would institutionalize consideration of Latino interests in the making of American public policy across the board.

Ford had assumed the presidency on the eve of the 1974 fall midterm-elections campaign, with the benefit of a certain presumption of goodwill for a fresh start. But he also came in with serious disadvantages, following what he called the "long national nightmare" of Watergate, and Nixon's unprecedented resignation. Having joined that beleaguered regime less than a year before, as the appointed vice president, the former congressional minority leader then became the only president to have never run in a national campaign, nor did he have a transition period to prepare his own administration. He needed to overcome the lost stature and isolation of Nixon's government, whose relations with virtually all constituencies had shriveled since 1972. Furthermore, regarding Latinos, the former congressman from Grand Rapids, Michigan had none of the experience, familiarity, or ties that his immediate predecessors from California and Texas, Nixon and LBJ, brought to Washington. He would have to work with a Congress controlled by the opposition party that had been about to impeach Nixon. Like never before in his career, Ford suddenly and urgently needed to reach out, listen to, and develop relationships with people and groups from far-flung regions of the country.[8]

Ford's own party had just officially institutionalized Hispanics as an organized constituency the month before he took office, in the form of the "Republican National Hispanic Assembly."[9] The very first major legislation Ford faced and signed as president in August 1974 included expansion and increased funding for bilingual education, one of Roybal's highest priorities.[10] Ford then authorized a White House Office of Hispanic Affairs, appointed the first presidential special assistant for Hispanic affairs to head it, convened a joint meeting of Hispanic members of Congress and his principal Latino appointees, and agreed to meet with heads of Hispanic organizations.[11] Even more consequentially, the next year Ford supported and signed the 1975 extension and expansion of the Voting Rights Act to include "language minorities."[12] But Roybal, by then in his third term as one of the 13 "cardinals" of the powerhouse Appropriations Committee, would not shy away from using his clout against the president, if needed. When Ford tried to cut education spending that year, Roybal led House Democrats in defying the president to restore the funds.[13]

In Congress since 1949 and having never faced voters beyond his own Midwestern district, in recent years Ford seemed to run into California and Californians at every turn. Nixon had headed Ford's party for half a decade when he summoned the congressman to replace disgraced Vice President Spiro Agnew. Now, as Ford struggled to survive the 1976 primaries and win his first presidential election, another Californian, Ronald Reagan, threatened to deny him the Republican nomination. In May, when the "Roybal Act" passed the Senate, Jerry Brown made a surprise late entrance into the presidential campaign on the Democratic side, with critical support from the UFW. The union's top organizer, Marshall Ganz, was put in charge of field operations, and Brown promptly won primaries in Maryland and Nevada.[14]

The "favorite son" on both parties' ballots in the California primary, ex-Governor Reagan and new Governor Brown, each crushed their opponents — incumbent President Ford and Democratic front-runner Jimmy Carter — on June 8. A week later, the House agreed to the amended Roybal bill and tossed it to Ford. The White House invited leaders of major Hispanic organizations to join him and members of Congress for the Rose Garden signing ceremony on the very morning that Public Law 94–311, "Relating to the publication of economic and social statistics for Americans of Spanish origin or descent," was passed.[15] In his remarks, Ford thanked "all of you who have participated in and worked hard to bring this resolution to completion. It is so important that we in government listen to the ideas and concerns expressed from outside government and that we maintain a constant dialog with many parts of our dynamic and diversified society."[16]

The Democratic National Convention was due to start in New York City in less than a month. Jerry Brown had no prospect of winning his party's top prize; he was in the race to make a showy statement before falling in line behind the inevitable nominee. Nonetheless, it was a grand and historic statement, live from Madison Square Garden, on primetime national TV. Brown insisted on getting this moment, and his command of the biggest state and a national base of supporters, mobilized by the UFW, secured it for him. He would go big, and shatter precedent, before going home. Some 50 million viewers watched Cesar Chavez deliver the speech placing Brown's name in nomination. The union leader's biographer would write that "the hottest item on the convention floor was the black eagle flag."[17]

Latinos had long been an overwhelmingly urban population, but with the union's boycotts of grapes, lettuce, and Gallo wines, and its backing of pro-union candidates, Chavez had strategically taken the farmworkers' struggle into the cities, where it came to symbolize the Chicano civil rights movement, and developed impressive organizational capacity with extensive support networks.[18] Latinos were taking on a political salience not seen since the Viva Kennedy campaigns of 1960 and 1968. A week after Cesar Chavez made his nominating speech to the biggest television audience ever addressed by a Latino leader, President Ford nominated Ignacio Lozano, Jr., the publisher of *La Opinión*, the Spanish-language daily newspaper in LA and largest in the country, as US ambassador to El Salvador. At the end of that month, Ford delivered the keynote address to the first annual banquet of the Republican National Hispanic Assembly.[19]

We do not know if Ford's various efforts may have helped him narrowly carry California in 1976, just that he did so while losing the election nationally. What is evident is that Latino political mobilization, leadership development, and policy influence advanced during the Ford interlude. A month after Jimmy Carter's win that November, Ed Roybal would lead his colleagues in founding the Congressional Hispanic Caucus, which soon began pressing the new administration on Latino appointments and issues.[20]

In line with the Roybal Act, the Office of Management and Budget of the new Carter administration issued what has become famous as its "Statistical Policy Directive 15" the following May, to this day reproduced in the manuals and on the websites of many federal agencies with the cumbersome title "Race and Ethnic Standards for Federal Statistics and Administrative Reporting." The directive defines "basic racial and ethnic categories," specifying, as would the next census, that "Hispanic" and "Hispanic origin" denote an ethnicity, distinct from the category of race. Although issued in May 1977, this regulation did not appear in the Federal Register for another year.[21] In another apparent direct line of descent, all 1980 census forms — one or another of which would be sent to every household in the country — contained the new, capitalized instruction to answer "BOTH" the question about Hispanic origin and the question that followed about race. This instruction included a comment about Hispanics being of any race, followed by the numbered question, "Is this person of Spanish/Hispanic origin or descent?" which in turn was followed by the options of "No"; "Yes" to one in the series of different national origins; or "Yes, another Hispanic" origin to be filled in. Immediately following was the next numbered question, about race.[22]

The significance of this census reform would not get widely noticed until the results began to be reported later in 1980, 1981, and beyond. The big aggregate numbers of Latino population growth would impress and even shock some, but for many others the impact would hinge precisely on having a complete count and not just a sampling of Latinos from a lofty altitude. The complete count would reveal population changes on the ground, in every little town and village, every neighborhood and district, in many cases far surpassing the 60 percent national growth figure and generating breathless reports in local papers, on TV, and on the radio. The heavy cloak of Latino statistical invisibility had been whipped off and set ablaze.

Implications for politics were profound and unavoidable. All geographically defined systems of representation where Latinos lived would eventually have to be reconsidered. Both the status quo and proposed revisions were subject to challenge. An astonishing combination of factors converged: there was a census, as always, and the need to redistrict, as usual, but now there was also an extraordinarily fast-growing group in the mix that was being fully counted for the first time, and that was also inventing itself politically and flexing new muscles. At the same time, this group was acquiring the benefit of new legal protections and the support of its own dedicated communications media.

The same year that Roybal introduced his bill requiring all relevant agencies to pay heed to Hispanics and address their needs, he was also deeply involved in extending and amending the historic Voting Rights Act of 1965. It had been extended once before, in 1970, but still only covered discrimination based on "race or color." The 1975 extension included an amendment protecting specified "language minorities," defined as "American Indians, Asian Americans, Alaskan Natives, and Spanish Heritage Citizens."[23] Those amendments were useful in some jurisdictions and made ballots and voting information available in Spanish and other languages. But the VRA would become a much more powerful legal weapon when it was amended and extended again in 1982. For purposes of the immediate redistricting based on the 1980 census, the VRA was less a basis for litigation than a rhetorical threat useful to a skilled political negotiator wrangling with legislators over their district lines.[24] In another element of convergence, California Latinos would happen to get the benefit of such a negotiator.

¡Cuéntese![25]

LATINO DEMANDS TO BE IDENTIFIED AND COUNTED BY THE CENSUS in the 1970s seem paradoxical in light of painful history. Immigration and refugee-driven growth of the Mexican-origin population in the 1920s provoked a surge in studies of "the Mexican problem."[26] That was a boom decade for "race theory" — aka "scientific racism" or "race science" — and intelligence testing, which was widely adopted, not least of all by Los Angeles public schools.[27] Severe restriction of immigration from southern and eastern Europe — rationalized with IQ-test data — and the complete cutoff of immigration from Asia by the early 1920s, increased employer demand for labor from Mexico, the flow of which, in turn, drew the attention of the country's robust nativist lobby.[28] It is in this context that the Hoover administration's Census Bureau established a "Mexican Race" category for the 1930 national count — the country's fifteenth decennial census, and the only one to classify Mexicans as a "race." The Depression-era campaign to repatriate Mexican immigrants and their US-born children to Mexico, promoted by Hoover's Departments of Labor (which then housed the Office of Immigration) and of Commerce (home of the Census Bureau), got underway the very next year.[29]

For the 1950 Truman administration census, the bureau opted for identifying all Spanish-surnamed individuals in the four states bordering Mexico plus Colorado, using a list compiled by the Immigration and Naturalization Service — the agency created in 1933 and charged with enforcing immigration laws.[30] The Eisenhower administration came in two years later, and with the fresh census data in hand, in 1954 launched "Operation Wetback."[31] In spite of this history, by the late 1960s, Latino leaders and organizations came to see accurate and detailed data on the Hispanic population to be in the community's vital interest. Their efforts to push the Census Bureau and all government agencies to collect and report such data were joined in the 1970s by business and especially Spanish-language media. When they succeeded in getting the census to add a Hispanic-origin question, all concerned — the bureau, advocates, elected officials, and the media — agreed that a concerted outreach campaign was needed to overcome understandable suspicions and promote public cooperation with the official count.[32] Immigrants in particular, and especially the undocumented, would need reassurance that personal information given to the census would not be shared with immigration authorities.

A mix of interests drove the various actors — public, business, and nonprofit — to lobby for a complete census count under the unified "pan-ethnic" Hispanic label. Of particular interest to our story are the motives of political actors, which fell under at least two categories: policy and elections. On the policy front, census data became key in the 1960s to both the allocation of resources for antipoverty programs and for measuring underrepresentation in employment.[33] It could not be shown, for example, that Latinos were underrepresented in local, state, and federal jobs or at particular levels of public employment without official data on the population in each jurisdiction.[34] Undercounting — whether due to not being counted at all or not being accurately identified as part of an underrepresented segment of the population — was a chronic and costly problem for Latino communities.

On the electoral front, politicians and activists were necessarily interested in equal access to the ballot and how districts were drawn and redrawn for legislative bodies — typically to the advantage of some groups and candidates but not others. Here again, undercounting by the census was disempowering. Furthermore, the most local-level census data possible would serve as an indispensable guide to both policy and electoral considerations on the ground, as well as basic currency in potential legal challenges to the allocation of resources and enforcement of civil and voting rights.

At a higher level, not only were district lines in play, but the "apportionment" of numbers of districts between states, regions, and localities were as well. The state legislature was responsible for dividing the state into both its own legislative districts as well those for Congress. Adjusting these plans every 10 years following the decennial census involved a colossal amount of painstaking work, immensely complicated by having to win majority support for a plan that affects every legislator's career. This work and its politics was all about redistricting, the adjustment of those district lines. But the job fell to what was called the Reapportionment Committee. The dictates of the census showed that this committee's name made sense, specifically in California.

In the first instance, the census determines the apportionment of the fixed number of seats in Congress among the states by population — which means reapportionment every 10 years when new, authoritative data becomes available. California's vertiginous growth, just since WWII, earned the state seven new congressional seats after the census of 1950, eight new seats after 1960, and five more new seats after 1970.[35] Clearly, for California, congressional redistricting meant redrawing the map with these newly apportioned seats, taken from other states, each time — but there was more. The "Golden State" was born in the midst of the nineteenth-century Gold Rush in the north, which powered San Francisco into the top 10 of American cities by 1870 — a list Los Angeles would not appear on until it suddenly edged San Francisco for tenth place in the 1920 census.

Out of the 80 seats in the state Assembly, San Francisco was able to hang on to 13 in the 1920s, but fell to nine in the '30s, eight in the '40s, and six in the '50s. By population, San Francisco would only merit three and a half Assembly seats in the 1960s, but "Baghdad by the Bay" political wizard Phil Burton managed to salvage not only four but five.[36] The seats that San Francisco and Northern California in general were losing were, in effect, "reapportioned" to fast-growing Southern California. The location of the lines would then determine a district's social, economic, and political profile, and thereby the sort of candidate who could compete in it, and what sorts of policies an incumbent could (and could not) pursue while representing it and getting reelected.

In either the case of reapportionment of legislative seats between states, or between regions within a state, any undercount of Latinos would deprive them, and their state or region, of the representation they are constitutionally entitled to. Inaccurate data can also distort both the profile of districts and the number of residents they contain.

What's in a Name? Strategic Rebranding

THE ULTIMATELY SUCCESSFUL, DECADE-LONG LATINO STRUGGLE to reform the census was a transformative experience. It brought together Latinos of different origins and forced them to become a team, in a competitive arena, none on his or her home turf. They had to work out their differences to impose their will on a vast federal government that did not know them. They were not a community when they began arriving in Washington in significant numbers, in the 1960s with Kennedy and Johnson, and especially the 1970s with Carter; they were representatives and emissaries of a variety of widely separated communities. Even within national-origin groups, there were serious differences between the "Texas Mexicans" and the Californians, the Nuyoricans and the Islanders. The mundane, overarching, unifying goal of this one particular policy struggle was inescapable: What was their name? What would they be called on the census? By its nature, the census in a continent-sized country of enormous diversity is a huge undertaking, in addition to being highly technical, even scientific, and still subject to innumer-

Photo by Armando B. Rendon, census promotion specialist for 1980 census and author of the "Cuéntese Censo '80" campaign.

able political pressures. But the challenge, though daunting, contained a structural advantage. And Ed Roybal brought to this challenge advantages of his own.

The director of the bureau during the most intense years of this journey would decades later call the issue of the Hispanic category in the 1980 census "the toughest question" of his service in Washington.[37] In time it would become clear that in the 1970s the bureau really had no idea how significant the Hispanic population would become nor how fast. The structural advantage in the policy challenge of starting to count Latinos for the first time, however, resided in precisely the decennial nature of the census. The stakes were so high that as soon as the various disputes over the 1970 census could be put aside, the players were ready to focus intently on the next one. Yet there was time for debate, research, testing, more testing and more debate, and a clearly understood objective: the 1980 census had to be improved, and the improvement needed to be lasting. In this way, the census functioned like an elongated electoral cycle: it *repeats* at regular intervals, the same participants can return having learned from previous iterations, and there will always be a next time to prepare for.

Roybal brought considerable advantages to this struggle — besides his having had the experience of learning from a loss in his first election, and overpreparing to come back the second time to win. Both sides of his family had centuries of forebears in New Mexico. In one interview he said his family could not trace their ancestry any further back.[38] The people of his regional culture had come to call themselves "Hispanos." But Roybal's family moved to Los Angeles, where he grew up and came to maturity among Mexican Americans. He became a leader of his community and started one organization after another. He had been part of lengthy naming debates. He struggled for inclusivity but accepted when a majority of one of the organizations he started insisted on its being called Mexican American.[39] He could see his community from both the inside and the outside. They came to elect and reelect him their representative time and again. And in Washington he would find himself among more Hispanic diversity than ever.

The decennial census gave Roybal time to start more organizations and advance more related policies between one enumeration and the next. The main players in the extended struggle over the 1980 census all had time for multiple extended projects, experimenting and bringing together those who agreed with one vision or another. Roybal co-convened with his congressional colleagues a "National Spanish-Speaking Coalition Conference" in 1971. In 1976, he led the formation of both a National Latino Association and the Congressional Hispanic Caucus.[40] Given Roybal's background, experience, values, and discreet, self-effacing authority, it is hard to imagine someone better to help guide and bring to fruition a process of unification around practical common goals.[41]

Once the Hispanic category was committed to, the parties to the effort undertook the mammoth job of selling census participation to their respective constituencies across the country and to the emergent national Hispanic/Latino public. The basic objective was to convince all these different people in all these diverse communities to complete their census forms, choose their particular Hispanic signifier, and send the thing back, considering that the data generated were critical to funding community programs and to their political representation. But even if viewed in a pragmatic, instrumental way, and even if untold numbers of census participants clung to the Mexican or Puerto Rican or Cuban box they checked beneath the question about Hispanic origin, the promotional campaign had the inescapable quality of a historic, collective self-rebranding exercise — a rebranding that faced resistance, most of all in California.[42]

The new brand would not be rigid, at least insofar as many would use Hispanic and Latino more or less interchangeably, along with other, more particular labels. But the ongoing creation of an immense variety of organizations with either term in their name, the institutionalization of one identifier in federal government and the other in many other arenas, and the ubiquity of these terms in every sphere and level of American life together made a compelling case for the success and permanence of this *cambio de piel*.[43] The collision of Latino California's leadership and direction with the anti-Latino and anti-immigrant wave that would come to power in Washington in 2017 would provide the paramount early-twenty-first-century test of the political clout developed using this pan-ethnic unification, mobilization, and branding strategy.

Back and Back Again to the (Hispanic) Future

AFRICAN-AMERICAN ELECTED OFFICIALS, GATHERED IN LAS VEGAS at the end of Thanksgiving weekend 1979, had their minds on the approaching 1980 census and the increasingly common talk in some circles that Hispanics would soon displace African Americans as the country's largest minority group. The National Black Caucus of Local Elected Officials of the National League of Cities was meeting in conjunction with the NLC's big annual "Congress of Cities" — a convention of mayors and other urban-area local officials of such weight that the Carter administration sent three cabinet secretaries to address it.[44] But in this case the sidebar Black Caucus event and a lowly specialist in minority statistics from the Census Bureau stole the headlines from the larger "congress."

Although the bureau did not customarily rank minority groups by population, the director sent a staff expert to the meeting armed with a special letter to the caucus that addressed the city officials' concerns about projected Hispanic growth — a matter on which the bureau had up to then not issued any public estimates. The conference-goers were pleased to hear from the government's top authority in these matters that the burgeoning Hispanic population would not come to outnumber blacks in their lifetimes.[45] But this would be just the first of many instances, over several ensuing decades, in which the Census Bureau — which had to be pushed for so many years to begin counting Hispanics — would get this aspect of the country's demographic future quite wrong.

Accounts of the conference differed on the bureau's announced estimate of the Hispanic population at that time, but agreed that Hispanics were projected to not surpass the black population until after 2057 — some 78 years in the future.[46] The bureau had yet to conduct a complete count of Hispanics, but even when it had that data in hand from the subsequent 1980 census, it continued to project that African Americans would not be displaced as the country's largest minority group until far-off 2058.[47]

The Census Bureau published that second projection well after the Las Vegas meeting in 1986, when it also forecast that the US Hispanic population would reach 30.8 million by the census year of 2010. The bureau's next set of projections was released after the 1990 census, and that time it must have provoked both consternation and excitement in different quarters. In 1992, the bureau projected that the Hispanic population would surpass the African-American total some 45 years sooner than previously expected — by midyear 2013 — and raised its official projection of the 2010 Hispanic population to 39.3 million.[48]

The bureau did not wait for the next census to once more revise its population projections in the 1990s. In 1996, it again moved the year that the two biggest minority groups would flip numerical positions, now putting Hispanics on top by 2005 — more than half a century sooner than had its first two forecasts. In that projection, Latinos were now expected to reach 41.1 million by 2010.[49] After that, the bureau passed on the next opportunity to issue mistaken, short-lived forecasts and waited for the actual 2010 census to have the last, or latest, word. The actual 2010 count of Hispanics came in at 50.5 million, marking 43 percent growth since 2000.[50]

Strategy, Personality, Both?

IS THERE A STRATEGIC LESSON TO BE FOUND IN THE LONG STRUGGLE to get the US Census to count Latinos — and in particular the route taken and role played by Congressman Ed Roybal? His advocacy and the legislative steps he took were strongly suggestive of a long-term strategy in the face of establishment resistance to reforms that could be employed to redistribute political power. But the route he took was also consistent with his style and personality.

Roybal and a close ally had met resistance from Democratic Party leaders when they sought nomination for statewide offices in different elections in the 1950s. They both won those nominations — Roybal in 1954 for lieutenant governor and Enrique "Hank" Lopez in 1958 for California secretary of state — but then both experienced a lack of support from their party in the general election and lost to Republicans. Roybal's frustration with what he perceived to be discrimination at the hands of his own party led him to call for the creation of MAPA, the independent, statewide Latino political organization, in 1959.[51]

When considering another run for higher office in 1961, he complained to the Assembly Reapportionment Committee about the fragmentation of Mexican-American neighborhoods among multiple legislative districts, and he repeated his complaints in the state Senate's committee hearings in 1970, declaring that he was "disgusted at the way the committee, controlled by Democrats, ignored the community."[52] Roybal evidently saw political empowerment as the prerequisite for other changes that would address Latino needs; but he also saw that entrenched resistance called for a sustained strategy of practical steps, some or many of which would not appear to be overtly political.

This sort of appreciation of how to effect change certainly seems to have informed the route Roybal took and the advances that would contribute, in the end, to a redistribution of political power. This is at least one way to understand what was arguably Roybal's first step in this direction — in the midst of the upheaval of 1968 — the establishment of the anodyne National Hispanic Heritage Week. On Tuesday, September 17, of a year that was marked by high-school walkouts, assassinations, and riots, and in which President Johnson suddenly withdrew from running for reelection, Congress hustled to approve the joint resolution designating that week, and henceforth every week including September 15 and 16, one in which "the people of the United States, especially the educational community" would observe "with appropriate ceremonies and activities."[53] The next year Richard Nixon issued his own declaration, as each president has ever since, including Donald Trump in 2017 — who went on to seemingly mock the pronunciation of "Puerto Rico."[54]

The Bilingual Education Act, which Roybal worked on with other legislators and the White House, had been signed into law in January 1968, but it had evolved from an initial bill concerning Spanish-speaking students to a general policy on language minorities.[55] Roybal and his many Mexican-American colleagues, who were struggling to win advances for their community on par with the historic strides blacks were taking in civil rights, saw in LBJ a unique ally, but one whose time was fast running out since his withdrawal from the presidential race.[56]

President Johnson issued the proclamation of the first Hispanic Heritage Week the same day it was authorized by Congress — having already just missed the Central American and Mexican independence days of the 15th and 16th of September that the commemorative week was pegged to. Nevertheless, this resolution and proclamation established a critical first beachhead in the battle to win official recognition of Hispanics as a national minority in federal policy. These early first steps — bilingual education for children and symbolic cultural recognition for a community that the president, a Texan whose first job had been teaching rural Mexican-American kids, was personally touched by — would be hard to oppose. The civil unrest and disorder of the times called for ameliorative action on every front, and among the many demands Mexican-American activists and organizations were making, these measures were innocuous and fiscally cheap. Even the original education bill primarily involved private foundation funding.[57]

The demands and pressure exerted over the next census in 1970, and Roybal's frustration with the minor progress made, sharpened considerably. In the decade that followed, frustration continued mounting, and Roybal's policy proposals turned more openly political. The 1975 extension of the Voting Rights Act, with amendments concerning language minorities, are a case in point. The convergence in time of this VRA amendment and the Roybal Act requiring all agencies to collect data on Hispanics is telling. Roybal was one of many legislators and advocates involved over a long period of time in the VRA extension and amendments; the legislative push for that would begin the first month of the new 94th Congress, coming right out of the gate after the Nixon resignation and the election of the class of Democratic "Watergate babies" in 1974.[58] Roybal apparently developed his stand-alone data-collection bill toward the end of this process, and introduced it in the House on January 14, 1975 — the same day as the first introduction of a bill amending and extending the VRA. The VRA extension would pass and be signed by the president that year, while the Roybal Act would take until mid-1976 to become law.[59]

That same year, Roybal took the first steps in creating the Congressional Hispanic Caucus (CHC) and the National Association of Latino Elected and Appointed Officials (NALEO), which went on to develop programs enlarging the Latino electorate by promoting naturalization among immigrants, voter registration, and voting.[60] But in the short term, these entities added new voices to the chorus demanding reform of the census, and the new and revised legislation gave those voices powerful new arguments.

The "language minorities" provision in the amended VRA is notable for covering three racial groups plus one, "Spanish Heritage," defined as not a race. The political significance of this, and the complication it posed for policy execution, is that while the census provided thorough data on what it accepted as racial minorities, it did not (yet) for the Hispanic population, however defined. The Roybal Act the following year furthermore called for the collection of data on Americans "of Spanish origin or descent." Together, these laws added substantially to the pressures being brought to bear on the Census Bureau to accept some version of a Hispanic category in its next complete count — which it finally did.

Were these steps, and this measured pace, all by design — Roybal's intricate, three-dimensional long game? Did he start with relatively unobjectionable policies regarding culture and kids in the 1960s, in order to lay the basis for more concrete and aggressive empowerment moves in the 1970s? Or was he pushed into a more aggressive stance by the activists and social unrest? His biographer would later repeatedly make the point that Roybal preferred to work behind the scenes, unconcerned with credit or glory, acting methodically to "keep up the pressure" to advance social legislation.[61]

In retrospect, and knowing the ongoing consequences of his efforts, Roybal's persistence and inventiveness seem remarkable. Membership in the CHC, and presumably in NALEO as well, grew to record size as a consequence of the 2016 elections.[62] The CHC's annual conference and gala in Washington, DC developed over time into the most important regular gathering of Latino leaders in the country, often addressed by the incumbent president of the United States and presidential candidates.[63] Whether Roybal's approach was astutely strategic, a trajectory forced on him by outsiders, an expression of his personality, or a combination of all three, the long journey he undertook and his dogged efforts along the way resulted in indispensable contributions to the quest for Latino empowerment.

Notes

1. After first garnering 59 percent of the vote to unseat the incumbent in 1949, in his first three reelections to city council, Roybal obtained 70, 73, and 74 percent landslides. See Berumen, *Edward R. Roybal*, 99, 125–26, 129, 130–32, 148, 157–60.

2. Burt, *The Search for a Civic Voice*, 203–07; Berumen, *Edward R. Roybal*, 277, 181, 189, 191, 194–195; Jacobs, *A Rage for Justice*, 89–90.

3. Berumen, *Edward R. Roybal*, 277.

4. Mora, *Making Hispanics*, 87–88.

5. Ibid., 98–99; *Joint resolution relating to the publication of economic and social statistics for American of Spanish origin or descent*, Public Law 94–311, 94th Congress (June 16, 1976), see text at http://uscode.house.gov/statutes/pl/94/311.pdf.

6. There had been only one other Democratic governor in California in the century, and he was thrown out after a single term, before Edmund G. Brown, Sr., known as "Pat," was elected in 1958. After losing the presidential election in 1960, former Vice President Richard Nixon returned to California and challenged Brown, Sr. in 1962. Nixon's loss was seen at the time as ending his political career. Brown's governorship was ended by his loss to Ronald Reagan in 1966, which appeared to mark the beginning of a conservative Republican comeback, helping revive Nixon's career and win him the presidency two years later. But when Nixon resigned and returned to California in 1974, he saw Pat Brown's son Jerry win the governorship.

7. Garcia, *From the Jaws of Victory*, 129–30; Pawel, *The Crusades of Cesar Chavez*, 306–07; Edmund G. "Jerry" Brown, First Inaugural Address, January 6, 1975, *The Governors' Gallery*, http://governors.library.ca.gov/addresses/34-jbrown01.html. The text of the ALRA, also known as the Alatorre-Zenovich-Dunlop-Berman Agricultural Labor Relations Act of 1975 (California Labor Code Section 1140–1166.3), along with related regulations and information about the Agricultural Labor Relations Board (ALRB) established by

the act, can be found at https://www.alrb.ca.gov/content/pdfs/statutesregulations/statutes/ALRA_010112.pdf and www.alrb.ca.gov.

8. Historian Craig Alan Kaplowitz deftly touches on all these considerations in *LULAC, Mexican Americans, and National Policy*, 163–67.

9. Republican National Hispanic Assembly, "About" tab, "History," www.rnhnational.org.

10. McAndrews, *The Era of Education*, 31. According to Kaplowitz, "The unanimity of Mexican American and Spanish-speaking organizations" on this bill, which Ford encountered in his very first days in office, "gave him few options if he hoped to engage them during his administration" (*LULAC*, 174).

11. Kaplowitz, *LULAC*, 165–66, 240–41 notes 28, 31, and 35. Nixon was already moving in this direction before he resigned; Ford took the Deputy for Hispanic Affairs to Nixon's Counselor Anne Armstrong and made him his Special Assistant to the President for Hispanic Affairs, in charge of his own Office of Hispanic Affairs. See "Introduction," Fernando De Baca Files, 1974–76, Gerald R. Ford Presidential Library and Museum, www.fordlibrarymuseum.gov.

12. Berumen, *Edward R. Roybal*, 301–03.

13. Richard D. Lyons, "House Defies Ford, Adds Billion to First Fund Bill," *New York Times*, April 17, 1975, http://www.nytimes.com/1975/04/17/archives/house-defies-ford-adds-billion-to-first-fund-bill.html?mcubz=1; see also White, *The Functions and Power of the House Appropriations Committee*, 525–27.

14. For some detail on the UFW's primary efforts in different states, see Bardacke, *Trampling Out the Vintage*.

15. Public Law 94–311, 94th Congress, June 16, 1976, House Joint Resolution 92, "Americans of Spanish Origin or Descent. Economic and Social Statistics, Publication."

16. Gerald R. Ford, Public Papers of the Presidents of the United States: Gerald R. Ford, 1976–1977, April 9 to July 9, 1976 (United States Government Printing Office, 1979), 596–97.

17. See Jensen, "Cesar Chavez," for a detailed discussion of the speech and context.

18. In what Alatorre and Grossman call Chavez's "landmark address" in 1984 to the Commonwealth Club in San Francisco, he declared, "The union's survival, its very existence, sent out a signal to all Hispanics that we were fighting for our dignity . . . that we were challenging and overcoming injustice, that we were empowering the least educated among us, the poorest among us. The message was clear. If it could happen in the fields, it could happen anywhere: in the cities, in the courts, in the city councils, in the state legislatures. I didn't really appreciate it at the time, but the coming of our union signaled the start of great changes among Hispanics that are only now beginning to be seen." Quoted in Pawel, *Crusades of Cesar Chavez*, 2–3; Alatorre with Grossman, *Change from the Inside*, 179.

19. Gerald R. Ford, "Text of Remarks by the President to be Delivered to the National Hispanic Assembly," White House Press Releases, July 29, 1976, Box 29, Gerald R. Ford Presidential Library and Museum, https://www.fordlibrarymuseum.gov/library/document/0248/whpr19760729-016.pdf.

20. See news reports cited in note 51 of "The Congressional Hispanic Caucus and Conference," *History, Art and Archives, U.S. House of Representatives*, http://history.house.gov/Exhibitions-and-Publications/HAIC/Historical-Essays/Strength-Numbers/Caucus-Conference/.

21. Mora, *Making Hispanics*, 97–98, 200 fn. 57.

22. Ibid., 108. See also Prewitt, *What Is Your Race?*, 3–5, 174–76, on the 2010 census questions language.

23. "About Language Minority Voting Rights," *United States Department of Justice, Civil Rights Division*, updated August 8, 2015, https://www.justice.gov/crt/about-language-minority-voting-rights.

24. Cain and MacDonald, "Voting Rights Act Enforcement."

25. President William Howard Taft launched the first census publicity campaign with his Census Proclamation of 1910; Anderson, *The American Census*, 125. Public efforts urging Latino cooperation with each decennial census date to the late 1970s, involving the bureau, Latino organizations, and Spanish-language media in branded, national campaigns. The full slogan for the 1980 census appears to have been "*Cuéntese — Responda al Censo '80,*" for which lapel buttons were distributed, but there is also evidence of the slogans "*¡Vamos a Contar! We Are Going to Count in the 1980s!*" and "*Yo Cuento.*" UCLA demographer Leo Estrada discussed the "*Cuéntese*" slogan in a syndicated column for *Hispanic Link* titled "My Favorite Day? You'll Never Guess," *Garden City Telegram*, March 21, 1980. G. Cristina Mora cites the "*Vamos*" slogan in *Making Hispanics*, 110–14 and 203 fn. 113. MALDEF also used the simpler "*Yo Cuento*" at this time, complete with its own lapel buttons; Oliveira, "Mexican American Defense and Educational Fund," 457–58. The 2010 campaign, more aptly branded as "*Ya Es Hora: Hágase Contar!*" (It's Time — Make Yourself Count!) retains an extensive presence online.

26. Young, *Mexican Exodus*, examines the relatively little-known refugee and exile components of Mexican migration.

27. McWilliams, *North from Mexico*, chapter 11; Prewitt, *What Is Your Race?*; Valencia, *Chicano Students and the Courts*.

28. In his classic *Factories in the Field*, Carey McWilliams traces how California "recruited, exploited, and excluded" one immigrant group after another, starting with the Chinese in the nineteenth century, shifting to the Japanese, and then East Indians and Armenians before settling on Mexicans and Filipinos in the twentieth century. The preeminent historical treatment of US nativist movements is Higham, *Strangers in the Land*. Schrag, *Not Fit for Our Society*, serves as both a general introduction and important update. Young, "Making America 1920 Again?" is the most up-to-date review of both this history and literature.

29. Hochschild and Powell, "Racial Reorganization and the United States Census 1850–1930"; Gratton and Merchant, "*La Raza*"; Mora, *Making Hispanics*, chapter 3; Hoffman, *Unwanted Mexican Americans in the Great Depression*; Balderrama and Rodriguez, *Decade of Betrayal*; and Sanchez, "Disposable People." Hoover was a resident of California and had himself served as secretary of commerce in the preceding Coolidge administration.

30. Mora, *Making Hispanics*, 85–86; Fernandez, "Comparisons of Persons of Spanish Surname"; Hattam, *In the Shadow of Race*, 106–09; US Bureau of the Census, "U.S. Census of the Population: 1950." On later use of surnames by the census and evaluation of this method, see Perkins, "Evaluating the Passel-Word Spanish Surname List"; and Word and Perkins, Jr., "Building a Spanish Surname List for the 1990s."

31. Garcia, *Operation Wetback*. This is not to suggest that law-enforcement authorities had access to names of individuals enumerated in the 1950 census, but they certainly had access to aggregate census data that could be used to identify local concentrations and clusters of Spanish-surnamed individuals. President Taft's 1910 Census Proclamation was the first official pledge of the confidentiality of personal census data, which later was codified in law. See Anderson, *The American Census*; Gatewood, *A Monograph on Confidentiality and Privacy in the U.S. Census*; and "Events in the Chronological Development of Privacy and Confidentiality at the U.S. Census Bureau," *United States Census Bureau* (website), last revised July 18, 2017, https://www.census.gov/history/www/reference/privacy_confidentiality/privacy_and_confidentiality_2.html.

32. See especially Mora, *Making Hispanics*, 110–14.

33. Ibid., 83.

34. Welch, Karnig, and Eribes, "Changes in Hispanic Local Public Employment in the Southwest"; League of United Latin American Citizens (LULAC), *Recruiting Hispanics — Why Not? A Dialogue on Federal Public Service*, June 2002, https://lulac.org/assets/pdfs/recruiting.pdf; National Hispanic Leadership Agenda (NHLA), *An Evaluation of OPM's Efforts to Improve Hispanic Representation in the Federal Workforce*, 2006, https://nationalhispanicleadership.org/images/Scorecards/NHLAreportOPM.pdf. The availability of data, of course, would not by itself change embedded patterns in public employment, which have persisted into the twenty-first century in many sectors, as shown in the LULAC and NHLA reports. See also Darryl Fears, "Hispanics Underrepresented in the Federal Workforce," *The Washington Post*, January 3, 2006, http://www.washingtonpost.com/wp-dyn/content/article/2006/01/02/AR2006010201716.html; Jon Ortiz, "Hispanics Underrepresented in California State Government," *The Sacramento Bee*, January 6, 2015, http://www.sacbee.com/news/politics-government/the-state-worker/article5510283.html. For the most recent data on Latinos in the military, see Kim Parker, Anthony Cilluffo, and Renee Stepler, "6 Facts about the U.S. Military and Its Changing Demographics," *Pew Research Center Fact Tank*, April 13, 2017, http://www.pewresearch.org/fact-tank/2017/04/13/6-facts-about-the-u-s-military-and-its-changing-demographics/.

35. Jacobs, *A Rage for Justice*, 117–18, 280–81.

36. Richardson, *Willie Brown*, 119; Jacobs, *A Rage for Justice*, 118–20.

37. Mora, *Making Hispanics*, 84.

38. Roybal, "Interview no. 184."

39. Burt, *The Search for a Civic Voice*, 182–84.

40. The former is the National Association of Latino Elected and Appointed Officials (NALEO). The CHC is formally organized as the Congressional Hispanic Caucus Institute (CHCI). See Office of the Historian, *Hispanic Americans in Congress, 1822–2012*, 410–18; Rodriguez, *Latino National Political Coalitions*; Barreto, *Ethnic Cues*.

41. Cornel West memorably groups black political leaders into "three types: race-effacing managerial leaders, race-identifying protest leaders, and race-transcending prophetic leaders," in *Race Matters*, 39. West pointedly categorized LA Mayor Tom Bradley as "race-effacing." Sonenshein, the authority on Bradley and his role in LA politics, described Roybal as "so similar to Bradley in style and political base," in *Politics in Black and White*, 65.

42. In the preceding decade, the movement to rebrand and mobilize Mexican Americans as *Chicanos* had spread widely and, starting in Southern California, became institutionalized on scores of college campuses, especially in the form of student organizations but also as official student service and cultural centers, academic programs of Chicano Studies, and professional associations. See Acuña, *The Making of Chicana/o Studies*. The movement was, for most participants and many communities, a transformative cultural revolution that reached every medium. Griswold del Castillo, McKenna, and Yarbro-Bejarano, *Chicano Art*, remains an essential source.

43. This expression, used in Latin American and Latino literature and song, means literally "change of skin," but the metaphor may be inapt. The census questions contain clues to the serviceability, in spite of resistance, of the pan-ethnic category. The questionnaire plainly states that one can be *both* Hispanic/Latino *and* Mexican, or Cuban, or Puerto Rican, or something other, as well as simultaneously black, white, Native American, or Asian. The census thus embraces multiplicity, complementarity, and the additive, rather than supersessionist, nature of the pan-ethnic category, i.e., rather than the substitution of Hispanic for something prior or more specific. Eventually, a Latina scholar would fully theorize the connection between multiplicity of identity and the viability of Latino subgroups coming together politically. See Barvosa, "Multiple Identity and Coalition Building."

44. The Secretaries of Transportation, Energy, and Housing and Urban Development were among the principal speakers at the 1979 Congress of Cities. Maurice Landrieu, Secretary of Housing and Urban Development, "Memorandum for the President, Weekly Report of Major Departmental Activities," November 30, 1979. Jimmy Carter Presidential Library (Digital Library collection), Collection: Office of Staff Secretary; Series: Presidential Files; Folder: 12/3/79; Container 140.

45. Bill Boyarsky's "Hispanics Not Outnumbering Blacks, U.S. Says," *Los Angeles Times*, November 26, 1979, appeared on front page. NLC later renamed its annual conference "City Summit."

46. The newsletter of the Joint Center for Political Studies, *Focus* 7, no. 12 (December 1979): 7, reported that the census estimated the Hispanic population to be between 14 and 16 million at that time, with the black population pegged at 25 million. *Jet* magazine reported that the census expert at the Las Vegas meeting put the Hispanic population at 12.1 million; "Hispanics Will Not Outnumber Blacks Until 2057: Census Bureau," *Jet*, January 10, 1980.

47. Although the bureau was still not ranking minority groups, the projections for each can be found in separate tables and publications. See Spencer, *Projections of the Population of the United States by Age, Sex, and Race*, 36, which projected the 2058 black

population would reach 53.5 million. Spencer's subsequent *Projections of the Hispanic Population: 1983 to 2080*, 30, projected the 2058 Latino population to reach 53.6 million.

48. Cheeseman Day, *Population Projections of the United States by Age, Sex, Race, and Hispanic Origin: 1992 to 2050*, 3, 6.

49. Ibid., 12–13.

50. Ennis, Ríos-Vargas, and Albert, *The Hispanic Population*, 3.

51. Burt, *The Search for a Civic Voice*, 175–84; Berumen, *Edward R. Roybal*, 209–11, 306–08.

52. Berumen, *Edward R. Roybal*, 277.

53. Joint resolution authorizing the president to proclaim annually the week including September 15 and 16 as "National Hispanic Heritage Week," Public Law 90–498, 90th Congress (September 17, 1968). See text at http://uscode.house.gov/statutes/pl/90/498.pdf.

54. In the late 1980s, Esteban Torres proposed expanding the week to a month, which Ronald Reagan signed into law and declared in 1988; see "The Creation and Evolution of the National Hispanic Heritage Celebration," *History, Art and Archives, U.S. House of Representatives*, http://history.house.gov/HistoricalHighlight/Detail/15032398402. Regarding Trump, see Associated Press, "President Trump Adopted a Spanish Accent to Say 'Puerto Rico,'" *Time*, October 6, 2017, http://time.com/4972883/donald-trump-puerto-rico-spanish-accent/. Trump seemed to find the difference between "puerto" and the common "porto" mispronunciation to be amusing.

55. Skrentny, *The Minority Rights Revolution*, 192–93, 205.

56. Pycior, *LBJ and Mexican Americans*.

57. Ibid., 183.

58. See John A. Lawrence, "The Democrats' High-Water Mark Came 40 Years Ago," *Politico Magazine*, November 4, 2014, http://www.politico.com/magazine/story/2014/11/the-democrats-high-water-mark-came-40-years-ago-112492.

59. For legislative history of Roybal Act, see "H.J.Res.92 — Joint resolution relating to the publication of economic and social statistics for Americans of Spanish origin or descent," 94th Congress (1975–1976), https://www.congress.gov/bill/94th-congress/house-joint-resolution/92/actions. This resulted in Public Law 94-311. On the same day, Representative Peter Rodino introduced "H.R.939 — A bill to amend the Voting Rights Act of 1965 to extend certain provisions for an additional 10 years and to make permanent the ban against certain prerequisites to voting," 94th Congress. Several other bills extending the VRA were introduced that session. The one that became law is H.R.6219, which became Public Law 94-73.

60. See Office of the Historian, *Hispanic Americans in Congress, 1822–2012*, 410–14; Rodriguez, *Latino National Political Coalitions*, 129–32, 137–40; Barreto, *Ethnic Cues*, 1, 18–19.

61. Berumen, *Edward R. Roybal*, 203, 207, 288, 322, 327.

62. Mike McPhate, "California Today: Latino Power Rising," *New York Times*, November 15, 2016, https://www.nytimes.com/2016/11/15/us/california-today-latinos-congress-trump.html?_r=0.

63. See Suzanne Gamboa, "This Hispanic Heritage Month, What's There to Celebrate? We Asked." *NBCNews.com*, September 17, 2017, https://www.nbcnews.com/news/latino/hispanic-heritage-month-what-s-there-celebrate-we-asked-n801776; 2017 marked the first time in 40 years that the president was not invited to address this gathering.

CHAPTER 6

State Power

FLASH FORWARD — NOVEMBER 4, 1980 — RONALD REAGAN DID NOT WIN
the White House by anything like a landslide in the popular vote — failing to
crack even 51 percent in a three-way race. But by taking 44 states, Reagan nearly
wiped out President Jimmy Carter in the Electoral College 10:1 and claimed a
mandate to take the country in a radical new direction.[1]

In California, however, the greater shock was that a TV network projected
Reagan's win, and Carter conceded, *before polls closed* on the West Coast. Carter
was expected to lose, and former two-term Governor Reagan, although alarming
to many across the country, was well known here. The state was in a long streak
of voting for Republican presidential candidates that began in 1968 and would run
to 1988, but Sacramento remained firmly in Democratic hands. Jerry Brown had
two more years to go in his first life as governor, and the legislature would enjoy
an only slightly diminished Democratic majority in one house. This separate California reality would soon make possible a political earthquake that would have
great and lasting effects no one had imagined.

The gripe of the night for many West Coast Democrats was that Carter's early
concession, combined with NBC's even earlier call of the presidential race based
on exit polls, cost them votes and perhaps some seats. But the real focus of attention for state-Capitol watchers would prove unaffected by the presidential result:
the year-long revolt by Assembly Democrats against their own Speaker continued
unresolved, and the possibility that the impasse might be broken with a dramatic
breach of party discipline was growing by the day.

Reagan's election was certainly bad news for Latino appointees in the Carter
administration, for whom this was a termination notice. Notable names would
return to LA, starting with Esteban Torres. But, as the previous chapter recounts,
more compelling national realities, with great implications for the future, had
emerged in 1980: the US Census for first time included a complete count of
self-identified Hispanics; Latino organizations, media, and elected officials jointly mobilized to promote cooperation with the census; Latino advocates pressured
and sued the Census Bureau to ensure a thorough count; the popular response exceeded all expectations, with the 1980 total soaring 60 percent over the estimated
Hispanic population of 1970; and reapportionment and redistricting were about
to get underway at every level of government, not only utilizing the stunning

new population figures but also with Hispanics and other "language minorities" at least partially protected for the first time by an amended and extended Voting Rights Act, and now under the scrutiny of the Congressional Hispanic Caucus and the National Association of Latino Elected and Appointed Officials (NALEO), both founded since the 1975 VRA renewal.

The long-term meaning of the reforms forged in Congress transcended the outcome of that year's election: radically more precise population data combined with steps toward requiring that Hispanics, like blacks before them, not be subjected to election schemes that thwart their ability to elect representatives of their choice or that have the effect of diluting the impact of their votes.[2] The one person who had more to do with these advances than anyone else was the Eastside's cranky Old Man, Ed Roybal. And the only person in the months to come who would be able to apply these advances and remake the political landscape of the country's mega-state was LA's self-described "bad Mexican," Richard Alatorre.

Not quite visible to all was how the vastly improved Latino prospects in redistricting were connected to the ongoing battle for control of the California Assembly — but in fact, redistricting was a core issue in the speakership fight, in part because new census data typically affected fast-growing California more than any other state. For this reason, the role that the two newest Latino members of the Assembly had in this dispute could well become the most consequential power play in Latino political history — a play that stood to make or break the careers of Richard Alatorre and his "good Mexican" compadre, Art Torres.

* * *

THE 1980 CENSUS DID NOT MAKE THE LATINO POPULATION SOAR, it *revealed* soaring Latino growth in the country, and especially in California. While the nation as a whole had grown over 60 percent since 1970, the state's Latino population had grown over 90 percent — nearly doubling.[3] Accurately measuring this surge and making it known was critically important, but the political question was, what could make this development concretely *empowering*? The most direct but rather esoteric answer would be *control of the state's electoral reapportionment and redistricting*. The historic political news out of California in 1980 was that after the census revealed a big population shift, by the end of the year a dramatic *power shift* upended the state's politics: California's leading black and Latino politicians would be running the state Assembly, with the power to remake its political map.

The paths to Willie Brown's historic run as Speaker of the Assembly and his ally Richard Alatorre's critical role in it were marked from beginning to end by the seemingly arcane issue of electoral district lines. Alatorre learned in his youth from his father how the Mexican-American community of Eastside Los Angeles was politically hobbled by its division into six, seven, or eight districts. Years later, Alatorre's opportunity to launch a political career would be tied to the challenge of fashioning a Mexican-American state Assembly district.[4] Similarly, Willie Brown might not have had a political career, if not for his mentor's salvaging an Assembly district for him in San Francisco in the early 1960s.[5] Eventually, Alatorre's and Brown's paths would bring them together and, in league with other key allies, put them in a position to redirect California politics. But how did such an unlikely, interurban turn of events come about? How did this obscure dimension of politics work, and what effects did this have?

Alatorre returned to Sacramento in January 1973 with experience beyond his years, ready to take on the role of lawmaker. Having worked in the Capitol and developed a range of relationships there, including with then-Speaker Bob Moretti; earned degrees at both public and private universities; taught college students as well as federal prisoners; helped run nonprofit advocacy organizations, election campaigns, and a small business; worked in a unionized plant and for local government; and having faced voters four times to win his own seat, Alatorre took his oath of office about as knowledgeable about the state, its politics, and his constituents as were the veteran legislators then in charge of the Assembly.

Alatorre was one of three Mexican Americans new to the lower house, joining the two already there. Suddenly having five members, even in a body of 80, was a big leap. Alatorre proposed they form a group and call it the Chicano Legislative Caucus. The notion first came up the previous summer of 1972 in the heady atmosphere of the Democratic National Convention in Miami — the one that nominated George McGovern for president.[6] Epic conflicts and civil rights struggles of the 1960s had pushed the Democratic Party to require state delegations include substantial numbers of minorities and women, which turned the convention into a collection of historic national summits for these groups.[7] Between this reform of the Democratic Party and the about-to-be-felt electoral effects of redistricting based on the 1970 census, representation of women and minorities in elected office was set to rise that fall. Talk within each group turned to how to leverage greater representation, once in power, to advance their agendas.

In Washington, the Congressional Black Caucus, founded just the year before, had drawn immediate attention and succeeded in pressing for a special meeting with a reluctant President Nixon — after first boycotting his State of the Union address.[8] Alatorre had long been attuned to how African Americans advanced a black agenda, and he wanted Chicanos to do likewise.[9] The next year, both Alatorre and his California associates, and Mexican-American legislators in Texas, would form similar groups in their state Capitols. Richard, however, was the only one of his Assembly colleagues genuinely comfortable with the Chicano label. Having no idea what he might make of it, they happily let him chair the new group. Alatorre proceeded to launch his caucus with a reception for the whole legislature at an august Sacramento hotel, on the day of their inauguration. He was already on a roll before the gathering.

Recall that Speaker Moretti, who represented a white, San Fernando Valley district far removed from black and brown LA, had strongly backed Alatorre's first opponent in 1971. Alatorre crushed the Speaker's candidate in the primary but lost in the second round that year. When he came back months later with a more ethnically assertive campaign in the regular 1972 election cycle, Alatorre again won the primary and, facing no serious opponent in the fall that time, became the presumptive Mexican-American Assemblymember from Los Angeles — the first in many years. Now Moretti wanted Alatorre's vote in January for his reelection as Speaker, and his support in running for governor the following year. Cornering him at the Democratic Convention, Moretti forcefully demanded that Alatorre pledge him his vote for Speaker. Although he must have known that campaign funds were likely at stake, Alatorre refused. Wally Karabian's substantial support allowed Alatorre to play chicken with the Speaker.[10]

Relations among such ambitious males in this era were nothing if not complicated. Moretti's legendary predecessor as Speaker, Jesse Unruh, "skillfully used money to assure he would become and remain boss."[11] As a premier political journalist put it in his biography of "Big Daddy," before Unruh, lobbyists and business normally contributed directly to individual candidates. But Unruh managed to rig "a system in which the money would come to him, and he would pass it on to candidates who supported him. It was a brilliant invention, a breakthrough."[12] Assembly Speakers gave bags of cash to favored candidates and choked off contributions to their opponents. Alatorre's mentor, Wally Karabian, would say in an interview that he turned down Jesse Unruh's money in his first run for office in 1966, to retain his independence. In spite of their run-in at the Democratic Convention, Moretti had campaign cash for Alatorre, and Alatorre went dutifully to the Speaker's North Hollywood district office to pick it up, but they did not yet reconcile.

Come January in Sacramento, Moretti tried another approach. By then, Alatorre had put out word of the creation of the Chicano Caucus, which he chaired, and its inauguration-day reception for the legislature. No California Speaker or candidate for governor had ever faced a *group* of Mexican-American legislators before, and this bunch made the dark, gruff-sounding guy from East LA their first chairman. Moretti needed their support to win the speakership vote by the widest margin possible, and in the governor's race just a year away. He had no way of knowing if Richard controlled any votes other than his own, but it could be to his advantage if he did. Moretti decided to call Alatorre and offer him a plum no freshman member had received before: he asked Alatorre to make the seconding speech for his reelection as Speaker on the Assembly's opening day. The game of chicken was over, and Alatorre had won.

Alatorre proceeded to startle and dismay his fellow freshman colleagues when, following their mass swearing-in and the first nominating speech for Moretti, he was called upon and rose to give the seconding. The day would be topped with a beaming Alatorre hosting the whole legislature at his inaugural Chicano Caucus reception. The power game was well underway, and Alatorre was a player in it before the other freshmen knew what was going on.

Chairing the newly created caucus soon put Alatorre in demand around the state. He was experiencing by himself what the original members of the Congressional Black Caucus discovered two years before; as Representative Louis Stokes said, "In addition to representing our individual districts, we had to assume the onerous burden of acting as congressmen-at-large for unrepresented people around America."[13] Scholars have described this as "surrogate representation."[14] Moretti took note and called Alatorre into his office. With Alatorre looking ever more valuable as an ally going into a statewide campaign, Moretti offered him another unprecedented prize for a freshman: a seat on the Ways and Means Committee — chaired by none other than Willie Brown. This second plum would also mean more dismay from his colleagues, but most of all it meant that Alatorre could start building a historic political and personal partnership with Brown and devising ways to grow and leverage his newfound power.

His experience as a professor at campuses of both the University of California and California State University systems led to Alatorre's chairing of the Ways and Means subcommittee on higher education. With responsibility for holding hearings and making committee recommendations on annual budgets and capital improvement proposals, Alatorre soon got the hang of what he could accomplish. He was in a position to question representatives of various UC campuses — chancellors and deans — on their schools' records on recruitment and admission of minority students, in particular to their professional schools. As described in his state oral history and later his memoirs, Alatorre repeatedly heard the university educators explain, to his subdued annoyance, that affirmative action would be beneath the dignity of their world-class schools of law and medicine, and unfair to unqualified minority students. But Alatorre learned from his chairman, Brown, quoting him decades later saying that "you don't have to debate whether or not to achieve lofty, worthwhile goals if you got the votes; you just use the power you have. We had it as legislators; we just had to use it."[15] And use it Alatorre did.

Alatorre leveraged his budgetary power over university administrators' trophy projects — a teaching hospital here, an agricultural extension building there — to get them to commit to increased admissions of black and Chicano students. In one case, he said he zeroed out a UC law school's administrative salaries. In every case, the educators soon produced the plans he wanted. Willie explained, "We became better at it as we went along because people like Richard did not seek or need . . . social acceptance. . . . He never felt obligated to be diplomatic. He just felt obligated to be effective for the people and causes he cared about."[16]

Back in Los Angeles, Alatorre's chief deputy, Lou Moret, was busy for months organizing a splashy demonstration of the arrival of Chicano political clout, in the form of an unprecedented fundraiser on the city's Westside. He knew there was frustration among Latino administrators of the giant Los Angeles Unified School District, who could not seem to rise above the middle ranks of the vast bureaucracy. Moret set up a meeting for these administrators with Alatorre, where they recounted their experiences. Alatorre was no fan of the district, dating to his own experiences in grade school. He and Moret were committed to "substantive change," which had at least two dimensions: on one level, to social progress itself, including integrating the upper ranks of the district's leadership, a more equitable distribution of resources among schools, and reforming the curriculum to better serve Chicano students. The other aspect was the practical challenge of accumulating the political muscle needed to advance such reforms. For that, as Moret would often put it, they had to "build" — that is, get more Chicanos elected to office, to represent the community and fight for change. That would take money.

Alatorre's response to the administrators was simple: support me and I will support you. He offered no details; Moret would be in touch. In due course, Alatorre had a talk with the district superintendent. He explained his concern with the lack of advancement of Chicanos in the district bureaucracy and his interest in what could be done about it. One challenge the district faced repeatedly, over many years, was proposals in the state legislature to break up LAUSD into smaller districts. Bills to that effect, some with bipartisan support, had been introduced in previous sessions — one of which passed both houses and was only stopped by a surprise veto in the summer of 1970 by Governor Reagan. LAUSD fought that bill, which would have split it into a dozen subdistricts, and lost in the legislature, only to be saved by the governor after it had adopted a decentralization plan.[17] Alatorre mused to the superintendent that perhaps breaking up the district would create more opportunities for Chicano educators and more responsive schools for Chicano students. Republicans in Sacramento had a new bill in the works.

Nobody knew what influence Alatorre might have. He had arrived at the Capitol with a splash, heading up the new caucus and suddenly reconciling with the Speaker. Were he to support a revived Republican bill to break up the LA school district, it would at minimum give the district bad press and cost them more to kill it — which they failed at once already. According to Moret, every one of those administrators who met with Alatorre moved up in the LAUSD hierarchy in the ensuing years. One in particular, William "Bill" Antón, would become the district's first Latino superintendent in 1990.[18] Moret stayed in touch, in part because he had that mammoth fundraiser to sell on the Westside, which he built into a landmark gathering of Mexican-American professionals, executives, and entrepreneurs.

"Para Español, Oprima Dos"

1973 TURNED TO '74, A MIDTERM FOR DC BUT A GUBERNATORIAL ELECTION YEAR FOR SACRAMENTO. Assembly Speaker Bob Moretti launched his bid to succeed Reagan as governor of California, but lost to Secretary of State Jerry Brown in the primary. Suddenly, the Speaker who made Willie Brown and Richard Alatorre into a power duo on Ways and Means was himself on the way out. The succession battle pitted Willie, who seemed to have the advantage, against another San Franciscan, Leo McCarthy. Richard was unshakably committed to Willie, but the rest of the Chicano Caucus defected to McCarthy, in a deal that Alatorre would describe as payback, a revolt against his high-profile leadership.[19] A McCarthy speakership would consign both Alatorre and Brown to Capitol oblivion.

McCarthy managed to push Bob Moretti out of way fast and beat Willie Brown for the speakership in mid-June 1974. But oblivion was postponed, at least for a few weeks, while Brown's committee finished work on the budget, and even after that the fight with McCarthy went on.[20] Brown, with Alatorre's determined support, continued the fight through November, trying to get Assemblymembers elected who would support him in another bid for the speakership at the start of the new session in January. Alatorre would later recall that he devoted all the money he was able to raise since joining the Assembly to this effort for Brown, never giving up or seeking a deal with the new Speaker, as many of his colleagues did. "Brown will always be my choice as Speaker," he declared.[21]

The one Alatorre was helping most in this cycle was his *compadre* Art Torres, who was trying for a second time to make it to the Assembly — but this relationship would matter beyond Alatorre's commitment to Willie Brown. Torres was already part of Alatorre's team, and not only for having supported him in the 1971 special election. After losing in his own first primary campaign in 1972, Torres became part of Alatorre's inner circle, helping develop legislation that Alatorre would introduce after taking office the following year.

The first working sessions of Alatorre the lawmaker & co. had taken place after hours at the watershed 1972 Democratic National Convention in Miami. Willie and Richard, for all the strength of their coming partnership in Sacramento, were not on the same team at the '72 DNC — Alatorre was there as a Humphrey delegate, while Brown co-chaired McGovern's California contingent. With his impassioned "Give me back my delegation!" speech, Willie won a convention credentials fight in recognizing California's primary as winner-take-all. The state's Humphrey delegates had to leave. Although Wally Karabian was able to get Alatorre back onto the convention floor, Alatorre and his closest associates had fewer parties to go to and more time to focus on what he should do when he got to the Assembly. Right off, he proposed forming a Chicano Caucus to his new colleagues, but what else? In the middle of the Nixon era nationally, soon to be reaffirmed with a landslide reelection, and of the Reagan era in the state, the upstart Eastsiders — including Alatorre, his campaign manager Lou Moret, Art Torres, and others — began sketching out a California Chicano legislative agenda.[22]

First up was a proposed law that, as the opening shot of a language-rights offensive, would have the most "far-reaching impact on state and local government" of any in Alatorre's career.[23] This push started with a "bilingual services" bill, which set the goal that state agencies provide services in the dominant language spoken by 10 percent or more (or above a certain number) of its residents. The bill lacked teeth in the form of penalties for noncompliance, but the state would conduct audits and could make it known if agencies were failing to provide bilingual services.

Alatorre's bill, which became the Dymally-Alatorre Bilingual Services Act, "carried" by Mervyn Dymally on the state Senate side, aroused private-sector opposition, which rightly feared that bilingual services would soon be demanded of business as well. Follow-up laws covered local government and compensation for the personnel providing the services, and eventually imposed penalties for noncompliance.[24] Alatorre built on his own precedent with bills requiring translators in medical facilities and for businesses to provide contracts in each language they advertised in.[25] These laws broke into the private sector, eventually leading to a day, forevermore resented by nativists throughout the land, in which one could "[p]ick up the phone and call any customer service number and you are likely to hear, 'Press one to continue in English,' followed by '*Oprima dos para español.*'"[26]

Chicano Bobbseys

ART TORRES HAD ADVANTAGES RUNNING AGAIN FOR STATE ASSEMBLY in 1974 over his first bid. Well known in his Eastside district for working it door to door until his back gave out right before the '72 primary, he believed he could have toppled the incumbent with just a couple more days walking.[27] Back then, he seemed to be following Alatorre's route to office, running as an aide to a state legislator, but his last boss, State Senator Dave Roberti, came out against him, choosing instead to stick by his colleague, incumbent Assemblymember Alex Garcia — a former aide to Roybal — whom Torres aimed to take out. But now in '74 Torres was working for Sen. Mervyn Dymally — Alatorre's ally in Sacramento and a pioneer African-American backer of Chicano empowerment — and had his support. Better yet, the incumbent Garcia was now running for state Senate, leaving his Assembly seat open. Redistricting, furthermore, which had been put off until 1974, helpfully made Alatorre's district more Hispanic, but decisively made the one Torres was running in the most proportionately Latino of any district in the state.[28] To top things off, Torres had Alatorre's successful campaign manager and chief deputy, Lou Moret, running his second effort — precisely as he had done for Alatorre two years before.

After his 1972 primary loss, Torres served as the United Farm Workers legislative director, but after a year joined Dymally's staff to position himself for his second run. The union was his primary backer the first time and endorsed him again in '74, but Torres evidently chose to hew even more closely to the Alatorre model, and Richard's support, in his second run. This also meant that he was part of Alatorre's all-out effort that year to make Willie Brown Speaker. That would be Torres's very first and most fateful vote in the Assembly — one for which he joined Willie and Richard in the oblivion they were cast into when Leo McCarthy's speakership was reaffirmed. "I was a very bad boy," Torres would recall, and rue his small office on the sixth floor of the Capitol, "next to the cafeteria."[29] In the vast Capitol building, with the governor's horseshoe suite of offices at ground level and legislative leaders one level above, status drained away with each passing floor up the elevators. All three legislators would suffer office retribution, what came to be called "dog house politics," with Willie getting the smallest space, but at least it was on the second floor.[30]

Getting spanked by the Speaker was a tradition said to go back to Jesse Unruh — and one that Willie Brown would himself later be seen as practicing to perfection, once he had the power.[31] But these three losers in this particular speakership battle were not cowed. "Since Richard and I never had anything to start out with in life, it really didn't matter," Willie later recalled, "we knew it was only a matter of time before some day we would be in charge of everything."[32] Under Speaker Moretti, Brown and Alatorre had exercised power on the Ways and Means Committee together and now were on the outs together. Audacity followed by adversity only served to cement their alliance, but Torres was coming in fresh and, at 28, would be the youngest member of the Assembly. He and Alatorre, all of 32, would be deskmates on the floor of the chamber. Alatorre's and Brown's alliance with Moretti put them at odds not only with the new Speaker, McCarthy, who had pushed Moretti out, but also with the new governor, Jerry Brown, who Moretti opposed in the gubernatorial primary. Thus Torres, by virtue of his tight relationship with Alatorre, started his Assembly career as an opponent of both his Speaker and his governor, the two most powerful figures in state government.[33]

The LA Eastsiders, out of the leadership loop, consigned to undesirable offices and committees, and allowed only minimal staff support, still charged ahead. Their opposition roles defined them, and they were not without cards to play. Alatorre had helped Torres get elected, which for the first time in his career gave him a junior partner, one with impressive skills and qualities that complemented his own. Alatorre still headed the Chicano Caucus, even after being betrayed by the others in the speakership fight. The caucus was down to four members in the lower house, and was arguably more divided than ever, but now had two senators — the first Latinos in the state Senate in over 60 years — for a total of six lawmakers.[34] And noticeably, with the addition of Torres, the number of assertive *Chicano* legislators on the floor of the Assembly had doubled, albeit it from just one to two.

So the pair of Chicano "Bobbseys" decided to come in with guns blazing, as elected spokesmen of their community and generation. Brown took office on the first Monday of 1975 with an inaugural address that included a bold statement of support for farmworker rights. Alatorre and Torres scheduled a press conference for the next morning, to slam the new governor for failing to consult with them before appointing a Mexican-American lawyer from Texas to his cabinet.[35] But given who they were, the relationships they had, and their approach to dealing with power, it was inevitable that they would soon clash with the new governor, most of all over how to reform relations in California agriculture, which had been in turmoil for years.

Torres had first immersed himself in farmworker issues and forged a relationship with Dolores Huerta of the UFW while in law school at UC Davis, when he worked for the state agency California Rural Legal Assistance.[36] His bond with the farmworkers deepened with their backing of his first Assembly run in 1972 and his subsequent work for them, which made Torres a card-carrying union member. Alatorre and many others would forever say that Cesar Chavez came to regard Torres like a son.[37] Chavez led the press conference at Torres's campaign headquarters to announce his and the union's support. The endorsement editorial in the union newspaper noted poignantly, "We have not come to Los Angeles to campaign for a political candidate since 1968, when farmworkers worked long and hard in the Democratic presidential primary for our beloved brother, the late Senator Robert F. Kennedy."[38]

Alatorre had waded into farmworker issues upon his arrival to the Assembly in 1973, when he was assigned to the Select Committee on Agriculture, Food, and Nutrition.[39] At that time, he was thrust into a scene of raucous political theater and combat involving both the UFW and the Teamsters union, Art Torres, then-Speaker Moretti, and the media. The committee held hearings in Los Angeles on pesticide residue found on lettuce shipped and sold in markets, and the dangers it posed for both farmworkers and consumers. The first hearing quickly "exploded" in shouting and insults traded between a consumer advocate, lawmakers, representatives of the UFW, and pesticide manufacturers. Torres, there as the union's legislative director, helped negotiate a restoration of order; Alatorre used his time as a member of the committee to grill a representative of the Teamsters union, which was in league with agribusiness in an effort to contain the United Farm Workers throughout the state.[40]

The UFW's struggle to protect farmworkers from pesticides marked the beginning of Latino activism and leadership in the emergence of the environmental justice movement.[41] Alatorre, however, moved on from the pesticide front to strategically using his position to advance the UFW's objectives regarding "a comprehensive legislative solution to the farm labor problem." He persuaded Speaker Moretti to name him head of his own new Assembly Select Committee on Farm Labor Violence.[42] Moretti would soon be out of the picture, but Alatorre would labor on, using his select committee to push a strategic debate on farmworker labor rights and fashion the instrument of a limited, stalking-horse bill that Cesar Chavez would not want to ever see become law. That one would precede another, quite different, *maximalist* stalking-horse bill that would serve as the union's extreme bargaining position a year later. This convoluted, game-within-a-game approach would eventually yield historic legislation, but the ultimate consequences for both the union and the workers in the fields would be endlessly questioned and debated.

The Labor-Law Puzzle

> *The greatest accomplishment of my administration was the enactment of a farm labor relations law.*
> —Jerry Brown
> California Governor, 1975–83[43]

GREAT BOOKS ON CESAR CHAVEZ AND THE FARMWORKERS, Jerry Brown and California, and Fred Ross and grassroots organizing recognize the state's 1975 Agricultural Labor Relations Act as a historic landmark, a breakthrough in American labor relations, and a turning point in California history. But few mention, and even fewer explain, the ALRA's opening sentence: "This part shall be known and may be referred to as the *Alatorre*-Zenovich-Dunlap-Berman Agricultural Labor Relations Act of 1975." Who are these people? Why does Alatorre come first?[44]

The politics of the farm labor law were devilishly complex for everyone concerned. Topping the list of the inherent difficulties in organizing workers in agriculture, both farm and domestic workers had been excluded — a full 40 years back — from the New Deal's National Labor Relations Act (NLRA) of 1935.[45] This exclusion, which made the unionization of millions of workers of color nearly impossible for the ensuing decades, is widely seen to have been racially motivated.[46] But for a combination of reasons, the UFW's organizing efforts in 1960s–1970s California were able to take advantage of a weapon most unions were not allowed to use: the secondary boycott.[47] Precisely because farm work was not covered by the NLRA, as amended by the 1947 Taft-Hartley Act that bans secondary boycotts, the UFW was able to mount an international consumer boycott, "which brought the entire table grape industry under union contract in July 1970."[48]

The growers signed the contracts, but their farm lobby and its allies in the Capitol went to work to strip the UFW of its boycott instrument.[49] The American Farm Bureau Federation took note of the union's unprecedented success in California and rightly feared labor breakthroughs in other states, as did growers in neighboring Oregon and Arizona, as well as in far-off Florida. The union found itself in legislative battles on all these fronts.[50] Over a dozen farm labor bills were also introduced in Congress. In California, however, the farm lobby had another recourse when its bill died in Willie Brown's Assembly Ways and Means Committee in 1971; they repackaged the measure as an initiative on the 1972 ballot, which precipitated one of the greatest statewide political battles to that point.[51] In a remarkable demonstration of the muscle the union had developed, Chavez called back to California all boycott organizers and any volunteers they could bring along. Although Richard Nixon supported agribusiness, opposed the union, and was reelected by an immense landslide vote on the same ballot, the UFW's all-out grassroots campaign, anchored in Los Angeles, buried the growers' Proposition 22 with a landslide in the other direction.[52] This result appears to have checked further proliferation of anti-union measures in other states.[53]

Nonetheless, the UFW, which was still juridically an "organizing committee" subsidized and under the aegis of the AFL-CIO, not yet a full-fledged, chartered union with a constitution and executive board, was under mounting pressure from various quarters to institutionalize, push for legislation that would allow for widespread recognition elections, resolve its conflicts with the Teamsters, and bring an end to both costly strikes and the anomaly (and potential legal hazard) posed by secondary boycotts that were prohibited to the rest of the labor federation.[54] The AFL made Chavez promise to support legislation, in exchange for strike benefits for workers in the Coachella Valley where the union had lost contracts to the Teamsters, who had negotiated sweetheart deals with growers.[55] Chavez directed his chief counsel to develop a bill for farm labor similar to the NLRA, but he had a complicated strategy in mind. Chavez was leery of laws that would deprive his army of irregulars — his "nonviolent Viet Cong" — of latitude for guerrilla-style tactics, laws that would make the UFW adopt the approach of a traditional labor union.[56]

The UFW's stunning defeat of Proposition 22 in the big arena of the 1972 presidential-election cycle led Chavez to think that the next big one in 1976 could be used to get the voters to pass the union's own ballot initiative, a more favorable law than could be obtained through the legislative process in Sacramento. He could buy time and fend off pressure from AFL-CIO and others by pushing legislation that was too skewed in the union's own favor to pass, but that would establish markers for what he really wanted in the law and that he believed could be gotten from the voters with another climactic, statewide effort. Chavez, in fact, wanted more than the ideal farm labor statute — he wanted a farmworker bill of rights chiseled into California's Constitution, permanently beyond the reach of legislators, alterable only by the voters themselves in another statewide vote.[57]

Alatorre prepared the way for the union's ideal labor-law strategy with a smaller bill in 1974 that grew out of his select committee hearings the year before, although it appears that he saw his measure as leading to a "more comprehensive farm labor law" to be introduced later, not a ballot initiative in 1976.[58] He undertook a tricky challenge — to "win the arguments" in the Assembly over critical issues of bargaining units, the timing of elections, and the handling of objections to them, while counting on the state Senate to kill the bill, setting the stage for something bigger. In fact, Alatorre won those arguments well enough for his bill to pass the Assembly, but this news deeply disconcerted Chavez, who feared it just might become law.[59] The danger, however, was remote, since Reagan was still governor and would certainly veto it. But then Jerry Brown was elected and announced his goal, for his administration, the legislature, and the state, of a farm labor law, adding another layer of complexity to "the theater," as Alatorre would recall this episode in his memoir.[60]

Brown's stirring and historic call in his first inaugural address on January 6, 1975, "that we treat all workers alike, whether they work in the city or toil in the fields," and that they have "the right of secret ballot elections," had an aspect of theater to it in that he had not been in touch with the UFW since his own election fully two months before. The governor's speech made it clear that new legislation was coming that would be much more likely to become law than the previous failed efforts. But Chavez remained fearful of any statute negotiated in Sacramento. He wanted to express to Brown that "legislation wasn't what we were after. We wanted damn contracts more than anything else. Legislation could screw us."[61] But the union also had to act to protect its interests both concerning the content of any new law as well as its timing. The UFW would have to be part of the lawmaking game and needed to maneuver to enhance its leverage.

Alatorre's role in the new Assembly session was to introduce the union's comprehensive bill, what General Counsel Jerry Cohen called "our stalking horse . . . our extreme negotiating position," intending to set the stage for a grand debate and bargain.[62] Alatorre proceeded to campaign for the bill, "traveling all over California" to "relentlessly attack the new governor."[63] With Brown having neither introduced a bill nor contacted him, at the end of February Chavez led a march from San Francisco 110 miles to Modesto, where it converged with contingents from Fresno and Stockton for a rally of 15,000 supporters, according to police, in front of the Gallo winery. Afterwards, he told journalist Jacques Levy that he had heard certain rumors,

> The governor had said that he was going to introduce "fair" farm labor legislation that no one was going to like. So I was concerned. And since we had about twenty thousand people at the Modesto rally, I warned them about the legislation. . . . I pointed in the direction of Sacramento and said that we like Governor Brown, but we liked the farmworkers more, and that maybe we would have to go to Sacramento. . . . [T]he governor didn't like that. . . . But at that point he became very interested in legislation and started working almost full time on it.[64]

Chavez and the governor did not meet until mid-March in Los Angeles, where they apparently worked out a deal. Brown and Chavez would push aggressively for their separate bills, leading ultimately to negotiations between all parties and a historic law.[65] Until then, the theater — meaning attacks on the governor — would intensify. Alatorre continued barnstorming after Brown's bill was introduced in April, while the governor rounded up, in his words, "the bishops and the religious groups that had supported Chavez," supermarket executives, growers, union officials, and "sheriffs, school board members, city councilmen, county supervisors to enlist the broadest possible support and make the bill that I had introduced the vehicle for compromise."[66] All of this mobilizing and theatrics culminated in a marathon series of meetings in the governor's offices the first weekend of May, with agreement reached late Monday night. The governor then called a special

Governor Jerry Brown and Assemblymember Richard Alatorre speak to press after the signing of the historic Agricultural Labor Relations Act of 1975. Lieutenant Governor Mervyn Dymally, an Alatorre ally, on the left. (AP Photo.)

session of the legislature, which would allow for the law to take effect and union elections to begin that same year — but the tugging and pulling was not entirely over.

Speaker Leo McCarthy, who had no role in reaching the farm-labor grand bargain, was nevertheless in charge of the special session to be covered on live TV, and he was against letting a wayward member who he was punishing either speak on the Assembly floor or have his name "tomb stoned" on the bill, in the argot of the legislature. But Chavez insisted Alatorre's role be so recognized. Thus, the Alatorre-Zenovich-Dunlap-Berman Agricultural Labor Relations Act of 1975 was passed, signed by the governor, and incorporated into the California Labor Code.[67]

The Reckoning

RICHARD ALATORRE'S "McCARTHY ERA" WENT ON — for himself, Art Torres, and Willie Brown — for another five and half years after the governor signed the farm labor bill into law, but he managed to make his mark at the outset, in spite of the Speaker, and it would come to a surprising end.[68] The Agricultural Labor Relations Board was formed and ready to start approving petitions for farmworker elections by the end of August, and then to hold each election within a week, as mandated by the law. Chavez summoned boycott organizers and volunteers back to California again, effectively shutting down the union's boycott machinery and suspending its support networks across the country and Canada — a decision that Cesar, toward the end of his life, would bitterly regret, as Alatorre would later recall.[69]

The UFW had to target hundreds of ranches and farm operations and get pledges of support from a majority of workers in each one to petition for an election. Pressure was on to schedule elections at peak harvest season for every operation, when the greatest number of workers would be around to vote, and not allow the Teamsters to beat them to it. Then they had to mobilize each location to win the vote, be ready to spot irregularities and file complaints and challenges, and defend against the complaints made by the competition and other opponents. The UFW hired 500 organizers for this offensive, on top of those recalled from the boycott network. Once elections were certified and disputes settled, there remained the task of negotiating a contract with the grower and getting the workers to approve it. California's ALRB conducted over 300 elections in the first three months of operation that fall, and continued to conduct more until it expended its budget and had to temporarily shut down operations in early 1976.[70]

The elections hiatus due to the budget shortfall revived Chavez's plan to take a stronger version of the farm labor law to the voters as a proposed constitutional amendment. The party primary season had started back East, and as long as petitions for farmworker elections could not be filed, the union had the capacity to gather the hundreds of thousands of signatures needed to qualify the proposition to appear on the same ballot as the November presidential contest — which it accomplished with even more hundreds of thousands to spare.[71] It was also able to lend its top organizer and his staff to the Jerry Brown presidential campaign for his run in a string of late primaries.

At least some believed that the ballot initiative drive, for what was labeled "Proposition 14," was meant to pressure the legislature to adequately fund the ALRB, but that turned out not to be the case. The lawmakers eventually came through with additional funding, sparking a debate within the union, and with others, over whether to proceed with a costly, all-out proposition campaign, or get back to organizing elections and negotiating contracts. Both the governor and the Speaker urged Chavez and his board to drop the proposition. But the union was riding high in the summer of 1976, after qualifying the proposition with twice the signatures needed and aiding Jerry Brown win a series of Democratic primaries — including a landslide victory over Jimmy Carter in California — capped by the thrilling, national publicity boost of Chavez's nominating speech at the Democratic Convention. When they put the question to a vote, the board decided to forge ahead with the drive to amend the constitution of the state of California on behalf and in the name of the state's farmworkers.[72]

Brown had so tied his unconventional political brand and national aspirations to the UFW that he kept his objections private, and publicly endorsed Prop. 14. Speaker McCarthy, however, openly opposed "14" — a position that would come back to haunt him. The farm lobby's "no" campaign spent heavily on media and buried the UFW's initiative by more than two-to-one on Election Day.[73] After all the near-miraculous advances that came before, many both inside and outside the union would consider this setback to be a decisive turning point in the UFW's and Cesar Chavez's fortunes.[74]

* * *

THE COLORLESS MCCARTHY WAS A LIBERAL, SAN FRANCISCO DEMOCRAT two years into his speakership. His city and much of the Bay Area were strongholds of UFW support, but McCarthy was cautiously sensitive to the interests of rural Assemblymembers who helped bring him to power in 1974 over his flamboyant fellow San Franciscan Willie Brown, and who he needed to remain Speaker. Governor Brown, also a native San Franciscan, was in a fundamentally different position, able to win statewide elections by running up the urban liberal vote.[75] The distance between McCarthy and the union was attenuated by his appointment of Howard Berman as majority leader, the youngest member to ever serve in that position.[76] Berman was a Westside LA liberal, close to the UFW, and a co-author with Alatorre of the farm labor bill.

Chavez heeded the advice of Alatorre and others and tried to reach out to the Speaker two years after their split over Prop. 14, when McCarthy was seeing to his majority's fortunes in the 1978 elections. Chavez delivered a substantial campaign contribution to McCarthy on behalf of the UFW, asking that the Speaker protect the Agricultural Labor Relations Act and Board against continuing efforts to undermine them on behalf of growers. But the next year, McCarthy appointed a progrower member to chair a joint committee overseeing the ALRB. Between McCarthy's opposition to Prop. 14 and this appointment, his relations with the UFW were damaged beyond repair.[77] The Speaker's caution, paired with his ambition, would also make him enemies.

That year, 1979, it became clear that McCarthy planned to run to succeed Jerry Brown as governor in 1982. The stage was set for more intrigue, as this was a circumstance similar to when McCarthy engineered the end of Bob Moretti's speakership in 1974, but with an added twist. In both cases, Democratic members began feeling that their Speaker was more focused on his next career move than their interests in the Assembly. But in 1979 there was the additional factor of the next cycle of redistricting, to follow the fast-approaching 1980 census. McCarthy had begun raising money for his gubernatorial race further down the line, and seemed to not be taking clear steps in preparation for the redistricting challenge just ahead. But his majority leader, Howard Berman, who was certain to be in line to succeed McCarthy as Speaker at some point, was perceived to be an especially strong partisan leader on redistricting. Berman's brother Michael was part of an aggressive and sophisticated Democratic political-consulting firm expected to play a central role in drawing California's new district maps. Following a big fundraising event that left some of McCarthy's fellow Democrats feeling as if they had been used to advance the Speaker's bid to become governor, Berman made the move to set a succession plan and date.

Timing would be key. Of course, McCarthy wanted to remain Speaker as long as possible, to continue using that position to advance his gubernatorial bid. He had been steadily shoring up his support, making amends with his 1974 nemesis Willie Brown and his Chicano friends Alatorre and Torres. For Chavez and the UFW, Berman could not replace McCarthy soon enough. But the Republicans feared getting especially hurt if Berman was Speaker during redistricting. As the two sides dug in for extended battle, Willie saw an opportunity: he and Alatorre could play a profitable swing role in the speakership war. For now, Willie was better served by McCarthy hanging on.

Art Torres, who had known McCarthy since his college days, when he spent weekends at his roommate's highly political family home in San Francisco, saw his opportunity and seized it. Torres was promised a leadership position, majority leader, for standing with the Speaker — the same man who punished him a few years previous for having voted with Alatorre for Willie Brown. This time around, it would be Torres talking Alatorre into joining him in backing McCarthy.

Torres was deeply involved with McCarthy's 1980 effort to extend his speakership when Chavez called Alatorre and asked to meet with the two of them. Alatorre was nominally with McCarthy, but had no great difficulty going along with Chavez's request in advance of the meeting. Alatorre sensed on the way that Chavez intended to ask them to support Berman's challenge to the Speaker, and he dreaded the whole scenario. Nevertheless, Torres succumbed to the pressure and placed the call to McCarthy with the news of his defection to Berman. But things would still get curiouser.

Resisting Berman's pressures pushed McCarthy from playing for time to never wanting to see Berman become Speaker. Willie became McCarthy's preferred successor. Party discipline called for a vote in the caucus, after which all were expected to back their party's caucus choice in the definitive vote on the floor of the Assembly. But a never-Berman vote among the Democrats, combined with strong Republican opposition to him, meant that he could not reach the 41 votes needed to become Speaker. Enter Willie Brown.

Brown called Alatorre to say that with his and Torres's votes, he could put together enough Democrats and Republicans to reach 41. Alatorre never doubted that he wanted Willie as Speaker, but needed assurances before undertaking to get Torres to switch again. Brown had a deal with the Republican minority leader for the votes he would need. In another dramatic meeting, Torres was turned around. But this time the outcome was worse. Breaking with Berman to go with Willie meant also breaking with Cesar, Dolores, and the UFW. After this, Torres and Chavez never spoke again.

* * *

THE VOTE THAT MADE WILLIE BROWN SPEAKER OF THE CALIFORNIA ASSEMBLY came in December 1980 after Ronald Reagan was elected president, which left no doubt about the country's change of direction. But the deal that made the vote (that made Willie Speaker) would be contested for many acrimonious months into 1981. Brown had made a deal with the Republican leadership to get the votes he needed to resolve the speakership war. Their core concern was the upcoming legislative redistricting of the state. Brown pledged to be fair, and then appointed Richard Alatorre chair of the committee in charge of redrawing the political map. There were Democrats as well as Republicans who were shocked and appalled by his choice. The entire process was fraught from beginning to end — and even after the end, when the Republicans challenged the adopted plan with a ballot initiative.

The redistricting plan ended up being the most important issue of the first year — and perhaps for the duration — of Willie Brown's speakership. If the plan itself accommodated the interests of Republican members, which in districting could only come at the expense of Democratic members, it would give Brown's tenure a particular stamp and likely have consequences for its durability. Putting his East LA Chicano deputy in charge of the process shrouded it in mystery for everyone — even to a certain extent Willie — but in the end Alatorre would make his goals clear. He deemed it politically imperative to delink Brown's speakership from the Republicans, which meant winning as many Democratic votes as possible for the new plan. Doing so would put the bipartisan vote that elected Brown behind him and make his hold on the speakership more stable. And if done astutely, taking growth and development trends into account, the plan would make Brown's speakership as long as possible. In a similar vein, Alatorre aimed to lay the basis for sustained growth of Latino representation, with a politically workable balance between the maximum possible number of Democratic districts and the maximum number of Latino districts. Several elements make it possible for Alatorre to meet his goals and produce a plan that could garner the needed 41 votes for approval.

The breakthrough in the US Census that provided complete count data on Hispanics for the first time came in tandem with developments in computer technology and, in particular, systems for the geographic mapping of diverse sources of data. Alatorre looked for a cutting-edge political-data genius, and found one at California Institute of Technology, CalTech. Young Assistant Professor Bruce Cain found that existing operations that legislators and political operatives thought were capable of performing the redistricting were, in fact, backward to nonexistent. He would have to throw himself into the task full time and hire hundreds of students to work in double shifts, 24 hours a day, to receive and process all the relevant census and political precinct data.

In effect, Cain organized a version of what has come to be called a "Big Science" approach to modern political geography, a small but intensive Manhattan Project to meet the challenge of squeezing mountains of data through a nonvariable political opening in a period of several months. This required a large space and walking distance from the CalTech campus, which provided another key element — distance and isolation from the Capitol and the affected lawmakers. Alatorre kept the operation he sponsored in Pasadena secret. The only other legislator to step into the pop-up redistricting data operation was Speaker Willie Brown himself, who arrived uninvited and unannounced, surveyed the operation, and created a great disruption. Cain got Alatorre on the phone, who proceeded to chew Brown out, ordering him to leave and never return.

Richard Alatorre advises Assembly Speaker Willie Brown at the 1982 United Farm Workers political convention in Salinas, publicly marking Brown's reconciliation with the union and Cesar Chavez following the bitter speakership struggle of 1980. See Alatorre with Grossman, Change from the Inside, *231.*

As Cain makes clear in *The Reapportionment Puzzle* — his unique, scientific account of the general problem of designing a defensible plan of legislative districts, and of the particular case of California in 1981 — Alatorre himself was another key element in making the process work. Alatorre functioned as an essential buffer between the Speaker and both his majority members, as well as with the Republicans — especially those who felt they had a claim on special consideration from Brown for having voted for him. Alatorre and Brown had more than one high-volume exchange over the issue, in which Alatorre prevailed.

Alatorre also played the main role in relation to organized Chicano efforts to influence the redistricting process, led by Californios for Fair Representation. Chicano pressure to redress a history of deliberate fragmentation by the electoral system had already become a factor in the previous redistricting, 10 years before. Now the pressure was enhanced by the new census data; districts and lines proposed by nongovernmental activists, organizations, and institutions; and the progress that had been made in adding language minorities to the Voting Rights Act. Alatorre articulated the complementarity between pressure from the outside and his role on the inside of the process — hence the title of his memoirs, *Change from the Inside*.

Visible outside pressures and the potential for a Voting Rights Act lawsuit served Alatorre well in dealing with Assemblymembers. He and Cain met with each one individually, to hear out their views on their needs and interests, and ultimately to present proposed district lines. The objective was clear: to get to

41 votes while balancing the core objectives Alatorre defined. The payoff of the whole effort came with the passage of a plan that met legal requirements, played a key role in Willie Brown's record-long speakership, and fashioned 16 districts of 30 percent or more Latino residents, six more than the previous court-ordered plan of 1973. Actually realizing the political potential of the combined effects of population growth, redistricting, and political mobilization would take time, and these Latino-influence districts were designed to grow; in fact, they were referred to as "growth districts." Alatorre's successor in the Assembly would play the next key role in advancing Latino clout in Sacramento and grow the Latino Caucus into the most influential grouping in the legislature after the two political parties themselves.

Notes

1. John B. Anderson polled nearly seven percent running as an Independent, but won no electoral votes; Jimmy Carter managed 41 percent of the popular vote, winning six states and Washington, DC, for 49 Electoral College votes to Reagan's 489.

2. See Davidson, *Minority Vote Dilution.*

3. Frederic Gey et al., "California Latino Demographic Databook."

4. Assemblymember Wally Karabian represented an Eastside district and wanted to help get a Chicano elected there, and to fashion a district that would keep him in office; Alatorre with Grossman, *Change from the Inside*, 91; Richardson, *Willie Brown*, 225.

5. Jacobs, *A Rage for Justice*, 121; Alatorre with Grossman, *Change from the Inside*, 238.

6. Alatorre with Grossman, *Change from the Inside*, 121.

7. Shafer, *Quiet Revolution.*

8. "Creation and Evolution of the Congressional Black Caucus," *History, Art and Archives, US House of Representatives*, http://history.house.gov/Exhibitions-and-Publications/BAIC/Historical-Essays/Permanent-Interest/Congressional-Black-Caucus/.

9. This and the ensuing account based on authors' interviews with Alatorre, Moret, and Karabian; Alatorre interview by Vásquez; and Alatorre with Grossman, *Change from the Inside*, 35, 112, 119–20.

10. Karabian both financed Alatorre's first campaign and lined up a bevy of big endorsements for him from other elected officials; see Alatorre with Grossman, *Change from the Inside*, 94–95.

11. Boyarsky, *Big Daddy*, 8.

12. Ibid.

13. Representative Louis Stokes quoted in "Creation and Evolution of the Congressional Black Caucus."

14. Swers and Rouse, "Descriptive Representation," 244–45.

15. Alatorre with Grossman, *Change from the Inside*, 125.

16. Quoted in ibid.

17. Ralph Frammolino, "Breaking Up's Been Hard to Do: For 23 years, people have tried to split the LA school district. It is a saga of flip-flops and feuds fueled by shifting political alliances and the city's big swing in demographics," *Los Angeles Times*, May 16, 1993, http://articles.latimes.com/1993-05-16/news/mn-36202_1_school-district/5; Lewis and Nakagawa, *Race and Educational Reform in the American Metropolis*, 67–70.

18. Howard Blume, "William R. 'Bill' Anton dies at 85; LA School District's First Latino Leader," *Los Angeles Times*, July 30, 2009, http://www.latimes.com/local/obituaries/la-me-bill-anton29-2009jul29-story.html.

19. Alatorre with Grossman, *Change from the Inside*, 149.

20. Jacobs, *A Rage for Justice*, 232.

21. Alatorre with Grossman, *Change from the Inside*, 201–02.

22. Ibid., 118–19, 121, 132.

23. Ibid., 132–41.

24. Ibid., 133–34.

25. Alatorre with Grossman, *Change from the Inside*, 135–40.

26. Delgado, Pera, and Stefancic, *Latinos and the Law*, 216.

27. Torres interview by Edgington, 24–26.

28. Frank del Olmo, "2 Chicanos War with Leaders," *Los Angeles Times*, August 22, 1975.

29. Torres interview by Edgington, 44.

30. Ibid.; Brown, *Basic Brown*, 118.

31. Stu Woo, "Mr. Gilmore's Capitol Punishment: He's Stuck in California's 'Dog House,'" *Wall Street Journal*, May 14, 2009, https://www.wsj.com/articles/SB124224825395716665; Michael J. Mishak, "State Lawmakers Toe the Line or Risk Losing Their Parking Spots," *Los Angeles Times*, August 1, 2011, http://articles.latimes.com/2011/aug/01/local/la-me-punishment-20110801.

32. Alatorre with Grossman, *Change from the Inside*, 150. Brown put the matter more starkly in his autobiography, writing, "I deserved being put in a fucking small office because when I got the chance I'd do the same thing to those who crossed me. I believe in the spoils system" (*Basic Brown*, 118).

33. del Olmo, "2 Chicanos War With Leaders."

34. Ruben Ayala of San Bernardino County, whose district included Pomona in LA County, took office first after winning a special election in January 1974; Mike Castro, "Ayala — Newest Voice in State Senate for Spanish-Speaking," *Los Angeles Times*, February 18, 1974. Both Ayala and Alex Garcia then won in the regular state Senate primary and general elections that year.

35. del Olmo, "2 Chicanos War with Leaders"; Alatorre with Grossman, *Change from the Inside*, 170–71. In his *Los Angeles Times* feature story, del Olmo explained that the Bobbsey Twins "nickname is supposed to bring to mind a pair of bratty youngsters, making noise and annoying their elders simply to bring attention to themselves." But del Olmo added that "some Mexican Americans" liked that the nickname implied that Torres and Alatorre were "brash young Chicanos who are taking on the powers-that-be in state government."

36. Torres interview by Edgington, 11–13.

37. Alatorre with Grossman, *Change from the Inside*, 217; Alatorre interview by Vásquez, 279–80.

38. "Editorial: Why do Farmworkers Support ART TORRES?" *El Malcriado*, June 6, 1972.

39. Alatorre with Grossman, *Change from the Inside*, 182–83, 186.

40. Ibid, 186; "Union Charges at Wild Pesticide Hearings: Poisoned Lettuce Still on Shelves," *El Malcriado*, March 23, 1973.

41. See Pulido, *Environmentalism and Economic Justice;* Shaw, *Beyond the Fields*, Chapter 5: "The UFW Battles Pesticides"; Tompkins, *Ghostworkers and Greens*; and Pawel, *The Crusades of Cesar Chavez*, 457–59.

42. Alatorre with Grossman, *Change from the Inside*, 186–87.

43. Quoted by Martin, *Promise Unfulfilled*, 1; and in prepared remarks in the presence of the governor by William B. Gould IV, "Agricultural Labor Relations act 40th Anniversary," June 24, 2015.

44. California Labor Code Section 1140–1166.3, Agricultural Labor Relations Board, https://www.alrb.ca.gov/content/pdfs/statutesregulations/statutes/ALRA_010112.pdf, 1140 (emphasis added). The first of the great books on Chavez and the farmworkers movement that follows developments through the passage of the ALRA (and in fact culminates with this breakthrough), Jacques Levy's mammoth, 550-page oral history titled *Cesar Chavez: Autobiography of La Causa*, makes no mention of Alatorre at all. The most recent and detailed Chavez biography (and just as long) by Myriam Pawel, *The Crusades of Cesar Chavez*, only makes cursory reference to Alatorre, without connecting him to either the ALRA or the union.

45. Often remote, rural settings and the spatially extensive nature of farm work are natural challenges to union organizing, compounded by a "maze of obstruction" in laws, policies, and practices by local and state officials; see Leggett, *Mining the Fields*, chapter 3 and endnote 54 on 112. By contrast, William Scott discusses the "great irony" that the urban-based industrial system of production, developed not only to increase productivity and lower labor costs but also to prevent unionization, actually had the effect of facilitating labor unionization in that sector and setting; see Scott, *Troublemakers*, 9–12. The National Labor Relations Act established the right of collective bargaining and a legal framework for recognition of labor unions, including supervised elections. See Strecker, *Labor Law*.

46. Perea, "The Echoes of Slavery." Farmworkers were excluded from a slew of New Deal programs, including the 1935 Social Security Act and the later Fair Labor Standards Act, a pattern of exclusion that "had become routine" by the time of the 1938 passage of the FLSA and that was "infected with unconstitutional racial motivation" (Linder, "Farm Workers and the Fair Labor Standards Act"). For a detailed, contrary historical treatment that argues that racism and sexism do not explain the exclusion of farm and domestic workers from the Social Security Act in particular, see Dewitt, "The Decision to Exclude."

47. Prohibited by Section 8(b)(4) of the NLRA and explained thusly by the National Labor Relations Board (NLRB): "The NLRA protects the right to strike or picket a primary employer — an employer with whom a union has a labor dispute. But it also seeks to

keep neutral employers from being dragged into the fray. Thus, it is unlawful for a union to coerce a neutral employer to force it to cease doing business with a primary employer." "Secondary Boycotts," NLRB, accessed September 9, 2017, https://www.nlrb.gov/rights-we-protect/whats-law/unions/secondary-boycotts-section-8b4.

48. Ganz, *Why David Sometimes Wins*, 6. Ganz examines the major factors that contributed to the UFW's breakthrough success, which contrasted with decades of failed efforts by others to organize farmworkers, as well as failed competing efforts by the AFL-CIO and the Teamsters. He offers a theory of the UFW's "strategic capacity" as the principal explanation; see 8–21.

49. Assembly Bill No. 964 was an elaborate, 23-page amendment to the state Labor Code introduced March 15, 1971. It would have become the "Agricultural Labor Relations Act of 1971," comprehensively regulating the rights of all parties to the "production, packing, processing, transporting, and marketing of agricultural products." Assemblymember Alex Garcia voted to pass the bill in the Labor Relations Committee, which led the UFW to encourage Art Torres to mount a primary challenge to Garcia in 1972; Alatorre with Grossman, *Change from the Inside*, 181–82.

50. Anti-union measures were passed in both Arizona and Oregon, but in the latter case the UFW helped pressure the governor to veto the bill. In Arizona, the governor refused to meet with Chavez and signed the bill within an hour of receiving it from the legislature. The UFW tried to mount a recall of that governor, for which it gathered over 100,000 signatures, but was blocked by the state attorney general. See Shaw, *Beyond the Fields*, 146–50; Pawel, *The Crusades of Cesar Chavez*, 239–41.

51. Pawel, *The Crusades of Cesar Chavez*, 243, 245–46; Alatorre with Grossman, *Change from the Inside*, 182; Shaw, *Beyond the Fields*, 150–53.

52. In his first year as president, Nixon backed anti-union legislation in Congress and acted to undercut the UFW's grape boycott by having the Defense Department more than double its purchases of table grapes, as well as pressing the government of South Vietnam to massively increase its imports of the fruit; see Garcia, *From the Jaws of Victory*, 133. Nixon won 49 states and surpassed 60 percent of the popular vote nationally, but just reached the 55 percent "landslide" threshold in California. Proposition 22 was rejected with a 58 percent landslide "no" vote. See Lee and Keith, *California Votes, 1960–1972*, and "Agricultural Labor Relations: California Proposition 22 (1972)" California Ballot Propositions and Initiatives, UC Hastings Scholarship Repository, http://repository.uchastings.edu/ca_ballot_props/773/.

53. Shaw, *Beyond the Fields*, 153.

54. Pawel, *The Crusades of Cesar Chavez*, 245, 264, 299–308. The UFW held its first constitutional convention in late September 1973 (ibid., 273–74). The AFL-CIO later came to support generalized consumer boycotts that did not engage in a secondary boycott. The UFW and its supporters saw such announced boycotts without grassroots pressure as "paper boycotts"; see Shaw, *Beyond the Fields*, 54–55.

55. Alatorre with Grossman, *Change from the Inside*, 185, 189; Pawel, *The Crusades of Cesar Chavez*, 299–300.

56. Both growers and the Teamsters disparagingly referred to Chavez and the UFW as "guerrillas" and the "Vietcong"; Chavez, however, embraced the idea of leading a "nonviolent Viet Cong"; see Pawel, *The Crusades of Cesar Chavez*, 138, 189, 260, 300. Chavez explained to writer Peter Matthiessen, "When the moment comes, we can just turn around and *hit it. . . .* We can go down the highway at eighty miles an hour and throw her into reverse gear and not even screech. . . . [W]e can be striking today, and tomorrow morning or a couple of days later we can move the effort into a boycott without missing a step. We have motion and we have rhythm. . . . [W]hen we see them make a mistake we move right in. That's why they call us the Vietcong — it's guerilla warfare. Institutions can't afford these methods. . . . [W]e can make them spend fifty dollars to our one, and sometimes more. And we're still developing our tactics" (*Sal Si Puedes*, 158–59).

57. Pawel, *The Crusades of Cesar Chavez*, 300–01.

58. Alatorre with Grossman, *Change from the Inside*, 191.

59. Ibid., 193.

60. Ibid., 196.

61. Pawel, *The Crusades of Cesar Chavez*, 305. Leroy Chatfield, who ran the UFW's 1972 campaign against Proposition 22, worked on Brown's 1974 election and then joined the governor's staff, explained this view directly to Brown, "I was opposed to legislation," favoring instead "a negotiated settlement, using the power of the governor's office to try to bring people together and to hammer out a settlement that all sides would agree to" (Levy, *Cesar Chavez*, 529).

62. Edmund G. "Jerry" Brown, First Inaugural Address, January 6, 1975, *The Governors' Gallery*, http://governors.library.ca.gov/addresses/34-jbrown01.html; Alatorre with Grossman, *Change from the Inside*, 194–95.

63. Alatorre with Grossman, *Change from the Inside*, 171.

64. Levy, *Cesar Chavez*, 527–28.

65. Pawel, *The Crusades of Cesar Chavez*, 305–07; Alatorre with Grossman, *Change from the Inside*, 195–96; Levy, *Cesar Chavez*, 528.

66. Levy, *Cesar Chavez*, 531.

67. Alatorre with Grossman, *Change from the Inside*, 197–98.

68. Ibid., 116.

69. Ibid., 199.

70. Pawel, *The Crusades of Cesar Chavez*, 311–22; Thompson, *America's Social Arsonist*, 211. According to Pawel, in the five months of operations before shutting down in February 1976, the ALRB conducted 423 elections, with the UFW winning twice as many votes and 192 contests in preliminary results to the Teamsters' 119, and with both unions rejected in 25 cases. Garcia, in *From the Jaws of Victory*, writes that the agency held 354 elections by the end of 1975, of which the UFW won 189 and the Teamsters 101, shifting 58 ranches from the Teamsters to the UFW (160–61).

71. Thompson, *America's Social Arsonist*; Pawel, *The Crusades of Cesar Chavez*, 329.

72. Pawel, *The Crusades of Cesar Chavez*, 330–32; Thompson, *America's Social Arsonist*, 212.

73. Pawel, *The Crusades of Cesar Chavez*, 332–33, 433.

74. Leroy Chatfield, "A Turning Point," in Chatfield Essays, UC San Diego Farm-worker Movement Documentation Project, accessed October 16, 2017, https://libraries.ucsd.edu/farmworkermovement/essays/essays-by-author/chatfield-essays/, 3–5.

75. Alatorre recognized McCarthy's strong record of support for labor, but also under-stood, "Something happens when you become Speaker. Now all of a sudden you can't just consider your own politics; you have to reflect the politics of everybody else who is part of your caucus. That's what comes with the leadership" (Alatorre with Grossman, *Change from the Inside*, 209).

76. Ibid., 202.

77. Ibid., 208–09.

Part III

Multiple Shifts

PART III

Multiple Shifts

As THE REAGAN ERA DAWNED IN THE 1980s, with century's end in sight, the political progress of Latinos and other historically subordinated groups in California appeared bleak and at best uneven. The Golden State had not been golden for all. In the twentieth century, there had never been a Latino, African-American, Jewish, or woman governor or senator. In fact, no Latino had been elected to any statewide office to this point in the century, or to any citywide office in Los Angeles, nor to the county board of supervisors. No Latino had served on LA City Council since Ed Roybal left in 1962. California had the country's largest Latino population, registering substantial growth with every census, but Roybal was approaching his third decade as the sole Latino in the nation's biggest and steadily expanding congressional delegation.

African Americans had managed much greater progress, in spite of the fact that Latinos were over two-to-one more numerous in the state. Tom Bradley was running for his third term as LA mayor in 1981, and would become the leading candidate for governor the following year. Willie Brown was just starting a record-setting tenure as Speaker of the California Assembly — a position that, since the office was established in 1849, had been the exclusive province of white men.

That lower house of the state legislature would prove to be the indispensable instrument of Latino political empowerment in California, and especially for Greater Los Angeles. It was from a state Assembly base that Latinos would stage their comeback to the Los Angeles City Council in the 1980s, and from there finally gain representation on the county board at the dawn of the '90s, and before the century turned, also conquer the pinnacle of power in the Assembly itself — the speakership — for the first time ever. That achievement, in turn, would lead to another pinnacle, the mayoralty of Los Angeles, early in the new century. The journey of Latino political empowerment in California would return, triumphantly, from Sacramento to Los Angeles, where it began, after having taken a long way home.

CHAPTER 7

Barrio Dreams

JUNE 1982 — POLITICAL CHANGE BEGAN SPEEDING UP with this year's primary elections, bringing greater competition and the promise of more representation for the Eastside. Making noise in background was Los Angeles Mayor Tom Bradley, running for governor of California. Reapportionment finally brought the area a new majority-Latino congressional district and with it an open race. Esteban Torres returned from Washington to claim the seat, eight years after his unsuccessful first try against an incumbent. Then, political maneuvering involving players in Washington, Sacramento, and Los Angeles suddenly opened yet another congressional seat to run for; if won, it would triple the number of Eastside Latinos in Congress in less than six months. And there was more.

After four terms in the California State Assembly, Art Torres decided to again take on his old political nemesis, the incumbent he lost to the first time he ran, who had moved up to the state Senate. Torres's renewed challenge to Alex Garcia, in turn, set up a race to fill the seat he was vacating in the Assembly — and *that* was the contest that would create divisions that would last for years, if not decades: Gloria Molina vs. Richard Polanco, both originally from East LA. Few knew that the path to their collision had been set nearly eight years before, in the pivotal year of 1974.

* * *

LA's "GREATER EASTSIDE" HAS ITS OWN EAST AND WEST SIDES — OF INDIANA STREET, along the original eastern boundary of the pueblo in 1781 and still a city limit today, where one street after another ends, and many of those that continue do not align with their namesake on the other side. Approaching Indiana, whether in Boyle Heights or East LA, you have to turn left and then right to proceed down what is, in name, the same street. Most strikingly, nearly every Boyle Heights street slopes down to Indiana at an angle, while nearly every East LA street is perfectly perpendicular to the ramrod north-south boundary. The clashing street grids reflect deep historical differences and make plain that the two sides are distinct communities and jurisdictions — LA city and unincorporated LA County.[1]

When Gloria Molina and Richard Polanco were born in the mid-twentieth century, Ed Roybal and his supporters were busy organizing the highly diverse, west, Boyle Heights, city side of Indiana — LA Police Department territory. That was where modern Latino politics was born in California and where the action was on the Eastside at least until the 1960s, marked by interethnic and interracial coalitions and focused on the LA City Council.[2]

On the other side of Indiana, the "Census Designated Place" of East LA was bigger when Gloria was born than it remains today. Some residents, including Polanco's uncle and later Richard, too, waged campaigns to incorporate it as a city in its own right, what would have made for — at least initially — a very Mexican-American city. In fact, residential East LA was developed from the beginning to attract working-class Mexicans. The Janss Investment Company developed tony Westwood, which surrounds UCLA, and "established new standards for race and class exclusivity"; the company also subdivided the first East LA barrios of Belvedere Heights and Belvedere Gardens, offering prospective residents "either a humble dwelling or an empty lot."[3] At one time, "a two-room shack with no bathroom" went for $625, while a somewhat larger empty lot could be had for $10 per month. Buyers could live in tents on their property while putting a house together.[4] Belvedere quickly grew to be "the fifth largest Mexican urban community in the nation," home to "twenty to thirty thousand Mexican residents" by 1930.[5]

In those days, some business interests pushed for incorporating the area, with the intention of raising taxes on the low-income residents and thereby "forcing the largely working-class community to sell their property in a depressed market."[6] Such a move would have echoed the first imposition of property taxes in 1851, which facilitated the massive transfer of land from the ranch-owning *Californio* Mexican families "to the new American businessmen who began to subdivide them."[7] But the later, recurring incorporation efforts always failed, from the 1920s to the twenty-first century, and East LA would persist, at nearly 97 percent, as the most Latino neighborhood in the county, out of the 265 ranked by *Los Angeles Times*.[8]

In the late 1960s and early '70s, organizing and reforming part of a particular East LA neighborhood known locally as Maravilla would take precedence over incorporation. It would bring Polanco, Molina, and many other Chicano-era activists, leaders, and organizations together — among them George Pla, in his first job out of college — and establish a new Latino power base on the Eastside, independent of Roybal and his Boyle Heights organization. Skills learned and relationships forged in this experience would propel Latino empowerment in California for a generation. But the common cause that initially seemed to unite them on a rising team would prove unable to prevent their splitting into bitterly opposed factions for long stretches of time.

The Molinas of the Brickyard Pueblo

GLORIA, WHO DECADES LATER BECAME THE FIRST LATINA TO WIN one major elected office after another in California, was from a family that started out in a decaying, southern part of unincorporated East LA, later annexed by the towns of Montebello and Commerce. Her neighborhood was known by the name of Simons, short for Simons Brick Yard No. 3, a giant family-owned business that had built the town for its Mexican workers and was said in the 1920s to be the biggest producer of bricks in the world.⁹ Her father, Leonardo, having found a little place to live in the declining company town just after WWII, brought her mother Concepción to LA from a rural area near Casas Grandes, Chihuahua, about 120 miles south of the border with New Mexico. Leonardo Molina did not work in the brickyard; there were few who still did, those who remembered the days of when Simons sponsored Friday-night dances, weekend picnics, baseball teams, and bonuses for having babies.¹⁰ Those days were gone.

The Simons brothers, in building this little company town for their Mexican workers a couple of miles beyond LA city limits, offered a paternalistic industrial counterpoint to the considerably less organized *colonias* of citrus-belt San Gabriel Valley nearby. In many ways, they provided a benevolent community, albeit segregated and strictly anti-union. Some of the shanty-like houses abutted *el hoyo*, "the hole" created by decades of shoveling tons of red clay out of the ground. The village had its company store, school, restaurant, pool hall, train station, post office, and a little Catholic church built by the workers from brick donated by Simons. At its peak in the 1920s, the workers and their families totaled some three thousand residents of *El Pueblo de Simons*. The plant's colossal production of 600,000 — or as many as a million — bricks per day helped build the better part of Pasadena and a good deal of Los Angeles through the 1920s. For many among the waves of Midwestern Anglos arriving with the completion of the railroads, good red brick "meant progress as against dirty, ugly, unprogressive adobe."¹¹

The Great Depression hurt the Simons Company, but the Long Beach earthquake of 1933 did even more so. Public-school authorities had favored brick construction, but hundreds of brick school buildings in the Southland were destroyed or damaged beyond repair by this temblor, which fortunately hit late on a Friday afternoon. Ed Roybal, on the Roosevelt track team, had just finished a meet at Jefferson High in South LA at the time of the quake. He would recount to his family that when the shaking started, the boys ran out of the showers with no clothes.¹² The entire high school, six buildings' worth, crumbled into ruins. A month to the day later, the state mandated that public schools be designed and built earthquake-resistant, spurring a shift to reinforced concrete. Then the construction boom that followed the war brought a further shift to prefab and stucco residences as well as more modernistic commercial-building designs. Simons went out of business altogether in 1952, shortly after the county declared its worker housing substandard.¹³

* * *

"Everything that we did, everything I did, everything I asked for had to fit into what the goals were of the family. But it was good."

GLORIA, THE ELDEST OF A BROOD THAT GREW TO TEN, WAS A SHY GIRL who led a busy, controlled, sheltered life. She began acquiring responsibilities for her younger siblings at the age of three, when the sound of machinery stamping every sixth brick with the company name could still be heard, 12 hours a day. Simons was an entirely Spanish-speaking community, but Molina's family lived near the edge of the company's 350 acres that bordered Montebello. She and her siblings were among the few living there who were able to attend Greenwood Elementary, a couple of blocks into Montebello, instead of going to what was informally known as the "Mexican school" by the brick yard. Yet until she learned to speak English, going to Greenwood was traumatic. Fluency brought her more responsibilities by the age of eight, when Gloria's mother taught her to take the bus by herself to go pay the family's bills in Montebello. By the time she was in third grade, Gloria had two younger sisters at Greenwood; they hurriedly practiced speaking English together every day during recess. Many years later, her ability to teach would connect Molina with a new generation of East LA youth.

Gloria's parents had a frontier traditionalism that seemed to rule her home life, but they also had long experience in dealing with urban life. Her mother, Concepción, was from an impoverished *ranchería* in the northern reaches of Chihuahua, outside the village of Casas Grandes. She met Gloria's father, Leonardo, who lived on a nearby ranch, when they were children. An aunt headed the extended Molina family from an early age, after her parents — Leonardo's grandparents — were killed in an Apache raid on the ranch. Back then, this was still Mexico's frontier. But Leonardo was actually born in downtown LA in the 1920s. His own father had migrated to California, married, and was successful, from the looks of a photograph they posed for, sharply dressed and standing in front of what might be his car. But Gloria's father was returned to the ranch in Chihuahua at the age of three and never saw his parents again. Knowing he was a US citizen and believing that his mother, perhaps divorced, might be living in California, Leonardo ventured north as a teenager in the 1940s, working his way by the end of the war from El Paso to New Mexico to LA. He was by turns a miner and a farmworker until he got to Los Angeles and found work with a landscaping company. Once he had secured his own place to live, he went back to Casas Grandes to marry his childhood sweetheart, Concepción, and bring her up to LA.

Gloria's father had finished primary school in Mexico, but her mother was sent off to work in the big bordertown of Ciudad Juárez, about 180 miles to the northeast, when she was still an adolescent. Tradition and urban life intertwined in their Simons household. Gloria was to come straight home from school every

First Person: Growing Up Gloria*

We . . . lived in the back of a little grocery store. . . . I remember being brought up always with the fact that we were going to . . . go back to Mexico. My mother came here under protest. . . . It was always the idea, "When we have enough money, we're going back." . . .

She didn't like the things that went on. We lived not far away from a little pool hall and things of that sort. She always just felt that . . . in Casas Grandes, everything was right. She used to have lots of problems with people drinking and partying . . . the looseness of everything. Everything was right in Mexico; everything was wrong here. The values were very different. I was very, very sheltered. We weren't allowed to participate in a lot of things. You went to school and you came home, and you had a whole list of things to do.

You couldn't stay after school and play. That's what Anglos did. Mexicans came home, and they helped their mothers wash clothes. And that bothered her that others didn't . . . because then that would set a bad example for us. . . . All of it, all the upbringing was always very different from kids that I went to school with . . . even sometimes kids in our own barrio . . . little things like joining Girl Scouts . . . that my parents didn't allow.

That was something that took away from the responsibility to the family. . . . If you went off and did things after school, then you didn't come home and take care of the rest of the kids or help with whatever was going on. . . . Everything was always back to the family. The responsibility of the family . . . that was foremost. . . . It was like that all of the time. Everything that we did, everything I did, everything I asked for had to fit into what the goals were of the family. But it was good.

---

* *Molina interview by Vásquez, 7–8.*

day, to make tortillas and help with other chores. Leonardo had an idea of the difference between city women and those from the country. He would encourage his daughters to speak up for themselves and not to scurry and hide when someone came to the door. He laughingly called his girls *rancheras* for their social reticence.

Gloria's father advanced from landscaping work to construction, as a unionized hod carrier. He strove to never miss voting but could not read his union's political literature — their election "cheat sheets," as Gloria called them — which was all in English. He would ask her to translate for him. Gloria's mother was a devoted fan of talk-radio personality Elenita Salinas on the Spanish-language station KALI, which kept her informed. Not a citizen and unable to vote, Concepción nevertheless helped inform Gloria's dad about coming elections, from her constant radio listening — all talk, no music. Gloria was a child who liked to listen to adult conversation, and she recalls hearing that a Mexican man with a name that did not sound Mexican, Edward Roybal, was an elected official in Los Angeles, and a source of pride.

Although Leonardo had a union job, the Molina family "couldn't get anything or do anything" during long years of saving for a down payment on a house that would take them out of Simons. But for a few years at least, Leonardo did take the family, "like all Mexican families," back to the district he was born in, downtown LA, to the movies at the Million Dollar Theater. With no television at home, Gloria looked for another window on the outside world, and found one in old copies of *Life* and *Look* magazines that had been discarded by a neighbor.

The day came, just as Gloria transitioned to junior high, when the family was able to buy a house and move further east, to Pico Rivera, which back then was an English-speaking suburb. The new surroundings frightened and intimidated her. But they got a TV set, and watched John Kennedy debate Richard Nixon in 1960. Between her magazines and now TV, Gloria developed a fascination for perennial Academy Award-nominee Edith Head. Within a couple of years, the Molinas had their first telephone.

* * *

SHYNESS ACCOMPANIED GLORIA TO HIGH SCHOOL AND BEYOND, at Rio Hondo and East LA Colleges, in her work as a secretary downtown, and her early years as an activist. But her will to overcome reticence grew steadily, and she developed an arsenal of skills to draw upon when she would later emerge as a famously assertive and outspoken leader.

Family need was a constant motivator: Molina had to work. At 14, she jumped at the chance for a job, but she had to lie about her age to get it. She became a telephone solicitor for the Fred Astaire Dance Studio, working for 75 cents an hour in a "boiler room" phone bank with blacked-out windows. She was trained, practiced the pitch, and acquired a professional telephone voice; this amounted to months of rehearsal for the sort of systematic work she would eventually do in political campaigns.

Before "critical pedagogy" was introduced to American education, and a generation before the term "fake news" was coined, Molina had a memorable civics teacher who demanded his students read a daily newspaper and constantly challenged them with made-up stories. Molina was determined to get ahold of a newspaper every day and not fall for any of her teacher's preposterous and provocative tales. She acquired a taste for verbal combat and longed to be on the school's debate team. She yearned to speak confidently, not just pitching dance lessons in the dark on the phone but on controversial issues, like the death penalty, in front of whole groups.

From her first years practicing English at Greenwood Elementary with her sisters to her cold-calling sales work, Molina knew that performance required practice. She studied the season's national debate topic and play-acted in front of a mirror, but never worked up the nerve to try out for the team. Expected to live at home and help her family until she got married — even if she was 38 years old, as her father once proclaimed — Molina dreamed of a professional career and independence, a life of her own, like Doris Day in the movies, or perhaps like Edith Head, designing costumes for the movies.

Years later, working for law firms downtown, she reached a tipping point, with experiences that challenged and changed her forever. Intimidated by a panhandler who regularly stationed himself outside her office building, Molina felt obliged to give him something, instead of saying no. One time, when they were walking out together at the end of the day, Molina shared her discomfort with a coworker as she tried to avoid contact with the beggar. Her colleague — a strong woman who happened to be married to Richard Alatorre, but in the midst of divorce — sharply admonished Molina for her lack of assertiveness; the words stung and stuck with her.

Then came an occasion when the personal secretary to the head of the firm implied that Molina might have pocketed the boss's missing plane tickets instead of placing them in his mail slot, as she said she had done after taking delivery of them. Molina looked frantically for the tickets, when another coworker admonished her even more strongly, asking how she could let herself be accused, even implicitly, of theft, and not defend herself. Molina worried and stewed for hours, until the end of the day, and finally decided to confront the secretary who had accused her. She figured she was going to be fired anyway, so she told the woman that she resented the implication that she might have stolen the plane tickets. The other secretary replied nonchalantly that the boss had found the tickets in his coat pocket. Molina was appalled that this woman had let hours pass without informing her that the issue had been resolved.

The experience was transformative. Molina vowed to never again shrink from a challenge or allow anyone to treat her unfairly. She also decided to get her own apartment and move out of the family home, over her parents' vehement objections.

The Polancos of Old Maravilla

RICHARD POLANCO WAS BORN NOT QUITE THREE YEARS AFTER GLORIA MO-LINA, and grew up in what would come to be known as one of East LA's "hard core" neighborhoods, Barrio Maravilla.[14] From a sports-mad childhood in a big, religious family, Polanco developed an abiding dedication to combating the social ills that came to plague his old neighborhood and others like it, and to overcoming the powerlessness and lack of opportunity he felt held them down. He would rise from community activist to policy wonk to politician, and in the 1990s become a wide-ranging power with considerable influence over more than half the state's budget. Said at that time to be "the architect" of Latino clout in Sacramento, Polanco developed into an advocate and law-making machine of seemingly boundless energy and a master at winning elections near and far in California.[15]

Polanco grew up on a couple of long blocks just south of Brooklyn Avenue, between the Maravilla housing project and Brooklyn Elementary. According to Carey McWilliams, Mexican immigrants arriving in the 1920s found Los Angeles to be a wonder, a *maravilla*, and took to calling this area by that name.[16] Many thousands settled here, well east of the LA River, and by the time Polanco was growing up, most of the neighborhood lay also just east of the wide divide created by the Long Beach Freeway, a torrent of heavy trucks rumbling south to the harbor. His parents were not immigrants but did not speak English. With eight children — Richard was the fourth — it was a busy household. Then two cousins came to live with them as well, which made the Polancos move to a bigger house on the next street over. The cousins, two boys, lived with the Polancos until they were old enough to join the military.

Two daily constants at home were that Polanco's mother was always up by 5:00 and his father always worked two jobs: one in a steel foundry, making manhole covers, and another in a bakery. He recalled accompanying his father one summer to the "horrific," blazing-hot foundry, with its roaring vats of molten steel. His dad came home every day exhausted, covered in salt from sweat. At night his moans from *calambres*, cramps, could be heard through the house.

There was never a time Polanco himself was not working to make some money. In certain ways his earliest, informal work as a kid laid the foundation for his grown-up political career and unrivaled success in getting Latinos elected. He had his routes, to pick up bottles on Fridays and selling oranges door to door after school. Hawking fruit picked by Mexican workers in the citrus belt to urbanites beyond his own barrio, young Polanco learned to speak effectively and efficiently to strangers, figuring out in seconds if he had a sale. He got to know people and neighborhoods he would campaign in and come to represent decades later in the state legislature. With this experience, rounding up votes and even campaign contributions would feel easy to him.[17]

Delinquency and crime were not prevalent in Maravilla when Polanco was a child, and alleys on two sides bounded his family home on North Kern Avenue. That would change by his teenage years, living on Arizona Street, with more drugs around and its own signature gang. But it seems no adversity could keep Polanco from fashioning himself into a marvel of political energy and skill, not even an inadequate education. The old neighborhood's maladies seem to have given him a mission, and propelled him into becoming an avatar of vigorously activist, problem-solving government.

Baptized Catholic, Polanco was raised evangelical Protestant, as a result of his mother's conversion by a friend. Church three times a week was a major influence, conducted entirely in Spanish, including Bible study. Friday evenings were spent at church, but there was one time when it seemed that Polanco's mother was not herself and not mobilizing them to go to the usual services. He approached her and noticed there was something truly wrong, which he would later describe as her having a breakdown. They were the only *aleluyas* on the block and all Richard could think to do was to run to their church about a mile away and pull the pastor from the pulpit to come help. When they got back to the Polanco home, paramedics had Richard's distressed mother strapped to a gurney. Contributing to the agonizing situation was the language barrier — the paramedics spoke no Spanish and Polanco's mother no English. The experience would inform his work as a state legislator decades later.

An even stronger pull on Polanco was the school playground just three blocks from home, and later the Boys Club next to it. Polanco would remember the playground director, Mr. Orozco, as "phenomenal" and "an amazing man," to which he might have added, freakishly well organized. Alex Orozco ran after-school sports programs, apparently on his own initiative, for hundreds of kids at a time, including two baseball leagues (American and National, of course), flag football, and basketball. He held a draft to form the teams. He raised money for uniforms and for the trophies all the players would get in the season-ending ceremony in the school gym.

Besides sports, Orozco started a Junior Optimist Club at Brooklyn, and Polanco became its president. Heading the club gave him his first experience running meetings. Around this time, he also became aware of community politics, when his uncle got involved in one of the periodic attempts to make a city out of unincorporated East LA. That campaign, like those that came before and after, would fail, but it planted a seed for the future.[18] In junior high, Polanco would also become president of his class.

Orozco's programs had competition from the Boys Club that the school shared the block with. Polanco was drawn to it as well. He learned to box there and got to leave the barrio to go camping in the mountains and to Dodger games at the LA Coliseum, before the stadium was built in Chavez Ravine. The club brought Polanco into contact with African-American boys for the first time. He boxed for a year and then gave it up when he came home with a black eye that he tried to hide from his mother, but the skills he learned would serve him well in the years to come. Boys Club gave Polanco opportunities beyond sports and recreation. When still in grade school, he was asked to participate in a fundraising banquet at the Ambassador Hotel, where a member of the California State Assembly was being honored. The first time Polanco stood in front of a real audience, he led the room of some 500 grownups and California Assemblymember Jack Fenton in the pledge of allegiance.

By junior high, Polanco had graduated to Pop Warner football, with its higher level of commitment and recognition: contact football, with practice and games now at a distance away, a park in Montebello, and each player announced at the start of the game. If he lacked a ride, Polanco would huff to the park on his bike, carrying his uniform. His whole team in Montebello, both the first and second squads, hailed from East LA.

Polanco got into a number of fights in junior high, and at least one other in high school. There was one fight that stood out. The other guy had "zeroed in" on Polanco, for reasons he could not understand. The fight was set for after school. Polanco came away from it with a broken finger, but he got the better of his opponent. Polanco had fast hands and knew how to study and maneuver who he was up against. The ground was slightly inclined, and Richard managed to work his way to the higher position, and from there pummeled the other boy, who never bothered him again.

* * *

Looking back, Polanco would realize the sportsmanship and teamwork Mr. Orozco taught had become part of him. What Polanco learned on the Brooklyn Elementary playground flowered in his three seasons as a varsity basketball point guard at Garfield. He started out junior varsity and broke two scoring records in his fifth game — records set the previous decade by none other than Richard Alatorre — which got Polanco moved up to varsity. He was the smallest guy on the squad but excelled at the consummate team-player position.

Richard Polanco turned 17 the first Monday of March 1968, his junior year at Garfield. The next day, March 5, he joined approximately 2,000 of his fellow students in the first of that week's organized Chicano high-school walkouts that swept across the Eastside.[19] The organizers, assisted by college students, had prepared their indictment of LA schools, how they failed Chicano students, and a lengthy list of demands. But in spite of taking part in this mass protest against the schools, Polanco would not fully realize the inadequacy of his own education at Garfield until a couple of years after graduating.

Polanco married right away and had to find full-time work. Early in the 1970s, he applied for a warehousing job with the city of Los Angeles and failed the test.

He would recall the experience, some 45 years later, as "devastating" and "shattering." That is when Richard learned how much he had not learned in school.

Another experience Polanco had while in high school, but largely outside of it, would lead to a series of opportunities, in retrospect a virtual path to the political career he would embark upon in the 1980s. Before the demise of the Teen Post program — President Johnson's "War on Poverty" antigang initiative that provided small "safe haven" activity centers for teenage boys, whether gang members or those who would later come to be called "at risk youth" — David Lizarraga had been hired to open a Teen Post in Maravilla.[20] Separately, Polanco had a writing teacher whose assignments were the most stimulating academic experience he had in high school, and the only class in which he ever made an A+. He found daily journaling "eye opening," and also had to do a community project and report. He picked graffiti removal, which Polanco executed through Lizarraga's Teen Post. The connection would prove fateful.

"I'm a product of Machado Market Teen Post," Polanco would declare when recalling his class project, referring to the small store the "post" was located next to. He became heavily involved with Lizarraga's operation, joining its council and helping plan activities and fundraisers.

A couple of years would pass during which Polanco got married, had children, worked a number of jobs, and took classes at various colleges. Eventually he found his way to Casa Maravilla, the youth center Lizarraga had started in the dilapidated projects in Polanco's old neighborhood, and started working there. This was Polanco's first full-time community job, as a gang worker. Historic developments would ensue in East LA while Polanco was based at Casa. Gloria Molina would do her first community volunteer work there as well, as a tutor, when she started taking classes at East LA College (ELAC) just three blocks away, and find herself drawn into the rising Eastside Chicano activist network.

* * *

REDEVELOPMENT OF THE MARAVILLA HOUSING PROJECT IN EAST LA — in the early 1970s-context of a burgeoning Chicano movement and cultural awakening, political turmoil, and mobilizations, as well as concessions and efforts by policymakers to relieve social and political pressures — pulled leaders, activists, and institutions through a series of historic tests and crossroads in the course of the 1974 election year. By year's end, with construction of *Nueva Maravilla* done and the housing complex of over 500 units ceremonially opened, an array of Eastside leaders had taken on new positions and begun charting new directions. As they entered the second half of the 1970s, East LA as a community and its rising leadership had in many ways reached a new maturity, leaving behind much of the lingering politics of the 1960s, as more professional approaches gained favor and began showing results.

First Person: Polanco's Maravilla Neighborhood Makeover[*]

My first full-time community work was at Casa Maravilla, working for David Lizarraga. . . . I was very much involved with the gang work that was going on at Casa. I worked with pretty hardcore kids who weren't making it.

Then came the Maravilla housing redevelopment. And then came the Maravilla NDP program, which is different from the housing projects . . . another federal program, urban renewal. . . .

My real organizing came into play, as I became executive director to the citizen component, one of the federal requirements of the NDP. That was a 218-acre, $24 million redevelopment. It was a big leap. We organized on a daily basis to create a land use that would be compatible. The land use that existed then — we had junkyards next to elementary schools. We had the [meat processing plant] across the street from my elementary school, with the stench, the blood in the gutter coming from the cows. What we did was in organizing we convened three meetings a day, Monday through Saturday. We put up the butcher paper and said, "This is how our community looks today. If you had a magic wand, how would you want it to look?"

"I want these junkyards out of here."

"We want daycare here."

From that we developed the land-use plan that became the ordinance that was adopted by the county board of supervisors. . . . I learned and mastered redevelopment law on my own. My board of directors was composed through the organizing, we had a seat for social service organizations that included the religious groups; Father Olivares was part [of it] at one time. . . . It was called a project-area committee; under federal statute, under state statute, you must have them. We organized the homeowners [and] the renters. We structured the ordinance . . . to make sure that urban renewal was not going to repeat itself here. . . . I had to protect every interest, the families there, property owners, renters, the business community. . . . It was my responsibility to make sure they didn't get screwed. Our contract said if we do not enter an agreement with the county, to implement, there is no activity, and therefore no federal funds.

We created a youth summer program; I had three hundred kids working for us. I had to know relocation law, I had to know what the benefits were, how they were calculated. I had to make sure that if there was property being acquired, it was not done by eminent domain. I saw it as a real big responsibility. If I was not prepared, it would cause harm to somebody. My parents' house was there, they lived in that area, they were affected by it.

---

[*] *Polanco interview with authors, March 5, 2013.*

The top bosses of public affairs in unincorporated areas of LA County, its board of supervisors, controlled by a decidedly conservative majority, signaled at least their acquiescence to the emergent participatory model of redevelopment in East LA by approving a major new project in the Maravilla neighborhood, greatly expanding the area of TELACU's federally financed community action.[21] Once the reconstruction of the 60-acre public housing project was successfully underway, the board approved a Department of Housing and Urban Development "Neighborhood Development Project" (NDP) to improve or replace homes in 218 acres of mixed, private housing west of Nueva Maravilla. As it did in the case of the public housing project, TELACU managed the community-participation dimension of a robust new planning process, as required by federal statute, organizing over 70 block meetings and 15 "town halls."[22] Between them, the two processes of community consultation in Maravilla, organizing the participation of hundreds of families and touching thousands of residents, built TELACU a strong political base ready to be activated in elections.

Their roles in the community-participation aspects of the Nueva Maravilla public housing redevelopment had drawn David Lizarraga and Richard Polanco of the Casa Maravilla youth center to start working directly for TELACU.[23] The 21-year-old Polanco was put in charge of the new NDP community-based planning process.

Working at TELACU further involved Polanco and Lizarraga in the various political objectives that the agency was pursuing or supporting under Esteban Torres. These included a major new effort, in preparation since 1972, to incorporate East Los Angeles as a city, to which Torres added, early in 1974, his own surprise bid to unseat the incumbent congressman representing the area, as well as his decision to take sides in what the *Los Angeles Times* called a "bitter contest" to represent the surrounding county District 3 on the board of supervisors. A first step of the Eastside leadership transition was thus already taken that spring, when in launching his congressional challenge, Torres stepped aside as director of TELACU, the nonprofit he founded in the seemingly revolutionary days of 1968 and had grown into a community development corporation. David Lizarraga, the former activist organizer of antigang programs, assumed the role of interim director of the now federally funded CDC.[24]

The spring primary also featured Art Torres's second effort, strongly supported by Richard Alatorre, to reach the state Assembly on behalf of East LA, as well as the incumbent Alex Garcia's bid to move up to the state Senate. Thus, in addition to the high-profile open-primary race for governor that year and the first open race in the area for county supervisor since the 1950s, the residents of East LA were being mobilized by Esteban Torres and Art Torres in their separate races, both with the backing of the United Farm Workers, which had worked the area intensively in 1972 and 1968. In addition to his NDP job, Polanco managed his new boss Esteban Torres's primary campaign, while also building support for the cityhood referendum in the fall general election. In the county supervisor's race, the TELACU network was actively supporting LA City Councilman Ed Edelman, even though Alatorre, Art Torres, and their circle backed Edelman's main rival in that election.

Esteban Torres had assembled a new coalition for the incorporation campaign, which would culminate in a vote on the fall ballot that would also feature a long list of candidates for the proposed East LA City Council. Besides the campaign waged by the coalition, which was seen as effectively replacing the Congress of Mexican American Unity that Torres also headed, and the individual efforts made by some 39 East LA candidates, that fall the Raza Unida Party also supported the cityhood vote and entered the councilmanic race with a slate of candidates for the five hypothetical seats. Although welcoming Raza Unida's support for East LA incorporation, Torres and his new coalition countered the more radical group with their own slate of city council candidates, headed by Richard Polanco.[25]

The primary election results added to the leadership transition precipitated by Esteban Torres's run for office. First, when Esteban lost to the incumbent congressman and chose not to return to lead TELACU again, Lizarraga's interim elevation to CEO became permanent. Second, Art Torres's primary win in his heavily Democratic and Mexican-American district made him its designated assemblymember, whereupon he chose to offer his chief deputy position to Gloria Molina, affecting her first key step in what would become a fabled political career.

In the fall, the cityhood referendum failed, which, in combination with Esteban's congressional loss in the spring, brought an end to the Esteban Torres-led era in East LA community politics of the 1960s–1970s. Torres returned to Washington and the United Auto Workers. But his decision to support Ed Edelman paid off with Richard Polanco's appointment as the new supervisor's chief Eastside deputy. Thus, Polanco's political career was quickly and more conventionally launched, or relaunched, immediately following his run for the hypothetical East LA City Council.[26]

On Her Own

The Molina family had sacrificed for years to buy a house of their own in the suburb of Pico Rivera, a dozen miles southeast of downtown LA. For Molina this meant coming of age at El Rancho High and then, over her mother's objections but with her father's support, continuing her studies at the brand-new campus of Rio Hondo College. Decades later, she would recall believing there were three things she was determined *not* to do with her life: become a secretary, teacher, or politician. But at Rio Hondo Molina soon concluded that she did not have the talent for her particular interest in fashion design; she would not become the Chicana Edith Head. She needed both to get full-time work and develop marketable skills.

Molina was able to land a full-time job as a receptionist in a downtown law firm and switched to classes at East LA College to equip her for secretarial work.

This previously undesired career track led her step by step to a position as a legal secretary in a prestigious firm, her own apartment in East LA, and continuing higher education, but at a politically restive campus a couple of blocks from the Maravilla housing projects.

Moving out on her own got Molina banished from her family, until she forced her way back in on a Thanksgiving Day. To her, the prospect of marriage would have meant passing from being under one man's authority to another's. She had chosen instead to liberate herself and move back to the *barrio* in more ways than one. Molina was now at ELAC almost every evening after work, where she was exposed to the Chicano movement, joined a student organization, on the spur of the moment participated in the 1968 walkouts, began volunteering at Casa Maravilla, and started connecting with movement leaders and activists.

Volunteer tutoring at Casa — which her father objected to for putting her in the projects, some place he had worked his whole life to keep his family away from — led Molina to a stint at TELACU as a jobs counselor, which in turn led her to a teaching position at the East Los Angeles Skills Center of the LA School District in nearby Lincoln Heights. She had never wanted to become a teacher any more than a secretary, but now her second previously undesired career put her in a government job in full-time service to the Eastside community.

All the while, Molina was developing, in her words, as a designated and dedicated *follower* of the Chicano movement, a loyal soldier doing backroom chores — from making menudo for fundraisers, to mimeographing flyers, to serving as an election campaign "licker and sticker." By the time an annual Mexican American National Issues Conference was held in Sacramento in the fall of 1970, a critical mass of such follower-activists gathered for a workshop on women's issues and formulated a challenge to what they saw as a male monopoly on leadership in the Chicano movement — an "exclusion" they resolved to "terminate." Although unbeknownst to her at the time, the idea of the Comisión Femenil Mexicana Nacional was born, and with it the seed of Gloria Molina's third (and final) undesired career, one that would turn her into a builder of Chicana Power and a pioneering Latina politician.[27]

Notes

1. The area of the original pueblo of Los Angeles, encompassing today's downtown and several adjacent neighborhoods, was a planned, Spanish colonial, civil settlement (unlike the more numerous Catholic missions or the military presidios), guided by the city planning mandates of Spain's sixteenth-century Laws of the Indies. Pueblos were to be anchored by a central plaza, setting the pattern for the surrounding street grid. But contrary to the later Anglo-American custom of streets running uniformly north-south and east-west, the *corners* of every Spanish colonial plaza were to be aligned with the cardinal points of the compass, yielding an equally symmetrical grid, but one that appears from an Anglo perspective to be tilted 45 degrees to the right, with diagonal streets running northeast-south-

west and northwest-southeast. Hence the clashing grids joined at the buried and otherwise forgotten limits of the old LA pueblo. See Reps, *The Making of Urban America*, 29, 51, 216–17; Mundigo and Crouch, "The City Planning Ordinances of the Laws of the Indies Revisited. Part I"; Crouch and Mundigo, "The City Planning Ordinances of the Laws of the Indies Revisited. Part II"; and Estrada, *The Los Angeles Plaza*, 33.

2. This assessment is strongly supported by Burt's exhaustive historical account, *The Search for a Civic Voice*. Burt, however, sometimes conflates Boyle Heights and East LA, as people often do when referring to the Greater LA Eastside. Also, Burt traces the birth of modern Latino politics to Eastside activism of the 1930s that continued into the 1940s, prior to the advent of Ed Roybal in 1947. The key Hispanic leader and organization in those years, Eduardo Quevedo and the Congress of Mexican and Spanish-American Peoples of the United States, achieved genuine influence, but Quevedo ran for office several times without success, and El Congreso, as it was known, was only active from 1938–39. See Burt's chapters 1–2.

3. Scott Kurashige, "Between 'White Spot' and 'World City,'" 57–59; Nicolaides, "'Where the Working Man is Welcomed,'" 538. According to USC historian George J. Sanchez, Belvedere "was developed in the 1920s as an exclusively Mexican community largely because developers could ignore city statutes concerning lot size, sewage, and other services" (*Becoming Mexican American*, 201).

4. Nicolaides, "'Where the Working Man is Welcomed.'"

5. Sanchez, *Becoming Mexican American*, 75; Romo, *East Los Angeles*, 78–81.

6. Sanchez, *Becoming Mexican American*, 3.

7. Crouch and Mundigo, "The City Planning Ordinances of the Laws of the Indies Revisited. Part II," 412.

8. "Mapping L.A.: Rankings: Ethnicity: Latino," *Los Angeles Times*, last accessed October 4, 2017, http://maps.latimes.com/neighborhoods/ethnicity/latino/neighborhood/list/. Westwood, which the Janss Company is most famous for, is ranked 236 out of the 265 in Latino population, at 7.0 percent. East Los Angeles is measured at 96.7 percent.

9. Cecilia Rasmussen, "Brick Firm Cemented Lives, Communities," *Los Angeles Times*, November 6, 1995; Deverell, *The Whitewashed Adobe*, 138. This section based on authors' interview with Molina; Molina interview by Vásquez; Molina interview by Guerra; and other sources as noted.

10. Deverell, *Whitewashed Adobe*, ch. 4.

11. Ibid., 135.

12. Berumen, *Edward R. Roybal*, 37.

13. Alquist, "The Field Act and Public School Construction," 7; Deverell, *Whitewashed Adobe*, 168.

14. Chávez, *Eastside Landmark*, 81. This section primarily based on multiple original interviews conducted with Richard Polanco, David Lizarraga, and Lou Moret. All quotes come from these interviews unless otherwise noted.

15. Ted Rohrlich and Dan Morain, "The Man Driving the Latino Machine," *Los Angeles Times*, October 14, 1999, http://articles.latimes.com/1999/oct/14/news/mn-22198.

16. McWilliams, *North from Mexico*, 202–04.

17. Rohrlich and Morain, "The Man Driving the Latino Machine."

18. Chávez, *Eastside Landmark*, 93–94.

19. "East Los Angeles Students Walkout for Educational Reform (East L.A. Blowouts), 1968," *Global Nonviolent Action Database*, last accessed October 4, 2017, https://nvdatabase.swarthmore.edu/content/east-los-angeles-students-walkout-educational-reform-east-la-blowouts-1968.

20. See chapter 3 for a more detailed history of the Teen Post program and the Casa Maravilla youth center that followed. See also Vigil, *The Projects*, and *Gang Redux*; Martinez, *Rising Voices*; and Bauman, *Race and the War on Poverty*, 105.

21. Maravilla and most of the Eastside were in county supervisorial District 3, represented by conservative Democrat Ernest E. Debs. For decades, the five supervisors were referred to as "little kings," exercising both legislative and executive powers and largely deferring to each other's prerogatives within their districts; see Bill Boyarsky, "The 5 Little Kings Who Are No More," *Los Angeles Times*, December 7, 1990. Debs had served on the LA City Council alongside Edward Roybal, and won a bitter election, marked by allegations of fraud, for county supervisor over Roybal in 1958. Although not a liberal like his supervisorial predecessor, John Anson Ford, or his successor, Ed Edelman, Debs had a history of supporting public housing, before the advent of the Chicano movement and the Eastside disturbances of 1967–70 that took place in his district. As de facto "mayor" of unincorporated East LA, he took personal pride in the Nueva Maravilla redevelopment, but late in life Debs soured on public housing, unless the tenants were well organized, as they were in Nueva Maravilla. See Debs interview by Vásquez, 94–99.

22. Chávez, *Eastside Landmark*, 116–17; Chávez does not seem to be aware of TELACU's lead role in the planning of the Maravilla NDP that he describes, but this was reported on at the time by Frank del Olmo, "Corporation's Goal: Improving Life in the Barrio," *Los Angeles Times*, January 15, 1973. Also discussed in Torres, "New Spirit in the Barrios," and confirmed by Richard Polanco in our first interview with him, March 5, 2013.

23. TELACU landed a $500,000 planning grant to develop the proposal for a Housing and Urban Development Department (HUD) Neighborhood Development Project, based on exhaustive consultation with residents of a large area (218 acres) west of the Maravilla public housing projects; del Olmo, "Corporation's Goal."

24. Jocelyn Y. Stewart, "Ed Edelman, Crusading L.A. County Supervisor, Dead at 85," *Los Angeles Times*, September 12, 2016, http://www.latimes.com/local/obituaries/la-me-ed-edelman-snap-story.html; Chávez, *Eastside Landmark*, 92–99, 101–05, 173.

25. Chávez, *Eastside Landmark*, 102–04.

26. Although the East LA cityhood proposition failed, Polanco succeeded in getting the second-highest vote total among the 39 candidates — second only to Raul Ruiz, who was on the ballot three times in 1971 special elections and had been on the ballot again in the 1974 state Senate primary; Frank del Olmo, "Defeat of East L.A. Plan Laid to Fear of High Property Tax," *Los Angeles Times*, November 7, 1974.

27. See "Guide to the Comisión Femenil Mexicana Nacional Archives," UC Santa Barbara Library, California Ethnic and Multicultural archives, www.library.ucsb.edu/spe-

cial-collections/cema/cfmn; Bauman, *Race and the War on Poverty*, 110–14; and Nieto Gomez, "Chicana Service Action Center."

CHAPTER 8

Chicana Power

"WOMEN ARE NOT ACCEPTED AS COMMUNITY LEADERS, either by the Chicano movement or by the Anglo establishment. . . . THEREFORE, in order to terminate exclusion of female leadership in the Chicano/Mexicano movement, be it RESOLVED that a Chicana/Mexican Women's Commission be established. . . . " So stated the unanimous resolution of the women's issues workshop at the October 1970 Mexican-American issues conference in Sacramento. The declaration went on to name the *Comisión* in Spanish and define its primary purpose as "organizing women to assume leadership positions within the Chicano movement and in community life."[1] A new activist and leadership network — a movement within a movement conceived to effect a shift within a shift — was born. Eventually, this development would make itself felt on LA's Eastside, draw in Gloria Molina, and change her life.

For a couple of years, the Comisión Femenil Mexicana Nacional (CFMN), which also referred to itself more modestly on paper as a steering committee and later became a governing board, was less a formal membership organization than a current within the emerging Chicana movement and a growing activist network around the key figure of Francisca Flores. With the support of close allies, including in government, for years Flores had also been developing a proposal to address the job-training needs of Mexican-American women, coupled to her critique of the neglect of women's issues by established Mexican-American organizations and programs designed to serve the community. Encouraged by her governmental contacts, she proposed to address some women's needs by tapping federal resources still available in the early 1970s after the official end of the War on Poverty, much like TELACU and other organizations were doing.[2]

In March 1972 in Phoenix, at the U.S. Labor Department's first-ever "Consultation for Spanish-Speaking Women," Flores and her associates pressed a Mexican-American official on urban Chicanas' dire need for job training. The official apparently tried to both impress and brush them off by allowing that he had a discretionary fund of $50,000, but it would take a formal proposal to consider the issue. Flores surprised him by pulling just such a proposal out of her purse. A commitment of funding ensued that required the Flores group to register as a nonprofit organization with a fiduciary board. Thus, the Comisión was urgently formalized to be able to receive the Labor Department's demonstration grant.

A Chicana Movement "Founding Mother":
Francisca Flores

Originally from San Diego, Francisca Flores was just a few years older than Ed Roybal, but her activism and leadership bridged generations in a way "the old man" never dreamed. Among World War II-era Mexican Americans, Flores was unusually familiar with earlier political struggles in Mexico, having connected in her youth with veterans of the Mexican Revolution in the tuberculosis sanitarium she shared with them for years. She helped found Hermanas de la Revolución Mexicana, her first women's organization.

Flores moved to LA in the 1940s, and for decades she went on to inspire, network, and catalyze empowerment efforts among both older Mexican Americans and younger Chicanas, comparable to the transgenerational impact of the much younger Esteban Torres in the 1960s–70s. Flores became involved with Roybal's Community Service Organization and with him was among the founders of the Mexican American Political Association (MAPA). But Flores found MAPA unsupportive of the rise of women, prompting her to take independent action — not unlike how Roybal had called for creating MAPA in response to the Democratic Party's failure to support the development of Mexican-American leadership. Flores and her allies founded what may have been the first Mexican-American women's organization dedicated to mainstream political empowerment — the League of Mexican American Women (LMAW) — in 1966. The LMAW was a key precursor to Flores's later Chicana-movement brainchild — Comisión Femenil Mexicana Nacional — the call for which was issued at the historic conference workshop she organized in 1970.

A tireless writer, editor, and publisher, Flores founded the political newsletter Carta Editorial *in 1963, which, in tune with the times, she rebranded in 1970 as the magazine* Regeneración, *after the famed publication of the radical Flores Magón brothers of the Mexican Revolution. The name change signaled she had shifted gears to reach out to the new generation in what was for Flores a pivotal year, when her Comisión vision was formulated and announced to the world.*

The difference in name between the Comisión and the LMAW reflected both changing times and Flores's approach to organizing. "Comisión" means commission or committee, which, unlike "league," does not suggest a mass-membership organization. Until the first meeting of the LA chapter in 1972, the Comisión activist network Flores was building had not had an open convening. Giving her new initiative a name in Spanish and calling it simply "Mexicana" was also relevant in its break with the Mexican-Amer-

*ican generation's respectability politics and fear of being seen as unpatri-
otic. Writing about the Comisión project in* Regeneración, *Flores declared,
"Chicanas are fighting for their own identity, and they do not care who does
not like it."*

*Committed to community empowerment, Flores resisted attempts to re-
cruit her to work for government or run for office, which to her would be to
join "the system." She had participated in election campaigns and was hap-
py to press for public funds to run autonomous community agencies and programs, but in time she soured on officeholders. "I've never felt that putting
women, or men for that matter, in a political position of leadership has really helped the community," she told the* Los Angeles Times *in 1981, "They
seem to be more interested in promoting themselves than the community."*

Within five months, in August of that year, the Chicana Service Action Center
(CSAC) — a vision Flores had been cultivating since the mid-1960s — opened in
Boyle Heights, focusing on job training and placement.[3] Francisca Flores's activ-
ist network had suddenly become a new Eastside LA institution.

* * *

IN THE GLOW OF THE CSAC OPENING RECEPTION, Gloria Molina, her close
friend Yolanda Nava of United Way, and many other Eastside Chicana activists
connected for the first time with Flores and others who had called for creating
the Comisión in Sacramento. Molina and Nava, in particular, were eager to join,
but the CFMN around Francisca Flores had evolved from a network to a steering
committee to a board, not a membership organization. Flores challenged those at
the reception to organize an LA "chapter." Some 40 women had put their names
to the original idea at the 1970 conference workshop; 200 women showed up for
the first open Comisión chapter meeting in Los Angeles in August 1972.

The Comisión, as an LA-based membership organization, was now on its
way, anchored and bolstered by the existence of a growing CSAC, and propelled
by the birth of what would always be its biggest local chapter. The combined
CFMN and CFM-LA drew some 300 women to their first national conference the
following year, held near Santa Barbara. By the end of 1973, additional state and
local funds allowed the Comisión to open two daycare centers, one of which later
spun off into its own nonprofit and became the first bilingual child development
center in East Los Angeles. The Centro de Niños, led by CFM-LA founding member Sandra Serrano-Sewell, still serves the Maravilla public housing development
and its surrounding neighborhood in East LA today.[4]

Also late in 1973, fresh and shocking evidence of the urgent need for specifically Chicana activism and leadership found its way to this still new Eastside net-

work; the issue took the group by surprise, tested its capabilities, and unexpectedly revealed a serious policy difference with white feminism. A young doctor who sought to complete his residency at the LA County-USC Medical Center, which loomed on a knoll just across the I-10 freeway from Boyle Heights and East LA, observed staff surgeons there congratulating residents on the number of sterilizations they performed per week, and encouraging interns "to press women into agreeing to a sterilization procedure."[5] Equipped not only with a social conscience but also a PhD in psychology, Dr. Bernard Rosenfeld was not the average medical intern when he had previously observed sterilization pressures in an Oakland hospital, which motivated him to write to a member of Congress. In his LA residency, Rosenfeld began researching hospital records, taking notes, and reaching out to journalists and advocacy organizations with his observations and findings.[6]

Rosenfeld found his way to a Chicana attorney fresh out of UCLA Law School, Antonia Hernández, then in her first job at the new Los Angeles Center for Law and Justice. He presented Hernández and her colleagues his documentation of over 180 cases of women sterilized during childbirth at county hospital — whose files contained no signed consent form. He argued that in combination with the attitudes and practices he witnessed, this was evidence of "targeted and coercive sterilization of African-American and Mexican women."[7] Thus began a wrenching journey of discovery for Hernández, whose own mother had experienced pressure to undergo a sterilization procedure at the same hospital when she was there for the birth of Antonia's younger sister.[8] The accumulated evidence led Hernández to reach out to Comisión and embark on an extended legal battle. First, she undertook to find and interview as many of the Chicanas identified in Rosenfeld's informal investigation as she could, which would take her "all over East LA," starting across the freeway from the hospital in City Terrace.[9]

Hernández and her colleagues decided to prepare a federal class-action suit on behalf of low-income, Spanish-speaking Chicana patients — a formidable challenge for any lawyer, but especially for green attorneys assembled in a new organization, representing a disadvantaged community that, unlike African Americans, was not well-known to the federal judiciary or mainstream legal profession. They would need resources, allies, a community strategy, and more.[10] Hernández contacted and met with the LA board of Comisión, and as she later recalled, said to them, "I need you, now!"[11]

This was how Gloria Molina and Antonia Hernández met and initiated a close personal and professional relationship that would last through the decades to come. Hernández needed an organizational client for the class-action litigation; Molina immediately formed and led Comisión's special committee on sterilization. They announced the lawsuit together in a press conference in June 1975, intending to educate the community and the wider public, win the case, and also win in the court of public opinion.[12] The federal district court judge ruled against the plaintiffs in the case of *Madrigal v. Quilligan*, but the lawsuit succeeded in winning changes in policy and practices regarding the handling of sterilization consent and the information provided to patients, as well as the institution of a waiting period for patients under 21 years of age.[13] The waiting-period reform, however, provoked a split between white feminists and the Chicana movement against sterilization abuse.

Antonia Hernández's 1976 law-review article indicated in its subtitle the core objective of the lawsuit she led: "Reforms Needed to Protect *Informed Consent*."[14] The movement exposing and combating coerced sterilization, from the whistle-blowing Dr. Rosenfeld, to the LA Center for Law and Justice, to the Comisión and the other organizations that mobilized on this issue, considered it fundamental to delink sterilization from childbirth, a time of obvious stress for the mother.[15] While allowing for the possibility that an emergency sterilization might be medically indicated at the time of childbirth, as a general practice, unpressured, informed consent would, at minimum, require the expectant mother's agreement in writing sometime prior to her entering into labor — that is, a waiting period between consent and sterilization. Because the sterilizations that most concerned the Chicana activists were "recommended" by hospital personnel, the waiting period was also intended, and needed to be long enough, to allow time for the expectant mother to become adequately informed about the surgical procedure and her alternatives, which might require obtaining a second opinion. But to white feminists, the idea of a waiting period violated the right to sterilization on demand; they objected to the measure in principle, as they did in the case of the anti-abortion movement's pressures to require a waiting period and "counseling" prior to a legal abortion.[16]

The disagreement turned into open conflict in the context of a series of public hearings on the state's proposed official sterilization guidelines, agreed to by California's Department of Health in 1977. As reconstructed by historian Elena Gutiérrez, "A lasting tension was born" over the waiting-period issue, specifically between Comisión and the California chapter of the National Organization for Women (NOW). According to Gutiérrez, several discussions were held between the two groups prior to the hearings; NOW agreed to research the issue and reconsider its position, but the dispute was never resolved. Gutiérrez quotes Molina as saying that NOW, "didn't want the 30-day waiting period or the three-day waiting period. They were just not willing to compromise on any of it. . . . [F]eminist women together working on these issues and here's a group of women . . . who don't seem to understand our issues and aren't sympathetic."[17]

While the lawsuit dragged on, the Chicana activist network developed by the Comisión and the Chicana Service Action Center continued to develop. By the end of 1977, CSAC was operating five centers in all and had trained or provided service to over fifteen thousand women. In 1978, CSAC established three more centers, two for battered women and a family crisis center. The CSAC-Comisión network had been consolidated as a fourth power base on the Eastside, after Roybal-CSO, TELACU, and Alatorre-Torres.

As both Comisión and CSAC strove to develop Chicana leaders, as well as advocate on issues and deliver services, Molina emerged as "the primary example of Chicana leadership emanating from CSAC."[18] Her leadership roles in Comisión, combined with this network's activism in election campaigns and voter-registration drives, gave her the salience and credentials to be picked in 1974 by Assemblymember-elect Art Torres to be his principal field deputy, also known as administrative assistant.

In 1976, Molina took a leave from the assemblymember's staff to head the Chicano outreach effort for Jimmy Carter's presidential campaign in California, and in 1977 was named to a White House job in the Carter administration's Office of Presidential Personnel. She returned to California in 1979 to take a position with the federal Department of Health and Human Services in San Francisco, a job that came to a sudden end when Carter lost his reelection bid to Ronald Reagan in November 1980, bringing Molina and other Latino appointees back to LA, where they refocused on further developing leadership opportunities and advancing their careers.

Collision Course

THE NOVEMBER 1974 COUNTY BOARD OF SUPERVISORS ELECTION had a reward for East LA and TELACU, and for Richard Polanco personally, when he was named new Supervisor Ed Edelman's field deputy for the Eastside. But Richard Alatorre and his circle, including Art Torres and Lou Moret, had backed Edelman's main opponent in the hard-fought race.[19] This split — between what had become East LA's preeminent Mexican-American institution and the new generation of Chicano elected officials — meant not only that some of the Eastside's emerging leadership's resources and energy were for naught in this election, its perceived clout could be undercut if such a split were to be repeated over another important contest or issue.

Moret reached out to David Lizarraga and George Pla with the idea of coordinating the rising Eastside leadership's support in future elections. A series of conversations reached this understanding, at least in the memory of some who participated. For electoral purposes, Alatorre's finance committee would serve as the hub. Democratic powerhouse and Latina leader Carmen Perez, longtime Alatorre ally, would be a central figure at the table. TELACU would be represented on the committee, which implied an ongoing commitment to pooling financial backing for agreed-upon candidates. David Lizarraga had a specific request to make going in: if and when either Alatorre or Art Torres decided to move on from their seats in the Assembly, Polanco would be first in line as the successor.

With or without specific knowledge of this agreement, in the coming years Polanco began preparing the way for his own run for elected office. He believed he would have a shot at taking out state Senator Alex Garcia, a former aide to Ed Roybal, who would be up for reelection for the first time in 1978 and then again in 1982. Polanco had worked the area almost continuously since he was a kid selling oranges door to door, and he could boast an astonishing community-service resumé: volunteer at Teen Post during high school; organizer and coach of a Pop Warner-style football team; full-time staffer at Casa Maravilla; intensive work with TELACU on the two housing redevelopment efforts and the Neighborhood Development Project; and as Esteban Torres's campaign manager in the '74 congressional primary, which was followed that fall by the East LA incorporation drive and Polanco's own campaign for its proposed city council. Polanco had worked closely with the UFW field efforts, especially in Esteban's campaign, and the union had considered Garcia an enemy of farmworkers — at least in the early 1970s when they backed Art Torres against him. After all that history, Polanco continued working the area at the highest level as field deputy to elected officials, first for Supervisor Edelman and then for Governor Jerry Brown.

By 1981, Polanco was ready with his plans and preparations to run in the 1982 primary and began making the rounds of key people. Willie Brown was now Speaker of the Assembly and Richard Alatorre was a top lieutenant. Both Alatorre and Art Torres had earned the ire of Cesar Chavez and the UFW for having abandoned the union's candidate for Speaker. Since Art's Assembly district was contained within Garcia's Senate domain, Polanco went to him first with his plan, but did not win his support.[20] Polanco's strategy could work, however, whether he ran against Garcia or, alternatively, if Art chose to do so and freed up his Assembly seat.

If Art had given any thought to challenging Garcia again — and even if he had not — it would be against his interests for Polanco to preemptively replace the old pol. Garcia's Senate seat was the next logical step in Art's plans to eventually run for statewide office. As Polanco would recall decades later, Art publicly announced his own challenge to Garcia without informing him of his decision. This was by now a strained relationship, but Polanco had his plan B of running to succeed Art in the Assembly. His carefully developed strategy was already working: instead of challenging a Mexican-American incumbent in the larger arena of a state Senate district election, he would run for the open Assembly seat vacated by Art Torres. Polanco had managed to strategically create his own opportunity.

* * *

GLORIA MOLINA RETURNED TO LA AFTER REAGAN'S NOVEMBER 1980 WIPE-OUT WIN over Jimmy Carter — and more importantly after the dramatic transfer of power in the California Assembly that crowned Willie Brown as Speaker and put his ally, Richard Alatorre, in charge of redistricting. With the support of Alatorre and Art Torres, who played key roles in the long speakership fight, Molina landed the job as Brown's chief deputy in Southern California, managing a small staff to liaise with various communities, including ethnic groups, labor, and gays. The basic purpose of the office was to strengthen support for the Speaker, whose own goal "was very clear." Molina later recalled in her state oral history, "He intended to be Speaker for life . . . he said that. And believe me, I had the same goals as the Speaker did . . . I didn't have a problem with that."[21]

From the earliest releases of state-level 1980 census data, it became clear that California would pick up two more seats in Congress going into the 1982 elections. Although Alatorre's greatest influence would be over the redistricting of the Assembly, he was in a position to also push to get one of the new congressional seats allocated to LA's Latino Eastside.[22] Ed Roybal had been in Washington by himself for going on 20 years, serving as the only Latino member of Congress from California. The state's Democratic leaders faced pressure on a number of fronts to show concrete support for greater Chicano/Latino representation. The Mexican American Legal Defense and Educational Fund, or MALDEF, was seen as ready to lodge a voting-rights lawsuit challenging any district plan that failed to adequately address the problem of Latino underrepresentation, and now the Republicans were adding to the pressure both vocally and by concretely supporting a Latino coalition pushing the cause.[23] Alatorre felt the pressure and conveyed it to his superiors, but also used it, and the threat of a Voting Rights Act lawsuit, in dealing with his fellow legislators' personal demands and recalcitrance in redistricting.

For a combination of reasons, it would be easier to quickly accommodate Chicano demands on the congressional level than in the state Assembly. The congressional delegation had new seats to work with, and the Democratic head of the delegation, Phil Burton, was both free and inclined to wrest still more seats from the Republicans. Unlike his protégé Willie Brown, who was elected Speaker with more Republican than Democratic votes in the Assembly, Burton did not owe California Republican members of Congress any special consideration. In fact, he wanted to create more Democratic seats to help him realize his ambition to become Speaker of the House of Representatives. He also wanted to protect Willie Brown's Assembly speakership by making room for his Democratic opponents — the rival faction Brown beat with Republican votes — to move up to Congress. The stage was set for Burton to devastate the California congressional Republicans. In this, the first year of the age of Reagan, Burton took a delegation with a bare 22 to 21 majority of Democrats and raised it to 28 to 17, restoring the 11-vote margin they held before the 1980 Reagan landslide.[24] For LA's Eastside, the big surprise was that Burton's new congressional district map contained not one but two predominantly Latino districts with open seats, in a deal Burton, in part, brokered directly with MALDEF.[25]

For decades to follow, Molina would recount excited conversations she had with her friends and allies about the prospect that two new Eastside districts would make possible the election of the first Latina to ever serve in Congress. But she would also recount being told that the positions were already spoken for. The complicated deal-making behind redistricting protected certain incumbents while sometimes harming others, and it produced new districts designed for particular candidates, in this case for Latinos, both men. Esteban Torres and Matthew "Marty" Martinez would be running for the two seats, with consensual backing of the elected Eastside Latino leadership, which at that time consisted of only men.[26] Thus, two stubborn facts were in collision: on one hand, an essential part of negotiating the creation of the new open seats were the reference points of recognized, ready-to-go candidates seen as able to raise money and win, matched to districts fashioned to make them viable. On the other hand, the negotiators and the beneficiaries of this process were all men.

Molina's Comisión network and friends were disappointed, of course, but would soon be even more so. She learned next from Art Torres that he would be giving up his Assembly seat in order to once again challenge Alex Garcia, who was completing his second term in the state Senate. Members of Comisión, led by Sandra Serrano-Sewell, rallied around the opportunity to elect the first Chicana to the Assembly. They convened a series of meetings to select a candidate among them to run, and Molina emerged as the logical choice. After all, she had been Torres's first administrative assistant, in charge of his district, the position that had developed for over a decade as the best springboard for a Latino Assembly run. The women also had a strong card to play: Comisión member Yolanda Nava was the wife of Art Torres — and as a television reporter and newscaster, just as articulate. Nava would prove instrumental in securing Torres's backing of Molina, a big gesture of support for the aspiring women of the Comisión as he entered his own tough election. According to Serrano-Sewell, who became campaign strategist for Molina's Assembly run, "Art Torres's endorsement of Gloria Molina was crucial to the campaign."[27]

Some of the Eastside team, especially Lou Moret and David Lizarraga, remembered the understanding they had reached following the 1974 election, in which Latino support had been split in the District 3 county supervisorial race: Polanco was supposed to be their consensual candidate, as Lizarraga requested, if either Art Torres or Richard Alatorre moved on from the Assembly. A series of meetings — some the stuff of legend — was convened on what to do about this 1982 Assembly race and others, in which the team found itself once again divided.[28]

Lizarraga stood by Polanco, of course, but the TELACU forces had an even greater stake in Esteban Torres's congressional race, managed by George Pla. Art Torres went with Molina, but others delayed an open commitment as they focused on the two new congressional races and Art's especially bitter, renewed fight with Alex Garcia. The UFW supported their old ally Polanco, but made punishing Art their top priority in this election, for his perceived betrayal in the 1980 Assembly speakership battle. What's more, divisions extended above and beyond the Eastside. Speaker Willie Brown remained neutral, in spite of Molina's receiving endorsement not only from his Assembly ally Art Torres, but also by his top lieutenant Maxine Waters, who was on board with Molina "right at the beginning" and had tried to win Brown over.[29] Alatorre split with both his *compadre* Art and

*Gloria Molina in her first campaign for California State Assembly in 1982, district map in back. (*Los Angeles Times *Photographic Archives. Collection 1429. UCLA Library Special Collections, Charles E. Young Research Library, UCLA.)*

fellow Assembly-leader Waters when he came in with a late endorsement for Polanco.[30] State Senate President Dave Roberti again strongly opposed Art, his former aide, as he had in 1972. The UFW contributed to Polanco's campaign, and Cesar Chavez lent his name to a stinging letter attacking Molina.

The Eastside Latino political world had suddenly gotten crowded and complicated in this primary, with all the subnetwork power centers that had emerged over the preceding third of a century committed and engaged — plus one "new" force, which had been developing for a dozen years, at least since that women's issues workshop at the conference in Sacramento in 1970 that called for the creation of the Comisión.

.   That an organized base of Chicana power existed on the Eastside was evident — in the institutional success of the Chicana Service Action Center and its multiple facilities, in the daycare centers established by Comisión and its capacity to convene hundreds of women in conferences, and in this network's ability to mobilize in support of campaigns (up to now) for male candidates, election after election. But this movement within a movement had not yet undertaken to elect one of its own to office, and in that sense it remained untested; it had not yet shifted electoral power in its own direction. Then the *Los Angeles Times* entered the fray, making the race into a test of the community, and of its men, and women.

The WASP Newspaper's Gaze

Los Angeles Times AND ITS FAMILY OWNERS PLAYED A COMMANDING ROLE in the city's rise beginning in the 1890s, but they had a long and troubled history in relation to people of color, their countries of origin, their residential communities, and their leaders and organizations.[31] Harrison Gray Otis became publisher and took sole ownership of the paper in the 1880s. His son-in-law Harry Chandler took full charge in 1917 and led the *Times* for nearly three decades, to be succeeded by his son Norman, who in turn passed the baton to his 32-year-old son Otis in 1960.

Los Angeles Times — **Family Dynasty and Corporate Culture**

Ohio-born General Harrison Gray Otis founded the dynasty that shaped the paper, and with it Los Angeles. Once a young supporter of Abraham Lincoln — the freshman in Congress who had opposed the US war of conquest with Mexico in the 1840s — his role in the Spanish-American War turned Otis into a virulent imperialist in the 1890s. After Spain's quick defeat in the Philippines, Otis, a twice-wounded veteran of the Union Army that fought to end slavery, reportedly led a "campaign of extermination" against Filipinos who resisted becoming a US colony.

Fancying himself "the complete soldier," Otis returned to LA in 1899 to a hero's welcome, and he ruled the Times *"like a military commander." Adamantly anti-union, Otis called his staff his "phalanx," fashioned his building like "a fortress," where he maintained a stockpile of 50 rifles and a case of loaded shotguns, and ran military drills "during times of tension, such as major labor conflicts."*

Otis later passed control over the Times *to son-in-law Harry Chandler, who had risen to circulation manager. Chandler simultaneously managed to become a real estate magnate and marry one of the boss's daughters. The slow transition from Otis to Chandler (1912–1917) coincided with the Mexican Revolution. Chandler had acquired vast lands in Mexico and brought his father-in-law in as a partner. They became friendly with the dictator Porfirio Díaz, whom the paper called "a wise and benevolent despot." Otis urged US intervention to keep Díaz in power and protect the land holdings of foreign investors and Mexico's wealthy. After Díaz fled the country, and the revolutionary movement headed by future president Venustiano Carranza announced its aim to effect land reform, the* Times *demanded in a front-page headline that "UNITED STATES MUST INTERVENE TO SAVE MEXICO FROM HERSELF."*

When Otis died in 1917, Harry Chandler and his wife declared that "The Times *will continue to be* THE TIMES *— The Times of General Otis, The Times that he made. Men may die, but influences do not." Those influences had propagated the belief that white Americans could determine the fate of nonwhite nations like the Philippines and Mexico better than they could themselves. In time, as LA became more racially diverse, the domestic implications of this colonialist worldview would become evident.*

A big landowner on both sides of the border in the Imperial Valley and else-where in California, Harry Chandler favored unrestricted entry and hiring of Mexican migrant labor, which he called "peons," over blacks, Filipinos, and Puerto Ricans.[32] According to journalism scholar Melita Garza, Chandler preferred "'innocent, friendly' Mexican peons," who "were much less likely to stand up for their civil rights."[33] Under Harry, the *Times* campaigned for the internment of Japanese Americans during World War II and for years inveighed against their liberation from concentration camps and their return to the West Coast. An official editorial acidly commented, "The *Times* has likened the Japanese to rattlesnakes. This is to apologize to the rattlesnakes."[34] Not long after the relocation of the Japanese Americans, wartime racial hatred promoted by the *Times* and other newspapers was suddenly redirected by off-duty servicemen and LA cops toward young Mexican-American men in what were called the "Zoot Suit riots."[35]

Harry Chandler's Depression-era paternalistic racism was a quaint memory by the early 1950s, when the *Times* took to regularly calling Mexican migrant workers "wetbacks," cheering on the federal government's "Operation Wetback" with screaming, front-page headlines like "500 NABBED BY L.A. WETBACK RAIDERS."[36] At the dawn of the 1960s, the last Chandler publisher was abruptly installed. Otis Chandler's name signaled continuity reaching back to his imperialist great-grandfather General Otis. In announcing the transition, his father Norman pronounced the responsibility "a sacred trust . . . dearer than life itself."[37] On his first day, Otis stated in the paper, "No changes are in the offing."[38] Nevertheless, he would become famous for half-allowing and half-promoting the modernization of the *Times*, its staff, and its outlook — within the boundaries of business.

Under Otis Chandler and his editors, the paper began paying greater attention to LA's minority communities. But even before he became publisher, and before a torrent of developments of the rollicking 1960s contributed to the paper's transformation, market studies oriented both the *Times* and its advertisers to "the growing middle-class sophistication of the suburbs," whose readers "were not interested in 'inner city' news."[39] Chandler sang the same tune all the way to the eve of his retirement in 1980, describing the *Times*'s target audience as middle and upper class. "We are not trying to get mass circulation, but quality circulation," he said in a television interview in the fall of 1979.[40] A couple of years earlier, he had echoed to *The Washington Post* an old market-survey finding that the *Times*'s readers were disinterested in coverage of minority communities, adding that the paper had deliberately "cut back some of our low-income circulation" because "that audience does not have the purchasing power and is not responsive to the kind of advertising we carry."[41]

Journalism scholars Félix Gutiérrez and Clint Wilson reported in 1979 that *Times* executives had been worrying that better coverage of minorities could cost the paper by loosening its "hold on the affluent, mostly white readers coveted by advertisers."[42] They also quoted a *Times* marketing specialist who, while denying racial considerations, explained, "It just happens that the more affluent and educated people tend to be white and live in suburban communities."[43] The implications of the paper's business model, despite efforts to overcome its traditionally right-wing and frankly racist corporate history and culture, would seem to have contributed to a virtual revolt in the early 1980s by the handful of Latino journalists on staff, as we will recount later in this chapter.

* * *

JUST AS THE UNPRECEDENTED SURGE OF EASTSIDE ELECTORAL CAMPAIGNS got underway in March of 1982 — and without consulting any of the few Latino journalists on its staff — the *Times* ran an explosive investigation into the management of what had emerged since the late 1960s as the Eastside's most salient and autonomous Mexican-American institution, the community development agency known as TELACU. That series opened on the *Times*'s biggest stage, the Sunday front page, under the headlines "Anti-Poverty Agency: Leaving Barrio Behind / East L.A. Community Union's Spending Runs into Millions and, Now, Official Suspicion." The lead article was augmented by a second piece scrutinizing TELACU's political activism and campaign contributions.[44]

The *Times* investigation ran parallel to and was sparked by what was then a two-year-long federal audit of TELACU that would continue well into the fall.[45] According to historian John Chávez, the newspaper's series "dealt a shattering blow to TELACU's image and threatened [its] very survival."[46] In his detailed reconstruction of the episode, Chávez highlighted the handling and effects of a grossly exaggerated estimate of the federal funds in question.[47] While the audit caused TELACU to shut down some important operations and spin off another, according to Chávez the worst damage was inflicted by the *Times*.[48] Perhaps the central problem with the paper's coverage was its unrelenting characterization of TELACU as an "anti-poverty agency," when in fact it had been a community development corporation (CDC) for a decade.

Ultimately, TELACU not only survived the dual assault by auditors and the *Times*, it actually came back to thrive. In addition to the family of companies it began growing in the 1970s when it officially became a CDC, in 1983 it established a leading community education foundation in response to the critically high numbers of Latino students dropping out of college, targeting its efforts at college readiness and achievement. TELACU is now celebrating its fiftieth year of job creation and service to tens of thousands of Latinos and first-generation students.

* * *

WITH TWO WEEKS BEFORE THE '82 PRIMARY ELECTION TO GO, THE *TIMES* ran an analytical piece that asked slyly, "Is Gender the Issue in Latino District?"[49] In retrospect, this framing cannot have helped Polanco, and likely energized support for Molina. The *Times* reporter portrayed Polanco as the front-runner in the race, with the lead in fundraising, support from TELACU, "and other key advantages."[50] Pointing out that Molina had made "only mild attempts" to exploit the sensationalized TELACU issue and attach it to Polanco, the piece seemed to urge her to make it a "major issue" of the campaign. Then, after summarizing Molina's strengths, the article turned to her vulnerabilities, "not the least of which is her sex."[51]

The *Times* report defined Molina's candidacy as an effort to elect the first Latina to the state legislature, which, it said, helped her raise money from women's groups but could potentially "hurt her overall chances." Citing unnamed sources in both campaigns, it suggested that "a woman has a built-in disadvantage competing with men for Latino votes," and that Polanco's financial lead ensured "a strong direct-mail appeal in the crucial final week."[52] The report went on to seemingly alert readers to the prospect of a late hit piece on Molina, presumably designed by Polanco's direct-mail specialist. A week later the paper summarized the election contest in this way: "Molina is trying to be the first Latino woman elected to the Legislature. Polanco is running with the blessing of The East Los Angeles Community Union (TELACU), the controversial anti-poverty agency."[53] Right between these two reports, the *Times* ran a fresh, front-page story revisiting its attempted take-down attack on TELACU.

A late hit piece did indeed materialize in this contest, but it was directed at Polanco, not from him. The *Times* reported the day before election day that Molina, "assuming a tough last-minute stance," mailed letters to voters attacking Polanco, and that the Molina campaign had benefited from a surge in "last-minute" contributions, including from members of the LA City Council.[54] Molina would later recall in her state oral history that council member Joy Picus phoned her, after reading the *Times* piece on how Molina's gender could hurt her chances of winning, to express her anger and to pledge to raise money for her. Molina agreed with her oral history interviewer that being a woman and running as a woman candidate actually benefited her campaign. She explained that towards the end, the campaign was "short on money that we really needed . . . to do a last-minute mailing. . . . We were getting ready to send out a letter."[55] The *Times* article powered a final appeal to "women's groups all over again for a second hit of money. . . . It worked. We quickly got in an awful lot of money," more than the campaign needed for the last mailing. They spent the extra funds on radio ads.[56]

When the vote counting began the next evening, Molina jumped out to an early lead that diminished only slightly in the course of the night.[57] Thus began what would become a pattern in each of her breakthrough elections: domination of vote-by-mail — cast early, first counted, and first reported.[58] When 100 percent of precincts were in, Molina had won by 842 votes, 52 to 48 percent.[59] The movement within a movement launched and developed by the Comisión and the women it rallied reached a new level. Molina not only became the first Latina to join the California Legislature, she and the Comisión network made Chicana power an electoral reality and accomplished something that Roybal, Alatorre, Art Torres, Esteban Torres, and now Polanco could not: she won her first time out.

The *Los Angeles Times*'s Big Eastside Story

MEXICAN-AMERICAN JOURNALISTS AT THE *TIMES* were frustrated and angry at the paper's coverage of their community. Half of the few Latino staff journalists at the *Times*, "about eight" writers, photographers, and an editor, gathered in February 1982 at a satellite office southeast of LA to discuss what to do.[60] The eventual result was a colossal, three-week, Pulitzer Prize-winning series titled "Latinos" in July-August 1983.[61] Ultimately some 17 *Times* staffers — all Mexican Americans — produced 27 illustrated parts to the series. Frank Sotomayor, who as the *Times*'s Southeast Section editor hosted the first meeting of the unhappy staff, co-edited the series and a third of a century later compiled a remarkable online account of the experience. He was unsparing in summarizing the project's backstory:

> For the first sixty-plus years of the twentieth century, the *Los Angeles Times* was no friend of Mexicans and Mexican Americans. . . . In Los Angeles, the *Times* consistently took positions that ran counter to the interests of Mexican American working people . . . it staunchly opposed labor unions. . . . *Times* coverage either ignored Mexican Americans or tended to cover them in stereotypical terms. In some instances, it demonized them and made them scapegoats. Some older Mexican Americans vowed never to allow the *Times* to enter their homes. They knew the history.[62]

Sotomayor continued with historical specifics, touching on the early years of the Great Depression, when "the *Times* fed a media hysteria that made scapegoats of Mexicans for supposedly being a drain on California's economy."[63] He quoted one of the staff writers on the Latinos series, Victor Valle, who said that the paper "whipped the hysteria that forced my grandmother and my dad to return to Mexico and lose their legal residency." Sotomayor noted that a decade later, after Pearl Harbor, the *Times* again contributed to racial hysteria in "accusing young Mexican Americans of being delinquents not supportive of the World War II effort." He cited a 1943 headline on the extended frenzy of assaults on Mexican Americans in LA by roving mobs of uniformed US sailors and soldiers: "Zoot Suiters Learn Lesson in Fights with Servicemen."

Mexican-American journalists at the *Times* saw the makeup of the editorial staff as a cause of the problems with its coverage and a manifestation of a larger issue. As Sotomayor put it, "No one at the *Times* seemed concerned about staff diversity. In fact, the word 'diversity' was not used at all."[64] This condition became a crisis for the paper when the 1965 Watts riots broke out — and the *Times* had no black journalists. Its white reporters covering the riots were threatened, attacked, and chased out of the area.

On the Latino side, the *Times* at least had Ruben Salazar by then, but after several years of his reporting on issues relating to "Mexican Americans, the Border, and Braceros," Salazar was reassigned in 1965 as a foreign correspondent, just months before the Watts riots.[65] When Sotomayor started at the *Times* a few weeks after Salazar was killed in 1970, the paper "contained about as much color as a loaf of Sarah Lee white bread. You could count the number of journalists of color on two hands. We were like the brown crusted edges of the nearly all-white newsroom."[66]

It was not until the 1980s that the *Times*, in Sotomayor's account, "had finally assembled a small corps of outstanding African-American reporters" and "a critical mass of Latino staff members." "Still," he added, "it had not learned the lessons of diversity." In 1981 the paper ran an investigative series on "the underclass," reported, written, and edited entirely by white staff, and which led off with the infamous front-page headline: "Marauders from Inner City Prey on L.A.'s Suburbs." Nearly a decade later, the *Times* itself would look back at its history in another series it called "Minorities and the Press." Recalling the "Marauders" article and headline, a reporter wrote, "Critics were equally upset by the illustration that accompanied the story and ran across the top of a full page, with large arrows leaping like panzer divisions from South-Central Los Angeles into predominantly white suburbs. The National Assn. of Black Journalists voted that story the 'most objectionable news story' of the year and called it 'reckless . . . preposterous . . . unpardonable journalism.'" The black journalists might have mentioned the paper's publicly acknowledged business model, with its focus on the interests of middle-class suburbs that happen to be white, exemplified by the "Marauders" headline and graphic. The *Times*'s reporter, writing in 1990, added that the paper's "coverage of gang activity, drive-by shootings, and other inner-city violence continues to give the front page of its metropolitan section a police blotter feel at times."[67]

The "Marauders" episode led to the paper's black reporters producing a very different series in 1982, the precedent-setting "Black L.A./Looking at Diversity." This was the immediate context in which the group of Mexican-American *Times* staff met to discuss coverage of Latinos. They were aware of the project that their black colleagues were embarked upon, which appeared later in the year. They were not aware, however, of another lengthy *Times* investigation, then in its final stages, that would be published the following month as a series — the paper's sensational exposé of a major Latino community institution on the Eastside.

* * *

BEFORE LA TIMES EDITORS APPROVED THE PAPER'S HISTORIC "LATINOS" SERIES — and while they considered what their Mexican-American staffers had proposed to them — the *Times* ran its famous assault on TELACU. Thus, the most proximate antecedent to the *Times*'s "Latinos" project was the "Black L.A." series, while the direct context of its development, reporting, and writing was the extended scandal, driven by the paper's coverage, that engulfed the most prominent Latino institution in East LA and the Greater Eastside. That coverage included a highly critical article on participation in electoral politics by the agency, its management, and its workers. The cloud the *Times* floated over TELACU cast shade on Eastside politics as a whole. At the very least, the investigations by both the paper and the Labor Department appear to have greatly complicated the challenge that the *Times*'s Mexican-American staffers were tackling with their proposed Latinos series: how to correct the paper's traditional focus — when it covered Latinos at all — on alleged delinquency, corruption, and deviance on the Eastside.[68]

Several parts of the "Latinos" series touched on political themes. The newspaper's highest-ranking Latino, Frank del Olmo, wrote the two articles most directly about political empowerment, which were striking in the message they conveyed by omission: while most of the series focused on aspects of the Latino community in Southern California, del Olmo's pieces on politics centered on the different paths taken by three Mexican-American leaders in San Antonio, Texas. For all its merits, the historic "Latinos" series did not even hint at the political impact LA-based Latino leaders and their community were already having on the metropolis, the state, and the nation, and anticipated not at all where LA-led Latino political empowerment might be headed — or that it was headed anywhere. Latino leadership invisibility remained the order of the day at the *Los Angeles Times*.

A couple of years before work started on the "Latinos" series, del Olmo had graduated from the Metro reporting staff to become a columnist, writing frequently about Latino politics. That was the pivotal year of 1980, when the US Census undertook its first complete count of the nation's Hispanic population, thanks to the long reform effort spearheaded by Ed Roybal in Washington. Del Olmo, along with a couple of his Mexican-American colleagues, played a role in the decision by the *Times* in 1981 to defy the federal government's adoption of "Hispanic," opting instead for "Latino." Thereafter, del Olmo went on "a personal campaign" against what he called the "ugly and imprecise word 'Hispanic.'"[69] The *Los Angeles Times*'s greatest contribution to Latino politics was undoubtedly the role it played in establishing the term "Latino" in mainstream American media. But another legacy of the newspaper's historically biased coverage of Latino political and business leaders has also endured; when a pointed and stingingly negative *Times* headline is directed at one of them, their colleagues routinely quip, "It's your turn!"

LA Prison Blues

LONG-DEVELOPED PLANS TO ELECT RICHARD POLANCO TO THE STATE LEGIS-LATURE needed updating after his relatively near miss in 1982. Alatorre, Torres, and Molina had all served as administrative assistant to one or more legislators at some point prior to their first election to the state Assembly. So, when Polanco took the same position under Alatorre, after his 1982 loss, the clear implication was that now, at last, he was locked into a position to move up when Alatorre moved on.

Molina had worked as a field deputy for Art Torres and Speaker Willie Brown, but she had never served in Sacramento. Despite her experience, and the fact that Maxine Waters had strongly supported her, Molina was headed for the Capitol, but would have no prospect of rising to a leadership position. She was also arriving to a changed state capital that, after two terms under Governor Jerry Brown, had again reverted to Republican control, in the person of Governor George Deukmejian. Molina's legislative career would thus unfold in a relatively constrained space, which three years later would become more so when Richard Alatorre did indeed move on to the LA City Council, and her old adversary Richard Polanco arrived in the Capitol as his successor.

By that time, two issues had developed that would also come to define Molina's career. The first was the Deukmejian administration's plan to build the first state prison in LA County and locate it on the eastern edge of the downtown area, separated from Boyle Heights by railroad tracks and the LA River.[70] Molina and her office were instrumental in elevating community activism against this plan, which would have put the prison in her district without prior consultation. A historic new organization emerged on the Eastside, the Mothers of East Los Angeles (MELA), aided by Monsignor John Moretta.[71] They organized a community mobilization against the prison that quickly became self-sustaining and continued long after Molina left the Assembly.

Another issue went practically unnoticed in the mid-1980s, one that put Molina and Alatorre on the same side; would go through various deaths, revivals, and transformations; and not become realized for another quarter of a century. There was no museum in town of either California or Los Angeles history, and, in particular, no museum devoted to the experience and contributions of people of Mexican origin to either the state's or the city's history and culture. It would be well into the next millennium before such a specialized cultural institution, albeit in modest, incipient form, would open to the public; but when it did, LA Plaza de Cultura y Artes, adjacent to the historic Los Angeles Plaza, the city's oldest church, and the architectural monument that is Pico House, would tie today's Latino metropolis to its beginnings as a Spanish-Mexican pueblo, and be indelibly marked as a legacy achievement of Gloria Molina's political career.[72]

* * *

A BEFORE-AND-AFTER HALLMARK OF LA AND CALIFORNIA HISTORY is the bad old habit of government officials developing and announcing plans for major projects without first securing the support of affected communities or their elected representatives. When the Deukmejian administration's Department of Corrections revealed plans to build LA County's first state prison in a marginal downtown location, apparently without having consulted anyone other than the property owner, the reaction was — at least in part — fast and furious.

According to the first report in the *Los Angeles Times*, which later supported the plan editorially, neither Senator Art Torres, nor members of LA City Council, nor apparently the county supervisor, all of whom represented the area, had been briefed on the decision to site the prison in or next to their districts.[73] The *Times* article did not mention Molina, who also represented the area, and a week later the paper made brief mention, at the end of another piece about an issue in another county, that Molina had introduced a bill in the Assembly that would block the planned LA prison location.[74] Torres also introduced an amendment blocking the downtown LA site for the prison.[75]

Molina's reasons for opposing the prison in her district seem not to have appeared in the pages of the *Times* until the paper published her letter to the editor, a month and a half after first breaking the story.[76] Molina's staff, however, undertook to inform her constituents on the issue through mailings and calls, encouraging the community to resist the prison. Torres succeeded in winning a number of concessions to the community, and the Senate passed its version of the prison construction bill later that year. Molina was able to block the bill from coming out of committee on the Assembly side until 1986. The community mobilization led by the Mothers of East Los Angeles held weekly protest marches that began that summer and continued into 1987.[77]

In the meantime, much more Eastside politicking unfolded. Richard Alatorre left his leadership position in the Assembly in 1985 to run in a special election for LA City Council, and in winning became the first Latino on the council since Ed Roybal left for Congress at the end of 1962.[78] As expected, Alatorre's administrative assistant, Richard Polanco, ran to succeed him in the Assembly in another special election in 1986, this time with Willie Brown's open support, and to no one's great surprise, Gloria Molina defied Brown and invested heavily in Polanco's main opponent.[79] Nonetheless, Polanco was elected and sworn into office in June 1986.

One of the impressive aspects of the prison fight in the Assembly up to that point was Molina's success in keeping the bill that would authorize its construction in her district stuck in a deadlocked committee. The prison plan finally made it out of committee after a year's delay, but only after the community had been roused and organized, and the rallying slogan "No Prison in East LA" had been firmly established.[80]

*Richard Polanco casting absentee ballot in person in the 1986 California State Assembly special election that marked the start of his career as a legislator. (*Los Angeles Times *Photographic Archives. Collection 1429. UCLA Library Special Collections, Charles E. Young Research Library, UCLA.)*

The response that the proposed site was not in East LA or even in Boyle Heights, but in fact on the west bank of the LA River, fell on deaf ears. "That doesn't matter," Frank del Olmo wrote in his *Times* column, "because the technicalities of the prison project long ago became less important than its symbolism. California Latinos are so opposed to Deukmejian's prison that he couldn't make them any madder if he suggested building it in the Vatican."[81]

The prison fight not only went on after Molina had left the Assembly, it continued past the Deukmejian governorship, and into the Pete Wilson administration. At a 1992 news conference at the Capitol calling on Wilson to yank the prison plan, Art Torres declared, "The governor has a historic opportunity to right a wrong . . . of such symbolic proportions to the Latino community, not only of East Los Angeles, but across the state of California."[82] The drama finally ended when Wilson, grappling with a fiscal crisis, signed the legislation backed by Torres and Polanco that killed the project.[83] Ultimately, Polanco and Torres's legislative maneuvering and relationships with Senate and Assembly leaders finished off the East LA prison.

* * *

BEFORE THE SPECIAL ELECTION THAT PUT A LATINO BACK ON THE LA CITY COUNCIL in December 1985 after a 23-year absence, the Reagan Justice Department surprised many in the political world by suing the city for violating the Voting Rights Act with the redistricting plan the council implemented in 1982. Congress had considerably strengthened the VRA that same year, and on that basis the Justice Department considered the LA City Council to be districted in such a way as to violate the rights of Hispanic voters.[84]

Based on Richard Alatorre's successful shepherding of the state Assembly's redistricting in 1981, the city council asked him to do the same for LA. The plan was to redistrict and settle the federal lawsuit out of court rather than fight it. The result, after extended and bitter wrangling — ultimately resolved by the unexpected death of an elderly white councilman — was that Alatorre and his expert colleague, Dr. Bruce Cain, were able to produce a politically viable scheme that created a new, predominantly Latino district to be filled in the short term by another special election, and that also fashioned yet another Latino "growth district" in the San Fernando Valley, then occupied, but one that would be likely to elect a Latino in the future.[85] MALDEF joined the lawsuit and assembled a multiracial coalition, to ensure unity and a place at the negotiating table for the expected settlement.[86]

The resolution of this case led to the scheduling of the special election for February 1987 — an opportunity for Gloria Molina to leave behind the limited horizons around her at the state Capitol while doubling Latino representation on the LA City Council. She would once again face a male opponent backed by her former Eastside political friends and colleagues, another war. This time, however, Molina would win a landslide victory in the context of markedly low participation.[87] She had added a broad base of Latino support to the Chicana network that backed her in 1982, and it showed.

Back in Sacramento, Richard Polanco was starting his first full term, still four years away from taking command of the Chicano Legislative Caucus. More great challenges, opportunities, setbacks, and comebacks lay ahead for Molina, Polanco, and the Latino Eastside. Los Angeles was on the verge of an accelerated period of change, as a major immigration-reform law passed in 1986 was about to go into effect.

Notes

1. Bauman, *Race and the War on Poverty*, 112; Cotera, "Chicana Conferences and Seminars, 1970–1975," 114–18.

2. This discussion and the Flores sidebar are based mostly on the work of Marisela Rodríguez Chávez, especially chapter two of her dissertation, "Despierten Hermanas y Hermanos!"; her subsequent paper, "We Have a Long, Beautiful History"; and original interviews with Gloria Molina, Yolanda Nava, Sandra Serrano-Sewell, and Deena J. González (see references). Yolanda Nava coined the "founding mother" moniker for Francisca Flores. See also Bauman, "Gender, Civil Rights Activism, and the War on Poverty in Los Angeles," and chapter six of his *Race and the War on Poverty*; del Castillo, "Comisión Femenil Mexicana Nacional"; and Flores, "Comisión Femenil Mexicana." The Flores quote in the sidebar appeared in Marita Hernandez, "Stirrings of Independence among Latin Women: Chicanas Rejecting Their Stereotyped Roles," *Los Angeles Times*, September 23, 1981.

3. Bauman, *Race and the War on Poverty*, 118–19.

4. Ibid., 125. For more on Centro de Niños see http://www.centrodeninos.com.

5. Gutiérrez, *Fertile Matters*, 40. As an internal medicine intern at Highland General Hospital in Oakland, Dr. Bernard Rosenfeld was immediately troubled when he first noted staff doctors urging sterilization of women of color who were there to deliver (Lombardo, *A Century of Eugenics in America*, 175). When Rosenfeld switched to OB-GYN and a residency at Johns Hopkins Hospital in Maryland, he again found doctors pressuring women into surgical sterilization (Espino, *Women Sterilized as They Give Birth*, 208–09). Completing his residency at LA County Medical Center (LACMC), Rosenfeld further witnessed pressures on both residents and patients to perform or be subjected to surgical sterilization at the time of childbirth, and found in the hospital's records dramatic increases in the numbers of elective hysterectomies and tubal ligations since 1968 (Stern, *Eugenic Nation*, 227).

6. Gail Kennard, "Women Sterilized under Pressure, Nader Aide Says," United Press International, published in *Fort Lauderdale News*, September 16, 1973. Rosenfeld connected with the Southern Poverty Law Center (SPLC) and with Ralph Nader's Health Research Group (HRG); Gutiérrez, *Fertile Matters*, 140 note 1; Espino, *Women Sterilized*, 209–16. Collaboration with HRG led to the publication of Bernard Rosenfeld, Sidney M. Wolfe, and Robert E. McGarrah, Jr., *A Health Research Group Study on Surgical Sterilization* (Health Research Group, 1973), which produced immediate national publicity (Richard D. Lyons, "Doctors Scored on Sterilization," *New York Times*, October 31, 1973). The SPLC used Rosenfeld's work in its celebrated 1974 *Relf v. Weinberger* sterilization-abuse lawsuit against the Department of Health, Education and Welfare (Gutiérrez, *Fertile Matters*, 143 note 33). Curiously, in spite of Rosenfeld's efforts, his presence in the city, and his report's focus on the county hospital, *Los Angeles Times* resisted covering the Rosenfeld-HRG report for over a year before publishing Robert Kistler, "Women 'Pushed' into Sterilization, Doctor Charges," *Los Angeles Times*, December 2, 1974 (Espino, *Women Sterilized*, 216).

7. Gutiérrez, *Fertile Matters*, 35–36.

8. Espino, *Women Sterilized*, 249. The Hernández family was able to consult with their family physician and rejected the hospital's recommended sterilization.

9. Gutiérrez, *Fertile Matters*, 35–36. The 2015 PBS documentary *No Más Bebés* features interviews with the principal actors on each side of this story. Director Renee Tajima-Peña also published an account of the case and the making of her film titled, "'Más Bebés?'" The online series *Talking Biopolitics* of the Berkeley-based Center for Genetics and Society (March 2, 2016) conducted a discussion of the film and lawsuit with the director and with historian Virginia Espino, who served as executive producer, hosted by historian Alexandra Minna Stern, author of *Eugenic Nation* (https://www.geneticsandsociety.org/internal-content/talking-biopolitics-virginia-espino-renee-tajima-pena-and-alexandra-minna-stern). The Center for Healthy Communities of The California Endowment, based in Los Angeles, conducted a similar panel discussion titled "No Más Bebés: Latinas, Reproductive Oppression, and Resistance in Los Angeles" on January 14, 2016, also featuring Tajima-Peña and Espino; see "Panel Discussion of 'No Más Bebés' Documentary" posted on February 26, 2016, https://www.youtube.com/watch?v=RV-tPSTnWoU.

10. In her interview in the *No Más Bebés* film, Hernández framed the lawsuit she led in the context of a just-emerging Chicano civil rights movement. By contrast, the black

civil rights movement was gestated in the decades-long development and execution of a painstaking litigation strategy of national scope, which included a community strategy, that preceded the more visible, sustained street-protest phase of the movement and the federal legislation it brought about in the 1960s. The ground was not similarly prepared for the LA County Hospital Chicana sterilization case, although there was at least the advantage of enhanced scrutiny and debate over sterilization abuse at that time. On the long development of the black civil rights movement see Tushnet, *The NAACP Legal Strategy*, or Kluger, *Simple Justice*. On the LA case see Hernández, "Chicanas and the Issue of Involuntary Sterilization." Among the characteristics of the plaintiffs in the LA case, Hernández wrote, "All of the victims and near victims belonged to a racial minority, were poor, and could not readily understand the English language. . . . Many of the women encountered doctors and nurses who were openly hostile to them because of their ethnicity or poverty status" (9). See also Espino, *Women Sterilized*, 250, and fn. 201, on the use of the Civil Rights Act of 1871 in this case.

11. Gutiérrez, *Fertile Matters*, 100.

12. Espino, *Women Sterilized*, 252–53, 255; see the film *No Más Bebés* for footage of the 1975 press conference.

13. *Madrigal v. Quilligan*, No. 75–2057 (filed June 18, 1975); Espino, *Women Sterilized*, 253, 256; Gutiérrez, *Fertile Matters*, 106–08; Robert Rawitch, "State Enjoined in Sterilization Suit Filed by Women," *Los Angeles Times*, October 7, 1975.

14. Hernández, "Chicanas and the Issue of Involuntary Sterilization," 3 (emphasis added).

15. Espino, *Women Sterilized*, chapter 4, examines in detail the wide array of activists, organizations, and coalitions that made this case into a movement.

16. Gutiérrez additionally identifies an early overlap between the white feminist struggle for reproductive rights and white support for population control. A conflict had already broken out between white feminists and primarily male, black leaders over family planning and population control, which included access to contraception, sex education, abortion, and sterilization; see *Fertile Matters*, 27–34; see also Espino, *Women Sterilized*, 8–10, 282.

17. Gutiérrez, *Fertile Matters*, 103–05.

18. Bauman, *Race and the War on Poverty*, 127.

19. Alatorre and co. supported LA City Councilman John Ferraro against his colleague Edelman. It could, of course, be argued that having high-level Latino support for both candidates provided the community protection against being shut out of influence on the board, if its leadership had been united behind the loser, and in this case, having supported Ferraro enhanced Alatorre's relationship with the councilman, who soon went on to become council president.

20. In our interviews with him, Torres did not recall this meeting or otherwise knowing of Polanco's initial plan to run against Garcia in 1982.

21. Molina recalls the circumstances of her appointment by Brown, the nature of the office, and her staff in Molina interview by Vásquez, 154–61.

22. The legislature had to approve both its own and the congressional redistricting plans, which meant that the maps for each first had to clear both houses' reapportionment

committees, but the drawing of the congressional districts was left to the leader of California's Democratic delegation in Congress, the supremely crafty Representative Phillip Burton of San Francisco. Jacobs details the intricate politics of California's 1981 congressional redistricting in *A Rage for Justice*, 414–16 and 425–40.

23. Ibid., 436; MALDEF had enhanced its visibility and perceived focus on Mexican-American civil and voting rights issues in California in the 1970s after moving its headquarters from San Antonio to Phil Burton and Willie Brown's in San Francisco, and when Governor Jerry Brown appointed MALDEF co-founder Mario Obledo to his cabinet in 1975. In 1980, MALDEF's Los Angeles regional office effectively co-sponsored, with the Republican-backed Rose Institute of State and Local Government, a broad Latino coalition known as "*Californios* for Fair Representation," to lobby and push publicly for the drawing of predominantly Latino electoral districts, in the processes based on the 1980 census; see Huerta interview by Vásquez, 89–113. Huerta was executive director of the MALDEF Southern California Office in LA and became general counsel for the *Californios* coalition. Comisión and Gloria Molina personally participated in the coalition; see Molina interview by Vásquez, 168–85. Both Huerta and Molina discuss the Republican nature of the Rose Institute and the controversy over Latino Democrats working with it; see also Kousser, *Colorblind Injustice*, 109–11.

24. Jacobs, *A Rage for Justice*, 434. The 43-member state delegation grew to 45; Burton fashioned Democratic districts for both new seats, and through geographic consolidation reduced Republican districts to 17.

25. As in big-league baseball trades, Burton orchestrated a set of complicated deals, extracting a Republican congressman from the Eastside by arranging a judicial appointment for him by the governor, redrawing his district, and opening his seat to move a Latino Democratic opponent of Willie Brown's out of the Assembly and up to Congress, and fashioned another altogether new, half-Latino district from the gains of reapportionment. See Jacobs, *A Rage for Justice*, 436. Burton called MALDEF to lock in the organization's support for his plan and in the process agreed to add the Democratic House Caucus's endorsement of the Latino community's candidate in the primary elections in these districts, which would include fund raising. Huerta would recall that, in addition to winning MALDEF's support, the deal was "easy to sell" to the *Californios* coalition; Huerta interview by Vásquez, 114–21.

26. MALDEF was strongly supportive of fashioning a congressional district for Esteban Torres. Marty Martinez was a former mayor of Monterey Park who had been elected to the Assembly with Howard Berman's support, as part of Berman's drive for the Assembly speakership. A Martinez run for Congress would thus come with continuing support from Berman, who was also running for Congress, and serve to remove Bermanites from the Assembly, show Democratic support for Latinos in redistricting, and secure another vote for Burton in the House. See Jacobs, *A Rage for Justice,* 409, 415, 436, 440.

27. Author interview with Serrano-Sewell.

28. See Chávez, *Eastside Landmark*, 187–92; and Frank del Olmo, "Will Gloria Molina Lead Us into Decade of the Hispanic?" *Los Angeles Times*, November 11, 1982, reprinted in Sotomayor and Beltrán-del Olmo, *Frank del Olmo*, 27–29.

29. See Molina interview by Vásquez, 284–86; Kristina Lindgren, "Latino Candidates Make Mark in Primary, Win 5 Key Races," *Los Angeles Times*, June 10, 1982; and Kevin Roderick, "Is Gender the Issue in Latino District?" *Los Angeles Times*, May 23, 1982.

30. Molina's understanding was that Waters persuaded Willie Brown to ordain that no assemblymembers of his caucus be allowed to take sides in the Polanco-Molina race other than herself and Alatorre (Molina interview by Vásquez, 429).

31. Otis Chandler, the last of the *Times*'s family publishers, looking back in a 1975 television interview admitted, "We were a WASP paper"; cited in Gottlieb and Wolt, *Thinking Big*, 343 and 572. Except where otherwise noted, this section and accompanying sidebar are primarily based on Gottlieb and Wolt's magisterial, 600-page history. See especially 17–23, 123, 166–73 and 297–301. Born to a midwestern farm family, Otis entered the newspaper business courtesy of a brother who edited a small paper. He became an ardent Republican and delegate to the 1860 convention that nominated Abraham Lincoln for president. Otis then entered the Union Army as a private, rose to the rank of captain under the command of future Ohio governor and president Rutherford B. Hayes, a staunch abolitionist, and in his own unit commanded another future president, William McKinley. Military relationships and service shaped the rest of his life. Hayes honorifically made Otis colonel upon his Army discharge; another fellow Ohioan and Civil War veteran gave Otis the chance to move to Southern California in the 1870s, to become editor of a new paper in Santa Barbara, just as the railroads were reaching the area and launching its development boom. In the 1880s, he moved to Los Angeles, where he became editor of another new paper, the *Los Angeles Times*, which he came to own and turn into a rabidly anti-union and partisan Republican power in the region. When the Spanish American War broke out, Otis prevailed upon his former junior officer, and now President William McKinley, to commission him as general. Gottlieb and Wolt quote a witness to the "decisive battle of Caloocan" between US troops led by Otis and anticolonial Filipino insurgents: "The slaughter of women and children was frightful . . . the Americans burning and devastating all before them, conducting a war of extermination and shooting every Filipino" (23).

32. See Gottlieb and Wolt, *Thinking Big*, 166-67; Garza, *They Came to Toil*, 16, 80, 101, 178; 192, fn. 93.

33. Garza, *They Came to Toil*, 178.

34. Gottlieb and Wolt, *Thinking Big*, 298.

35. Ibid., 297–301.

36. See Matt Ballinger, "From the Archives: How The Times Covered Mass Deportations in the Eisenhower Era," *Los Angeles Times*, accessed March 9, 2018, http://documents.latimes.com/eisenhower-era-deportations/; and Kate Linthicum, "The dark, complex history of Trump's Model for His Mass Deportation Plan," *Los Angeles Times*, November 13, 2015, http://www.latimes.com/nation/la-na-trump-deportation-20151113-story.html.

37. Gottlieb and Wolt, *Thinking Big*, 323.

38. Ibid., 324.

39. Ibid., 326–27.

40. Quoted in Bagdikian, *The New Media Monopoly*, 231.

41. William H. Jones and Laird Anderson, "Press Concentration: Perhaps Fewer Than Two-Dozen Firms Will Own All Daily Papers by '90s," *The Washington Post*, July 24, 1977; see also *Washington Journalism Review* 2 (1980): 34. Chandler was apparently referring to an internal *Times* study of 1977 titled *A Report on the Los Angeles Spanish Market*, cited in Gutiérrez and Wilson II, "The Demographic Dilemma."

42. Gutiérrez and Wilson II, "The Demographic Dilemma," 53.

43. Ibid., 53–54.

44. This series by Claire Spiegel and Robert Welkos ran without an overall title from March 28–30, 1982. The lead-off installment continued onto five more pages in the first section of the paper, each segment ending with "Please see POVERTY, Page x; the succeeding headlines were led by all caps "POVERTY:" followed by "Barrio Agency Probed," "East L.A. Agency Leaves Barrio Behind," "Barrio Agency Investigated," "Leaving the Barrio Behind," and "Barrio Agency Trots Globe." At the first jump on page 3, a second article by the same authors (with names reversed) was added: "Politicking: Another Murky Area for TELACU," which continued on two more pages with headlines anchored by "POLITICS:" followed by "More Problems for Agency" and "A Murky Arena for Agency." The two stories thus ran with these headlines on a total of eight pages of the Sunday paper's first section. The series continued on the Monday front page with the story "Far-Flung Empire Is Built on Federal Grants," and the Tuesday front page with "Giant Anti-Poverty Agency Did Little to Create Jobs." Follow-up articles continued into 1983.

45. This discussion based on Chávez, *Eastside Landmark*, 195–223, and other sources as noted.

46. Ibid., 198–99.

47. According to Chávez, "The auditors later admitted that they had exaggerated the figure to draw attention to TELACU's misconduct" (ibid., 205, 213).

48. Chávez argues the *Los Angeles Times*'s story on the complete audit report "amounted to a retraction of its March investigative series" — but a retraction without apology (ibid., 214–15). The artist who served as chairman of TELACU's board, along with his wife, pled guilty to making "false statements concerning his CETA employment" (207), but the US Attorney who supervised the investigation of potential charges stemming from the Labor Department's 285-page audit report concluded, according to the *Times*, that TELACU "successfully argued," in its 104-page rebuttal and "in meetings with prosecutors and auditors," that federal grants invested in private businesses by a community development corporation (CDC), lose their "character as federal funds" and are no longer subject to federal control as long as they are used "within the scope of the project" (Chávez, *Eastside Landmark*, 215). See also Spiegel and Welkos, "Poverty Agency Largely Immune from Corruption Probe: Taxpayer Dollars Invested in TELACU's Businesses Became Private Funds," *Los Angeles Times*, November 12, 1982; Howie Kurtz, "Audit Says Anti-Poverty Agency and Subsidiaries Misused Funds," *The Washington Post*, August 12, 1982, https://www.washingtonpost.com/archive/politics/1982/08/12/audit-says-anti-poverty-agency-and-subsidiaries-misused-funds/c3a2368f-6660-4cb8-9028-d5e6798c-7d69/?utm_term=.0f19b7a6f361. That was "the way the project was set up," US Attorney

Stephen Trott said, "to act as a capital enterprise and investment operation" (Spiegel and Welkos, "Poverty Agency").

49. Roderick, "Is Gender the Issue in Latino District?"

50. Ibid.

51. Ibid.

52. Ibid.

53. Ibid. Jerry Gillam, "Record Spending Seen in State Senate, Assembly Contests," *Los Angeles Times*, May 30, 1982.

54. Kevin Roderick, "Candidate Says Foe Was Late on Child Support," *Los Angeles Times*, June 7, 1982.

55. Molina interview by Vásquez, 276–80.

56. Ibid.

57. Tables of election results in early edition of the next day's *Los Angeles Times* from June 9, 1982, reported that with 22 percent of precincts counted, Molina held a lead of 53 percent to Polanco's 47 percent. "California Assembly" table, *Los Angeles Times*, June 9, 1982, p. 20.

58. In her state oral history, Molina discussed the vote-by-mail campaign strategy, in the context of her first LA City Council race in 1987 (Molina interview by Vásquez, 437–39).

59. "California Assembly" table, *Los Angeles Times*, June 10, 1982, p. 17. District 56: 10,061 votes to 9,219.

60. See Sotomayor, *The Pulitzer Long Shot*; and Gudiño, *Below the Fold*. Discussion also draws on Sotomayor interview with authors.

61. Published in book form as Ramos and Sotomayor, *Southern California's Latino Community*.

62. Sotomayor, *The Pulitzer Long Shot*, chapter 2. This electronic document has no page numbers.

63. All quotes in this paragraph from Sotomayor, *The Pulitzer Long Shot*, chapter 2.

64. Ibid.

65. Salazar, *Border Correspondent*; the quoted phrase is Garcia's heading for the selection of Salazar's writings in the *Times* from 1961–65.

66. Sotomayor, *The Pulitzer Long Shot*, chapter 3.

67. David Shaw, "Newspapers Struggling to Raise Minority Coverage: Journalism: Guidelines Have Been Set Up to Alter Perceptions of Blacks, Latinos, and Asian-Americans," *Los Angeles Times*, December 12, 1990, http://articles.latimes.com/1990-12-12/news/mn-5876_1_minority-communities.

68. This is a tendency that academic analysts refer to as the "criminalization of Latinos" and of others. See David E. Hayes-Bautista and Gregory Rodriguez, "The Criminalization of the Latino Identity Makes Fighting Gangs That Much Harder," *Los Angeles Times*, September 15, 1996, http://articles.latimes.com/1996-09-15/opinion/op-44051_1_latino-identity.

69. Sotomayor, "Foreword," 19; del Olmo, "Hispanic, Latino, or Chicano"; del Olmo, "Latino *Sí* — Hispanic, *No*," 85.

70. See Pardo, *Mexican American Women Activists*, 53–55; Rich Connell, "Downtown Prison Site Selected," *Los Angeles Times*, March 21, 1985, http://articles.latimes.com/1985-03-21/local/me-20727_1_prison-plan.

71. Louis Sahagun, "The Mothers of East L.A. Transform Themselves and Their Neighborhood," *Los Angeles Times*, August 13, 1989, http://articles.latimes.com/1989-08-13/local/me-816_1_east-los-angeles.

72. See Reed Johnson, "New Focus for Latino Culture: A $54-million Center in L.A. Will Mix Exhibitions, Education and Performance," *Los Angeles Times*, April 11, 2011, http://articles.latimes.com/2011/apr/11/entertainment/la-et-la-plaza-20110411.

73. Connell, "Downtown Prison Site Selected"; "A Prison in the Neighborhood?" unsigned official editorial, *Los Angeles Times*, May 1, 1985, http://articles.latimes.com/1985-05-01/local/me-11647_1_new-prison.

74. Kenneth F. Bunting, "We Want a State Prison, Adelanto Officials Insist," *Los Angeles Times*, March 28, 1985, http://articles.latimes.com/1985-03-28/news/mn-29069_1_prison-construction.

75. Ted Vollmer, "L.A. County Prison: Now a 2nd is Being Planned," *Los Angeles Times*, April 26, 1985. In this article the *Times* also reported that the state Department of Corrections had initially chosen a different site for the prison, in the far north of LA County, but that the conservative county supervisor there — a Republican Party leader with close ties to the governor — strongly opposed the plan and, according to his own chief deputy, "steered corrections officials to the downtown site that eventually was selected."

76. Gloria Molina, "Proposed Prison Site in L.A.," *Los Angeles Times*, April 30, 1985, http://articles.latimes.com/1985-04-30/local/me-19952_1_boyle-heights-prison-los-angeles-county.

77. Pardo, *Mexican American Women*, 55–56, 264 note 36. Molina interview by Vásquez, 411–12.

78. In his 2016 memoire, Alatorre explains the longevity of the white LA city councilman representing the Eastside, Art Snyder, who endured multiple attempts by Latino challengers to dislodge him, but who then decided to resign in 1985. Alatorre also explains his decision, in consultation with his closest allies, to leave his power position in the Assembly to run for city council, succeeding Snyder; Alatorre with Grossman, *Change from the Inside*, 274–82.

79. See Molina interview by Vásquez, 419–26.

80. See Pamela Varley, "'No Prison in East L.A.!' Birth of a Grassroots Movement," John F. Kennedy School of Government, Case Program, Reference no. HKS1541.0.

81. Frank del Olmo, "Prison Issue Inspires Eastside to Do Battle," *Los Angeles Times*, September 22, 1986, reprinted in Sotomayor and Beltrán-del Olmo, *Frank del Olmo*, 34–36.

82. Mark Gladstone, "The California Legislative Showdown: Latinos Press Wilson to Sign Bill to Kill L.A. Prison Plans," *Los Angeles Times*, September 2, 1992, http://articles.latimes.com/1992-09-02/local/me-6391_1_lancaster-prison.

83. Pardo, *Mexican American Women*, 56.

84. See Ronald J. Ostrow, "U.S. Inquiry Targets 1982 L.A. Council Redistricting," *Los Angeles Times*, February 26, 1985, http://articles.latimes.com/1985-02-26/local/me-24976_1_advisory-committee; Associated Press, "U.S. Sues L.A., Charging Anti-Latino Redistricting: Plan Called Violation of Rights," *Los Angeles Times*, November 26, 1985, http://articles.latimes.com/1985-11-26/news/mn-2217_1_los-angeles-city-council.

85. See Alatorre with Grossman, *Change from the Inside*, 291–302.

86. George Ramos, "Latinos Seek to Join Suit on L.A. Redistricting," *Los Angeles Times*, January 7, 1986, http://articles.latimes.com/1986-01-07/local/me-13930_1_latino-voters; Rich Connell, "3 Ethnic Groups to Join Forces in Fight for New City Council District Boundaries," *Los Angeles Times*, May 2, 1986, http://articles.latimes.com/1986-05-02/local/me-3142_1_city-council.

87. Associated Press, "Hispanic Woman Wins City Seat in Los Angeles," *New York Times*, February 5, 1987, http://www.nytimes.com/1987/02/05/us/hispanic-woman-wins-city-seat-in-los-angeles.html.

CHAPTER 9

"They Keep Coming":
Labor, Politics, and the New Immigrant Wave

FLASHFORWARD — FALL 1994 — BEFORE THIS SEASON, THE '90S WERE SHAPING UP as a boom decade for Latino empowerment as seen from LA — especially compared to the political landscape of 1980. Growing numbers, voting rights, and electioneering were combining to drive Latino advances in the city, county, and state, and in Congress as well. Millions of immigrants legalized in the late '80s were becoming eligible to turn into citizens and voters. The presidential candidate that Latinos favored in '92, Bill Clinton, won both the White House and California for the first time in a generation, heralding new opportunities for progress in Washington.[1] Clinton's predecessor, George H. W. Bush, set the stage for a historic reinvention of US relations with Mexico. On the 1994 California ballot, a newly created statewide office appeared within reach, which could serve as a springboard for the long-sought Latino assault on the governorship. But then disaster struck.

They called 1992 the "Year of the Woman" in American politics, but the '94 wave election was dubbed the "Year of the Angry White Man."[2] This was a wave of reaction that swept Democrats out of power in the US Senate and in the House of Representatives they had controlled for 40 years. Willie Brown lost his majority in the Assembly, although through deft maneuvering was able to hang onto the speakership for another six months.[3]

There was even worse news for California Latinos. Resorting to a regressive tradition in the state's politics, Governor Pete Wilson hitched his difficult, come-from-behind reelection in 1994 to the aggressively anti-immigrant Proposition 187 and won both by wide margins. His signature campaign commercial used grainy, black-and-white footage of Mexican men "scurrying across the border" while a narrator intoned "they keep coming."[4] Art Torres, after 20 years in the legislature, gambled his seat and lost in a bid for the new post of state insurance commissioner, abruptly ending his career in elected office at the age of 48. The once-future Latino breakthrough governor began looking for another line of work.

There had been warning signs in the 1980s that thinly disguised racial appeals, issued from the platform of a statewide ballot-initiative campaign, could still be employed in California to undo progress and advance reactionary policies and politics, and that this strategy could be turned specifically on the increasingly visible Latino population. There would be more of this to come in the 1990s. At the same time, however, the combined Wilson and Prop. 187 campaigns had the unintended effect of further politicizing Latinos and spurring their entrance into the electorate as never before — now as a decidedly pro-immigrant and anti-Republican force. Days before the election, Los Angeles had its biggest protest march ever, made possible by the rise of Latino leadership and swelling ranks of immigrants in the city's resurgent labor movement. A historic threshold was crossed: the country saw, for the first time in American history, mass, organized resistance to deportations, repatriation pressures, and campaigns scapegoating immigrants. The nativists had unintentionally summoned 100,000 protestors into the streets of LA. Much more of this also lay ahead.

Driving this dialectic were both the accelerated immigration of the 1980s and its suddenly enlarged presence in the cities. Policy debates over undocumented immigration dating to the '70s had ultimately resulted in historic reform in the mid-'80s that legalized millions — legislation in which then-Senator Pete Wilson ironically played a major role.[5] This reform had far-reaching effects and greatly bolstered diametrically opposed social and political forces. On one hand, the large undocumented population was openly mobilized to acquire newly available legal status within a limited time period, and the immigrants became more assertive Californians as a result. On the other, Wilson stoked resentment and even alarm among whites, especially in Southern California, encouraging them to see the growing Latino population as a threat.[6] Many newly legalized migrants who did not already live there gravitated to major cities, at first between harvest periods and then dropping out of farm work altogether and settling down. An economic downturn completed the old recipe for an upsurge in nativist sentiment, but this time, unlike in the past, the Latino community was capable of organized resistance. As LA continued to attract immigrants, it had also attracted new leadership that fashioned the means to turn immigrant numbers into political power. Enter Maria Elena Durazo and Miguel Contreras. The last decade of the twentieth century would yet fulfill its promise of Latino empowerment in California and LA.

Labor and Love

THEIRS WAS A MIXED MARRIAGE, A UNION OF ONCE-OPPOSING SIDES in a historic dispute in organizing Mexican-origin workers. The role of Cesar Chavez and the United Farm Workers is by far the most famous dimension of Mexican-American labor organizing, but another, little-known current shaped some of the most important Latino leaders of our time in California. This latter movement, too, is associated with a legendary figure, leftwing activist Bert Corona, and his great cause that has loomed ever-larger with the years: the defense of undocumented immigrants. Chavez and Corona split bitterly over what to do about undocumented workers — whether to organize them or support their deportation.[7] The organized Latino community, including the UFW, would in time overcome past divisions and unite to defend the immigrants.[8] But the old dispute between Chavez and Corona would softly echo between Durazo and Contreras all the years they were together.[9]

In the middle of both the state and its vast San Joaquin Valley lies Fresno, the big city of the hot farming region. Most of California's agricultural production comes out of this valley, reliant on migrant labor of various origins since the late-nineteenth century. Grapes are the valley's signature crop — but overwhelmingly table grapes and raisins, not the wine grapes of the cooler coastal regions. Since the 1920s, mainly Mexican and Mexican-American farmworkers have brought in the harvests of grapes, other fruits and vegetables, and cotton.[10] The Durazo and Contreras families were among those farmworkers when Maria Elena and Miguel were born, in small towns just about a half hour to the northwest and to the southeast of Fresno, in the early 1950s.

The Durazo and Contreras children were part of their families' migrant farmworker crews from an early age. The intensity of summertime work and the need to earn enough money to get through the winter usually meant the Durazo children would start late at a different school every fall, as their family plied its trade, harvesting one crop after another, up and down the state. For months at time, the Durazos would sleep under a tarp in the back of their flatbed truck and occasionally in labor-camp tents. One summer, at a remote camp, the youngest of the children, Maria Elena's infant little brother, took ill and died before they could get him to a doctor.

Miguel's family, living on a ranch his father managed, was not migratory. When the UFW grape boycott peaked in 1970, the ranch owner, along with many other growers, capitulated and signed a contract with the union. The Contreras family became active in the UFW, with Miguel, still a teenager, serving on the ranch committee that his father headed. When the union contract expired in 1973, the ranch owner fired Miguel's father and his whole family. Miguel found himself blacklisted, unable to find work in the area. He had planned to go to college, but the UFW wanted him to work the renewed international consumer boycott in Toronto, where he spent three years.[11]

The Durazos had twice as many kids as the Contreras, which turned out to Maria Elena's advantage. Her father was proud and conscientious about his work, but believed strongly in education. Maria Elena was the seventh of her parents' 11 children. The family was able to settle down in Fresno as she and her next-older brother entered junior high. Their summers were still devoted to farm work, but she was able to attend a single Catholic school from eighth grade until finishing high school. By then her brother was the first in the family to go to college. His assistance and example helped her get into Saint Mary's College, just east of the Oakland hills, taking Maria Elena out of Fresno, the valley, and the fields for good.

Maria Elena's family knew about Cesar Chavez and the union he and Dolores Huerta founded, but they had already settled in Fresno when the UFW began extending their organizing work around the state. While Miguel was in Toronto working the grape boycott, Maria Elena was at Saint Mary's studying politics and Latin America. She entered college primed to be politicized, since her brother had taken her to a Chicano protest rally when she was still in high school. At Saint Mary's, and in occasional contact with nearby Oakland and Berkeley, Maria Elena learned about an organization called CASA and its founder, Bert Corona; his message of solidarity between Mexican-American and Mexican-immigrant workers was compelling.[12]

Corona had worked with Ed Roybal's Community Service Organization in the Bay Area, along with Fred Ross and Cesar Chavez, and later headed the Mexican American Political Association that Roybal founded in 1959. The younger Chavez, who went to school only as far as junior high, was emotionally, even spiritually, attached to rural life and identified strongly with his fellow Chicano farmworkers.[13] Corona, on the other hand, was born and mainly raised in inner-city El Paso, finished high school there, and won a basketball scholarship to attend USC in LA.[14] Bert worked urban union jobs all along and developed his own social consciousness and commitment — a studied internationalist, socialist outlook, and an unwavering belief that Mexicans and Mexican Americans were a single people who needed to unite to defend themselves and advance, without regard for borders. This viewpoint was central to CASA and became popular for a time in the 1970s among Mexican-American activists in LA and Chicago.[15] Corona's differences with Chavez were many; although he did not finish his college program, Corona would go on to teach at universities and had a number of published writings.[16]

* * *

AFTER FINISHING COLLEGE, DURAZO MARRIED AND SETTLED IN OAKLAND, but her interest in social activism continued developing. She was torn between her dream of becoming a lawyer and professional advocate for people like her family, which would take several years of law school, or plunging directly into workplace organizing. Her marriage to a man less interested than she in such causes ended in divorce and her move, along with her young son, to Los Angeles, where she had friends involved in CASA. In LA, Durazo could pursue both of her passions at once. She was hired as an organizer for a heavily immigrant union, and then also began attending People's College of Law, along with fellow CASA activists Antonio Villaraigosa and Gilbert Cedillo. The three came to fervently believe in solidarity with undocumented immigrant workers and the need both to organize them and redeem the historically nativist labor movement by turning it into an ally and champion of immigrant rights.

As she advanced in her legal studies, Durazo moved on from her first union gig to take a job at a law firm, but remained torn over her path forward. After a time at the firm, she was drawn back to working for a union, now for one of the firm's clients, Local 11 of the Hotel and Restaurant Employees, known as HERE. But to Durazo's dismay, she found that this local was not actually organizing workers, especially not the immigrants who now dominated the hospitality-industry workforce in LA; in fact, the local's old-guard, white, male leadership acted to marginalize immigrants in various ways. They refused to translate the union's printed materials into Spanish or provide translation at union meetings, and they maintained office hours that made it impossible for the local's members to access union services.[17]

In 1986, Durazo took a leave from her second union job to join in the coordinated field efforts of the California Democrats and Senator Alan Cranston's last reelection campaign, working under former UFW heavyweights Marshall Ganz and Jessica Govea. Considered the best in the business, Ganz and Govea's experience working the Eastside dated to the legendary Robert Kennedy campaign of 1968.[18] Democrats were fighting across the country to take back control of the Senate, lost in the Reagan landslide of 1980, and the 72-year-old, three-term "liberal war-horse" Cranston had to fend off a strong challenge from a much younger opponent, the high-tech, libertarian-leaning, entrepreneurial congressman from "Silicon Valley," Ed Zschau.[19]

Cranston's Latino field effort delivered critically needed votes, and the Democrats won more than enough seats that fall to retake the Senate. But even if the "Reagan Revolution" appeared to be winding down, the 1986 cycle also carried another, rather ominous, message. Already in 1984, California voters had approved, by a far greater margin than Reagan's reelection, the state's repudiation of the bilingual ballots provided for by the federal Voting Rights Act.[20] Now in 1986, the sponsoring organization, "U.S. English," and California voters went considerably further, amending the state constitution to establish English as the exclusive language of government.[21] In a seeming political paradox, in this same year Congress culminated a 10-year effort, extending from the Jimmy Carter administration to Ronald Reagan, to pass immigration reform, which Reagan cautiously held off from signing until two days after the November election.[22] Thus, while Congress and Reagan came to agreement on legislation that eventually provided "amnesty" for 2.7 million undocumented immigrants, California voters, with their two "largely symbolic" official-English ballot measures, "rehearsed language through which far more punitive attacks on immigrant rights would be made in the future."[23]

When Maria Elena Durazo returned to Local 11, the president of the union — whose position depended on keeping the immigrant majority among his members disempowered — and who was evidently fearful of Durazo's now-proven organizational abilities and formidable allies, became suspicious of her intentions and fired her. Durazo's moment of truth had arrived.

Jessica Govea, also from a Central Valley farmworker family, had given her life to the UFW but felt pushed out.[24] She reacted bluntly when Durazo recounted the story of her firing as a tearjerker: the local was just a few months away from a leadership election; if Durazo wanted to empower immigrant workers and reform unions that failed to serve them, this was her chance. She knew how. She needed to stop whining and get on with organizing the electoral overthrow of the local's useless board and president, which she then set about doing.

* * *

The big corner LA turned, as 1986 gave way to 1987, was hard to see at the time. But looking back, how these two years formed a hinge of history, how the developments in this stretch set up great social, political, and policy battles of the 1990s and 2000s, jumps out. A locally born and raised journalist writing for a prestigious East Coast paper characterized the rancorous 1986 dispute over the creation of an "ugly little Los Angeles City Council district" as a "war" between councilmen Richard Alatorre and Michael Woo. On one hand, the reporter saw this as "the first great battle of twenty-first-century California politics, a contest of Latinos against Asians in the state they will one day govern." But on the other, he called the redrawn district "a holiday gift from the city's black and Anglo leaders to their Latino and Asian colleagues, one more sign of how far the immigrant communities still are from real power."[25] State Assemblymember Molina jumped into the contest to represent that new District 1, made it, and joined Alatorre on the council in February. Corner turned.

And just as Republicans and Democrats in Washington were coming together to pass immigration reform in 1986, polling showed that nativism and racism were boosting the campaigns to recall the only Latino that, up to then, had ever been appointed to the state's Supreme Court, and to constitutionally enshrine English as California's sole official language.[26] Those winning forces in the balloting of November 4, 1986, were still celebrating when Reagan signed the immigration-reform bill two days later. The new law started a countdown to May 5, 1987, precisely six months out, the day undocumented immigrants could start applying for "amnesty."[27] A broad coalition was formed in LA to launch a campaign to urge immigrants to come forward, and to assist with their legalization; over 300,000 applications were filed in the Los Angeles district in the first five months.[28] Another corner turned.

Durazo was fired from her union organizing job in 1986, but came storming back to unseat the local's anti-immigrant leadership in 1987 — just as the campaign devised by the "amnesty coalition" to legalize LA's longtime undocumented residents was getting underway, and just as the city's demographically white century was coming to an end. Los Angeles had been founded in 1781 by people that historians of the region call "Spanish-Mexican" settlers.[29] A short century later, certainly by the 1870s, the city had an Anglo-American majority.[30] But

Miguel Contreras and Maria Elena Durazo at the Memorial Garden of the César E. Chávez National Monument, north of Los Angeles.

in 1987, when the process of legalizing the undocumented population was just starting — before both the drift of former agricultural workers to the cities and the boost to immigration by family members of the newly legalized — the long century of a majority "Anglo/white" LA came to an end.[31] Henceforth, no racial or ethnic group could claim to be the majority in Los Angeles.

The old-guard white leadership of HERE Local 11 apparently subscribed, and depended on, the supposed "unorganizability" of immigrant workers — especially the low-wage, Spanish-speaking recent arrivals that had come to dominate the hospitality industry of late.[32] When Durazo's insurgent slate won the election, the incumbents cried foul and called for national HERE officials to throw out the results. The national union sent a team of trustees to fix the broken local, most significantly among them, Miguel Contreras.[33] Although Durazo initially saw Contreras as illegitimately depriving her and her slate of their victory, she came to see that he intended to manage a transition period during which they could work together to reform the local. The process worked so well that they ended up getting married, and in 1989 Durazo again ran for and won the local's presidency by landslide.[34]

Déjà Vu All Over Again?

SOMETHING WAS AFOOT AMONG LATINOS IN LA IN 1986–87, but a range of officials and authorities kept missing it. Deukmejian's Department of Corrections thought it could build a prison in an urban area without the support of its elected leaders, but inadvertently set off a sustained community mobilization instead. Heads of a union thought they could hang onto power while treating their members with contempt, but sparked an insurgency that swept them away. Molina took office in February 1987, giving a part of the city transformed by new immigration from Central America something entirely new: an activist Latina representative on the LA City Council. Later that year, with the fight over the prison that she helped launch still intensifying, Molina was treated to an elaborate presentation of a regional agency's bold redevelopment plans for that Central-American immigrant neighborhood in her district. Bad move.

One of the immigrants to the MacArthur Park area, who arrived with his family from Guatemala as a child, brings a highly unusual perspective to what happened in his neighborhood.[35] When Gerardo Sandoval was growing up, the small park and surrounding area was the most gang- and crime-infested part of LA, and indeed one of the most violent in the country. Although it had its distinctive culture and a struggling "Mesoamerican" community, he disliked MacArthur Park's criminality, and he had the smarts to be able to leave LA altogether for his college and graduate school studies. What became known as LA's Metropolitan Transportation Agency, the mighty MTA, built a subway line running underneath the neighborhood, with a MacArthur Park station that opened in 1993, shortly before Sandoval left for college. In the years that followed, he became an expert in city and transportation planning and studied the impact of similar subway stations on neighborhoods as far afield as Chile and Japan.

Sandoval thoroughly expected LA's Metro Red Line to displace the low-income residents of MacArthur Park, redeveloping and gentrifying the neighborhood. His studies showed this to be a global pattern that accompanies major transportation systems in such urban areas. He could have predicted the sort of redevelopment plan that Metro authorities presented to Molina in 1987, and would have expected it, or something like it, to be carried out, with the effect of not only eliminating, or simply evicting, his old neighborhood's social problems, but also wiping out its Mesoamerican culture, incipient "ethnopolitan" economy, organic community institutions, and "immigrant milieu." But when he returned after a decade away, Sandoval was "extremely surprised to find that the Central-American neighborhood was still there but was very different from the one [he] had known."[36]

Sandoval was now an advanced PhD student in city and regional planning at UC Berkeley. He could instantly read the transformation he saw in MacArthur Park but was puzzled to find it this way — cleaner, with gang members and drug dealers no longer in sight, relaxed cops on bikes, street vendors now with attractively decorated carts who seemed "less apprehensive and more self-assured." Sandoval undertook to investigate the *revitalization* of MacArthur Park and the development of its "New Mesoamerican" community, instead of its expected gentrification, and devoted his dissertation and first book to this experience.

The young scholar found that a fundamental part of the new MacArthur Park story dated back to the meeting that LA Metro officials had with City Councilmember Molina in 1987, who was still relatively new at that point. He learned that they had developed their plan for the transformation of the area in conjunction with the opening of the subway station, but without regard for the existing community. A transportation expert for the city was in the room and recalled Councilmember Molina's reaction: "She was pretty upset."[37] The regional transportation agency's MacArthur Park redevelopment plan crashed and burned such that, in his research, Sandoval has had to "piece together" descriptions from interviews, because the plan itself is "nowhere to be found."[38]

What ensued from that point were years of tugging and pulling, redesigns and delays, community engagement and a process of mutual "adaptation and co-evolution between the neighborhood's endogenous organizations and city institutions." Sandoval attributes the revitalization of MacArthur Park's immigrant neighborhood, as opposed to its expected displacement, to a set of "critical factors," including the area's community organizations, which mobilized against gentrification, and the rise of "Latino citywide political power," which arrived in 1987 in the person of Gloria Molina. [39]

Invisible No More

MARIA ELENA DURAZO WENT ON TO LEAD HERE LOCAL 11 IN A SERIES OF CAMPAIGNS that succeeded in sparking the revitalization and reform of the labor movement in the 1990s, and in significantly changing Los Angeles. A three-year campaign of resistance to the Hyatt hotels' attempts to severely undercut employees' rights drew national attention and recast the image of Latina immigrant workers — previously considered the most unorganizable of all — as determined, courageous, and effective defenders of their own gains in the workplace. In an inspired burst of innovation, Durazo introduced high-profile civil disobedience tactics to the effort to pressure the Hyatt Corporation. Her strategy not only succeeded over Hyatt, it transformed her union and its members.[40]

A critical human resource for this breakthrough, uniquely available in LA throughout these transformative years, was the Rev. James Lawson, a legendary architect of the civil rights movement in the South. Lawson was the principal figure to introduce Gandhian tactics, strategy, and philosophy to the United States in the 1950s and 1960s, both separately and in collaboration with Dr. Martin Luther King. From his base in Nashville, Lawson was the premiere teacher of and trainer in nonviolent direct action for an array of future leaders of the movement and legions of their activist followers. He moved to Los Angeles in the 1970s, and in the 1980s trained a corps of new leaders who would come to the fore in LA in the following decade, including Durazo, Villaraigosa, and Cedillo.[41]

The "Rodney King riots" of 1992 made plain the exhaustion of Mayor Tom Bradley's leadership, coalition, and model of development focused on downtown LA. The poly-ethnic, black-Latino character of the mass looting that took place over several days revealed that, in economist Manuel Pastor's words, "this was as much a 'bread riot' as it was a 'race riot.'" The city's now-evident, multidimensional crisis set the stage for a self-described "tough enough" Republican businessman to succeed Bradley for two terms, but also for the emergence of a successor to Bradley's coalition, one that to be sustainable and ultimately come to lead LA, "would have to have the burgeoning population of Latinos at its core."[42]

In the early 1990s, Durazo helped bring together forces that, through multiple channels of organizing and mobilization, begat a broad coalition that culminated in the passage in 1997 of a "living wage" ordinance, by unanimous vote of a city council that went on to also unanimously override Mayor Richard Riordan's veto.[43] In the course of this effort, Durazo's husband Contreras was appointed political director of the Los Angeles County Federation of Labor, deepening an overall shift in the character and direction of unionism in the metropolis, and to a significant extent in its politics as well. The "County Fed's" secretary treasurer at the time had come to see that Latinos and immigrant workers were both a challenge and an enormous opportunity, and the only future for organized labor in LA. That leader, Jim Wood, was understood to be grooming Contreras as his successor, in a process that would likely take a decade. But Wood was stricken with cancer and died in 1996, precipitating a premature succession struggle. Contreras won the top position, shifting the transformation of LA labor and politics into a new gear.[44]

In addition to the success of the long-term living-wage effort, 1997 marked the first full implementation of a largely immigrant-labor-based strategy of electoral mobilization in LA. Durazo's Local 11 had been developing a multiphased approach to the union's role in elections, combining the promotion of naturalization of immigrants, registration of new citizens, and field campaigns to mobilize their votes.[45] The most innovative aspect was the training and deployment of noncitizen immigrants, including the undocumented, in voter-engagement operations such as phone banking, precinct walking, and the range of physical tasks of a campaign's field effort. In conjunction with Contreras, first in his role as the County Fed's political director and later as its secretary treasurer, Durazo succeeded in stimulating a new era of labor-movement electioneering in Los Angeles that has since been replicated elsewhere in the country — most notably in Las Vegas. "We have this vast army of activists," Contreras said in a filmed interview, "many of them who are undocumented here. . . . They can still help us get out the vote, help us educate the voters, they can still register voters, they can still go out there and get their relatives who are voters to come out and vote."[46]

Using this strategy, Contreras and Durazo were able to take election-campaign field efforts to new levels. By the 2000 election cycle, the County Fed was going after Republican members of Congress in potential swing districts with only a relatively small minority of Latino voters — and succeeded in knocking off two out of the three who were targeted. In the same cycle, Contreras unveiled a surprising weapon that would later, in Republican circles, become known as "getting primaried." Contreras targeted an incumbent Latino Democratic member of Congress who had been in office for 18 years, "who had an 80 percent union voting record, but you know what, 80 percent was not good enough for the kind of blue-collar district" he represented, Contreras explained.[47]

The next year, the County Fed put two thousand volunteers on LA city streets on a summertime local election day, walking precincts in an all-out push in the mayoral race. This effort to elect a union-man mayor — and the first of Mexican origin in Los Angeles since the 1800s — did not prosper in 2001, but the ground was laid for a future breakthrough.[48] Throughout the twentieth century, LA had been known as a company town, but back in 1910, San Francisco trade unionists had dubbed it more vividly, "in spite of its name . . . a *wicked city*."[49] The moniker has stuck as a historical point of contrast with what has so widely come to be called, for want of a better handle, the New LA.

* * *

PERHAPS THE WIDEST IMPACT THAT THE IMMIGRATION-BASED TRANSFOR-MATION of organized labor in Los Angeles had was in driving a change on immigration policy by the union movement as a whole. With Miguel Contreras in charge, the LA County Fed hosted the AFL-CIO's biennial national convention in October 1999. Unions representing immigrant-heavy labor sectors called for the AFL-CIO to follow their lead in organizing immigrants, supporting immigration reform, and junking its dated support for sanctions on employers found to knowingly employ undocumented workers. The national federation's leadership chose to put a committee in charge of examining the proposals and conducting forums on the issue around the country.

The County Fed took charge of organizing the labor immigration forum in LA, for which the designated committee would return. Scheduled for the old Sports Arena in Exposition Park, the Fed packed the venue with twenty thousand union members calling for immigration reform. When the AFL-CIO Executive Committee convened the following February in New Orleans, it adopted the immigration proposals as the federation's official policy.[50] Although a new immigration reform would prove to be politically fraught, this big institutional change on labor's part helped make possible a breakthrough in the tone and approach of the next Republican presidential nominee and his subsequent administration.[51]

In California, the Latino shift in labor also made possible a corresponding shift, most notably in the state Assembly, and later in the state Senate, and ultimately in Los Angeles mayoral politics. Since Contreras took over the LA County Federation of Labor, three Speakers of the California Assembly, a President pro Tem of the California Senate, and a two-term mayor of Los Angeles have been Latinos who emerged from the city's resurgent labor movement. Every aspect of anti-immigrant state law from the 1990s has been reversed. The city, county, state, and educational-district governments have established immigrant-friendly policies. LA's development model has been reformed to serve community needs. All this is a major part, but still only part, of the overall Latino power shift in Los Angeles, California, and the country.

Notes

1. The last such candidate, who in a single election won the Latino vote, the state of California, and the presidency, was Lyndon Johnson in 1964. Had he lived, Robert F. Kennedy might have done the same in 1968.

2. See online introductions to "the year of the woman," and other topics related to women in Congress at "The Year of the Woman, 1992," House of Representatives, Office of History, Art and Archives, http://history.house.gov/Exhibitions-and-Publications/WIC/Historical-Essays/Assembling-Amplifying-Ascending/Women-Decade/. For a summary of the 1994 cycle see Richard L. Berke, "The 1994 Elections: The Voters; Defections among Men to G.O.P. Helped Insure Rout of Democrats," *New York Times*, November 11, 1994, http://www.nytimes.com/1994/11/11/us/1994-elections-voters-defections-among-men-gop-helped-insure-rout-democrats.html.

3. Jacobs, *Rage For Justice*, 491.

4. See Daniel M. Weintraub, "Wilson Ad Sparks Charges of Immigrant-Bashing," *Los Angeles Times*, May 14, 1994, http://articles.latimes.com/1994-05-14/news/mn-57650_1_illegal-immigrants.

5. See Gibbs and Bankhead, *Preserving Privilege*, 77; and Waldinger and Lee, "New Immigrants in Urban America," 36–37. As a favor to the farm lobby, Wilson sponsored amendments to the Immigration Reform and Control Act of 1986 (IRCA) that extended legalization beyond longtime undocumented residents to hundreds of thousands of seasonal agricultural workers who were not settled residents in California.

6. See Chavez, *The Latino Threat*.

7. For an account that is both highly sympathetic to Chavez and the UFW as well as to undocumented migrant workers, see chapter 9, "The Mexican Dilemma," in Griswold del Castillo and Garcia, *César Chávez*. For Corona's account of the dispute, see chapter 15, "¡Raza Sí, Migra No!" in García, *Memories of Chicano History*. We treat this topic further in the next chapter.

8. See Gutiérrez, *Walls and Mirrors*, 190–203, and "'Sin Fronteras?,'" 16–17.

9. This section primarily based on authors' interviews with Maria Elena Durazo and Kent Wong; also, Wong and Viola, *Miguel Contreras*; Hillel Aron, "The Wage Warrior," *LA Magazine*, December 23, 2013, http://www.lamag.com/longform/the-wage-warrior/; Parker, "Hotel Workers Transform the Labor Movement," and other sources as noted.

10. The last great wave of non-Mexican migrant farmworkers was the Filipinos, who played a key role in the founding of the United Farm Workers union. With the Philippines under US colonial administration following the Spanish-American War, up to 1934, Filipinos were able to migrate to the United States as American "nationals," but like other Asian immigrants were barred from becoming US citizens; see Baldoz, *The Third Asiatic Invasion*. Other recent studies that also examine the interaction of Filipino and Mexican-origin workers in California include Ocampo, *The Latinos of Asia*, especially chapter 2, and Wald, *The Nature of California*, chapter 5.

11. Also based on "Beyond the Dream," interview with Miguel Contreras by Lyn Goldfarb, which she and her frequent co-producer Alison Sotomayor kindly made avail-

able. Goldfarb interviewed Contreras for her 2006 documentary *The New Los Angeles*; also see her tribute video *Miguel Contreras: Warrior for Working Families* (Los Angeles Alliance for a New Economy, 2005).

12. Acronym for *Centro de Acción Social Autónoma*, often paired with *Hermandad General de Trabajadores* (CASA-HGT) — Center of Autonomous Social Action – General Brotherhood of Workers — an association founded by Corona and others in Los Angeles in the 1960s as a Mexican-immigrant-focused mutual-aid organization, but one that in the 1970s attracted a new wave of formerly Chicano student-movement activists drawn to the defense of undocumented immigrants.

13. Chavez was born on the family farm near Yuma, Arizona, lost to foreclosure when he was 12. They moved to California in 1939 and became migrant farmworkers. Chavez was said to often talk about the loss; see Tony Perry, "Chavez Died Near Birthplace, Site of Property Lost in Depression," *Los Angeles Times*, April 24, 1993, http://articles.latimes.com/1993-04-24/news/mn-26700_1_cesar-chavez. On life on the Chavez farm see Pawel, *The Crusades of Cesar Chavez*, 7–14.

14. Significantly, Corona also lived for a time in his youth in Mexico.

15. See Garcia, *Memories of Chicano History*; Sergio Muñoz, "Guided by a Vision: How Bert Corona Met The Challenges of Latino Leadership," *Los Angeles Times*, October 9, 1994, http://articles.latimes.com/1994-10-09/books/bk-48092_1_bert-corona; and George Ramos, "Bert Corona: Labor Activist Backed Rights for Undocumented Workers," *Los Angeles Times*, January 17, 2001, http://articles.latimes.com/2001/jan/17/local/me-13397.

16. Corona's intellectual range is displayed in Hammerback, "An Interview with Bert Corona."

17. Parker, "Hotel Workers Transform," 88.

18. Ganz headed Cranston's field effort throughout the state, while Govea and Durazo worked the LA Eastside. Cranston had a deep background in political organizing and was unusually adept at soliciting campaign contributions. See Harold Meyerson's retrospective assessment, "The Organizer," *LA Weekly*, January 10, 2001, http://www.laweekly.com/content/printView/2132872. Govea's father was a leader of CSO in Bakersfield; as a child she accompanied him in his organizing efforts (Pawel, *The Crusades*, 358–59).

19. See James Ridgeway, "New Faces, Key Races, and Votes to Remember," *Mother Jones* (October 1986), 42; R. W. Apple, Jr., "California Senate Race Reflects Electronic Era," *New York Times*, October 19, 1986, http://www.nytimes.com/1986/10/19/us/the-political-campaign-california-senate-race-reflects-electronic-era.html?pagewanted=all.

20. Reagan won California in 1984 with 57.5 percent of the vote to Walter Mondale's 41.3 percent, but the state's Proposition 38, "Voting Materials in English Only," a declaration of sentiment to the federal government in opposition to the "language minority" mandates of the Voting Rights Act, passed by 70.5 percent to 29.5 percent; UC Hastings Scholarship Repository, California Ballot Initiatives and Propositions, Propositions, 938, http://repository.uchastings.edu/ca_ballots/; *David Leip's Atlas of U.S. Presidential Elections*, 1984 Presidential Election Data – National, https://uselectionatlas.org/.

21. Dyste, "Proposition 63." At the local level, English-only activists also sought to ban signs, billboards, and other advertising in Spanish. See also Frank del Olmo, "*Se Habla Inglés*: Prop. 63, a Cruel Joke, Could Cost Us Dearly," *Los Angeles Times*, August 28, 1986, http://articles.latimes.com/1986-08-28/local/me-13908_1_cruel-joke; also reprinted in Sotomayor and Beltrán-del Olmo, *Frank del Olmo*, 32–34.

22. For a detailed, meticulously documented account of this extended effort, see Osuna, "Amnesty in the Immigration Reform and Control Act of 1986," 153–61.

23. Martinez HoSang, *Racial Propositions*, 132.

24. On Govea see Elaine Woo, "Jessica Govea Thorbourne, 58; Organizer for UFW Sounded Alarm on Pesticides," *Los Angeles Times*, February 2, 2005, http://articles.latimes.com/2005/feb/02/local/me-thorbourne2; and Pawel, *The Union of Their Dreams*, 294–96.

25. Jay Mathews, "Los Angeles Election 21st Century Preview: Latinos, Asians Vie for Redrawn District," *The Washington Post*, February 1, 1987, https://www.washingtonpost.com/archive/politics/1987/02/01/los-angeles-election-21st-century-previewlatinos-asians-vie-for-redrawn-district/6d8a287a-66fd-49b6-8ab6-4c32fee8dd64/?utm_term=.e53f715081c0. Coincidentally, at the time Mathews filed this piece, he was also "stalking" (his word) and writing his book, *Escalante*, about the Garfield High calculus teacher who would be made famous by the movie of the same year, *Stand and Deliver*. Mathews celebrated Escalante's celebration of *ganas*, "a Spanish word that he said meant the urge to succeed," but took a more jaded view of the Latino drive for political representation and empowerment; see Mathews, "Jaime Escalante Didn't Just Stand and Deliver. He Changed U.S. Schools Forever," *The Washington Post*, April 4, 2010, http://www.washingtonpost.com/wp-dyn/content/article/2010/04/02/AR2010040201518.html.

26. George Skelton and Bill Boyarsky, "Racism Has a Hand at the Ballot Box: State's Minority Candidates Hindered by Bias, Studies Indicate," *Los Angeles Times*, August 24, 1986, http://articles.latimes.com/1986-08-24/news/mn-17293_1_racial-bias. Cruz Reynoso was the recalled Latino California Supreme Court justice; for a compelling portrait, see George Acero and Brian López, "Justice Cruz Reynoso: The Dawn of Justice for California's Latino Population," Sacramento County Bar Association, *Live Blog*, July 5, 2016, https://blog.sacbar.org/2016/07/05/justice-cruz-reynoso-the-dawn-of-justice-for-californias-latino-population/.

27. Per the terms of the Immigration Reform and Control Act of 1986, Public Law 99–603, also known as the "Simpson-Mazzoli" bill and the "Simpson-Rodino" act, after sponsors of two versions. See Humel Montwieler, *The Immigration Reform Law of 1986*.

28. See Ayón, "Mobilizing Latino Immigrant Integration"; and North, "Immigration Reform in its First Year."

29. See, for example, the preface and note on terminology in González, *Refusing the Favor*; Weber, "Spanish-Mexican Rim"; and Pitti, *The Devil in Silicon Valley*, ii, 16, 38.

30. Historians Philip J. Ethington, in "Spatial and Demographic Growth of Los Angeles," and Lawrence B. de Graaf, in "The Changing Face and Place of Race in Los Angeles City Government," differ on this question. According to Ethington, "Sometime in the middle of the 1870s the Anglo/white population became a majority in Los Angeles" (670); but

de Graaf writes, "The Anglo-American population . . . was swelled by the influx of former gold seekers and by 1870 was a substantial majority of the city's inhabitants" (730).

31. Pastor, "Contemporary Voice," 253.

32. For a breakdown of the components of "the myth of unorganizability," see Milkman, *L.A. Story*, 126–33. There was vivid evidence at the start of 1987 of growing assertiveness among undocumented immigrant workers in LA, in the form of a strike at a textile plant, prior to the Durazo campaign and election; see Stansbury "L.A. Labor & the New Immigrants."

33. Henry Weinstein, "Parent Union Takes Over at Troubled Hotel Local," *Los Angeles Times*, April 8, 1987, http://articles.latimes.com/1987-04-08/local/me-255_1_international-union.

34. Marita Hernandez, "Organizer Wins Post of President: Latina Leads Takeover of Union from Anglo Males," *Los Angeles Times*, May 6, 1989, http://articles.latimes.com/1989-05-06/news/mn-2087_1_durazo-s-english-union-from-anglo-males-maria-elena-durazo.

35. This discussion is primarily distilled from Sandoval, *Immigrants and the Revitalization of Los Angeles*. See also Sandoval, "Transforming Transit-Oriented Development Projects."

36. Sandoval, *Immigrants and the Revitalization of Los Angeles*, 11.

37. Ibid., 67.

38. Ibid., 258 note 26.

39. Ibid., xxiv.

40. Key sources for this discussion are Parker, "Hotel Workers Transform the Labor Movement." A parallel struggle also treated in *The New Los Angeles*, known as the "Justice for Janitors" campaign and developed in relation with locals of the Service Employees International Union (SEIU), also contributed significantly to reforming organized labor in Los Angeles from the 1980s to the 1990s. See Milkman and Wong, "'Sí, Se Puede.'"

41. Kent Wong, "Preface," in Wong et al., *Nonviolence and Social Movements*; Stephanie Ritoper, "Q&A: UCLA's Kent Wong on the Life and Legacy of a Longtime Civil Rights Activist," *UCLA Newsroom*, April 6, 2016, http://newsroom.ucla.edu/stories.

42. Pastor, "Contemporary Voice," 256–58.

43. For a general introduction to the living-wage policy concept, its implementation, and effects in several cases, see Levin-Waldman, *The Political Economy of the Living Wage*; the political story of the passage of the living-wage ordinance in LA is summarized on 154–67; see also Gottlieb et al., *The Next Los Angeles*, 45. For a more detailed assessment of the effects of living-wage ordinances, see Luce, "Living Wages, Minimum Wages, and Low-Wage Workers."

44. See Frank and Wong, "Dynamic Political Mobilization," 156–57; Harold Meyerson, "The Architect," *LA Weekly*, May 12, 2005, http://www.laweekly.com/news/the-architect-2139950; Ted Rohrlich, "Miguel Contreras," *Los Angeles Times*, January 31, 1999, http://articles.latimes.com/1999/jan/31/opinion/op-3359; Matea Gold, "L.A. Power Broker Faces Test," *Los Angeles Times*, March 21, 2005, http://articles.latimes.com/2005/mar/21/local/me-contreras21.

45. Refers to a special election in November 1997, discussed further in the next chapter. George Ramos, "Cedillo Beats Castro in 46th District," *Los Angeles Times*, November 20, 1997, http://articles.latimes.com/1997/nov/20/local/me-55960.

46. Contreras interview by Goldfarb, 33–34.

47. Ibid., 27.

48. The subsequent election of Antonio Villaraigosa as mayor is recounted in the next chapter.

49. Cited and discussed by Milkman in "New Workers, New Labor, and the New Los Angeles," 104–05; emphasis added.

50. Briggs, "American Unionism and U.S. Immigration Policy"; Contreras interview by Goldfarb, 29–30.

51. See Tichenor, "Splitting the Coalition."

CHAPTER 10

Eastside–Westside: To UCLA and Back

LA POLITICS LOOKED LIKE A TV RERUN WHEN 2005 GOT STARTED, WITH
THE SAME TWO CHARACTERS AS IN 2001 — both liberal Democrats — once again
battling for the town's highest office. But this rematch turned seismic for Los
Angeles and well beyond. The big story, here and for politically attuned Latinos
across the country, centered on a handsome and deceptively young-looking man
with an unusual name. At historic downtown gatherings and processions of civic
heavyweights, eyes this year were on Antonio Villaraigosa — for what his mayoralty might bring, certainly, but even more for what his ascendency would *mean*,
the broad shift in underlying power it revealed to the world. For half the year,
Villaraigosa was on a course to oust the sitting mayor of this fabled global city,
but the winding, sometimes treacherous road to his breakthrough had been under
construction since before he was born on LA's Eastside.

Just over a decade earlier, when Villaraigosa first ran for office, another Latino social and political quake sent shock waves from coast to coast. In the first
recorded instance of organized mass resistance to repatriation pressures, as many
as 100,000 Angelenos, mainly Mexican immigrants, marched against the ballot
initiative Proposition 187, a reactionary move that was itself born in this metropolis. Prop. 187, as it was called, would have denied nearly all public services to undocumented residents of California — a measure that, among other things, would
have expelled scores of thousands of immigrant children from the state's public
schools. More than anyone else, another young man from the Eastside made the
scale of this unprecedented protest possible: Gilbert Cedillo, then-head of Local
660 of the Service Employees International Union, representing legions of Los
Angeles County workers. Cedillo and Villaraigosa were high-school, college, and
law-school buddies turned political comrades and labor-movement "brothers."
Their achievements in real life early on surpassed their youthful dreams of changing and redeeming not just their own Eastside but all sides of LA and the world
beyond.[1]

Cedillo and Villaraigosa, joined after college by their movement sister from
the Central Valley, Maria Elena Durazo, and later also by Miguel Contreras, truly
marked the advent of a new generation of Latino activists in LA. Like many other
urban Mexican Americans of their era, Villaraigosa, the car club tough, and Cedillo, the varsity quarterback, came to call themselves Chicanos in their youth and

217

plunged into the Chicano student movement by their early college years. Tony became known as Antonio, and Maria as Maria Elena. Like most of their generation, they had fervently supported the United Farm Workers' cause; actively promoted the union's consumer boycotts; and regarded Cesar Chavez and Dolores Huerta with reverence. But unlike most, Villaraigosa, Cedillo, and Durazo were also shaped and forged by even more profound experiences and influences that combined to guide the rest of their intertwined lives. By the mid-1970s they shifted in their views and source of inspiration from Chavez to the more radical, intellectual, old-time activist leader Bert Corona, became members of the evolving organization called CASA that he founded in the 1960s, and began to identify as *mexicanos* rather than as Chicanos.[2] This transition was of a piece with a commitment to the defense of undocumented, Mexican-immigrant workers, and an insistence that there was no difference between Mexicans and Mexican Americans, who were all, in CASA's slogan, *un pueblo sin fronteras* — one people, without borders.[3]

Navigating LA's extraordinarily diverse worlds, networks, and communities of labor and politics took them far beyond the radicalism and *mexicanismo* of the 1970s, but they carried into the twenty-first century and onto the national stage an unwavering commitment to the cause of immigrant rights. And at each level — that of their unions, the metropolis, the mega-state, and the country — they would fully realize their predecessors' devotion to building and maintaining interracial and interethnic coalitions, which would remain as central to their new era of modern Latino politics as they were at the beginning, back in Boyle Heights.

Tony's Story

VILLARAIGOSA — "VIA LIKE VIA AIRMAIL, RYE LIKE RYE BREAD, AND GOSA," HE WOULD SAY WHEN RUNNING FOR MAYOR — hailed from an unincorporated, county-run barrio on LA's eastern fringe. The ironically named City Terrace, with wide views of Los Angeles from the outside, was symbolic of how the town's Mexican population had been shunted out of neighborhoods in and around what became the city's modern downtown, making way for the civic center, freeways, office towers, cultural palaces, and sports venues. Much as hills were leveled, and the erratic river sunk firmly into its assigned place, surging numbers of Latinos had been redirected to the other side of the concrete channel and even beyond city limits — for a good while, at least.

Villaraigosa's family moved east from Boyle Heights to City Terrace when he was four. About a year later, around the time he started kindergarten at a Catholic school, his immigrant father abandoned the family to return to Mexico. From then on, his was an English-speaking home, headed by his US-born and well-read single mom, Natalia. Antonio — known then as Tony — grew up bookish, as his mother made the local park off limits, to keep him away from gangs. Natalia was a secretary at a downtown financial firm. He was to go to the public library on City Terrace Drive every day after school. His mother believed in absorbing the classics. She especially loved *Black Beauty* and, when Antonio was in about fourth grade, she urged him to borrow and read it.

Antonio got home without the novel. He told his mother that the librarian refused to lend it to him, alleging that he was not capable of reading it. Natalia, furious, charged off to the library, confronted the librarian and had Antonio read aloud from the book. "She was a fighter like that for us," he would recall. Decades later, as mayor, Villaraigosa would return to his old neighborhood to speak at a grade-school morning assembly of two hundred students and tell them, "The *key*, everybody, the *key*: You've got to *read every day*."[4]

In all the years he spent there, Villaraigosa would remember only ever finding a single book about Mexican Americans. But in a corner of the library he found a section of books by and about black people, and he began learning about the civil rights movement. He would say he read them all, voraciously, and found themes in the books resonant with his mother's views and tastes. Back then, the neighborhood was still ethnically and racially mixed, and her diverse set of friends included Jewish and black neighbors. Natalia was a big fan of Sidney Poitier and his topical race dramas like *Lilies of the Field* and *A Raisin in the Sun*. These influences would follow Villaraigosa all the way to Cathedral High, where he became friends with African Americans on the football team and joined with them in creating the school's Black Student Union, before it had a Mexican-American organization.

After years of shining shoes as a kid, Villaraigosa had a paper route that took him to the top of the hills of City Terrace. He could not make it all the way without having to walk his bike, especially with the load of fat papers on Sundays. From there he lingered at the sight of downtown, marked by its lone white tower. City Hall was still the tallest building around, a familiar sight from *Dragnet*, and Sgt. Joe Friday's badge, but Villaraigosa did not know what it was.

Concerned about her son's lack of a father, Natalia worked at keeping Antonio busy and supervised by responsible men. She involved him in Boy Scouts, YMCA, and Boys Club. Nevertheless, Villaraigosa was unathletic and, he would think in retrospect, outwardly unmasculine, which got him picked on. He had two formative fights in junior high. In the first he got pummeled, never landing a punch of his own, but he refused to go down. In the second, right off the other guy hit him in the eye, nose, and mouth, drawing blood. Villaraigosa managed to hit him back hard in the face, which made the boy stop fighting and start crying. Later in life, Villaraigosa would often repeat what these fights taught him: every blow to the face hurts, but he knew he could take a punch; but not everyone else can take a punch, even if they can throw one. These lessons allowed him to defend himself and never shrink from a fight — and as a consequence, Villaraigosa had "dozens and dozens and dozens of fights."

The self-described "angry kid," quick to throw down, expelled from the last Catholic school he attended, Cathedral High, reported to Roosevelt High in Boyle Heights a month into the fall term of junior year. He showed up still dressed like a Catholic schoolboy, was promptly picked on by a gang member larger than him, and got into his first fight on his first day. Villaraigosa's considerable experience had developed his hand speed and a feel for the psychological dynamics of fighting. The other guy pulled the clichéd, deliberate run-in, knocking Antonio's books to the stairs, which he followed up with the challenge to meet him after school. Antonio, knowing the gang member would have friends there, immediately threw a flurry of punches, picked up his books, and walked away.

By spring of that academic year, Villaraigosa stopped going to school and failed all his classes. But Natalia's motherly anguish was the greater crisis for Villaraigosa, pushing him to go back to Roosevelt the next fall with the intention of climbing out of the hole he had fallen into, and still graduate with his classmates. The steep challenge he faced somehow combined with the desire to not let his mother down again, setting Antonio's life on a new course. And there was another element, one quite unlike Ed Roybal's experience at the same school four decades earlier, or Richard Alatorre's at Garfield, one that Villaraigosa would recall time and again in the course of his political career, including in his first mayoral inauguration address over three decades later: a teacher who cared.

Villaraigosa had the good fortune to connect with an especially committed high-school counselor. Herman Katz made the arrangements Villaraigosa needed to meet the requirements to graduate on time, taking classes day and night, including one taught by Katz. He would often grab dinner at Cedillo's house nearby, before returning to Roosevelt for his night classes. In the course of a grueling year, the counselor-teacher came to see Villaraigosa's ability, drive, and potential. Katz prodded the former dropout to apply to college and succeeded in getting him through the process and admitted into East LA College, the famous ELAC, starting immediately in the first summer session.[5] Continuing with his newfound discipline and determination got Villaraigosa admitted to UCLA as a transfer student the following year, where he reunited with his high-school friend Cedillo, who was just starting as a freshman.

Organizer of the Ball Box

ALL OF GILBERT CEDILLO'S GROWING UP WAS IN BOYLE HEIGHTS, and until he left for UCLA, sports were a constant influence. His father had been a competitive boxer since serving in the army, stateside during the Korean War, and he maintained a vigorous workout regimen. Following his father's jogs, Cedillo became a runner, developing speed and endurance that served him into high school. The main house he grew up in was on a hillside, propped up in back by stilts, leaving an open area under the house. His father worked out there, often on a speed bag, the rhythm of rapid punching and the bag whipping back reverberated through the house. The heavy bag and the rope jumping had their own steady rhythms but were not as noisy.

The grade-school playground gave Cedillo his first experience as an organizer. What peddling oranges door to door was for Richard Polanco, and selling dance lessons over the phone was for Gloria Molina, keeping track of sports equipment was for Cedillo, forming a template of order and discipline in his mind. In fourth grade he was put in charge of the big "ball box" cabinet, where all the playground gear was stored and locked at the end of the day. This was a big-deal assignment that distinguished Cedillo as a good student, and he performed in it. He devised a system for keeping track of all the balls and related gear — one that the neighborhood kids would deeply resent. He took a complete inventory, numbered the shelves and spaces in the cabinet, and drew up a chart that identified all the gear, to record the checking in and out of each piece. This resulted in a full box but put an end to the neighborhood kids' own sly system, which was to hide balls in the bushes so they could resume playing after school. The kids hated Cedillo's new playground order, but it got him recognized for "citizenship" at a school assembly. He was also given a special opportunity for enrichment activities during the summer, and without his knowing, he was placed in the small college track at his junior high.

* * *

CEDILLO'S FATHER WAS KNOWN TO THE NEIGHBORHOOD AS A TOUGH GUY, gruff and physically intimidating. He was a union man, a steelworker, who labored at a fearsomely noisy American Can Co. plant, where he was part of a racially diverse crew that constantly joked around like an army platoon. Cedillo benefited from his dad's athleticism, which underlay his own public-school career that culminated in making starting quarterback at Roosevelt. He enjoyed his dad's protection from gangs, which knew better than to touch him, at least since a big kid from the projects took Gilbert's baseball mitt and faced the scary Mr. Cedillo when he showed up at his home to retrieve it. And Gilbert enjoyed his dad's ban on his kids taking jobs, which gave him time to concentrate on schoolwork, sports, student government, and the special benefit in high school of the UCLA-based Upward Bound college-bridge and enrichment program.

His father's stern, imposing demeanor also meant little conversation at home, which made Gilbert into a quiet kid. But this, too, had an upside — it turned the boy into a reader. Like Villaraigosa, Cedillo developed the habit of regularly spending time at the public library in the neighborhood, this one named for the Scottish fabulist Robert Louis Stephenson, same as his junior high. But Cedillo's library experience diverged sharply from Villaraigosa's. The Stephenson librarian would have a stack of books ready for Cedillo to read every time he showed up. His parents were not equipped to help him with his homework, or introduce him to the world. Books took Cedillo out of Boyle Heights. His parents' role was to provide and protect. The full development of his potential would depend on his own efforts, and the influence of others.

Villaraigosa would remember Cedillo first seeing him at Roosevelt on his dramatic first day, precisely in his fight with the gang member. But Cedillo would recall first seeing Antonio in the middle of a crowd of students listening to him talk, true to his nickname at the time, "Tony Rap." Antonio would say that he earned this handle because other students saw that he could talk back to teachers like no one else.

Playing high-school varsity football, especially as starting quarterback, had a profound effect on Cedillo, imbuing him with a confidence that he would say makes athletes walk in a different way. In Boyle Heights, the greatest aspiration of male youth was to be a Roosevelt High Rough Rider — meaning to make the varsity football team — to be part of the program that took Mike Garrett from the projects *right there* and catapulted him to USC, a Heisman trophy, and the NFL, where he won a Super Bowl ring. The annual season-ending rivalry match with Garfield High of neighboring East LA, *el clásico*, as *La Opinión* called it, played at East LA College stadium, was said to be the most-watched, regular-season high-school game in the country. Cedillo found himself up against almost all his old teammates from his Pop Warner football days, who made Roosevelt suffer both times that he got to start in the East LA *Classic* in 1970 and '71.[6]

But if such a thing is possible, Upward Bound at UCLA would have an even greater impact on Cedillo than football. This particular program, another lingering benefit of the War on Poverty, was specifically geared to Mexican-American students. The summer he spent living in a dorm at UCLA for six weeks not only socialized Cedillo to college, it transformed him. He was in the middle of high school, between sophomore and junior year. Among the counselors in the program were two Chicano law students, future lawyer-leaders Antonia Hernández and Samuel Paz. Paz would have a stellar career as a civil rights attorney. Hernández would go on to battle the county hospital over sterilization abuse, serve under Ted Kennedy on the Senate Judiciary Committee staff, head the Mexican American Legal Defense and Educational Fund, known as MALDEF, and move its headquarters to LA. The two challenged Cedillo like he had never been challenged before, and made him see the world and his place in it in a new way.

For the first time, Cedillo not only learned a load of new material and perspectives, he also started to speak up, express himself, something that never happened at home. In a span of six weeks, he embraced a politicized, Chicano identity and returned to Roosevelt feeling himself to be a changed person. He would still play football and serve in student government, but those things no longer mattered like they had before — much less things like his friend Villaraigosa's car club. Like Esteban Torres in his return to East LA in 1968, but at a much younger age, Cedillo came to believe in the '70s that he was living in revolutionary times, and the part of the world he lived in was overdue for fundamental social change. He had mentally moved into the next phase of his life as a Chicano student activist and part of a movement, with a significant role to play in it, in Los Angeles, in

California, and in a couple of years, at UCLA. It would genuinely mean the start of the rest of his life, a political life, however many forms it would now take.

Go Westside, Young Man

VILLARAIGOSA GRADUATED FROM ROOSEVELT IN 1971 AND CONTINUED his academic comeback by going straight to East LA College. He saw less of Cedillo, who remained at Roosevelt and unexpectedly won the starting quarterback position for his senior season, but they still occasionally cruised together on weekends in Villaraigosa's '65 Chevy Malibu. Cedillo was set on going to UCLA; while at ELAC, Villaraigosa focused on getting grades good enough to transfer there. He put in his application during his first and only year as a junior-college student, instead of completing the usual two-year program.

Villaraigosa devoted his UCLA application essay to the story of his expulsion from Cathedral, the turn that sent him to Roosevelt and on a downward spiral until he hit bottom. But two years of disciplined, academic rehabilitation paid off. He had studied his own life story and was determined to become its author. Both Antonio and Natalia experienced his admission to UCLA as another turning point in his life, a fulfillment of her dream, and his proudest moment, even while acknowledging having benefited from Affirmative Action. "There he was, on the first day," Cedillo would recall of Villaraigosa, who had completed a triple jump from East LA — through Roosevelt, night school, and ELAC — to the Westwood campus. He began crashing, rent free, at the apartment Cedillo shared with other students.

For Villaraigosa, UCLA "opened up a whole new world," but for Cedillo, finally starting his coursework there marked a continuation of the path he had been on since entering Upward Bound two years before. Fully four decades earlier, Ed Roybal had taken a similar route, from Roosevelt to UCLA, but as an extension student. It so happened that Cedillo's first real job, starting the summer that followed his freshman year, was working for Roybal's original organization, CSO. Upward Bound helped Cedillo overcome his family's unfamiliarity with college, but he would still experience considerable personal as well as intellectual challenges.

Cedillo majored in sociology, a department dominated by radicals, and "really jumped into it." Among his classes, he took on a three-quarter graduate seminar on Marxism, directed more by its teaching assistant — a "brilliant" graduate student — than by the course's esteemed professor. The class plowed through Marx's *Capital* and grappled with its economic "formulas." Being good at math, the algebraic expressions did not intimidate Cedillo, but he observed quietly, "trying to learn the language." He knew he was the only one in the seminar to have seen the inside of a factory, but he did not invoke his background, family, or experience in the discussions. The teaching assistant, however — who wrestled with being a Marxist from a wealthy family — saw promise in Cedillo that transcended his own academic radicalism.[7]

Unlike most UCLA undergrads, Cedillo started a family and became a father by his sophomore year. Now it was his turn to stop going to school. He moved back to Boyle Heights and tried to figure out how to properly start a family. The phone rang near dinnertime one day at his parents' small, crowded home. The radical grad student TA had tracked Cedillo down. "You need to come back," said the voice over the phone. "You *get* this. I can *never* go to where you can go. You need to do this. You get how this works, and you can use this to help your people." The intervention took Cedillo by surprise and left him amazed. He was in low spirits, and had never before received such validation from "someone so prominent." Without that call, Cedillo would have likely "rerouted," perhaps switched to ELAC, the reverse of Villaraigosa's progress. He returned to UCLA the next quarter.

Villaraigosa had withdrawn from almost all extraneous activity during his two-year academic detour. But once having made it to the university, he started getting involved again. Now, however, he was in a whole new context. In the late 1960s and early '70s, UCLA developed into a stronghold of Chicano-movement activism. It was in fact because of the larger movement that Cedillo had enjoyed the benefit of access to the university via Upward Bound, and arguably that he and Villaraigosa were admitted to the school: UCLA's recruitment and admission of Chicano students soared the year after the 1968 Eastside high-school walkouts.[8] In short order, the university established a Mexican American Cultural Center on campus and a "Zapata Center" in Boyle Heights. The cultural center took on research and pedagogical functions; in 1970, it launched the academic periodical *Aztlán: Chicano Journal of the Social Sciences and the Arts*, and in 1971, it developed into the Chicano Studies Center.[9]

Also in the aftermath of the high-school walkouts and a series of conferences of students and Chicano youth, the university's United Mexican American Students organization joined the movement to rebrand all such groups with the name of MEChA.[10] Both Antonio and Gilbert became *mechistas*, developed as campus leaders, and were drawn into community-based efforts as well. A campaign to aid the legal defense of a trio of East LA activists in the projects known as "Los Tres," and to protest their criminal convictions and sentences, became the conduit by which numerous Chicano students and former students became further radicalized and started looking for an ongoing vehicle for their politics, beyond the campus.

Cedillo and Villaraigosa in LA, as well as Durazo in Northern California and many others in this period, wound up landing in CASA, which they participated in for several years out of college in the late 1970s. The wave of earnest, new, ex-student movement *casistas* adopted and intensified CASA's ideological and organizational commitment to defend and serve Mexican immigrants, especially the undocumented. This commitment would endure after internal divisions led to the demise of the organization, which meant that Durazo, Cedillo, and Villaraigosa had to keep looking for ways to realize their ideals.

Be the Best

IN THE 1980S, AFTER COLLEGE AND CASA, VILLARAIGOSA, CEDILLO, AND DURAZO became students again, and then again, first by attending what the *New York Times* called the country's only radical law school, a few blocks west of downtown LA, in the gritty, inner-city neighborhood of MacArthur Park. And later they participatied in a study group led by "civil rights icon" James Lawson, at his South Los Angeles church.[11]

Peoples College of Law was born in 1974, as the long Reagan era in state politics was coming to an end, the year Nixon was pushed out of office, when the first lawsuit was filed against LA County Hospital for sterilization abuse, and when for the first time Chicanos were leading a new effort to incorporate East LA as a city.[12] Law seemed to matter more than ever. "Radical criminology" and unaccredited law schools were flowering in California.[13] This was also the year that Rev. Lawson moved to LA to assume leadership of the "church of the bells," United Methodist, at the north edge of South LA.[14]

A progressive criminology movement had emerged at UC Berkeley and launched the journal *Crime and Social Justice*, based in San Francisco. At the same time, community activists and radical lawyers of the National Lawyers Guild in LA hatched a plan and raised money for a Guild Law School, which became formally named Peoples College of Law, an institution designed to be run by the students themselves. Ten years later, around the time that Durazo, Cedillo, and Villaraigosa were completing their legal studies there, PCL's admissions-and-recruitment officer declared the school to be "a dream and an ideal now realized." The organizers had aimed for two-thirds students of color, half women. The sort of pitch these former student activists responded to, as articulated by this administrator writing in *Social Justice*, was, "If you are an activist who would use your law degree as a tool of justice to represent the poor and oppressed, Peoples College of Law would like to hear from you."[15]

Cedillo, for one, applied to mainstream law schools, but felt blackballed for his radical political activism, the stances he had taken, and enemies he had made. But PCL sought in its recruits what other schools frowned upon. Villaraigosa, Cedillo, and Durazo answered the call and entered PCL within a year of each other, went on to begin working for labor unions, also within a year of each other, and continued drawing deeply from the currents and reserves of social knowledge and experience swirling all around them in 1980s LA. They would become the law school's best-known and most influential graduates, key players in shaping the politics of today's Los Angeles and California.

It may have been inevitable, with what was going on in LA in the 1980s and '90s — waves of Central-American refugees and migrants from Mexico; the transformation of the workforce and expansion of the low-wage economy; deepening inequality and rising nativism — that socially and politically committed Latinos like Durazo, Villaraigosa, and Cedillo would be drawn to labor issues and

---

First Person: Gilbert at Peoples College of Law, Day One

We had a guy named Sam Rosenwein . . . who had argued more cases at the Supreme Court than anybody. The casebook on the Constitution and the First Amendment, was his cases. He was a founder of the National Lawyers Guild. . . .

Right at the beginning, the first thing he said, "Look, if you don't aspire to be the best attorney in the country, if you don't aspire to represent your clients at the Supreme Court, you shouldn't be here. This school is about representing people who don't have a voice — you're going to be their voice. You should aspire to be the very best. They've already got enough problems . . . they don't need a poor lawyer." It was intimidating in some respects.

The first lesson in our Con Law course — this is Sam Rosenwein, a giant — he starts talking about World War II, the Soviet Union, the United Front against Fascism . . . I'm sitting there thinking this is really fascinating . . . but what the heck does this have to do with Con Law?

He does this whole deal that takes us to when that period ended and McCarthyism started, and then took us to the First Amendment. He took us all over the world and then brought it all back to the First Amendment, the fights to defend it and to expand it, the rights to organize, to unionize, to express yourself. It was just amazing. The guy was great, brilliant, and had a big influence.*

---

* For more on Rosenwein, see Rosenwein interview by Balter.

---

organizing. With the union movement in long-term decline across the country — a decline accelerated by Reagan — and with union leaders painfully out of touch with the new workforce, the whole landscape of labor relations needed shaking up. From a social-justice point of view, such as that shared by these ex-mechistas and ex-casistas, the times desperately called for new grassroots leaders with new approaches and skills, new or renewed movements, and perhaps even something that could be called a "new economy."[16]

Power Shift on the County Board

THE REAGAN JUSTICE DEPARTMENT'S SURPRISING VOTING-RIGHTS LAWSUIT on behalf of Latinos and against the city of Los Angeles in late 1985 was looking less remarkable by late summer 1988, when MALDEF and the ACLU of Southern California decided to stop waiting for the DOJ to similarly sue LA County. The two rights groups had prepared to join the expected suit challenging the county's 1981 board of supervisors districting plan, as they had successfully sued LA for its city council plan, and settled out of court in 1986. The DOJ's Civil Rights Division had informed the county in May of its intention to sue.[17] But by the end of August, with no indication as to when the Justice Department would act, if at all, MALDEF and the ACLU decided to go forward on their own with their class-action suit on behalf of Latino voters against the supervisors.[18]

It appeared not entirely coincidental that the Reagan administration, after having loudly trumpeted its support of the Voting Rights Act, chose to use it first against the city of LA, which was led by a council dominated by Democrats, and a Democratic mayor who was challenging a Republican governor in elections the next year. Now, however, the administration appeared to be dragging its feet on the way to suing a county board dominated by Republicans — the conservative-majority board that controlled the biggest county in the country.[19]

Half a month later, the Justice Department joined the MALDEF-ACLU suit, and the case went to trial in 1990.[20] Along the way that year, the heavyweight creator and leader of the county board's conservative majority, Supervisor Pete Schabarum, decided to retire after 18 years.[21] Schabarum's decision not to run again, in the midst of historic litigation in which he was heavily implicated, signaled that the conservative political era was ending in the county. The coming transition was ratified by the federal judge presiding over the case, who ruled for the plaintiffs.[22] That year's elections in Schabarum's district were cancelled, the district lines were redrawn, and a new election was set for early 1991, in a district designed to be predominantly Latino. That is when a new dynamic took over LA county politics.

In retrospect, it seems almost foreordained that Molina would run to represent the new district and complete a trifecta: first Latina in the California Assembly, on LA City Council, and on the LA County Board of Supervisors. The real question would be: who would oppose her? It seems scripted that Molina and the man she once walked precincts with, now-Senator Art Torres, who provided her with a professional start in politics, who was married to one of her best friends and hired her as his administrative assistant when he was elected to the Assembly, and who supported her first run to succeed him in that seat, would come full circle to oppose each other. A clash of titans was on, two veteran elected officials, both seen to have a great future ahead. The trifecta would not be denied, and on Friday, March 8, 1991, Molina was sworn into office by Congressman Edward Roybal, who had been kept from taking the same office in 1958 by a controversial series of recounts.[23]

As of Molina's first supervisor meeting the following Tuesday, for the first time in 10 years the board flipped from having a 3–2 conservative majority to 3–2 liberal majority. Two weeks later came the first heated showdown and "significant shift in county policy," according to the *Los Angeles Times*, for which a crowd of activists filled the hearing room in anticipation. Policy substance and heavy symbolism aligned, as the preceding conservative decade on the board coincided almost perfectly with the 10 years since the first report, by the Centers of Disease

Control, attempting to diagnose what would later become understood as AIDS, first detected in five Los Angeles men.[24]

On the board's agenda was a program that conservatives had blocked for years — kits of condoms and bleach to be distributed to intravenous drug users. In the previous 10 years the county had counted 11,534 people with AIDS, over two-thirds of whom had died. Although healthcare is a county responsibility, the city of Los Angeles, "tired of waiting for the county to act," stepped in with 100,000 kits. Now one of those city liberals was on the county board, aiming to change its course. Of the four male supervisors, the only one who did not attend Molina's swearing-in, conservative Mike Antonovich, said that "any supervisor who voted for distributing bleach and condoms to drug addicts was 'subsidizing the drug culture.'" Molina cut him off, declaring, "That is absolute nonsense," and accused the man of calling for more study of the program just to delay it. "We don't interrupt each other here," Antonovich shot back. "This is not the city council," he added, according to the *LA Times*, "red faced." The program won the vote and the crowd of AIDS activists "rose in a standing ovation," one of them proclaiming, "It's a new day at the county."[25]

Toward a New Economy: "The Most Astonishing Civic Transformation"

THE SAME YEAR THE "DREAM LAW SCHOOL" AND *SOCIAL JUSTICE* were launched, the Reverend James Lawson came to Los Angeles to lead an African-American congregation committed to progressive social change — which is why they hired this civil-rights-movement veteran. Lawson, with his multiple graduate degrees, got to work learning the local scene, and in the 1980s convened a study group at his church that amounted to an ongoing master class on social-justice philosophy, strategy, and tactics. As mentioned in the last chapter, these sessions involved Villaraigosa, Cedillo, Durazo, and others, as they continued preparing themselves to reshape and employ the labor movement to reform LA and its economy and empower its new Latino immigrant workforce.[26]

Around the same time, while also trying to study for the bar exam, Cedillo was drawn by a friend into taking a job as an organizer for the biggest union in town, Local 660 of the Service Employees International Union, representing over 40,000 workers — half of the LA-county government labor force. It so happened that Kent Wong, another friend and fellow student at PCL, headed the union's legal department. With his training at the same law school, Cedillo was soon promoted to legal, where his regular duties centered on weekly appearances at hearings of the county's Civil Service Commission.[27] In late 1990, as complicated contract-renewal negotiations approached, the union local's deeply divided board — primarily split between blacks and whites — suddenly turned to Cedillo, a talented, articulate young Latino, to serve as interim general manager. Cedillo got over his shock and took on the more-than-daunting challenge. Fortunately for him, in the preceding years he had become an avid reader of the business literature on leadership, departing dramatically from his radical college and CASA days.[28]

As the deadline for renewal of 21 separate contracts in a variety of departments approached, representatives of the county stunned Cedillo and his team by reneging on the deal they had already reached. Cedillo and his staff undertook frantic consultations with all of the local's diverse bargaining units. They devised a plan to pressure the county with an unpredictable series of one-day strikes by different segments of the workforce at a time, a strategy they dubbed "rolling thunder."[29] The battle was on and altogether dragged on week after week.

At a high point in the crisis, legendary septuagenarian County Supervisor Kenneth Hahn loudly insisted that he and the county board could settle the dispute directly with "Gil," the young and green, but well-spoken general manager. In a public hearing room full of reporters, Hahn demanded, "Get Gil in here! We'll settle it with Gil!" And thus, the contract dispute came to be settled, Gilbert Cedillo henceforth became known as Gil, and Local 660, headed by a Latino, emerged as the undisputed great power of labor in LA.

* * *

IN 1991–1992, SOCIAL-JUSTICE AND LATINO-EMPOWERMENT EFFORTS were making significant progress in LA, but were decidedly in a race against time. Before the political disaster of Proposition 187 for Latinos in 1994, the social disaster of the Rodney King riots exploded in 1992. The riots that broke out on April 29 on the Southside, which spread widely and continued for nearly a week, were the worst in US history.[30] But the primary election held less than a month after the smoke cleared set both the Eastside and the state on a course to a political leap into the future.

The coincidence of a presidential race with the first election cycle following a census and redistricting both offered new opportunities and relatively high Latino voter turnout. Assemblymember Richard Polanco had taken control of the Chicano Legislative Caucus in the Capitol, rebranded it as Latino, recruited candidates, and vigorously supported their campaigns. Polanco's efforts helped double the number of Latino assemblymembers, from four to eight, as well as LA County's Latino representation in the Assembly, from three to six, most importantly helping to launch Martha Escutia's political career, representing the county's southeast cities.[31]

A further significant, but not as apparent, aspect of the 1992 electoral cycle was that it was the first of the new era of term limits imposed on the state legislature by Proposition 140, which passed in 1990. This ballot initiative was also the first of the reactionary propositions of the '90s in California, sponsored by the rightwing power on the LA County Board of Supervisors, Pete Schabarum, as his last angry blow for conservatism in the state.[32] Prop. 140 was an undisguised attack on Willie Brown and "professional politicians," a venting of frustration with

Governor Jerry Brown signs the first (AB130) of two bills known as the California Dream Act on the back of the historic legislation's author, Assemblymember Gilbert Cedillo, at Los Angeles Community College in July 2011. (ZUMA Press, Inc./ Alamy Stock Photo.)

his long speakership of the Assembly, and more.[33] The initiative was intended to hobble the state legislature as a policymaking body, not only by severely limiting time in office, but also by cutting its operating budget by half.[34] But the big unintended effect of Prop. 140, according to an expert assessment of the succeeding half-dozen electoral cycles, was that it "accelerated trends of increasing female and minority representation that were already underway in California."[35]

The term limits established by Proposition 140 helped open a new era of Latino empowerment in California in combination with Latino population growth, redistricting, and the electoral mobilization orchestrated by Assemblymember and Latino Legislative Caucus Chairman Polanco. The advances of 1992 were dramatic but still in line with the pattern of increased Latino officeholding every 10 years, following redistricting. But the subsequent years showed sustained increases in Latino representation, without the usual 10-year lull. Almost immediately, in 1993, Polanco and the caucus helped Cruz Bustamante win a special election in an Assembly district representing Fresno — the first Latino legislator elected north of Los Angeles since 1972. In the course of less than a year, the caucus was suddenly established as a power unto itself in California politics.

Durazo's and Cedillo's success in the labor movement and the growing ranks of Latino elected officials, set against the decline of older forces such as Roybal's CSO and MAPA, and the United Farm Workers, constituted a remade Latino political landscape in the state. With enormous support from Cedillo's big, well-financed SEIU local, Villaraigosa would be the first of the three to make the leap to elected office in 1994. Three years later, with even more labor support directed by Durazo and her HERE Local 11, Cedillo would make his own leap and join Villaraigosa in Sacramento, where he would serve for 14 years.

In 1996, before Cedillo got to the Capitol, Polanco and the Latino Caucus provided a critical assist in taking control of the Assembly back from the Republicans. The payoff came when a member of the caucus, Cruz Bustamante of Fresno, became the 62nd Speaker of the California Assembly, and the first Latino. It was widely understood that the Latino Caucus, under Polanco's leadership, opted to

*Gilbert Cedillo, then in the state Senate and in the midst of a years-long estrangement from his high-school friend Antonio, received a public service award from LA Mayor James Hahn and City Councilmember Villaraigosa, on behalf of the city of Los Angeles and at the close of the city's celebration of Latino Heritage Month, 2003. (Photo by Myung J. Chun/*Los Angeles Times *via Getty Images.)*

promote one of its members with centrist (and Central Valley) appeal, and avoid pitting the LA area against the San Francisco/Northern California region in the bid for the first Latino Speaker. But with Villaraigosa positioned next to Bustamante as majority leader, the next step in the LA-based Latino quest for empowerment was only about 14 months away.

Cedillo was in the Assembly in February 1998 when Villaraigosa was elected Speaker, a position Villaraigosa held for over two years. By the time his speakership ended, it was clear what Villaraigosa's next move would be — a run for mayor of Los Angeles in the new century, 2001. When he embarked on his greatest leap of all to that point, Villaraigosa's friend and comrade Durazo would still be with him, but by then he and Cedillo, each other's oldest friend in politics, going back to high school, had parted ways. That rift would not be healed for a good many years.

Notes

1. This chapter is primarily based on multiple, original, separate interviews with Gilbert Cedillo, Antonio Villaraigosa, Maria Elena Durazo, Gloria Molina, Monica Lozano, and Kent Wong, as well as additional sources as noted.

2. In addition to Gutiérrez, *Walls and Mirrors*, and his "Sin Fronteras?" cited in the last chapter, the rise and fall of CASA in LA is summarized in Pulido, *Black, Brown, Yellow, and Left*, 117–22. *Sin Fronteras* was also the name of CASA's newspaper, edited by Carlos Vásquez, one of CASA's top leaders, then based at the UCLA Chicano Studies Research Center.

3. The classic statement of this identity shift is the essay "On Culture" by UCLA Prof. Juan Gómez-Quiñónez, first published in *Revista Chicano-Riqueña* in 1977 and expanded as a widely circulated booklet of the same name published by the Chicano Studies Research Center. In Spanish, terms such as *mexicano* are not capitalized.

4. Kevin Roderick, "Pop Star Mayor," *Los Angeles Magazine* (December 2006).

5. See Matea Gold, "His 'Second Chance' Shaped Villaraigosa," *Los Angeles Times*, May 31, 2001, http://articles.latimes.com/2001/may/31/local/me-4669; Robin Abcarian,

"Spotlight on a Longtime Villaraigosa Supporter," *Los Angeles Times*, July 2, 2005, http://articles.latimes.com/2005/jul/02/entertainment/et-teacher2; Brenda Gazzar, "Herman Katz, Long-Time Los Angeles Educator, Lived a Life of No Regrets," *Los Angeles Daily News*, June 14, 2015, http://www.dailynews.com/2015/06/14/herman-katz-long-time-los-angeles-educator-lived-a-life-of-no-regrets/.

6. See Mario Villegas, "A Classic for Many Reasons," ESPN.com, November 4, 2010, and the documentaries *Symbol of Heart* and *The Classic*.

7. The course professor was himself a caustic critic of his professional world of American, university-based Marxism at that time; see Horton, "A Contribution to the Critique of Academic Marxism."

8. See Rosalio Muñoz oral history interview in García, *The Chicano Generation*, 227. LA Mexican-American leaders complained angrily that War on Poverty programs early on overlooked their community's needs, which in California had a larger poverty population than the black community. Upward Bound, in particular, was launched in 1965 with 17 pilot programs, none of which were in California. See National TRIO Clearinghouse, "Do You Know TRIO? A TRIO History Fact Sheet," The Pell Institute for the Study of Opportunity in Higher Education, no date. Sal Castro, the teacher at Lincoln High School who catalyzed the student walkouts of 1968, was hired later that same year to direct the new UCLA Upward Bound program; see García and Castro, *Blowout!*, 236.

9. See UCLA Chicano Studies Research Center, "About the CSRC," last accessed October 6, 2017, www.chicano.ucla.edu/about. The journal subsequently twice modified its name, setting on *Aztlán: Journal of Chicano Studies*; see Lomelí, "Revisiting the Vision of Aztlán," 18, 23 fn. 38. The journal's most important offerings can be sampled in the three editions of Noriega et al., *The Chicano Studies Reader*.

10. Acronym for *Movimiento Estudiantil Chicano de Aztlán* (Chicano Student Movement of Aztlán); see Gómez-Quiñónez, *Mexican Students Por La Raza*; Muñoz, Jr., *Youth, Identity, Power*; García, *The Chicano Movement*; Acuña, *The Making of Chicana/o Studies*.

11. On the eve of Barack Obama's first inauguration as president, *Time Magazine* interviewed Lawson as one of "seven icons of the civil rights movement"; see "James Lawson — Civil Rights and the Obama Presidency," January 26, 2009. Lawson was a northerner who moved to the South at the request of Dr. Martin Luther King, Jr., where he spent 17 years in the civil rights movement; see "James M. Lawson (1928–)," *King Encyclopedia*, The Martin Luther King, Jr. Research and Education Institute, Stanford University, http://kingencyclopedia.stanford.edu/encyclopedia/encyclopedia_contents.html; and Heidi Hall, "Civil Rights Advocate James Lawson Was Rooted in Faith," *The Tennessean*, October 27, 2013, http://www.tennessean.com/story/news/local/2017/03/02/civil-rights-advocate-james-lawson-rooted-faith/98605166/.

12. A personal-injury lawsuit on behalf of three young women, *Andrade v. Los Angeles County*, was filed and reported on in late 1974, the year before the class-action suit discussed in chapter 8; see Mike Goodman, "3 Women Ask $6 Million from County in Sterilization Claim," *Los Angeles Times*, November 21, 1974.

13. According to an unbylined story in the *New York Times*, in its second year, PCL was "one of 36 unaccredited evening law schools that have sprung up in the last few years in California," charged $350 per semester, offered free childcare, but had trouble meeting its enrollment goals of half women and two-thirds black and Chicano students ("A Radical Law School Enters Its 2nd Year," October 16, 1975).

14. See Sharma, "The Philosophy of Nonviolence," 6–16; Ritoper, "Kent Wong"; and Slessarev-Jamir, *Prophetic Activism*, 56–57, 98–113.

15. See Gomez, "Peoples College of Law." On the focus of the journal see Schwendinger, "Editorial." This journal is often referred to simply as *Social Justice*.

16. The idea of a "new economy" is something of a double or even triple entendre in the useful analysis by USC Professor Manuel Pastor and his colleagues Chris Benner and Martha Matsuoka in *Something Big*. On one hand it is suggestive, as they say, of the "glitter of high-tech," but on the other, the social costs of deindustrialization, the decline of unions, and the growth of low-wage manufacturing and service sectors. They note the loss of over 300,000 manufacturing jobs in LA County between 1990 and 2005, and the decline of average hourly wages among the remaining jobs in that sector by over 12 percent between 1989 and 2002. This restructuring of the local economy was accompanied by the increase of over 200,000 immigrants in the workforce in the 1990s, concentrated in low-wage, nondurable goods manufacturing and services. This second sense of a "new economy" of declining fortunes set the stage for the various efforts described both here and in their earlier book to achieve what might be called a *reformed* new economy, which in LA required the mobilization, organization, and empowerment of Latinos and immigrants, in coalition with other social forces (111–12).

17. Victor Merina and Ronald J. Ostrow, "U.S. Sues to Get New Supervisor Districts Drawn," *Los Angeles Times*, September 9, 1988, http://articles.latimes.com/1988-09-09/news/mn-1925_1_senior-justice-department.

18. Victor Merina, "Latinos Sue, Charge Bias in Districting by Supervisors," *Los Angeles Times*, August 25, 1988, http://articles.latimes.com/1988-08-25/local/me-1323_1_latino-voters.

19. The White House invited leaders of all major civil rights groups — overwhelmingly made up of critics of the administration's civil rights record — to Reagan's signing of the 25-year extension and strengthening of the VRA in 1982. The president even seemed to have the VRA's use in the Southwest in mind when he said, "To so many of our people — our Americans of Mexican descent, our black Americans — this measure is as important symbolically as it is practically." See Howell Raines, "Voting Rights Act Signed by Reagan," *New York Times*, June 30, 1982, http://www.nytimes.com/1982/06/30/us/voting-rights-act-signed-by-reagan.html; and Herbert H. Denton, "Reagan Signs Voting Rights Act Extension," *The Washington Post*, June 30, 1982, https://www.washingtonpost.com/archive/politics/1982/06/30/reagan-signs-voting-rights-act-extension/b59370f1-fc93-4e2f-b417-2b614ea55910/?utm_term=.e28705682a12. According to author Peter Skerry, the 1986 suit against the city was "widely regarded as a Reagan administration move to embarrass Democratic mayor Tom Bradley, then running for governor" (*Mexican Americans*, 332).

20. *Garza v. County of Los Angeles*, Cal., 756 F. Supp, 1298 (C.D. Cal. 1991); Merina and Ostrow, "U.S. Sues."

21. Richard Simon, "Schabarum — End of an Era," *Los Angeles Times*, March 3, 1991, http://articles.latimes.com/1991-03-03/local/me-353_1_board-members.

22. Richard Simon, "Judge Finds Anti-Latino History," *Los Angeles Times*, July 26, 1990, http://articles.latimes.com/1990-07-26/news/ti-625_1_latino-history-judge.

23. Richard Simon, "Molina Sworn In as Supervisor," *Los Angeles Times*, March 9, 1991, http://articles.latimes.com/1991-03-09/local/me-2084_1_county-government.

24. Laurie Lucas and Susan Abram, "35 Years Ago, the AIDS Riddle Unraveled in Los Angeles," *Los Angeles Daily News*, August 28, 2017, http://www.dailynews.com/2016/06/04/35-years-ago-the-aids-riddle-unraveled-in-los-angeles/.

25. Amy Pyle, "AIDS Bleach, Condom Program OK'd," *Los Angeles Times*, March 27, 1991, http://articles.latimes.com/1991-03-27/local/me-965_1_intravenous-drug-users.

26. This discussion based on original interviews with UCLA Labor Center Director Kent Wong and with Gilbert Cedillo, as well as Ritoper, "Q&A: UCLA's Kent Wong"; Gayle Pollard Terry, "James Lawson: Standing Up for Rev. King's Beliefs — and His Convicted Killer," *Los Angeles Times*, January 19, 1997, http://articles.latimes.com/1997-01-19/opinion/op-20095_1_james-lawson; and Wong, et al, *Nonviolence and Social Movements*.

27. Chris Coates, "The Bridge Builder: Downtown-Based State Senator Gil Cedillo Has Made Skid Row a Focus, and the Work is Only Beginning," *Los Angeles Downtown News*, April 3, 2006, http://www.ladowntownnews.com/news/the-bridge-builder/article_8d67d551-f734-5296-b125-c8e72069cb86.html.

28. Cedillo would recall being "amazed" to discover that there was such a thing as leadership studies, and credited this literature with giving him the vocabulary he lacked but needed to understand and explain his own role. In discussing a number of business-leadership gurus and their books, including Lee Iacocca, Robert Green, John Maxwell, and others, Cedillo said, "Warren Bennis saved my life." But most of all, he came to embrace Robert Greenleaf's philosophy of "servant leadership," and established that as the model for his team and subsequent career in politics.

29. Irene Wielawski and Eric Malnic, "Nurses Vote to Return but Threaten a New Walkout," *Los Angeles Times*, October 31, 1991, http://articles.latimes.com/1991-10-31/news/mn-747_1_county-public-works-employees; "Strikes Cripple Los Angeles Hospitals," *New York Times*, October 30, 1991, http://www.nytimes.com/1991/10/30/us/strikes-cripple-los-angeles-hospitals.html; Richard Simon and Irene Wielawski, "Resumption of Strike Threatened," *Los Angeles Times*, November 7, 1991, http://articles.latimes.com/1991-11-07/local/me-1315_1_county-employees.

30. For a comprehensive examination from a range of perspectives, see Gerdes, *The 1992 Los Angeles Riots*.

31. See Becker, Hughes, and Morin, *The History, Development, and Policy Influence of the California Latino Legislative Caucus*.

32. See Swatt, *Game Changers*, chapter 12, "1990: Californians Punish Lawmakers with Term Limits," 233–51; Davis, *City of Quartz*, 133, 179. In an unsigned official edi-

torial the *Los Angeles Times* called Schabarum "a self-styled last angry man" and his 18 years in county office "a landmark conservative domination of the board." See "Post Pete: Let's Make a Deal?" *Los Angeles Times*, March 13, 1990, http://articles.latimes.com/1990-03-13/local/me-16_1_latino-leaders.

33. See Tribune News Service, "California's Proposition 28 Would Let Legislators Serve Longer Stints," *Governing: The States and Localities*, May 24, 2012, http://www.governing.com/topics/politics/Californias-Proposition-28-Would-Let-Legislative-Leaders-Serve-Longer-Stints.html.

34. Prop. 140 also stripped legislators of retirement benefits; see Paul Jacobs, "California Elections/Proposition 140: Initiative Cuts More Than Term of Office," *Los Angeles Times*, October 28, 1990, http://articles.latimes.com/1990-10-28/news/mn-4898_1_term-limits.

35. See Public Policy Institute of California, "How Have Term Limits Affected the California Legislature?," *Research Brief* 94 (2004), http://www.ppic.org/content/pubs/rb/RB_1104BCRB.pdf.

Part IV

The Latino Century

PART IV

The Latino Century

ON A SUNNY SPRING 2006 AFTERNOON, HUNDREDS OF LOS ANGELES LEAD-ERS, activists, and hotel housekeepers gathered by the old entrance to Paramount Pictures, the arched gate immortalized in the 1950 classic *Sunset Boulevard*.[1] After a reception charged with anticipation, they filed into the big studio-lot theater a few steps away for the premiere of *The New Los Angeles*, a documentary on the city's makeover from a politically conservative and exclusively WASP-led past to its progressive, multicultural present and future. Different segments of the crowd came to see something new: a movie about themselves and *their* version of LA.

The filmmakers strove to overcome a stubborn problem of the media-saturated and image-obsessed city, one memorably articulated in an interview early in the film: "*Los Angeles is a city that is profoundly invisible to itself.*"[2] The challenge of making visible the struggles, personalities, and achievements of a vast global city's working people and its reformers was daunting. The documentarians set out to tell key parts of the story of LA's transformation using the 1973 election of Mayor Tom Bradley as the pivot of modern LA social and political history. But the city's story kept unfolding in the course of their project. The filmmakers found themselves drawn to document the most recent dramatic turn in LA's ongoing evolution: the Latino political breakthrough and the associated rise of a vital, new, immigrant-based labor movement — thus the presence of the hotel housekeepers and their union leaders, also featured in the new film. Topping things off, Antonio Villaraigosa, elected mayor the year before, was on hand to speak. The image of the new LA had taken a somewhat different hue.[3]

Bradley famously led a black-Jewish coalition and served a record 20 years as mayor, although his legacy was tarnished toward the end by the Rodney King riots of 1992.[4] Following his second reelection in 1981, Bradley was at the peak of his power and favored to be elected governor the following year. Had he won the governorship while Willie Brown was still early in his record-breaking tenure as Speaker of the Assembly, California would have become the great national exemplar and stronghold of black political power and achievement. But Bradley lost both of his campaigns for governor, in 1982 and 1986.

Latinos were a junior part of Bradley's Los Angeles coalition, although increasingly important over time, especially after Richard Alatorre joined the city council at the end of 1985. Two white mayors followed Bradley, both indicating

Seen at Antonio Villaraigosa's inauguration, on the steps of Los Angeles City Hall, July 1, 2005. (Photo by David McNew/Getty Images.)

and contributing to a decline of black political clout in LA. *The New Los Angeles* filmmakers were committed to the story of Bradley's impact, but could not ignore what had emerged since the 1990s as LA's ascendant social and political narrative: the rise of Latino leadership and the mobilization of that community. They were fortunate that the key Latino figures they chose to highlight in the film, labor-warrior Maria Elena Durazo and her union-man-turned-politician ally Antonio Villaraigosa, acknowledged their great debt to the black civil rights movement. The film was able to cast LA's new Latino-empowerment narrative as an extension and renewal of the cause that Bradley and civil rights activists had pioneered.

During the screening, contingents of LA's various collective identities, some overlapping, some bunched in different parts of the theater, erupted in cheers when their heroes appeared onscreen — blacks for Bradley, labor for Durazo and her late husband Miguel Contreras, Latinos for Villaraigosa — and they united in booing former Governor Pete Wilson, though not all with equal vigor. The film described the new mayor as having assembled a Bradley-style multiracial coalition, and he was heard saying that he stood on the giant's shoulders. The documentary ended on this note of vindication of the Bradley legacy, but palpable tension hung in the air between the factions in the audience. The film was premised on the need to redress insufficient recognition and appreciation of Bradley, but there seemed to be more than a hint of Latino triumphalism in the final cheers for Villaraigosa's recent but also historic win. The new mayor rose to speak and addressed the tension.

Some people are saying, "It's our turn now," Villaraigosa began, easing into the unease in the room, "but it's not about that." He let his words sink in, allowing supporters to realize he intended to challenge such thinking. "It's about *change*," he said, referring to population shifts. "Today it's Latinos, but in a hundred years, it could be . . . Chinese." The unease seemed to move from one part of the theater to another. Villaraigosa then posed a question softly before answering it firmly, "And you know what? *It will be ok.*"

LA's narrative had changed, the youthful mayor seemed to be saying, and would continue to change. *Embrace the change.*

Notes

1. Steven Blingen calls Paramount's Bronson Gate the most famous in the world and "Hollywood's Arc de Triomphe" in his book, *Paramount.* The studio's double-arched Melrose Gate, which mimics the older Bronson, is mistaken by tourists and passersby for the gate of *Sunset Boulevard* fame. The single-arched Bronson is set back on the expanded studio lot and barely visible from the street.

2. From an interview with Harold Meyerson in *The New Los Angeles*, produced and directed by Lyn Goldfarb.

3. Account based on personal observation and Lynn Smith, "United in Their Hope for the City's Future: A Screening of the Documentary 'The New Los Angeles' Hits Home for a Diverse Audience of Civic Leaders, Activists and Workers," *Los Angeles Times*, April 21, 2006, http://articles.latimes.com/2006/apr/21/entertainment/et-newla21. Lyn Goldfarb and Alison Sotomayor went on to make another documentary that delves more deeply into the Bradley story, *Bridging the Divide: Tom Bradley and the Politics of Race.*

4. Sonenshein, *Politics in Black and White*; on the impact of the riots on Bradley, see 223–24.

CHAPTER 11

Delayed Dawn

In a state that has been dominated for more than two decades by white voters who lack confidence in public institutions and elected officials, nothing could have as profound an effect on politics and policymaking as trust among the growing Latino electorate.
—Mark Baldassare
Public Policy Institute of California[1]

THE MOST ELECTRIFYING CAMPAIGN RALLY VETERAN JOURNALISTS HAD SEEN unfolded in UCLA's fabled Pauley Pavilion and on live TV, Sunday morning before the 2008 "Super Tuesday" primary elections. What the *New York Times* called a "pitch-perfect event" featured Michelle Obama, Caroline Kennedy, Oprah Winfrey, and California First Lady Maria Shriver on a platform in the middle of the arena, surrounded by thousands of cheering supporters. Most media reports failed to note another woman on the platform, a national co-chair of the Obama campaign, a legendary Latina union leader who was about to ascend to what she had helped develop into one of the most powerful positions in California and in all of American labor.[2] Maria Elena Durazo, who introduced Kennedy, had led her burgeoning union of hotel and restaurant workers to endorse Barack Obama for president. She was the only one on stage with the proven ability to mobilize and deliver thousands of votes precisely where needed to decide elections, but much of the coverage of the rally rendered her invisible.[3]

Durazo's role in helping Obama secure the Democratic nomination was especially notable in a campaign in which the great majority of prominent Latino leaders across the country were committed to his primary opponent — and that opponent was a supremely qualified woman. Los Angeles was home to another such Latino exception in this primary season, state Senator Gilbert Cedillo, but this spectacular UCLA event was most of all by and for women. Recognition of Durazo and LA Latino labor's role in securing the nomination and presidency for Obama was not long in coming.

Still in 2008, a month before his first inauguration, President-elect Obama named Eastside Congressional Representative Hilda Solis his choice for Secre-

Michelle Obama, Caroline Kennedy, Maria Shriver, Oprah Winfrey, and Maria Elena Durazo at UCLA campaign rally in February 2008, two days before the "Super Tuesday" primary elections. (© Lisa O'Connor/ZUMA Press.)

tary of Labor, which made her the first Latina member of a president's cabinet in American history.[4] Solis, who had been among the Latinas and Latinos who served in the Carter administration and were sent back to California following the 1980 Reagan landslide, returned to Washington in 2001 as LA labor's candidate in a successful effort to "primary" a Latino Democratic member of Congress deemed insufficiently supportive of a working-class agenda.[5]

Four months into his presidency in 2009, Obama would on one day nominate the first Hispanic to the Supreme Court, a Latina New Yorker, Sonia Sotomayor, and on the next name another legendary LA Latina leader, Vilma Martinez, to be US ambassador to Argentina. The close, sequential timing of these announcements was not coincidental. Like the Obamas, both women were renowned, Ivy League lawyers. As a federal judge, Sotomayor did not endorse candidates, but Martinez, like Durazo, was a prominent Latina who came out in support of Obama in 2008. In her stellar career, Martinez had led the Mexican American Legal Defense and Educational Fund for a dozen critical years and had herself once been a contender for nomination to the Supreme Court.[6] The leading Latino candidate at that time was, like Sotomayor, a Puerto Rican jurist and a New Yorker, but Latino leaders and organizations failed to unite behind him.[7] Obama's temporal coupling of the Sotomayor and Martinez nominations with consensual Latino support marked both a breakthrough in American jurisprudence and a historic, attention-getting advance in Latino empowerment.[8]

Three years later, President Obama would announce an executive action protecting from deportation potentially over a million undocumented immigrants brought to the country as children — a cause equally dear to Durazo and Martinez.[9] This interlocking complex of support in an election campaign, on one hand, with high-level presidential appointments and dramatic policy change on the other, offered vivid evidence of the consolidation of national Latino politics significantly anchored in LA Latino political clout — institutional clout exemplified in 2008 most of all by the bold leadership of Durazo. But those still unfamiliar with the rise of Latino political power, its history, personalities, and nuances — including much of the media — did not know who that fifth woman was on the platform at the UCLA rally, why she was there, or how it mattered.

Recessions, Upheavals, Advances

IN SPITE OF THEIR GREATER NUMBERS, LATINOS IN CALIFORNIA IN THE EARLY 1990S were widely seen as, at best, politically lagging behind their counterparts in Texas. Prominent LA-based Mexican-American academics even argued that, compared with San Antonio, LA's Eastside was not truly a community.[10] In a separate, massive study, also comparative with San Antonio, a non-Latino scholar portrayed Mexican Americans in Los Angeles as pursuing a flawed and dysfunctional political strategy.[11] At worst, demographically changing California was a "Paradise Lost," in the process of becoming "Mexifornia," with Los Angeles as "capital of the Third World."[12] Multiple books argued that Mexican Americans, rather than seeking inclusion, equality, or civic integration and empowerment, were plotting with Mexico to affect a "*reconquista*" of the US Southwest.[13]

The eminent Harvard political scientist Samuel Huntington gave these once-fringe views a patina of scholarly respectability when he argued that there was a "trend toward cultural bifurcation" of the country, the "driving force" for which "has been immigration from Latin America and especially from Mexico." "Mexican immigration," he wrote, "is leading toward the demographic *reconquista* of areas Americans took from Mexico by force in the 1830s and 1840s, Mexicanizing them in a manner comparable to, although different from, the Cubanization that has occurred in southern Florida." Huntington portrayed Mexican immigration as a threat to American national unity, and as "blurring the border between Mexico and America, introducing a very different culture." As such, he held that Mexican immigration fundamentally "differs from past immigration and most other contemporary immigration" to the United States.[14]

Unbeknownst to Huntington, however, by the turn of the century what actually happened in California is that panic over demographic change subsided, even as Latino empowerment in the state surged ahead of that of Texas. The ongoing statewide survey of the authoritative Public Policy Institute of California (PPIC) began charting key trends in 1998. Like many other surveys, for several years it detected among the general population high and rising levels of distrust of government and growing pessimism about the future. But it also found a countervailing trend — that the state's burgeoning Latino population was strikingly optimistic and, of all groups in the state, expressed the highest level of trust in government. "Latinos may offer the best chance of changing the politics of government distrust that have dominated California politics for 20 years," PPIC survey director Mark Baldassare declared in 2002.[15]

Baldassare went on to see in the combined Latino political and demographic rise a transformation of politics in California. "The year 2000 was a turning point and could be viewed as the beginning of the 'Latino Century' for the state," he maintained. "Not only in sheer population size but also in shifts in public attitudes and political significance, there were signs that Latino growth was having statewide effects."[16] But Baldassare's heralding of a major Latino impact on California's politics at that time was at least premature and perhaps of two minds. He made much of the success of the 2000 election ballot initiative, Proposition 39, which made approval easier for local school bonds, as signaling perhaps a historic break with the anti-tax political culture established in the 1970s by Proposition 13. Baldassare rightly credited Latino, black, and Asian-American votes for making possible a narrow win "after two earlier defeats by an electorate dominated by whites, demonstrating the possibilities of new multiracial/ethnic coalitions in the state."[17]

Yet Baldassare recognized that economic conditions were key; the late-1990s prosperity enjoyed through the 2000 election cycle, which allowed for greater acceptance of demographic change, had as its counterpart the early 1990s downturn and anti-immigrant sentiment that produced Proposition 187 in 1994. "The ability to achieve any real, significant changes," he observed, "probably rests on the success of current efforts to improve the state's public educational system and on the hope of future periods of prosperity."[18] He did not know then that 2000 was the peak year of the "dot-com bubble" of the still-young high-tech economy. The extended collapse of that bubble, accelerated by the terrorist attacks of September 11, 2001, had severe consequences for California and the country. It especially roiled state government and politics; by 2003, the previous years' budget surpluses turned into crisis deficits projected at $35 billion over two years.[19]

Though Governor Gray Davis had managed to be narrowly reelected in 2002, as the crisis mounted, he was recalled 11 months later. Twice Davis had vetoed bills introduced by Cedillo to restore the ability of undocumented immigrants to obtain driver's licenses. But, in an effort to shore up Latino support ahead of the recall election in 2003, Davis signed a revised version of the bill. Republican movie-star Arnold Schwarzenegger's recall success that fall allowed him to immediately take office and intimidate the Democratic-controlled state legislature into repealing Cedillo's driver's license bill before it could take effect.[20]

Even less foreseen than the collapse of the dot-com bubble was the greater financial crisis yet to come in 2008, which would produce the "Great Recession" and turn Schwarzenegger's second term into a calamity nearly as bad as his predecessor's. That downturn would be so severe and so further contribute to political gridlock that a sense of chronic governmental crisis would become widespread among analysts and politicos. California would come to be seen as having experienced a "decline and fall" and as a politically "failed state." Analysts and policymakers increasingly saw the need for profound, constitutional change to turn the state around.[21] Nevertheless, as severe and fundamental as the state's recurring crises seemed to be, the intense nativism of the early 1990s did not return — at least not in California. Schwarzenegger's march to victory in 2003 was, in the first instance, launched on the basis of popular discontent with a tripling of the annual car registration fee, which he rescinded as his first act, right after his inauguration.[22] The Austrian-born actor's political termination of a freshly re-elected governor was certainly symptomatic of a crisis in California government and politics, and in the process he pledged to repeal the driver's license bill; but, this retrenchment, as frustrating as it was to Latino leaders, was not a full-blown replay of Prop. 187 or Pete Wilson's 1994 anti-immigrant campaign. In certain ways, however, the front end of the Schwarzenegger phenomenon in 2003–2005 in California seems to have anticipated the rise of Donald Trump in the rest of the country a dozen years later.[23]

Taming the Terminator

FEBRUARY 2004: WITHIN THREE MONTHS OF TAKING OFFICE, THE NEW GOVERNOR had to start contending with a new Speaker of the Assembly strongly backed by organized labor. Fabian Núñez, the first-term Latino member, was a former immigrant-rights activist and union leader representing Eastside and downtown Los Angeles. In the normal course of business in Sacramento, governor and Speaker were expected to negotiate the state budget and major legislation, but Schwarzenegger stormed into office swaggering and mocking, calling lawmakers (mostly Democrats) "girlie men" and vowing to upend the Capitol and its ways.[24]

Schwarzenegger immediately launched into governing in the style he was elected, by successfully sponsoring major initiatives in the March primary that came up right away, and using the threat of more such measures to bully the legislature into acquiescing to his demands. Núñez — young and green but a former high-school boxer — resisted loudly, leading Schwarzenegger to forge ahead with his plebiscitary strongman tactics to legislate without the legislators. Conservatives across the country, like columnist George Will, noted the irony of century-old Progressive Era reforms, such as the recall and referendum supposedly meant to empower the citizenry, being used "to magnify the power of the most powerful person in the state, the governor," who he characterized as "a mega-celebrity who can move multitudes to sign petitions to get propositions on the ballot, and who can attract millions of dollars to pass them."[25]

With back-to-back successes in the recall and the primary, Schwarzenegger was on a roll and kept on campaigning, taking official positions on the majority

of propositions that would be at issue in the next election in November and raising vast sums for a variety of committees to advance his agenda. His string of
wins with this approach led the governor to then go even further, opening 2005,
a nonelection year, with a call for the legislature to enact a new set of reforms in
a special session. He threatened to use his power to decree a special election to
take his spending, redistricting, and other proposals to the voters if the legislature
failed to act as he demanded.[26] Were he to succeed again in 2005, as he had in
2003–04, Schwarzenegger would have been, historically, the "most transformative" governor, positioning him for reelection in 2006, and reverberating across
the country.[27] Speculation extended to the possibility that a Republican Congress
in Washington "could suddenly get excited about a constitutional amendment to
allow immigrants to run for president."[28]

Núñez, however, maintained his resistance, made clear he would campaign
forcefully against any special election, and attended to the work of building the
coalition that could stop the governor.[29] Among the many avenues he pursued
or simply found himself on, one would prove to be historic: marriage equality.
Núñez had made a deal in 2004 to avoid having his Democratic majority vote on a
same-sex marriage bill during that election year. In early 2005, the Speaker added
his name to the reintroduced bill authored by San Francisco Assemblymember
Mark Leno. The gay marriage measure was approved by Assembly committees
and put to a floor vote in June. Although the bill was favored 37 to 36, it fell four
Democratic votes short of the majority of at least 41 of the full 80 members of the
Assembly required to pass legislation. Gay rights advocates were "incensed" that
Núñez failed to prevail upon a recalcitrant handful of his 48-member majority to
support the bill, but the story would not end there.[30]

The marriage equality measure, considered hazardous to Democratic lawmakers facing reelection in 2004, looked more like "a political weapon aimed
at California's Republican governor" in 2005, for whom "the politics of gay
marriage" were "a no-win" — especially if he intended to take his pet ballot
measures to the voters in the fall.[31] The bill's failure on June 2 appeared to give
Schwarzenegger a reprieve on that front, and less than two weeks later, in a Mon-
day-night address to the state from his office, the governor decreed the threatened
special election for November.[32]

Leno and Núñez proceeded to quietly reintroduce a renumbered gender-neu-
tral marriage bill, otherwise identical to the previous measure, and allowed it to
pass the state Senate at the end of summer before bringing it back to the lower
house. On the Tuesday following Labor Day 2005, the traditional first business
day of a fall campaign, debate on the reborn bill began in the Assembly and went
into the night. This time, much greater effort was employed to reach a different
result, with former Speaker Willie Brown working the halls of the Capitol while
freshly elected Mayor of Los Angeles (and also former Speaker) Antonio Villaraigosa worked the phones. The "Religious Freedom and Civil Marriage Protection
Act" squeaked by without a vote to spare, 41 to 35. "When the final vote was

called," the *San Francisco Chronicle* reported, "there was a moment of stunned silence before supporters broke out in cheers. Leno grabbed Assembly Speaker Núñez, D-Los Angeles, in a bear hug and lifted him off the floor with glee."[33] In the aftermath, there was widespread recognition that, as the *New York Times* reported, "it was a final drive by prominent Latinos and African Americans that ultimately moved [the bill] from the legislature to Mr. Schwarzenegger's desk."[34]

With a precedent going back to Richard Alatorre's support for Willie Brown's "Consenting Adult Sex" bill in the early 1970s, Latino and black leaders again succeeded in defining marriage equality as a civil rights issue and California as a national leader in social progress.[35] The governor now faced a dilemma: to accept the first legislation passed in the country on this issue that was not forced by a court decision, or to veto it. Schwarzenegger's constant conflicts with legislators, unions, and minority groups combined throughout the year with his endless campaigning to steadily erode his standing in the polls. Vetoing a measure that Californians were now evenly split on would not help him either in the special election that fall or in the general election in 2006. But between those two tests with the general electorate, he would have to face Republican primary voters — Republicans *only* — for the very first time; failure to veto a bill opposed by every Republican legislator in Sacramento would hurt him in that small, partisan arena dominated by far-right activists.

The governor chose to veto — and went on to lose on every proposition in the special election two months later.[36] That debacle forced Schwarzenegger to change course and from then on govern in a more normal manner, largely in negotiation with Núñez — whom he had previously dismissed as a "punk."[37] The muscle-bound, action-star governor would in time come to call the diminutive Speaker "one of my closest allies," but his turnaround and reconciliation with Núñez did not appear foreordained.[38] The Speaker was blunt the day after the election, saying, "You can't just move on. . . . Lessons have to be learned," moving a *Sacramento Bee* reporter to write that Núñez "sounded as if he were threatening retribution." [39] The Speaker went further in an interview with a onetime hometown newspaper, declaring that "all of the governor's economic theories of strangling government in order to balance the budget on the backs of schools and public servants failed miserably."[40]

Schwarzenegger dramatically pivoted days later in his next State of the State address, delivered before the entire legislature at the end of the first week of 2006. Núñez and the governor were seated directly next to each other behind the podium until Schwarzenegger got up to speak. Standing at the Speaker's rostrum, he tried to sound apologetic without explicitly apologizing, his opening remarks tracking closely with the Speaker's recently quoted pronouncements. He was quick to acknowledge "the mistakes I made and the lessons I've learned," adding "I have absorbed my defeat and I have learned my lesson." In case that was not sufficient, he went on to say that the people "always have the last word" and that they "sent a clear message." "So to my fellow Californians," Arnold intoned at his most contrite, "I say — message received."[41]

Substantively, in a significant break with conservatism, Schwarzenegger went on to outline a grand vision of investment in public works, his "Strategic Growth Plan for California's Future," premised on a plethora of needs: "We need more roads, more hospitals, more schools, more nurses, more teachers, more police, more fire, more water, more energy, more ports . . . more, more, more."[42] The first phase of his plan would involve $70 billion in bonds spread over the next 10 years to be leveraged for an investment of over $200 billion, which would need approval by the voters. In his speech, the governor also called for an increase in the minimum wage and ended with special recognition of Senator Martha Escutia, with whom he had worked to have California become the first state to ban sodas and junk food in public schools.

Democratic legislators were enthused with the governor's new approach, but of course they had their own ideas about the state's needs and priorities in this election year. Schwarzenegger and the legislature had until the end of March to come to agreement to put a comprehensive infrastructure bond initiative, or package of initiatives, on the ballot for the primary election, which had been moved back to June. They failed to meet the deadline.

Once again it largely fell to Núñez "to put the pieces and parts together," as another former Speaker, Robert Herzberg, put it. Núñez "was instrumental in taking what was a failure last time and putting it all together this time."[43] The agreements reached in May put a four-bond package amounting to $37 billion for transportation, housing, schools, and levees on the November ballot. A fifth bond concerning water resources was later added, bringing the total package to $42.7 billion.[44] There remained the matter of winning voter approval of the bonds, a year after all of Schwarzenegger's previous initiatives had gone down in flames. But the path to November, to the great benefit of the governor's reelection prospects, was eased by a remarkable series of legislative advances that originated in Schwarzenegger's year-opening speech. For the first time in six years, the state's budget was passed before the annual July deadline, the minimum wage was increased, and a measure adopted to decrease prescription drug prices — and then there was the Speaker's, the governor's, and the state's crowning achievement of 2006: Assembly Bill 32, the California Global Warming Solutions Act, the cornerstone of the state's internationally recognized environmental leadership role, "the first enforceable statewide program to cap all [greenhouse gas] emissions from major industries and penalize those that do not comply," mandating a 25 percent reduction in carbon emissions in the state by 2020.[45]

The bond measures all passed on November 7, 2006, and both the Speaker and governor were reelected. A year to the day later, Fabian Núñez was in Washington, DC to be honored as one of the prestigious *Governing* magazine's public officials of the year — the only legislator among the 2007 honorees. The magazine's profile characterized "his real importance" as his role "as the state's main policy fulcrum," calling the Speaker and governor an "unlikely pair" that became "real partners, leading to the flood of major legislation."[46]

Mark Baldasarre had foreseen in 2001, "If Latinos are able to achieve a more prominent role in politics in the next two decades, they will have a strong voice not only in their own destiny but also in the future of the Golden State."[47] When he took the position in February 2004, Núñez was the third Latino Speaker of the Assembly since December 1996, and just California's third Latino Speaker ever. The fourth and fifth followed with John Pérez in 2010 and Anthony Rendon in 2016.

Following the first general election with Núñez as Speaker in November 2004, the Latino Legislative Caucus, born in 1973 with five members led by a then just-elected Richard Alatorre, reached a new record strength of 27, 18 assemblymembers and nine senators, a total not matched again until after the 2016 elections.[48] The National Association of Latino Elected Officials (NALEO) had counted 460 Latino elected officeholders in California in 1984, and 796 in the fateful year of 1994. By 2014, the count reached 1,370. Evidently, the recessions of the early 1990s, the early 2000s, and the more recent Great Recession — along with the political waves that accompanied them, surfed by the likes of Pete Wilson and Arnold Schwarzenegger — did not arrest the advance of Latino political empowerment in California. But what might be the impact on Latino political progress of a Trump presidency — brought to power exploiting racial resentment, nativism, and hostility toward Mexico on a level never seen before?

Notes

1. Baldassare, *A California State of Mind*, 147.

2. This account is based on personal observation and Andrew Rosenthal, "Michelle, Maria, Caroline, and Oprah on the Hustings in California," *New York Times*, February 4, 2008, http://www.nytimes.com/2008/02/04/opinion/04mon4.html; Mark Z. Barabak, "State's First Lady is for Obama," *Los Angeles Times*, February 4, 2008, http://articles.latimes.com/2008/feb/04/nation/na-maria4.

3. On the movie industry's role in making LA's Latinos invisible see Duncan Campbell, "Hollywood's Hidden Hispanics: Why LA's Latinos Are Invisible on Screen," *The Guardian*, December 17, 2016, https://www.theguardian.com/us-news/2016/dec/18/hollywood-hidden-hispanics-los-angeles-la-la-land-brownout. Legal scholar Juan F. Perea has linked Latino invisibility to language and to the "Black/White binary paradigm" in "Los Olvidados," "Death by English," "The Black/White Binary Paradigm of Race," and "Five Axioms in Search of Equality." See also "Getting to Know LA's Powerful Labor Leader Maria Elena Durazo," A. Martinez interview with Hillel Aron, KPCC *Take Two*, November 26, 2013, http://www.scpr.org/programs/take-two/2013/11/26/34846/getting-to-know-las-powerful-labor-leader-maria-e/; Jim Newton, "Labor's Maria Elena Durazo and a Life of Activism," *UCLA Blueprint*, Spring 2017, http://blueprint.ucla.edu/feature/labors-maria-elena-durazo-and-a-life-of-activism/; the *Times* editorial board, "The Legacy of County

Fed Leader Maria Elena Durazo," *Los Angeles Times*, June 27, 2017, http://www.latimes.com/opinion/editorials/la-ed-1030-durazo-20141030-story.html.

4. Littler News & Analysis Reports, "Hilda Solis Officially Confirmed as Labor Secretary," *ASAP*, February 24, 2009, https://www.littler.com/publication-press/publication/hilda-solis-officially-confirmed-labor-secretary. Solis was first elected to represent a San Gabriel Valley district of the Greater Eastside in the California Assembly in 1992, moved up to the state Senate in 1994, and was elected to Congress in 2000.

5. See Ness, "Labor Keeps the Democratic Party Accountable"; Marc Haefele, "Solis Challenges the Democrats' Seniority System," *Los Angeles Times*, February 13, 2000, http://articles.latimes.com/2000/feb/13/opinion/op-64078; Frank and Wong, "Dynamic Political Mobilization," also available as a separate monograph titled "Intense Political Mobilization," published by Wayne State University, Center for Labor Studies (2004), http://community-wealth.org/content/intense-political-mobilization-los-angeles-county-federation-labor; Harold Meyerson, "Solis Steps Down," *The American Prospect*, January 10, 2013, http://prospect.org/article/solis-steps-down.

6. This was during the first Bill Clinton term. See the official, unsigned *Los Angeles Times* editorial "An Angeleno on the Short List?: Vilma S. Martinez would be a strong candidate for U.S. Supreme Court," May 6, 1994, http://articles.latimes.com/1994-05-06/local/me-54349_1_supreme-court; Buskopic, *Breaking In*, 66, 80.

7. Neil A. Lewis, "No Apparent Front-Runner to Fill Supreme Court Seat," *New York Times*, April 28, 1994, http://www.nytimes.com/1994/04/28/us/no-apparent-front-runner-to-fill-supreme-court-seat.html?mcubz=1; Juan Gonzalez, "Gore Ticket Needs Hispanic," *New York Daily News*, March 24, 2000, http://www.nydailynews.com/archives/news/gore-ticket-hispanic-article-1.873121.

8. Buskopic, *Breaking In*, 8; Ed O'Keefe, "Eye Opener: Obama's Hispanic Nominees," *The Washington Post*, September 2, 2009, http://voices.washingtonpost.com/federal-eye/2009/09/eye_opener_obamas_hispanic_nom.html; Karen Tumulty, "Why Obama Picked Her," *Time*, May 26, 2009, http://content.time.com/time/politics/article/0,8599,1900956,00.html.

9. In June 2012, Obama announced the policy of Deferred Action for Childhood Arrivals (DACA), a program based upon the landmark 1982 US Supreme Court case that barred discrimination against minors in basic public education on the basis of their immigration status, and pointedly did so on the thirtieth anniversary of this ruling known as *Plyler v. Doe*. This case was the critical breakthrough in the area of immigration policy that established the Mexican American Legal Defense and Educational Fund (MALDEF), then headed by Vilma Martinez, as "the major purposive player in immigration litigation" and Latino civil rights. See Olivas, "From a 'Legal Organization of Militants.'" On Durazo's views and priorities following the Trump election see Bobbi Murray, "Conversations on Trump's America: The Coming Immigration Wars," *Capital & Main*, November 30, 2016, https://capitalandmain.com/conversations-on-trumps-america-the-coming-immigration-wars-1130.

10. Navarro and Acuña, "In Search of Community."

11. Skerry, *Mexican Americans*.

12. Schrag, *Paradise Lost*; Davis Hansen, *Mexifornia*; Rieff, *Los Angeles*.

13. Buchanan, *State of Emergency* and *The Death of the West*.

14. Huntington, *Who Are We*, 221–22.

15. Baldassare, *California State of Mind*, 189.

16. Ibid., 150.

17. Ibid., 187. Proposition 39, its complicated politics and context are much more carefully dissected by Baldassare on 95–103, beyond the role of the minority vote. He makes clear on page 103 that the passage of Proposition 39 in 2000 was certainly historic "in effect," even if white voter confusion may have played a role. Proposition 13, passed in 1978, strictly limited local property taxes in California, with severe consequences for state and local public finance and services. Emulated in many other states, "Prop. 13" was widely considered to have powered the election of Ronald Reagan in 1980 and retrospectively to have been the opening shot of "the Reagan Revolution." See Citrin and Martin, *After the Tax Revolt*.

18. Ibid., 188–89.

19. John M. Broder, "California Ponders Big Loan in Deficit Crisis," *New York Times*, May 9, 2003, http://www.nytimes.com/2003/05/09/us/california-ponders-big-loan-in-deficit-crisis.html?mcubz=1.

20. Michael Hiltzik, "California Grows Up about Immigrant Driver's Licenses," *Los Angeles Times*, October 4, 2013, http://articles.latimes.com/2013/oct/04/business/la-fi-mh-licenses-20131004.

21. See the analyses and commentaries collected in Lustig, *Remaking California.*

22. Dave Downey, "Schwarzenegger Repeals Car Tax," *The San Diego Union-Tribune*, November 18, 2003, http://www.sandiegouniontribune.com/sdut-schwarzenegger-repeals-car-tax-2003nov18-story.html; Peter Nicholas and Joe Mathews, "Schwarzenegger Sworn In, Rescinds Car Tax Increase," *Los Angeles Times*, November 18, 2003, http://articles.latimes.com/2003/nov/18/local/me-inaugural18.

23. For a look at comparisons between Trump and Schwarzenegger and a response, see Abby Lunardini, "I knew Governor Schwarzenegger. Mr. Trump, you're no Governor Schwarzenegger," *The Washington Post*, January 6, 2017, https://www.washingtonpost.com/opinions/i-knew-gov-schwarzenegger-mr-trump-youre-no-gov-schwarzenegger/2017/01/06/5ae327ba-d2ca-11e6-a783-cd3fa950f2fd_story.html?utm_term=.036cdb68e668.

24. Schwarzenegger, *Total Recall*, 525.

25. George F. Will, "In Calif., Power by Plebiscite," *The Washington Post*, July 15, 2004, http://www.washingtonpost.com/wp-dyn/articles/A50503-2004Jul14.html.

26. John M. Broder, "Schwarzenegger Proposes Overhaul of Redistricting," *New York Times*, January 6, 2005, http://www.nytimes.com/2005/01/06/us/schwarzenegger-proposes-overhaul-of-redistricting.html?mcubz=1. The Associated Press, "A Timeline of Schwarzenegger's Tenure," *The San Diego Union-Tribune*, December 25, 2010, http://www.sandiegouniontribune.com/sdut-a-timeline-of-schwarzeneggers-tenure-2010dec25-story.html.

27. George F. Will, "California Revolution," *The Washington Post*, February 10, 2005, http://www.washingtonpost.com/wp-dyn/articles/A12489-2005Feb9.html?nav=rss_politics/specials/califrecall/opinion.

28. Carlos Watson, "Arnold's political thriller," *CNN.com Politics*, June 22, 2005, http://www.cnn.com/2005/POLITICS/06/22/schwarzenegger.election/.

29. Ina Jaffe, "Schwarzenegger's Troubles Deepen," National Public Radio *Morning Edition*, May 12, 2005, http://www.npr.org/templates/story/story.php?storyId=4648992.

30. Joe Dignan, "California Marriage Drive Persists," *Gay City News*, June 16–22, 2005, http://gaycitynews.nyc/gcn_424/californiamarriagedrive.html; Lynn Vincent, "Anatomy of a Victory: Inside A Razor-Thin Vote to Preserve Marriage in the Golden State," *World Magazine*, June 18, 2005.

31. Joe Dignan, "Marriage Bill Teeters in California," *Gay City News*, June 02–08, 2005, http://gaycitynews.nyc/gcn_422/marriagebillteeters.html.

32. Melissa Block and John Myers, "Schwarzenegger Calls for Vote on Plans," *National Public Radio*, June 13, 2005, http://www.npr.org/templates/story/story.php?storyId=4702082.

33. Lynda Gledhill, "Gay Marriage Up to Governor Now/Landmark Legislation Clears Assembly by Narrowest of Margins on Second Try," *San Francisco Chronicle*, September 7, 2005, http://www.sfgate.com/news/article/Gay-marriage-up-to-governor-now-Landmark-2610923.php; Joe Dignan and John Pomfret, "California Legislature Approves Gay Marriage," *The Washington Post*, September 7, 2005, http://www.washingtonpost.com/wp-dyn/content/article/2005/09/06/AR2005090602076.html.

34. Dean E. Murphy, "Schwarzenegger to Veto Same-Sex Marriage Bill," *New York Times*, September 8, 2005, http://www.nytimes.com/2005/09/08/us/schwarzenegger-to-veto-samesex-marriage-bill.html?mcubz=1.

35. Officially only named Assembly Bill 489 (AB489), the previous bill was also subject to contentious debate and a bare majority vote. It did not pass and become law until 1975. See United Press International, "Dymally Breaks Ties as Senate Passes Consenting Adults Bill," *Daily Independent Journal*, May 2, 1975.

36. Smith, "Direct Democracy and Candidate Elections"; Gerston and Christensen, *Recall!*; Harold Meyerson, "Arnold Terminates Himself," *The Washington Post*, November 10, 2005, http://www.washingtonpost.com/wp-dyn/content/article/2005/11/09/AR2005110901635.html.

37. "Schwarzenegger's Gun," *Los Angeles Times*, January 29, 2005, http://articles.latimes.com/2005/jan/29/opinion/ed-arnold29.

38. Schwarzenegger, *Total Recall*, 522.

39. Núñez statements quoted in a story by Daniel Weintraub and cited in Edward Barrera, "CA: Fabian Núñez Intends to Deal, Move On," *Inland Valley Daily Bulletin*, January 1, 2006; and David Caruso, "Terminated!" *David Caruso's Magical Island* (blog), November 10, 2005, http://dcmi.blogspot.com/2005/11/terminated.html.

40. Barrera, "CA: Fabian Núñez."

41. "California State of the State Address," *C-SPAN* (video), January 5, 2006, https://www.c-span.org/video/?190592-1/california-state-state-address.

42. Ibid.

43. Metro Investment Report (interview series), "Herzberg: State Infrastructure Bond Results from Consensus-Building & Need," *The Planning Report*, May 2006, http://archive.is/iDKe.

44. Elizabeth G. Hill, "Implementing the 2006 Bond Package: Increasing Effectiveness through Legislative Oversight," Legislative Analyst's Office, January 22, 2007, http://www.lao.ca.gov/2007/2006_bonds/2006_bonds_012207.pdf.

45. Tom Chorneau and Mark Martin, "Even Top Dems Help Governor with Turnaround: Assembly Speaker Especially Works Well with Schwarzenegger," *San Francisco Chronicle*, August 31, 2006, http://www.sfgate.com/politics/article/Even-top-Dems-help-governor-with-turnaround-2488798.php. See also Larry Morandi, "Tough Act to Follow," *State Legislatures*, March 2007, http://www.ncsl.org/Portals/1/documents/magazine/articles/2007/07SLMar07_ToughAct.pdf; California Air Resources Board, "Assembly Bill 32 Overview," last reviewed August 5, 2014, https://www.arb.ca.gov/cc/ab32/ab32.htm.

46. Alan Greenblatt, "Public Officials of the Year: Fabian Núñez," *Governing: The States and Localities*, November 2007, http://www.governing.com/poy/Fabian-Nunez.html.

47. Baldasarre, *A California State of Mind*, 189.

48. Becker, Hughes, and Morin, "The History, Development and Policy Influence of the California Latino Legislative Caucus," 22. As of December 2016, following the November elections, the caucus listed 22 assemblymembers and five senators; see Lawrence C. Becker, Tyler Hughes, and Jason L. Morin, "2016 Election Update," Center for Southern California Studies, CSU Northridge, https://www.csun.edu/sites/default/files/CLLC%202016%20Election%20Update.pdf.

CHAPTER 12

Counting on California

We're not in the business of deportation.
—Xavier Becerra
California Attorney General[1]

Californians do not need healing. We need to fight.
—Anthony Rendon
Speaker, California Assembly[2]

When the president says millions of illegal ballots are cast, that's simply not the case. It's a lie.
—Alex Padilla
California Secretary of State[3]

We're not going to back down, no matter what the president does.
—Kevin de León
President Pro Tem, California Senate[4]

LA-AREA HIGH SCHOOLERS CONNECTED LIVE WITH PARIS IN DECEMBER 2015, courtesy of their state senators, for an inside look at the historic United Nations Climate Change Conference then taking place. California legislative leaders, including Senate President Kevin de León, Assembly Speaker-elect Anthony Rendon, and State Senator Ricardo Lara joined Governor Jerry Brown on the nearly six-thousand-mile-long trip for the two-week summit. Campaigning for the Republican presidential nomination, Donald Trump just days before called the conference "ridiculous" and a "big scam."[5] The high-school students, however, learned not only that their governor had a seat at the table along with 196 sovereign countries and the European Union, but also that California was the only subnational participant so privileged.

Seeing US Latino leaders on the world stage addressing global environmental issues and linking them to local, stateside realities was something new, perhaps dramatically so, but generally unspoken and not apparent to those unfamiliar

Lara & the Southeast Side Story

*Firstborn son to work-
ing-class Mexican-immigrant
parents in one of the gritty, independent, industrial mini-cit-
ies just southeast of downtown
LA, Ricardo Lara's career
marked the convergence of
multiple currents of empowerment and means of ascent in
California Latino politics, propelling his quick rise to leadership in Sacramento. He began*

*as a field aide to Nell Soto, a suburban Latina member of the Assembly, and
joined her in the Capitol when she moved up to the Senate. There he jumped
at the opportunity to work for a dynamic, urban Latino Assemblymember,
Marco Firebaugh, who happened to represent the Southeastside district that
Lara was originally from.*

*Lara rose from legislative aide to Firebaugh's chief of staff, working
with him on historic legislation that provided access to public higher education for California "Dreamers," undocumented students brought to the
state as children. This job and relationship connected Lara to Firebaugh's
mentor, then-Senator and Latino Legislative Caucus chair Richard Polanco, and their close ally, Senator Martha Escutia, who represented the same
area as Marco. Firebaugh went on to succeed Polanco as chair of the Latino
Caucus and, as his mentor did in the Senate, he also served simultaneously
as majority leader in the Assembly. Lara was thus strongly linked, through
Firebaugh, Polanco, Escutia, and the caucus, back to the empowerment efforts initiated by Richard Alatorre (in association with incumbent elected
officials) and TELACU (rooted in community organizing) in the 1960s and
'70s.*

*After Firebaugh tragically succumbed to a liver ailment in 2006, be-
fore he would turn 40, a grieving Lara resumed his career as an aide to
then-Speaker Fabian Núñez and later to Kevin de León, also a member of
the Assembly. Núñez and de León, non-Eastsiders who rose through organized labor to public office, widened Ricardo's sources of support by helping
him connect to the Latino immigrant movement in LA's unions. By 2010,
his considerable experience, relationships, and backing served to catapult
the now openly gay Lara into the Assembly in his own right, representing
Firebaugh's and Escutia's old district. Lara was promptly elected to lead the*

Latino Legislative Caucus in his first term, and after that one term moved up to the state Senate. There, he was able to support de León, his last boss, in his historic bid for the position of Senate president. By the time Trump pulled the United States out of the Paris Climate Agreement in 2017, Senator Ricardo Lara had turned to running for state insurance commissioner, campaigning with the central message of resisting all the ways in which the Trump administration would try to impose a regressive policy agenda on the country's biggest and most progressive state.

with the Latino political experience.[6] In addition to being the featured guest on an internationally broadcast French TV interview program, de León conversed via Skype with an environmental science class and student government leaders at John Marshall High, a school in his district he had strong ties to because of its "large and active Environmental Club." He explained to them the concise message California took to Paris: that the state had been able to "de-couple carbon from GDP," reducing "our carbon emission while we have grown our economy."[7]

Senator Lara Skyped with advanced placement government and economics students at the sprawling, flagship high school of his district, known as Long Beach Poly.[8] Lara was barely in his first term on the state Senate, but was already part of that body's leadership as chair of its powerhouse Appropriations Committee. More importantly, he was in Paris to enlist the global summit in efforts to pull the governor and the state, long champions of traditional environmentalism, further in the direction of *environmental justice*.[9] Lara had previously authored legislation directing the state's Air Resources Board to study and devise a plan to combat short-lived air pollutants that harm particular communities, such as those in his district, more directly than the carbon dioxide levels that affect the planet as a whole. Brown moved in this direction in 2015 and in Paris joined Lara in announcing the senator's new bill to implement the strategy to reduce the emissions of pollutants with locally focused effects such as methane and black carbon.[10]

The 2015 Paris Conference marked a turning point not only for global action on climate change, but also for consolidating the emerging roles of California, and its Latino leadership in particular, in uniting and advancing the interrelated causes of traditional environmentalism and the more recent environmental-justice movement. In practical political terms, this point was reached in large measure by the expansion southward of Latino political mobilization in California, beyond its origins in Boyle Heights and East LA proper, into the vast warehousing and industrial region that stretches along the LA River channel, rail lines, and the I-710 freeway to the ports of Los Angeles and Long Beach. Lara and Rendon, whose positions of leadership and policy priorities are an expression of this area's empowerment, directly represented these heavily working-class Latino communities in Sacramento, along with all Californians in Paris.[11]

* * *

OF THE TOP LATINO OFFICEHOLDERS IN CALIFORNIA WHEN DONALD TRUMP was sworn in, two had already been in their prominent positions before he launched his campaign in New York City in June 2015. Senate President de León and Secretary of State Alex Padilla, sons of immigrants and the first Latinos to hold their respective offices, were unlikely, and probably unable, from Trump's notorious opening act of reality-show political theater, to regard his candidacy with anything but contempt.

De León and Padilla had spent decades not only preparing and pursuing their own political careers, they had both necessarily and by choice devoted their adult lives to organizing, defending, empowering, and serving their heavily immigrant, Latino communities. They now had as their sworn professional responsibility the interests of Californians of all generations and of the state as a whole — from the California of their parents' immigrant journeys and struggles, to their own urban-barrio upbringing, to their high-powered college educations away from home, to their plunge into LA political and labor organizing, to the making of laws and policies for the whole state in Sacramento. They had learned the history, the causes, the defeats, and the victories of those like themselves, who had given their lives to public service and the quest to overcome marginalization, exclusion, and powerlessness. They were heirs to what could be considered a modern Latino political tradition.

Early in 2016, Anthony Rendon, grandson of immigrants, another representative of a cluster of those small cities southeast of downtown LA, reached the top tier of state leadership, becoming seventieth Speaker of the California State Assembly – the fifth Latino – and from that position observed Trump's seemingly unstoppable march to power. At the start of 2017, Xavier Becerra, another son of immigrants, left his post as chair of the Democratic Caucus of the U.S. House of Representatives, that body's highest-ranking Latino, to return to his native Sacramento and become the state's first Latino attorney general. Even casual followers of politics understood that Becerra had come home to help lead the new and historic fight to defend the path of inclusion and progress that Californians had forged over the course of his life, and had recommitted to by landslide electoral margins in November 2016.

What was happening in California could be seen clear to Trump Tower in New York City. In the spring of 2017, Thomas Friedman, perhaps New York's leading newspaper columnist, reflected on the incessant discussion of the new regime's first 100 days — driven by Trump's many "bizarre" interviews on the topic — and asked, "As for the next 100 days, who will protect us?" Friedman, a three-time Pulitzer Prize winner, dismissed the Democratic Party as "too weak." Instead, this eminent New Yorker revealed, "On the issues I care about most, I'm actually counting on California." Friedman argued that the state's "market size, aspirational goals, and ability to legislate make it the most powerful opposition party to Trump in America today."[12]

"Ability to legislate" — a remarkable recognition of progress from just the end of the last decade, when the idea of California as a "failed state" morphed from "epithet," to question, to topic of self-serious debate, to internet meme, and for several years at least, to a commonplace slam.[13] January 2010 saw a full-blown, Oxford-style debate on this proposition at New York University, which the proponents won.[14] The University of California followed with a conference at its Davis campus titled "Failed State: Crisis and Renewal in California Politics and Culture," which served to launch UC Press's new online journal ironically named *Boom: A Journal of California*. The editors observed in the inaugural issue, "Leaders on all sides promise new directions. Still, the Golden State remains more adrift than at any time since the Great Depression. . . . But silence will not produce solutions." They went on to refer matter-of-factly to "the state's failed constitution and the dire consequences of its bitter racial politics." The featured analysis at both the 2010 conference and the 2011 debut issue of the journal was "How to Fix a Broken State."[15]

Six years after the appearance of *Boom*, Thomas Friedman did not try to account for the ability to legislate in California that he heralded, a quality so lacking in polarized Washington, but he ended the column with a series of clues, admiringly quoting Senator de León and citing priorities advanced by California's ascendant Latino legislative leadership: clean-energy jobs, of which the state has "far more" than all the coal jobs in the country; "resistance to Trump's draconian immigration policies [and] creating health care, education, and work opportunities for illegal immigrants who have been living here responsibly and productively"; and the legislature's hiring of Eric Holder to defend the state "against Trump suits." "We have made it very clear," Friedman quoted de León saying about California and its leadership, "we will protect our economic prosperity and our values from Trump."[16]

De León, Rendon, Padilla, and Becerra formed a corps of LA-based state leaders, augmented by legislators such as Senator Lara, Senator and Latino Caucus Chair Ben Hueso, and Assemblymember Lorena Gonzalez Fletcher, who were boldly guiding California in the early Trump era in tandem with the governor, at the head of "supermajorities" in the legislature and bolstered by a Latino Caucus once again at record strength in the Capitol. The main early test of Rendon and de León's ability to pass major legislation in league with the governor in 2017 came the first week of April. Context was all in understanding the significance of the fierce battle over raising taxes and fees to pay for sorely needed road repairs. In November, state voters had extended and increased certain taxes, and many jurisdictions, led by LA County, passed new taxes, signaling the possibility that now, at last, the anti-tax culture established by the 1978 Proposition 13 tax revolt was truly, finally over.[17]

Governor Brown and the legislative leaders agreed to push the state's first gas-tax increase in 23 years, coupled with a new annual vehicle tax, on a fast track before the legislature's spring break. As governor in 1978, Brown had vehemently opposed Prop. 13, but had to radically change his position when voters passed the measure by a landslide. His chief of staff at that time, Gray Davis, became governor two decades later and in 2003 was recalled from office, primarily for having pushed an increase in annual vehicle fees. Brown took the unusual step of appearing before the Senate Appropriations Committee to personally make the case for what he allowed was a "big lift" for legislators.[18] The measure, intended to raise over $5 billion a year, passed with the minimum number of votes required in each house. Rendon and de León each lost only one vote of their supermajorities in the contest.[19] Opponents vowed to block the tax increase by putting it on the ballot in a new proposition, but the Capitol's leaders had shown they could legislate big.

Public approval of the legislature had risen almost steadily since the dismal 10 percent low point it hit in 2010. By September 2016, the legislators' approval rating among registered voters reached 50 percent, anticipating the November election results that awarded supermajorities to the Democrats in each house.[20] By the time the lawmakers took their difficult votes raising gas taxes and vehicle registration fees in April 2017, their approval rating was measured at 57 percent — the highest found by the same pollster since 1988, a level that the *LA Times*'s "Capitol Journal" columnist called "astronomical" and "something I never expected to see again in my lifetime." The veteran *Times* journalist made his view of what was happening clear: "Unlike the gridlocked, Republican-controlled Congress, the Democrat-dominated state legislature exhibited an ability to pass significant, controversial legislation that required a supermajority vote."[21]

The General

A PROGRESSIVE LATINO POLITICAL TRADITION COMPOSED OF A NUMBER of distinct currents developed in Greater Los Angeles in the second half of the twentieth century. Community organizers, public-minded professionals, union activists, feminists, Spanish-language media, business leaders, and committed politicians all played key roles. In California politics, by the advent of the Trump administration, it was evident that leaders such as Rendon, de León, Padilla, Becerra, and their numerous Latino Caucus colleagues, represented, fused, and were extending the principal currents of that tradition from the twentieth century well into the twenty-first.

The new attorney general had directly succeeded the founder of the oldest current in Congress. Becerra was elected with Ed Roybal's blessing in 1992, as the old man prepared to retire, completing 15 terms — 30 years — of service in Washington. Becerra would take Roybal's baton and carry it forward another dozen terms, in the course of which he would labor on the signature cause of Roybal's entire working career: healthcare. Becerra was there as a freshman, pushing as best he could for the Clintons' failed healthcare reform in 1993–94. He was still there, but now part of the House leadership as special assistant to Speaker Nancy Pelosi, when they managed to pass the historic Affordable Care Act in 2010 on a strict party-line vote.

But Becerra had actually gotten his start with another Eastside political current, when he took his first government job as a Senate fellow, assigned to the Capitol staff of Art Torres in the 1980s, and later served as the senator's administrative assistant in Los Angeles. Thus, well before he ever met Ed Roybal, Becerra was already working for a legislator deeply committed to healthcare policy, a promoter of single-payer health insurance for California. The Sacramento boy, educated at Stanford, learned in his stint at the state Capitol that should he want to pursue an electoral career, LA was the place to be. To Becerra's benefit, Art Torres, by then a wizened veteran of Eastside and statewide political wars, was eager to bring promising new talent into the ongoing LA Latino-empowerment project.

Becerra made his first run in 1990 precisely in the manner pioneered by Alatorre and Torres, making his entry as a staffer and then running for an open Eastside seat in the state Assembly with his former boss's support. He was aware of the split that had emerged in Eastside politics in 1982 and tried to bridge it. Gloria Molina had been Art Torres's first administrative assistant, and she also followed the path of running for an open Assembly seat with her former boss's backing. Becerra reached out to Molina, who was by then on the LA City Council, and won her support as well. Still in his first year in office, he faced a major decision: his mentor, Torres, and his new ally, Molina, were headed for a climactic battle over who would represent the new LA County Supervisorial District for the Latino Eastside — the result of a successful voting-rights lawsuit. Becerra went with Molina. Later that year, the Assembly freshman saw the opportunity to run for the congressional seat Roybal was vacating. Having started his political career in Sacramento with Art Torres, Becerra continued it in Washington, identified more with Roybal's legacy and Molina's support, at least initially; but the two currents that had carried him were fused within a single, progressive, California Latino political tradition.

State Man

The emergence of an entirely different base of Latino political power in Los Angeles in the 1990s — the East San Fernando Valley — made it possible for Alex Padilla to become in 2014 just the second Latino elected to statewide office since the 1800s, when he won an open contest for secretary of state.[22] Padilla grew up in the core barrio of the area known as Pacoima, famous for having produced the tragic Mexican-American 1950s rock-and-roll star Ritchie Valens, of "La Bamba" fame.

Pacoima is in certain limited ways comparable to its Eastside counterpart of Boyle Heights. Both are located in corners of the city that border on heavily

Latino but non-LA jurisdictions.[23] A major difference is that while LA City Hall is visible from Boyle Heights, which is separated only by the concrete river channel from the eastern reaches of downtown, Pacoima lies 25 miles away to the northwest, past some rugged hills and much San Fernando Valley flatland. For good reason, the Valley looks and feels like a different city altogether. Unlikely as it may seem on the ground, however, Latino empowerment in the East Valley owes much to the development of Latino political power on LA's Eastside and the progressive tradition that it produced.

The first widely noticed step in East Valley Latino empowerment did not come until 1990, early in the fifth and last term of the Tom Bradley administration. That is when Bradley appointed Richard Alarcon, a young "mid-level city bureaucrat," to be his liaison to the entire Valley, a position that had been held by a diminutive Jewish woman activist for 17 years, since the mayor's first day in office. The conservative, suburban-styled Valley was always politically challenging for Bradley, and he had looked to its Jewish population as a source of support, but the city's steady demographic shift toward a Latino plurality, including in the East Valley, was both an inescapable reality and an opportunity.[24]

Bradley had learned the politics of multiracial coalitions back when he was a police officer and volunteer in Ed Roybal's campaigns from the late 1940s to the early 1960s.[25] As no Latino succeeded Roybal on the city council for decades following his departure to Washington in 1962, Latinos did not figure prominently in the Bradley coalition that came to power in 1973. But suddenly in the mid-1980s, in Bradley's fourth term as mayor, Richard Alatorre and Gloria Molina were elected to the council in relatively quick succession. Alatorre came in as a power, for his role in Willie Brown's Assembly speakership and in the 1981–82 redistricting. He was promptly put in charge of the city council's redistricting committee. After years of development through the channel of the state legislature, Latinos were now happening politically in City Hall.

After a lackluster fourth reelection in 1989, with an embarrassing scare from a little-known challenger, Bradley acted decisively to shore up his leadership and preserve the option of running for a sixth term. To advise him on Latinos, he named the highly competent Ed Avila to the position of deputy mayor at the start of 1990. Avila had been an aide to Roybal and served as the first executive director of the National Association of Latino Elected and Appointed Officials (NALEO).[26] Five months later, the youthful, Latino city bureaucrat, Alarcon, was appointed liaison to the Valley, where he had long resided and was a community activist. His first press in the *LA Times* noted, "Speculation abounds in the East Valley as to whether the high-visibility post will position Alarcon to run for city council."[27] Not coincidentally, Alarcon headed the Valley chapter of the Mexican American Political Association — another organization founded by Roybal — and in that capacity had "urged the consolidation of Valley Latino neighborhoods into one council district" in the 1986 redistricting that Alatorre was in charge of, which resulted in the drawing of a district "likely to produce the Valley's first Latino Los Angeles City Council member."[28]

Alarcon did in fact run in that district at the next opportunity, when it was an open seat in 1993. The Latino political mobilization of the East Valley was underway. After five years on city council, Alarcon ran for another open seat in the state Senate, with the young Alex Padilla managing his campaign. Padilla brought to that race the experience of having recently run an Assembly campaign in an overlapping district, and unique number-crunching skills acquired with his MIT engineering degree, augmented by a software programming job at Hughes Aircraft. "As he was managing those campaigns," the *New York Times* observed in a fawning profile, "he was also laying the groundwork to become a politician himself."[29]

After engineering Alarcon's step up to the state Senate, Padilla organized his own bid for the vacated city council seat, which he won in 1999. Two years later, his elder colleagues elected Padilla president of the council, making him the youngest council president in LA history and the first Latino in that position in over a century. Five years after that, he again succeeded Richard Alarcon, this time in Sacramento, when his former campaign client was termed out of the state Senate.

Alex Padilla's two full terms in the California Senate came to an end in 2014, just as the secretary of state's office became open, also due to term limits. He had good fortune in the race — an independent candidate in the primary that hurt the main Republican contender, and especially the arrest of his main Democratic opponent, which gave Alex the publicity benefit of a first-place finish. He went on to win the general election by a substantial margin, precisely 10 years after Art Torres lost his statewide bid in the wave election that included Proposition 187. The electorate had changed significantly, and now MIT-trained Alex Padilla would be in charge of the entire state's electoral system.

Lion of the Senate

OF THE FOUR MAIN CALIFORNIA LATINO LEADERS AT THE DAWN OF THE TRUMP ERA, Kevin de León exemplified the singular role of the labor movement in performing a trio of key functions: drawing new talent from throughout the state into the LA-based quest for Latino empowerment, forming such talent into skilled leaders, and advancing them directly onto an electoral political path. In de León's case, all three aspects worked doubly, as he came as one of a pair. De León and Fabian Núñez, who was the first of the two to take the electoral plunge and achieve high office, grew up together in a San Diego barrio and went to high school and college together. Their similar family experiences of having lived on both sides of the border led them step by step to a life of activism in defense of immigrant rights, and to Los Angeles, the center ring of the rights struggle.[30]

After finishing college in nearby Claremont, some 30 miles east of LA, de León and Núñez found themselves working together for an immigrant-rights organization in Boyle Heights in 1994, that pivotal year of Proposition 187. They took as their task the challenge of organizing a long series of protests against the measure, in an effort to mobilize visible, mass opposition. They invited Gilbert Cedillo to attend and speak at one of their rallies. The immigrant-rights organization was a threadbare operation that only had a bullhorn for sound and lacked the infrastructure or budget to produce and distribute materials, promote a major protest, or transport marchers. Cedillo's Local 660 of the SEIU, which represented over forty thousand LA County Workers, had its own public-address system, printing capabilities, and both the human and financial resources to organize a major event. Gilbert took the issue to his local's board and got approval to invest the union's resources in staging a large-scale climactic march against Prop. 187, to take place on the middle Sunday of October, three weeks before the election.[31]

The day after, *Los Angeles Times* called the demonstration "one of the largest mass protests in the city's history," estimating the number of protestors, who marched from the Eastside to City Hall, at 70,000.[32] As Proposition 187 went on to pass by a landslide vote — and its major backer Governor Pete Wilson was likewise reelected — the political impact of the eye-popping march sparked angry debates, but the organizational success was indisputable. With phone calls from Cedillo, Núñez and de León landed staff jobs at the County Federation of Labor and the California Teachers Association.

When Miguel Contreras became head of the County Fed in 1996, he named Núñez his successor as political director. With Contreras at the helm, the Federation greatly increased its involvement in electing committed supporters of labor to office, applying the new model of immigrant mobilization in campaigns to elect Gilbert Cedillo to the state Assembly in January 1998 and numerous others thereafter. Núñez became expert in the art of winning elections. When Cedillo left his Assembly seat open to run for state Senate in 2002, Núñez ran to succeed him, enlisting de León as campaign manager. Núñez achieved the speakership of the Assembly in record time, after just over a year in office. By Núñez's third year as Speaker in 2006, de León ran for Assembly in Antonio Villaraigosa's old district. Next stop, Sacramento: de León and Núñez would be working side by side again.

De León rose quickly to a leadership position in the Assembly, becoming head of the Appropriations Committee and positioning himself to make a bid for Speaker. That was not to be, and as is traditional in Sacramento, he found himself in the proverbial Assembly dog house in early 2010 — the reward for losing in a speakership battle. The president of the state Senate at that time, Darrell Steinberg, encouraged de León to come over to the Senate side, where term limits were making Gilbert Cedillo's seat an open race. He ran and won, and again rose to the leadership as head of Appropriations.[33] But he did not cut ties to the Assembly or to his origins.

California Senate President Kevin de León flanked by Governor Jerry Brown and former Governor Arnold Schwarzenegger at the signing of the extension of the state's carbon emissions control program known as "cap and trade," on Treasure Island in the San Francisco Bay, July 2017. (AP Photo/Eric Risberg.)

When Lorena Gonzalez was elected to the Assembly to represent the district where de León grew up in San Diego, he immediately partnered with her on legislation and did, in her words, "everything in his power" to ensure the novice legislator's success.[34] Gonzalez, who married and became Gonzalez Fletcher, quickly compiled a robust legislative record and, following in de León's footsteps, went on to become the first Latina to chair the Assembly Appropriations Committee.[35] By mid-2015, *The Atlantic* magazine characterized Gonzalez as "arguably the state's most influential female politician."[36] That was before her crowning achievement of 2016, in partnership with de León in the Senate, that for the first time established overtime pay for farmworkers.[37]

De León succeeded his colleague Steinberg as president of the state Senate, becoming the first Latino to hold this office since the 1880s. In the course of a decade since the protest march against Proposition 187, a reformed labor movement had taken newcomers to LA and made them first into more effective catalyzers of the Latino immigrant community, and ultimately, top-echelon leaders of the state. What has come to be known as LA's pioneering "Latino-labor alliance" compiled a remarkable record, not only getting a wide array of its cadre and allies elected to public office, but in the span of a dozen years helping four of them achieve the pinnacles of power in the California Legislature: Antonio Villaraigosa, Fabian Núñez, and John Pérez as Speakers of the Assembly in 1998, 2004, and 2010, respectively, and Kevin de León as President of the Senate in 2014.[38]

From his position of institutional and political authority, de León was empowered to represent California on the global stage afforded by the Paris climate summit. While featured there on an internationally televised French interview program, the state legislative leader spoke out about Donald Trump's pronouncements as a candidate, by then six months into his campaign. De León characterized Trump's statements regarding Muslims and other immigrants as repugnant, disgusting, anti-American, and unquestionably racist.[39] A year later, when the time came for de León to respond to the reality of a Trump presidency, he not only had his own experience and journey to fortify him, he had a column of direct predecessors in line stretching behind him, friends and allies he could call on and consult at any time, and a California Latino political tradition that reached back decades. Within eight months of Trump's inauguration, de León announced his goal of continuing to lead the resistance from a forward position in Washington, by running for the US Senate in 2018.

Philosopher King

WHEN ANTHONY RENDON TOOK HIS PLACE IN SACRAMENTO AS A NOVICE state legislator in December 2012, John Pérez of Los Angeles, the fourth Latino Speaker of the preceding decade and a half, had been in charge of the Assembly for almost three years. Rendon did not achieve elected office by rising through labor, nor by first serving on the staff of a politician who then sponsored him, nor by organizing his community and running with its backing. Latino representation was not constrained for him by district lines drawn to divide Latino communities. Latino legislators were not isolated, and the Assembly's leaders were not unfriendly or indifferent to the needs of his constituents. On the contrary, besides Latino Speaker Pérez, who was a union leader, other Latinos representing districts with similar needs as Rendon's by then chaired a slew of powerful legislative committees. But nothing demonstrated how much California politics had changed for Latinos — and how Latinos had changed California — more than the fact that while still in his first term, Rendon would make a bid to become the next Speaker, and that less than a year into his second term his Democratic colleagues would unanimously elect him to that position.[40]

His election in 2012 to the Assembly, taken together with Ricardo Lara's simultaneous election to the state Senate and his assumption of chair of the Appropriations Committee, and then Rendon's ascension to Speaker in 2016, marked the culmination of an extraordinary broadening of Latino empowerment on the Greater Eastside. That journey began with the redistricting process of 1990–91 and the election of Martha Escutia to the Assembly from this area in 1992.

What got Rendon to the Assembly, and in early 2016 to its highest office, was a combination of his life trajectory, the preparatory work he had undertaken, and the transformation of California politics in his lifetime. He was born in Los Angeles the very week that thousands of Chicano students stormed out of high schools across the Eastside and plunged the country's second-largest school district into crisis, dramatically enhancing pressures for reform. Yet by his teens, he too was completely alienated from school and on the verge of flunking out. Rendon spent a couple of years in entry-level warehouse jobs after high school before turning his life around, starting with classes at a community college that he passed on the bus going to and from work. A series of institutions later, his turnaround culminated with his earning a PhD in political theory, completing a post-doctoral fellowship across the country in Boston, and teaching for several years at the university where he got his BA.⁴¹

An advanced liberal education was the route to a different life for Rendon, a life of learning that opened his eyes to art, literature, philosophy, and environmental studies, but the academy itself was not his passion, and he limited his subsequent teaching to adjunct work. He wanted instead to address the dire needs of his community and those around it, of which two stood out: the literally sickening, industrial-corridor urban environment, and the lack of educational attainment by the area's youth. His part of metropolitan LA was and is a troubled area, known as the Southeast Cities and the 710 Corridor.⁴² Anthony got involved with the California League of Conservation Voters and served on its board for over a dozen years, at one point taking over as interim executive director. Thus, Rendon participated in the formative years of the environmental-justice movement.

After a brief but meaningful stint at the Museum of Contemporary Art in downtown LA, Rendon found his most compelling vocation in working on early childhood education programs at the Mexican American Opportunities Foundation. Anthony was just finishing his dissertation when he took the job at MAOF in December 1999. The organization's legendary founder, Don Dionicio Morales, had recently retired from the last of his positions there, but he wanted to be the new guy's first meeting each week. They met for breakfast one-on-one every Monday, Morales imparting a tutorial, an hour at a time, "about social service . . . about how you have an impact on communities and how you change communities."⁴³ Rendon's community certainly needed change. Years later he would tell an audience about his five cousins killed in gang violence. He would refer to his Assembly district's nine cities along the industrial corridor between LA's warehouses and the ports as a "corridor of corruption," explaining that former members of five of the city councils were in prison.⁴⁴

Rendon's experience at MAOF led to the CEO position at another Latino organization with dozens of centers throughout the county, providing preschool programs and related services. He was finally moved to run for office because of his anger and frustration at severe cutbacks in funding for programs like those he directed, as a result of the Great Recession. Rendon packed up his convictions about the critical nature of early childhood development, society's responsibility, and his particular concern for Latino children, and took them into the political and policymaking arenas — a system significantly opened to Latinos and transformed by generations of collective efforts — where he has been able to acquire the power and position to make a difference. In possession of, institutionally, the most powerful office held by a Latino in California, second in clout only to the governor, seventieth Speaker of the California Assembly Anthony Rendon can be said to be living and working in a world remade by the progressive Latino political tradition.

Notes

1. Becerra was asked for California's reaction to the notice that the Trump administration sent to the state and other "so-called 'sanctuary' jurisdictions" "demanding they help enforce federal immigration law or risk losing federal grants." Rebecca Savransky, "Becerra Fires Back: 'We're Not in the Business of Deportation,'" *The Hill*, April 23, 2017, http://thehill.com/homenews/state-watch/330113-becerra-were-in-the-business-of-public-safety-were-not-in-the-business.

2. "Speaker Rendon Strikes Defiant Tone for California as Assembly Reconvenes," Anthony Rendon Speaker of the Assembly Press Release, December 5, 2016, https://speaker.asmdc.org/press-release/speaker-rendon-strikes-defiant-tone-california-assembly-reconvenes.

3. John Myers, "President Trump's Voter Fraud Allegation Is 'a Lie,' Says California's Top Elections Officer," *Los Angeles Times*, January 25, 2017, http://www.latimes.com/politics/essential/la-pol-ca-essential-politics-updates-president-trump-s-new-voter-fraud-1485391926-htmlstory.html.

4. Alejandra Molina, "Sen. Kevin de León, Amid Taunts from Trump Supporters, Tells Riverside to Remain Defiant," *Riverside Press Enterprise*, May 6, 2017, http://www.pe.com/2017/05/06/sen-kevin-de-leon-amid-taunts-from-trump-supporters-tells-riverside-to-remain-defiant/.

5. "Donald Trump on Climate Change Policy," *The O'Reilly Factor*, Fox News, December 3, 2015, http://video.foxnews.com/v/4645149613001/?#sp=show-clips.

6. For a comprehensive survey of the broader issue see Taylor, *The State of Diversity in Environmental Organizations*.

7. Erin Hickey, "Senator de León Skypes with Marshall Students from Paris Climate Summit," *Los Feliz Ledger*, December 30, 2015, http://www.losfelizledger.com/article/senator-de-leon-skypes-with-marshall-students-from-paris-climate-summit/; Chris Megerian, "California Revs Up for Paris Climate-Change Summit," *Los Angeles Times*, November 4, 2015, http://www.latimes.com/politics/la-pol-sac-california-paris-climate-change-delegation-20151104-story.html; and Chris Megerian, "California's Paris Delegation: Who's Going and Who's Paying?" *Los Angeles Times*, November 4, 2015, http://www.latimes.com/politics/la-pol-sac-california-paris-delegation-donors-html-20151104-htmlstory.html.

8. Keeley Smith, "Long Beach Poly Students Get Behind-the-Scenes Look at Paris Climate Talks via Skype Q&A with Sen. Ricardo Lara," *Long Beach Post*, December 9, 2015, https://lbpost.com/news/education/2000007717-long-beach-poly-students-garner-presence-at-paris-climate-talks-in-q-a-with-sen-lara.

9. See Taylor, *Toxic Communities*; Walker, *Environmental Justice*; California Environmental Justice Alliance, "Mission and Vision," http://caleja.org/about-us/vision-and-history/; and US Environmental Protection Agency, "Environmental Justice," last updated August 8, 2017, https://www.epa.gov/environmentaljustice.

10. David Siders, "Why Jerry Brown's Shifting Focus on Pollutants Could Help the Planet — and His Political Causes," *The Sacramento Bee*, December 8, 2015, http://www.sacbee.com/news/politics-government/capitol-alert/article48700275.html; Keeley Smith, "State Sen. Lara Announces Climate Change Legislation from Paris," *Long Beach Post*, December 9, 2015.

11. For more on Lara, see Patrick McGreevy, "Point Man in the Push for Immigrant Rights," *Los Angeles Times*, July 27, 2013, http://www.latimes.com/local/la-me-ricardo-lara-20130728-dto-htmlstory.html; California Legislative Lesbian, Gay, Bisexual and Transgender Caucus, *LGBT Profiles*, "Ricardo Lara: A Few Miles, and a World Away – the Journey of Ricardo Lara," accessed September 25, 2017, http://lgbtcaucus.legislature.ca.gov/sites/lgbtcaucus.legislature.ca.gov/files/LaraProfile.pdf. It was reportedly Núñez and de León's elder colleague, Mayor Antonio Villaraigosa, who played the central role in lining up labor support for Lara's first campaign, conditioned on it being at the right time and in the right district; see Gene Maddaus, "The Chosen One," *LA Weekly*, June 3, 2010, http://www.laweekly.com/news/the-chosen-one-2165333. See also, Phil Wilson, "Trump-Bashing Begins in California's Race for State Insurance Commissioner," *Los Angeles Times*, May 8, 2017, http://www.latimes.com/politics/essential/la-pol-ca-essential-politics-updates-trump-bashing-begins-in-california-s-1494024656-htmlstory.html.

12. Thomas L. Friedman, "Trump: Crazy Like a Fox, or Just Crazy?" *New York Times*, May 3, 2017, https://www.nytimes.com/2017/05/03/opinion/trump-crazy-like-a-fox-or-just-crazy.html?mcubz=1.

13. Journalist Robert Kuttner appears to have first invoked the "failed state" tag in reaction to the crisis and recall election that made Schwarzenegger governor; "Failed State," *The American Prospect*, October 9, 2003, http://prospect.org/article/failed-state-0. A crisis later, in a summer 2009 interview with the *LA Times*, revered California historian Kevin Starr revived the characterization by ruminating that, "In our public life, we're on the verge of being a failed state," to which he curiously added that no state had failed before in US history; Pat Morrison, "Making History: A 2009 Interview with California Historian Kevin Starr," *Los Angeles Times*, July 11, 2009, http://www.latimes.com/opinion/la-oe-morrison-starr11-20090711-story.html. Around the same time, Starr told a class in a USC graduate program on leadership that Ricardo Lara took before his first Assembly campaign that "Mexican Americans are about to inherit a broken state" (Maddaus, "The Chosen One"). British journalist Paul Harris then kicked off a frenzy of slams and autopsies when he cited the earlier Starr quote in his article "Will California become America's First Failed State?" *The Guardian*, October 3, 2009, https://www.theguardian.com/world/2009/oct/04/

california-failing-state-debt. William Voegeli, of the deeply conservative *Claremont Review of Books*, went on to pen his own lengthy takeoff on the Starr quote (Voegeli, "Failed State"). In an extended paean to Governor Jerry Brown, former *Times* editor Narda Zacchino looked back at this discourse, characterized the tag an "epithet" and Starr as "revered" in *California Comeback* (6).

14. "California is the First Failed State," Intelligence Squared US, January 18, 2010, https://www.intelligencesquaredus.org/debates/california-first-failed-state. Governor Gray Davis led the losing team that argued against the motion.

15. "Failed State: Crisis and Renewal in California Politics and Culture," UC Davis, April 16, 2010, http://dhi.ucdavis.edu/failedstate/; "From the Editors," *Boom*, iii-iv; Mathews and Paul, "How to Fix a Broken State," 25–35.

16. Friedman, "Trump: Crazy Like a Fox, or Just Crazy?"

17. Dan Walters, "California's Tax Revolt May Have Run Its Course," *Sacramento Bee*, November 13, 2016, http://www.sacbee.com/news/politics-government/politics-columns-blogs/dan-walters/article114200903.html.

18. Patrick McGreevy, "Lawmakers Advance Proposal to Increase Gas Taxes and Vehicle Fees to Fund California Road Repairs," *Los Angeles Times*, April 3, 2017, http://www.latimes.com/politics/essential/la-pol-ca-essential-politics-updates-legislative-panel-sends-gas-tax-1491249099-htmlstory.html.

19. Patrick McGreevy and Melanie Mason, "California Legislature Votes to Raise Gas Taxes, Vehicle Fees … for Road Repairs and Transit," *Los Angeles Times*, April 6, 2017, http://www.latimes.com/politics/la-pol-sac-california-gas-tax-vote-20170406-story.html.

20. Taryn Luna, "State Legislature's Approval Rating Hits 50 Percent," *The Sacramento Bee*, September 28, 2016, http://www.sacbee.com/news/politics-government/capitol-alert/article104797076.html.

21. George Skelton, "Why Are California Legislators Getting Decent Approval Ratings? They're Getting Things Done," *Los Angeles Times*, April 10, 2017, http://www.latimes.com/politics/la-pol-sac-california-legislature-approval-rating-20170410-story.html.

22. At least in its beginnings, this story is really about the Northeast Valley, but as the Latino population has continued to grow and expand, it has come to refer more generally to the East Valley, in a manner analogous to the loose use of "East LA."

23. Pacoima borders the independent city of San Fernando.

24. Stephanie Chavez, "Profile: Richard Alarcon: Bradley Trains New 'Eyes, Ears' on Valley," *Los Angeles Times*, June 10, 1990, http://articles.latimes.com/1990-06-10/local/me-599_1_east-valley; Richard Simon, "Meyer Serves Bradley as 'Mayor of the Valley,'" *Los Angeles Times*, January 6, 1986, http://articles.latimes.com/1986-01-06/local/me-13556_1_stanley-meyer.

25. Burt, *The Search for a Civic Voice*, 88; Sonenshein, *Politics in Black and White*, 61–62.

26. George Ramos, "Que Pasa?: People and Events," *Los Angeles Times*, January 18, 1990, http://articles.latimes.com/1990-01-18/news/ti-1_1_east-los-angeles.

27. Chavez, "Profile: Richard Alarcon."

28. Ibid.

29. Barbara Whitaker, "Public Lives; A Quick Climb Up the Los Angeles Political Ladder," *New York Times*, July 7, 2001, http://www.nytimes.com/2001/07/07/us/public-lives-a-quick-climb-up-the-los-angeles-political-ladder.html?mcubz=1.

30. Patrick McGreevy, "Setback Put Kevin de León on the Path to Senate Leadership," *Los Angeles Times*, June 18, 2014, http://www.latimes.com/local/la-me-kevin-de-leon-20140619-story.html.

31. Wong, "Cultural Democracy," 76. This discussion also draws from separate original interviews with Gilbert Cedillo and Kent Wong.

32. Patrick J. McDonnell and Robert J. Lopez, "L.A. March Against Prop. 187 Draws 70,000," *Los Angeles Times*, October 17, 1994, http://articles.latimes.com/1994-10-17/news/mn-51339_1_illegal-immigrants. The 2014 *LA Times* article by McGreevy cited earlier put the number of protestors at 80,000.

33. McGreevy, "Setback Put Kevin de León on the Path."

34. Gonzalez Fletcher, in a social media statement welcoming de León's announced challenge to US Senator Diane Feinstein in the 2018 California primary, wrote, "From the day I set foot in the Assembly, Kevin de León has done everything in his power to make sure I was successful" (Lorena Gonzalez Fletcher Facebook post, October 15, 2017). Her hometown newspaper characterized her as a "social media maven," Michael Gardener, "Gonzalez: A Growing Capitol Profile," *The San Diego Union-Tribune*, July 21, 2014, http://www.sandiegouniontribune.com/news/politics/sdut-lorena-gonzalez-assembly-california-immigration-2014jul21-htmlstory.html.

35. Gardener, "Gonzalez"; "Biography," Official Website — Assemblywoman Lorena Gonzalez Representing the 80th California Assembly District, accessed October 17, 2017, https://a80.asmdc.org/biography.

36. Sara Libby, "The California Democrat Setting the National Agenda," *The Atlantic*, July 8, 2015, https://www.theatlantic.com/politics/archive/2015/07/lorena-gonzalez-california/397952/.

37. See Michael Smolens, "Lorena Gets Much More Than 15 Minutes," *The San Diego Union-Tribune*, September 16, 2016, http://www.sandiegouniontribune.com/news/politics/sd-me-politicalnb-0918-story.html.

38. On the "Latino-Labor Alliance," see Harold Meyerson, "What the Democrats Need to Know about Los Angeles," *LA Weekly*, August 9, 2000, http://www.laweekly.com/news/what-the-democrats-need-to-know-about-los-angeles-2132372.

39. "Kevin de León: 'Donald Trump Has No Place in the American Political Space,'" *The Interview*, France 24, December 10, 2015; http://www.france24.com/en/20151209-interview-kevin-de-leon-california-san-bernardino-attack-donald-trump.

40. Jeremy B. White, "Anthony Rendon Selected Next Assembly Speaker," *The Sacramento Bee*, September 3, 2015, http://www.sacbee.com/news/politics-government/capitol-alert/article33841500.html. Barring an extended speakership battle, the Assembly majority typically elects the next Speaker well in advance of the formal vote on the first day of the next session. Rendon's rapid ascent differed from that of Núñez because Rendon did not have the power of labor propelling his career, nor a patron like Polanco. See Willie Brown, "Anthony Rendon, New Assembly Speaker, Is No Machine Hack," *San Francisco*

Chronicle, April 1, 2016, http://www.sfchronicle.com/bayarea/williesworld/article/New-Assembly-speaker-is-no-machine-hack-7223919.php. The time had come when a Latino could reach high office in large part due to power of intellect, strikingly like the "philosopher king" theorized by Plato, who was in fact a key source of inspiration for Rendon. See Melanie Mason, "Punk Rock and Plato Are Touchstones for Incoming Assembly Speaker," *Los Angeles Times*, January 9, 2016, http://www.latimes.com/local/politics/la-me-pol-sac-anthony-rendon-20160110-story.html.

41. George Skelton, "As Next Assembly Speaker, Academic Late-Bloomer Anthony Rendon Aims to Focus on Education," *Los Angeles Times*, November 2, 2015, http://www.latimes.com/local/politics/la-me-pol-sac-cap-anthony-rendon-20151102-column.html; Koren Wetmore, "The Philosopher Politician, Anthony Rendon PhD '00," *UCR Magazine* (Spring 2016), https://magazine.ucr.edu/4779.

42. "Speaking Up for Education," *Titan Magazine*, August 29, 2016, http://news.fullerton.edu/2016su/Anthony-Rendon.aspx; "About 710 Corridor," *KCET Departures*, accessed September 25, 2017, https://www.kcet.org/shows/departures/projects/710-corridor; Janet Wilson, "Cancer Risk Rises for Those Near Rail Yards," *Los Angeles Times*, May 25, 2007, http://articles.latimes.com/2007/may/25/local/me-smog25; Margot Roosevelt, "A New Crop of Eco-Warriors Take to Their Own Streets," *Los Angeles Times*, September 24, 2009, http://www.latimes.com/local/la-me-air-pollution24-2009sep24-story.html; Monika Shankar, "Land Use in South L.A.: A Legacy of Environmental Crime," *KCET Departures*, November 14, 2014, https://www.kcet.org/shows/departures/land-use-in-south-la-a-legacy-of-environmental-crime.

43. Anthony Rendon, remarks in accepting the Mexican American Opportunity Foundation Community Award, published on YouTube October 10, 2016, https://youtu.be/IsD-iWn4KGl8.

44. Anthony Rendon, "Assembly Speaker Anthony Rendon Inaugural Speaker's Lecture Series," *Assembly Access*, Assembly Democratic Caucus (YouTube channel), streamed live September 8, 2016; https://www.youtube.com/watch?v=2d96T82DXjo; Alexei Koseff, "California Politicians Stole Their Money. Will That Make Them Care about Democracy?" *The Sacramento Bee*, May 7, 2017, http://www.sacbee.com/news/politics-government/capitol-alert/article148912624.html.

EPILOGUE

Invisible No More

WHEN DONALD TRUMP CLINCHED HIS PRESIDENTIAL NOMINATION at the end of May 2016, it was a given that, were he to win in November, at least one and most likely two of California's top Latino leaders in office at that time would be on the ballot two years later, in the midterm elections that would be considered a referendum on the new president — and in which the party in the White House usually takes a beating.[1] Both Secretary of State Alex Padilla and Assembly Speaker Anthony Rendon would be up for reelection in 2018. By the time Trump formally won his party's nomination in July 2016, second-term state Senator Ed Hernández had added his bid for lieutenant governor to the lineup. Two days after Trump won the presidency in November, Antonio Villaraigosa officially launched his campaign to top the 2018 California ballot as candidate for governor — making clear not only what he was running for, but also what and whom he was running against.[2]

By the first of December, when Governor Jerry Brown nominated veteran Congressman Xavier Becerra to fill the vacated office of attorney general, the next elections appeared destined to feature a record number of Latino candidates running statewide campaigns. Three weeks into Trump's presidency, Becerra confirmed that he was running for a full term as attorney general the next year. Six weeks after that, Senator Ricardo Lara launched his campaign for state insurance commissioner. Sacramento's *Capitol Weekly* noted that "having five Latinos as top-tier statewide candidates, including two incumbents, is unprecedented." The author of that observation, a prominent, non-Latino professional political analyst, columnist, and consultant, predicted that the state's voters would in 2018 "for the first time see an election where the majority of political mailers, commercials, and media coverage will be focused on campaigns for Latinos."[3] Seven months after those words were written, state Senate President Kevin de León formally announced his candidacy for the US Senate seat held by veteran Senator Dianne Feinstein, taking the 2018 California Latino political surge to yet a higher plane.[4]

That prospect, on the statewide level, did not take into account the dozens of other Latina and Latino members of Congress and the state legislature who would be campaigning for reelection, nor Latino candidates running for the first time. In metropolitan LA alone, notable incumbent members of Congress seeking reelection would include Linda Sanchez, vice chair of the House Democratic

Caucus; Tony Cardenas, head of the Congressional Hispanic Caucus political action committee; Lucille Roybal-Allard, the embodiment of the progressive Latino political tradition initiated by her father in California; and Norma Torres, former suburban mayor and state legislator and the first Central American immigrant elected to Congress. Of the eight Latino Assemblymembers representing Los Angeles County when Trump took office, seven would be seeking reelection, led by Speaker Rendon.

Of the candidates not yet in office, running for the first time, one towered over the rest. Maria Elena Durazo, after decades of getting labor allies elected, announced through *La Opinión* her own campaign to succeed Kevin de León in the state Senate.[5] *The Sacramento Bee* quickly followed, reporting that this news from LA "sent a jolt of adrenalin through the political establishment in Sacramento."[6]

Maria Elena's campaign would, of course, be conducted in de León's district, a fortieth of the state's political map, one of 13 Senate districts in LA County, the equivalent of two Assembly seats, but together with the other campaigns — especially the astonishing six statewide candidacies all also based in the county — the planets seemed to have aligned for a midterm election like no other in the Latino political experience and in state history. Did the trajectory of Latino empowerment in California just happen to find itself on a collision course with the rise of Trumpism nationally? Or was the Trump threat fueling and accelerating unprecedented Latino political mobilization? Would Californian voters in 2018 clearly reaffirm their 2016 rejection of Trump and their support for progressive, multicultural political leadership and activist government? Or might the appearance of a Latino political surge spark a backlash?

There had been significant Latino candidates for statewide office before, but the twentieth century nearly ended in California without a single success. Ed Roybal and Hank Lopez were frustrated in their runs for lieutenant governor and secretary of state in the 1950s. Art Torres's bid for insurance commissioner fell victim to the anti-immigrant wave of 1994. Finally, Cruz Bustamante was able to parlay his breakthrough turn as Speaker of the California State Assembly into a winning race for lieutenant governor in 1998. Although reelected in 2002, Bustamante lost in his attempt to move up the statewide ladder to governor in 2003, as well as down it to insurance commissioner in 2006. Other failed efforts included LA City Attorney Rocky Delgadillo for attorney general, state Senator Gloria Romero for superintendent of public instruction, former Assembly Speaker John Pérez for state controller — all based in LA. Padilla's 2014 election as secretary of state made him just the second Latino elected statewide since the 1800s. In 2016, Loretta Sanchez gave up her Orange County seat in Congress for an unsuccessful run for US Senate.

But none of those previous Latino statewide candidacies acquired the defining social, political, and cultural weight that Tom Bradley's runs for governor in the 1980s had for California, or that Antonio Villaraigosa's bids for mayor in the 2000s had for LA. The voters' turn against Bradley on Election Day 1982, when he had been leading in all the polls, gave rise to the political concept of the "Bradley effect" — when the actual vote for a minority group candidate falls significantly below his or her pre-election polling, without any late developments to account for the difference. Many analysts concluded that, in some elections with heightened racial implications, a significant number of white voters disguised their actual intentions to pollsters.[7]

The meaning of any election can be recast by later events. Following Villaraigosa's loss to James Hahn in 2001, some Los Angeles voters seemed to have experienced a kind of remorse that led them to reconsider and elect Villaraigosa mayor on his second try in 2005. Hahn's effort to win once again with a late smear campaign failed miserably, much as Mayor Sam Yorty's similar tactic did against challenger Tom Bradley in their 1973 rematch.[8] But it seems inevitable that the response to the six simultaneous Latino statewide candidacies in 2018 will be read as a key, and perhaps definitive, gauge of California voters' commitment to the idea and reality of Latino leadership, and as a signal of the support Latino leaders will have in the state's ongoing resistance to Trump.

We know in advance about the many barriers Latinos had to overcome and all that they had to accomplish, usually in coalition with others, to make such a field of candidates in a single upcoming election politically and historically possible. But we also know that as California emerged as the stronghold of resistance to Trump and his designs on immigration, healthcare, the environment, and relations with Mexico, Latino leadership had not yet jelled as a salient concept in the minds of many Californians — even among those particularly knowledgeable about politics and sympathetic to how the state has evolved. To take a prominent example, a veteran *Los Angeles Times* journalist who had served as the paper's politics and government editor, and as its bureau chief in Sacramento, painted a picture of Governor Jerry Brown as the state's savior in her otherwise detailed 2016 book *California Comeback*. Although this valuable account extensively discussed Latinos and immigration issues, just one top Latino leader rated a passing mention in it, in the author's look back to Proposition 187.[9] Furthermore, in this book, the extension of Medicaid health benefits in 2015 to undocumented children is described as a liberal gesture in the governor's budget, but the author and champion of the measure, Senator Ricardo Lara, is not even obliquely alluded to.[10] The landmark Global Warming Solutions Act of 2006 is described as creating "potentially one of the most important programs in California history," but is only credited as "signed into law by Arnold Schwarzenegger"; the authors of the bill and the role played by Assembly Speaker Fabian Núñez, who made its passage possible, did not even make it into a footnote.[11] It seems safe to say that many analysts of politics, even in California, are still unaccustomed to having readers who might notice and object to such lapses, or reviewers who might find them at least curious.

Of all the barriers in Greater LA that Latino empowerment efforts had to overcome to mount the electoral surge of 2018, perhaps the most difficult and

consequential has been the manifold fragmentation of the region. On the short-
est of lists of classic studies of Los Angeles is *The Fragmented Metropolis*, a
1967 interpretive tour de force that portrays what specialists call *municipal fragmentation* as being — along with booming growth itself — the defining feature
of the development of the LA metropolitan area.[12] The vast Mexican-American
population on LA's Greater Eastside was severely hampered in gaining representation at any level in the first half of the twentieth century by, along with other
factors, being geographically split among various local jurisdictions. Municipal
fragmentation was a dynamic structural feature of local politics and government
as new municipalities and governing authorities were formed at a rapid clip over
several decades.[13] Blatant racial considerations guided many of the municipal incorporation, annexation, and secession efforts.[14] From the perspective of Latino
wellbeing and empowerment, these fragmenting governmental structures were
exacerbated by land-use policies, the location of freeways and other public works,
and the drawing of electoral district lines. The segregation and division of communities acted to suppress minority and ethnic group voting and representation in
what Robert Fogelson called "the fragmented metropolis par excellence."[15] But
as a later generation of LA-based urban scholars noted about Latinos, "There had
always been some level of community organizing within this most fragmented of
communities."[16]

* * *

IRONICALLY, AS MINORITY GROUPS HAVE MADE STRIDES in overcoming the
various ways that municipal fragmentation and a panoply of other policies and
practices have long served to exclude and marginalize them, critics of collective
empowerment efforts have resisted by characterizing such endeavors as divisive
"identity politics." But precisely the opposite is evident in the Latino political experience, and it merits due recognition: the often unifying and integrative means
and consequences of Latino empowerment. We have seen how, in the first instance, Mexican-American political mobilization in Boyle Heights initiated by
Ed Roybal's first campaign in 1947 soon brought a diverse coalition together and
additional thousands of citizens into the electoral process, substantially advancing
political integration in LA, from the voter rolls to the city council, with Roybal's
election in 1949. In the early 1970s, Esteban Torres and TELACU brought thousands of East LA residents into the county's housing renewal process. Richard
Alatorre's first campaigns in those years not only brought additional Mexican
Americans into the electoral system, they also pulled in gay voters in an unprecedented fashion in Southern California. Gloria Molina's trifecta of election wins
from 1982 to 1991 advanced the integration of many more Latinas and Latinos
into civic life, policymaking, and government in the city, county, and state.

Alatorre's and Roybal's roles in leading Latino elected officials to act collec-
tively in Sacramento and Washington, founding their respective legislative cau-

cuses, obviously brought participating representatives together, but as we have seen, they also served to advance policies that, over time, helped bring millions more voters into the political system and integrate Latinos into hundreds of decision-making bodies across the country at every level. They also served to integrate Latinos into leadership positions in every branch of government. Prior to these efforts, no Latina or Latino had served in either the president's or the California governor's cabinet, on either the state or federal Supreme Court, or in a leadership position in Congress, the state legislature, LA City Council or school district, major political party, or labor union. Integration of Latinos into such high-profile public leadership positions was preceded by appointments to thousands of subordinate posts — as US ambassadors, deputy and assistant secretaries, judges, agency directors, local department heads, commission members, prosecutors, and leaders in public educational institutions from preschool to the University of California.

The integrative nature of Latino group action by legislators was evident when state Senator Richard Polanco served simultaneously as chair of the Latino Legislative Caucus and as majority leader of the state Senate — as his successor Marco Firebaugh did later. The unifying impact of enhanced Latino leadership in the legislature can be further seen in the two houses' election of Latinos as their current Speaker and president, their success in achieving two-thirds majorities in each house, their ability to deliver legislative results, and in the legislature's radically improved approval rating among the state's registered voters. The enlargement and rebranding of the California Legislature's Chicano Caucus to become the Latino Caucus was itself an inclusive, integrating step. In Washington, the Congressional Hispanic Caucus and the National Association of Latino Elected and Appointed Officials were inclusive in this manner from the start. Decades after its founding, the CHC went on to take a critical, further integrative step in joining in the creation of the "Tri-Caucus," along with the Congressional Black Caucus and the Congressional Asian Pacific American Caucus.[17]

The primarily integrative thrust of Latino empowerment efforts can be further seen in the routes these might have taken but never did: in spite of repeated attempts, East Los Angeles was never incorporated as a separate city; Mexican Americans did not significantly support the separatist Raza Unida Party; Latinos did not support the secession of the San Fernando Valley; and they never sought the breakup of the Los Angeles Unified School District.[18]

Furthermore, the rise of Latino leadership and the power shift they effected has done much more than advance Latinos themselves. This can be seen in how Latino activism and advocacy fostered the coming together of LA County's environmentally stressed but structurally fragmented southeast cities. When the time approached for the legislative redistricting process in conjunction with the 1990 census, the head of the Mexican American Legal Defense and Educational Fund at that time, Antonia Hernández, called practicing attorney Martha Escutia to urge her to work with that area's small cities to push for a common Assembly district, which would give them a voice in Sacramento. Escutia took on the challenge and led these municipalities into fashioning a district plan that was adopted by the committee of judges put in charge of that decade's redistricting. The able and rising attorney was then persuaded to run for the Assembly seat representing the new district, won the eager support of Richard Polanco and the Latino Legislative Caucus, was elected, and assumed formal, public responsibility for the area. In addition to her many policy initiatives that benefited the district in the ensuing years, the new assemblymember led the southeast cities in forming a joint community development corporation.[19] The forces set in motion by the various Latino leaders and groups in this experience ultimately made it possible for a later representative of the area, Anthony Rendon, to ascend to the Assembly speakership in 2016. Another consequence of Latino-led empowerment of the southeast cities has been the role their representatives have played in bringing environmental-justice measures into California's policy leadership in combatting pollution and climate change. Latino leaders, activists, and organizations have played similar roles in bringing together otherwise fractured communities of interest in other parts of the state.

The ongoing case of the advancing environmental-justice agenda illustrates the indispensable complementarity between social movements and reformist professional politicians — the critical interrelationship between the role of the outsiders and that of the insiders. Historians have documented how this has been a basic aspect of political and social progress since the movement that resulted in the founding of the United States.[20] The Latino quest for political empowerment traced in this book shows the essential connection between activism and mobilization on one hand, and the acquisition of professional political skills and elected office on the other, from Boyle Heights to the southeast cities, from redistricting to the immigrant rights movement and the role of revitalized labor.

The basic requirements for the journey we have examined, from political and social exclusion to an advancing role in leading the great, progressive city, region, and state, are as few as the fingers of a hand, but in combination have been able to pack a mighty punch: grassroots organization, regard for mentors and role models, the development of leaders with professional political skills, the embrace of newcomers and diversity, and the building of diverse coalitions. These factors, energized by the dynamic link between the work of the insiders and outsiders toward common ends, have proven capable of overcoming many daunting barriers and setbacks and achieving long-sought reforms.

In the course of this journey, politically active Latinos forged values, dispositions, and a perspective that can be seen as constituting not just a critical power shift, but a progressive political tradition, one that notably contrasts with the venerable precepts distilled by historian Richard Hofstadter in his classic *The American Political Tradition*. Writing during World War II, Hofstadter looked back and saw in American leaders, from the founders to Franklin Roosevelt, a dogmatic attachment to the inviolability of private property, a cult of individualism, and faith in the value of competition.[21] The roots of the modern Latino political tradition cannot be found there. We saw in the case of our first pioneer, Ed Roybal, a political origin that followed the same path as that of his New Mexico role model, Dennis Chavez. Roybal, like Chavez, was born into a Republican family, but both deliberately and consequentially abandoned the party of Herbert Hoover's "rugged individualism" in favor of the pragmatic, activist governing approach of the New Deal.[22]

It was common for Mexican Americans in the nineteenth-century Southwest to favor the Republican Party, as did most African Americans back East. Republicans of that era opposed slavery and supported civil rights. They were against the French invasion and occupation of Mexico in the 1860s, favoring the unyielding resistance of the besieged Mexican Republic led by Benito Juárez.[23] But a third of the way into the twentieth century, the Great Depression and the New Deal provoked a reconsideration of party loyalty and a turn against the free-market dogma of the post-Progressive Era Republican Party.

The view took shape and took hold over time that government can do people and communities great harm but can also be employed to do great good. The understanding developed that government can help solve social problems, but that certain social groups have been systematically excluded from the political processes that determine what government does and who it serves. The encounter with others of diverse origins, similarly situated as outsiders to the political system and dependent upon insider employers to survive, fostered a disposition to undertake joint collective action to compel government to be more responsive, and to restructure it if necessary.

Embracing some aspects of the New Deal was a pragmatic break with dogma, not a conversion to a new doctrine.[24] The emergent Latino political tradition, developed and institutionalized under the leadership of the figures introduced in this book, is pragmatic and nondogmatic; reformist and nonradical; supportive of activist government, coalition, and compromise; able to relate simultaneously to business, unionism, and, in its day, the antibourgeois Chicano movement; tolerant of differences in background and lifestyle; anchored in college-educated, professional, big-city urban life but able to identify with the agonies of clandestine migration, farm labor, and even gangs and the imprisoned.

Whatever the outcome of California's unprecedented Latino political surge of 2018 and the test of our collective character that it presents, the fundamental power shift that made getting to this moment possible, and those who have led and are leading the charge forward, will be visible as never before.

Notes

1. The Associated Press and CNN separately confirmed on May 26, 2016, that Trump had won the support of enough delegates to secure nomination at the Republican Convention in July. Kyle Cheney, "AP calls Republican Primary for Trump," *Politico*, May 26, 2016, http://www.politico.com/story/2016/05/trump-gop-primary-delegate-wins-223605;

M. J. Lee, "Donald Trump Has Delegates to Clinch Gop Nomination," *CNN Politics*, May 26, 2016, http://www.cnn.com/2016/05/26/politics/donald-trump-has-delegates-to-clinch-gop-nomination/index.html; on the pattern of midterm elections see Busch, *Horses in Midstream*.

2. For an inventory of elected officials and declared candidates, see "The Green Papers: California 2018 General Election," *The Green Papers*, last modified September 23, 2017, https://www.thegreenpapers.com/G18/CA.

3. Paul Mitchell, "CA120: High Diversity, But Low Turnout Looms in 2018," *Capitol Weekly*, March 15, 2017, http://capitolweekly.net/2018-elections-record-diversity-low-turnout-looms/.

4. Seema Mehta and Melanie Mason, "California Senate Leader Kevin de León Announces He Will Challenge Sen. Dianne Feinstein," *Los Angeles Times*, October 15, 2017, http://www.latimes.com/politics/la-pol-ca-kevin-de-leon-Senate-run-dianne-feinstein-20171014-story.html.

5. Araceli Martínez Ortega, "María Elena Durazo se lanza en campaña por el Senado de California," *La Opinión*, April 6, 2017, https://laopinion.com/2017/04/06/maria-elena-durazo-se-lanza-en-campana-por-el-senado-estatal/.

6. Christopher Cadelago, "Key Labor Leader Maria Elena Durazo to Run for Kevin de León's Senate Seat," *The Sacramento Bee*, April 6, 2017, http://www.sacbee.com/news/politics-government/capitol-alert/article143093544.html.

7. See Payne and Ratzan, *Tom Bradley;* and Payne, "Shaping the Race Issue."

8. Michael Finnegan and Mark Z. Barabak, "Villaraigosa's Support Goes beyond Latinos," *Los Angeles Times*, May 19, 2005, http://articles.latimes.com/2005/may/19/local/me-exit19.

9. Zachinno, *California Comeback*, 157. The book highlights the role played by Chicano cartoonist Lalo Alcaraz in the debate over Proposition 187; see 138–39.

10. Ibid., 272–73.

11. Ibid., 191. The original author of the bill ("AB32") was environmentalist and then-Assemblymember Fran Pavley, who was joined by Speaker Núñez as coauthor.

12. Fogelson, *The Fragmented Metropolis*.

13. See Hogen-Esch, "Consolidation, Fragmentation and New Fiscal Federalism."

14. Ethington, "Segregated Diversity."

15. Fogelson declared at the outset of his landmark opus, *The Fragmented Metropolis*, that "More than any other American metropolis — and with remarkably few misgivings — Los Angeles succumbed to the disintegrative, though not altogether undesirable, forces of suburbanization and progressivism. And as a result it emerged by 1930 as the fragmented metropolis par excellence, the archetype, for better or worse, of the contemporary American metropolis" (2). Nearly a half-century later, the authors of a leading textbook on local politics noted in their discussion of metropolitan fragmentation: "The Los Angeles Area is one of the largest and most fragmented of all areas. Los Angeles County has 292 towns and cities, of which 88 are incorporated as legally recognized municipal governments (cities)" (Donovan, Smith, Osborn, and Mooney, *State and Local Politics*, 419).

16. Gottlieb, Freer, Vallianatos, and Dreier, *The Next Los Angeles*, 164.

17. Tyson, *Twists of Fate*.

18. See O'Connor, "Public Benefits from Public Choice"; O'Connor, "These Communities"; and Ihn, "The Long Road to Self-Determination."

19. Mary Helen Berg, "Cities Join Forces to Tackle Common Problems While Cutting Costs: Government: Coalition Seeks to Give Communities More Clout and Access to Funding," *Los Angeles Times*, October 1, 1994, http://articles.latimes.com/1994-10-01/local/me-45283_1_common-problems; also based on authors' interview with Martha Escutia.

20. Wilentz, *The Politicians and the Egalitarians*. Other academic approaches to American politics have similar or complementary implications, such as Brown, *Moderates*; and Jonathan Rauch and Benjamin Wittes, "More Professionalism, Less Populism: How Voting Makes Us Stupid, and What to Do about It," *Brookings Institution*, May 31, 2017, https://www.brookings.edu/research/more-professionalism-less-populism-how-voting-makes-us-stupid-and-what-to-do-about-it/.

21. Hofstadter, *The American Political Tradition*. Hofstadter described the tradition in these sweeping terms at the outset, but in a final chapter portrayed Roosevelt as having had a "great receptivity" to ideas and proposals (327–28), an "experimental temper" antithetical to the social and economic philosophy that he and his Republican predecessor Herbert Hoover were both reared on (316), and as having been educated in politics with a "progressive optimism" that conceived of no social ill beyond the reach of government policy (324). In spite of FDR's affirmation of belief in free enterprise in his final campaign in 1944 (346), his disregard for "abstract principle" and the improvised nature of the New Deal — pursued against adamant conservative resistance — appear to have departed from, if not definitely broken with, the American political tradition as defined by Hofstadter.

22. Hoover's Madison Square Garden speech to close his 1928 presidential campaign expanded on his signature theme of "rugged individualism" and called for shrinking the federal government. Text available at http://teachingamericanhistory.org/library/document/rugged-individualism/. As president, Hoover went on to repeatedly invoke the phrase in the face of the deepening Great Depression. See Davenport and Lloyd, *The New Deal & Modern American Conservatism* and *Rugged Individualism*.

23. Hayes-Bautista in *El Cinco de Mayo* details support for Lincoln and the Republican Party by Mexican Americans in California. On the tradition of African-American identification with the Republican Party from the Civil War to the New Deal, see the first three chapters of Farrington, *Black Republicans and the Transformation of the GOP*.

24. The New Deal had decidedly racist aspects, as detailed by Sanchez in "Disposable People," and most recently by Rothstein in *The Color of Law*.

Acknowledgments

Our book would not have been possible without the generous cooperation of the eight living principal leaders who agreed to multiple interviews, in many cases coming to us and in others opening their offices and even their homes and sharing their memories: Richard Alatorre, Gilbert Cedillo, Maria Elena Durazo, Gloria Molina, Richard Polanco, Art Torres, Esteban Torres, and Antonio Villaraigosa.

Numerous other witnesses to the history covered here were similarly generous with their time and patient with our many questions: Ed Avila, Willie Brown, Bruce Cain, Tom Castro, William Deverell, Martha Escutia, Deena Gonzalez, Robert Hertzberg, Walter Karabian, David Lizarraga, Christine Marín, Lou Moret, Yolanda Nava, Sandra Serrano-Sewell, Frank Sotomayor, Cynthia Telles, Fernando Torres-Gil, and Kent Wong. Many others contributed to informing our work through less formal but no less illuminating conversations and email exchanges, including Kenneth Burt, Ernie Camacho, Mike Davis, Moctezuma Esparza, Leo Estrada, Victor Griego, Vilma Martinez, Cindy Montañez, Manuel Pastor, Robert Stern, Roberto Suro, and Arturo Vargas.

Special thanks are due to Marc Grossman, who shared the pre-publication manuscript he collaborated on with Richard Alatorre and was open to any number of questions and conversations. Jeff Penichet shared Frank Berumen's manuscript on Edward Roybal and put us in touch with him, who also cheerfully answered our questions.

George's Personal Acknowledgments

This book had its genesis over a decade ago when I began to fully understand that the history of California's Latino political genius was not being sufficiently told. I am grateful for my co-author David Ayón, a brilliant political scientist who shared my dream of telling this story and who worked tirelessly to make *Power Shift* a reality.

My thanks also go to Diane Gonzalez-Cibrian, who with her extraordinary energy and intellect provided editorial support, research, and management in her role as principal consultant. She was instrumental in moving this project forward along with our editor and publishing consultant Anitra Grisales, whose expertise proved remarkable and invaluable; together their focus and determination kept this project on track.

Thank you to Hector Cruz Sandoval, our talented cover designer; my Senior Executive Assistant Romie Vega and Executive Assistant Elaine Vega, who for 30 years have never wavered in their support and belief in what we do; Maria Mehranian and Randall Martinez, who work with me to make a difference where we live and work; Dr. Mireya Loza, curator at the Smithsonian Institution's National Museum of American History, for recommending our editor; Professor Bruce Cain for suggesting our publisher; Ethan Rarick and Maria Wolf at Berkeley Public Policy Press, who diligently took us through this process and believed this material should be recorded for American political history; and Secretary Mickey Kantor, friend and mentor, for advice and counsel.

I am grateful to have been a part of this history, and I dedicate this work to my family: my wife Gail, who has been supportive of my many projects for the past 45 years; my children Vincent and Lisa; my grandchildren Vanessa, Daniel, Patrick, Damian, and Kane; and my great grandchildren Noah and Kaden, so that they may learn about the great Latinos who reshaped California and American politics.

David's Personal Acknowledgments

George had the original idea for *Power Shift* and proposed we undertake this challenge together. Our book would be inconceivable without George's own contributions and witness to the history contained within these covers, his enduring relationships with virtually all of the players, the vast amounts of time and support he and his Cordoba Corporation staff put into the many interviews we conducted, and his great patience and high standards for every aspect of the book.

My thanks to Summer Azucena Wall, who contributed to this project first as a transfer student to LMU with a passion for immigrant rights, and then as a research assistant and collaborator on my Latina/o Politics class. Fernando Guerra and the staff of the Center for the Study of Los Angeles provided an academic home and many insights over the years of development of this project, including his own dialogs with half of the living principals of the book.

I am also indebted to my late college roommate, Jorge G. Castro, and to his big brother Thomas Castro, for my start in learning about Los Angeles and California politics, as well as to the late Jessica Govea and the legendary Marshall Ganz. The great American historian David Kennedy provided encouragement and astutely recommended *The Wise Men* as an exemplary model of group biography.

My most special thanks are to my *compañera* from long before this project began, Monica Lozano, and her parents Nacho and Marta, who over many years offered memories, insights, and loving support, and even sat for several formal interviews. The Lozanos and *La Opinión* played indispensable roles in the Power Shift. Much more of this experience remains to be chronicled — even as it continues to unfold every day.

Table of Abbreviations

AA	Administrative Assistant
ACLU	American Civil Liberties Union
AFL	American Federation of Labor
ALRA	Agricultural Labor Relations Act
ALRB	Agricultural Labor Relations Board
CAP	Community Action Program
CASA	Centro de Acción Social Autónoma
CFMN	Comisión Femenil Mexicana Nacional
CDC	Community Development Corporation
CHC	Congressional Hispanic Caucus
CIO	Congress of Industrial Organizations
CSAC	Chicana Service Action Center
CSO	Community Service Organization
DA	District Attorney
DOJ	Department of Justice
ELAC	East LA College
EOA	Economic Opportunity Act
EOP	Executive Office of the President
FEPC	Fair Employment Practices Commission
HERE	Hotel Employees and Restaurant Employees Union
IAF	Industrial Areas Foundation
LMAW	League of Mexican American Women
LAPD	Los Angeles Police Department
LAUSD	Los Angeles Unified School District
LDF	Legal Defense Fund
MALDEF	Mexican American Legal Defense and Educational Fund
MAPA	Mexican American Political Association
MELA	Mothers of East Los Angeles
MTA	Metropolitan Transportation Authority
NAACP	National Association for the Advancement of Colored People
NALEO	National Association of Latino Elected and Appointed Officials
NDP	Neighborhood Development Project
NLRA	National Labor Relations Act
NOW	National Organization for Women
OEO	Office of Economic Opportunity
PCL	Peoples College of Law
PPIC	Public Policy Institute of California
SEIU	Service Employees International Union

TELACU	The East Los Angeles Community Union
UAW	United Auto Workers
UC	University of California
UCI	University of California, Irvine
UCLA	University of California, Los Angeles
UCSC	University of California, Santa Cruz
UFW	United Farm Workers
USC	University of Southern California
VRA	Voting Rights Act

References

Original Interviews
(Recorded unless otherwise noted.)

Alatorre, Richard. Interview with authors, February 8, 2012; March 29, 2013; April 24, 2013; June 26, 2013; and July 28, 2015, Los Angeles, CA.
———. Interview with Fernando Guerra, November 17, 2016, Loyola Marymount University, http://studyla.org/podcast/change-from-the-inside-richard-alatorre.
Avila, Edward J. Interview with authors, January 16, 2013 (notes only); and May 23, 2013, Los Angeles, CA.
Brown, Willie. Interview with authors, August 1, 2015, San Francisco, CA.
Cain, Bruce. Interview with authors, April 30, 2013, Stanford, CA.
Castro, Tom. Interview with authors, June 16, 2013, Los Angeles; July 6, 2013, Pasadena, CA.
Cedillo, Gilbert. Interview with authors, September 15, 2014; September 29, 2014; February 9, 2015; March 9, 2015; April 2, 2015; July 30, 2015; and August 4, 2016, Los Angeles, CA.
———. Interview with Fernando Guerra, October 15, 2013, Loyola Marymount University, Los Angeles, https://www.youtube.com/watch?v=4jH9X9b_W1E&t=478s.
Deverell, William. Interview with authors, July 23, 2013, San Marino, CA.
Durazo, Maria Elena. Interview with authors, May 11 and May 23, 2016, Los Angeles, CA.
Escutia, Martha. Interview with authors by phone, June 11, 2017.
González, Deena J. Interview with authors by phone, March 30, 2018 (notes only).
Gonzalez, Diane. Interview with authors, January 27, 2016; March 4, 2016; and March 15, 2016, Los Angeles, CA.
Hertzberg, Robert. Interview with authors, June 22, 2014, Los Angeles, CA.
Lizarraga, David. Interview with authors, February 21, 2013; May 7, 2013; May 28, 2014; and July 24, 2015, Los Angeles, CA.
Lozano, Jr., Ignacio. Interview with authors, February 16, 2013; February 23, 2013; March 23, 2013; and May 4, 2014, Newport Beach, CA.
Lozano, Monica. Interview with authors, March 9, 2013 and April 4, 2013, Los Angeles, CA.
Marín, Christine. Interview with authors by phone, August 29, 2016.
Molina, Gloria. Interview with authors, October 16, 2014, Los Angeles; September 8, 2017 (notes only), Los Angeles, CA; September 10, 2017, by tele-

phone (notes only); September 11, 2017, by telephone (notes only); March 29, 2018, by telephone (notes only).

———. Interview with Fernando Guerra, October 23, 2012, Loyola Marymount University, Los Angeles, https://www.youtube.com/watch?v=48s6_TbCo5Q.

Moret, Lou. Interview with authors, April 25, 2013; June 20, 2013; and April 22, 2014, Los Angeles, CA.

Nava, Yolanda. Interview with authors by phone, March 29, 2018 (notes only).

Polanco, Richard. Interview with authors, March 5, 2013; April 19, 2013; April 25, 2014; July 7, 2015; July 24, 2015; and May 23, 2016, Los Angeles, CA.

Serrano-Sewell, Sandra. Interview with authors by phone, March 30, 2018 (notes only).

Sotomayor, Frank O. Interview with authors by phone, May 7, 2017.

Telles, Cynthia. Interview with authors, February 11 and February 22, 2013, Los Angeles, CA.

Torres, Art. Interview with authors, April 30, 2013 and June 17, 2015, San Francisco, CA.

Torres-Gil, Fernando. Interview with authors, April 2, 2013, Los Angeles, CA.

Villaraigosa, Antonio. Interview with authors, March 5, 2014, Washington, DC; March 13, 2014, Los Angeles, CA; and May 26, 2016, Los Angeles, CA.

———. Interview with Fernando Guerra, February 16, 2016, Loyola Marymount University, Los Angeles, https://www.youtube.com/watch?v=pSpesiBsUCQ.

Wong, Kent. Interview with authors, May 3, 2016, Los Angeles, CA.

Other Interviews and Oral Histories

Alatorre, Richard. Conducted by Carlos Vásquez, 1989–1990, California State Archives State Government Oral History Program, UCLA Center for Oral History Research Interview Collection.

Contreras, Miguel. "Beyond the Dream." Interview conducted by Lyn Goldfarb, July 23, 2004, Los Angeles County Federation of Labor. Transcript provided by Goldfarb.

Conway, Jack T. Interview by Larry J. Hackman, April 11, 1972, Robert Kennedy Oral History Program of the John F. Kennedy Library, ttps://www.jfklibrary.org/Asset-Viewer/Archives/RFKOH-JTC-02.aspx.

Debs, Ernest E. Oral History Interview, Conducted by Carlos Vásquez, 1987, UCLA Oral History Program, for the California State Archives State Government Oral History Program, http://archives.cdn.sos.ca.gov/oral-history/pdf/debs.pdf.

Huerta, John E. Oral History Interview, Conducted by Carlos Vásquez, 1990, UCLA Oral History Program, for the California State Archives State Government Oral History Program, http://www.oac.cdlib.org/view?docId=hb-8c6011pv&brand=oac4&doc.view=entire_text.

Molina, Gloria. Oral History Interview, Conducted by Carlos Vásquez, 1990, UCLA Oral History Program, for the California State Archives State Government Oral History Program, http://content.cdlib.org/view?docId=hb8b69p-65d&brand=calisphere&doc.view=entire_text.

Rosenwein, Sam. Interview Conducted by Michael S. Balter, 1989, UCLA Library, Center for Oral History Research, http://oralhistory.library.ucla.edu/Browse.do?descCvPk=27826.

Roybal, Edward. "Interview no. 184." Conducted Interview by Oscar J. Martinez, October 23, 1975, Institute of Oral History, University of Texas at El Paso, http://digitalcommons.utep.edu/cgi/viewcontent.cgi?article=1243&context=interviews.

Schrade, Paul. "Interview of Paul Schrade." Conducted by Michael Connors, March 1, 1990, UCLA Center for Oral History Research, Tape VIII, Side Two, http://oralhistory.library.ucla.edu/Browse.do?descCvPk=27993.

Torres, Art. Oral History Interview Conducted by Steve Edgington, 2003, California State University, Fullerton Center for Oral and Public History.

Published Sources

Acuña, Rodolfo R. *The Making of Chicana/o Studies: In the Trenches of Academe.* New Brunswick, NJ: Rutgers University Press, 2011.

Agrasánchez, Rogelio. *Mexican Movies in the United States: A History of the Films, Theaters and Audiences, 1920–1960.* Jefferson, NC: McFarland & Co., 2006.

Akenson, Donald Harman. *Surpassing Wonder: The Invention of the Bible and the Talmuds.* Chicago: University of Chicago Press, 2001.

Alatorre, Richard, with Marc Grossman. *Change from the Inside: My Life, the Chicano Movement, and the Story of an Era.* Berkeley, CA: Berkeley Public Policy Press, 2016.

Alquist, Alfred E. "The Field Act and Public School Construction: A 2007 Perspective." California Seismic Safety Commission (February 2007).

Anderson, Margo J. *The American Census: A Social History,* 2nd ed. New Haven, CT: Yale University Press, 2015.

Ayón, David R. "Mobilizing Latino Immigrant Integration: From IRCA to the *Ya Es Hora* Citizenship Campaign, 1987–2007." Woodrow Wilson International Center for Scholars, Mexico Institute, Research Paper Series on Latino Immigrant Civic and Political Participation, No. 1 (January 2009), https://www.wilsoncenter.org/sites/default/files/Ayon%20-%20Mobilizing%20Latino%20Imm%20Integration.pdf.

Bagdikian, Ben H. *The New Media Monopoly.* Boston, MA: Beacon Press, 2004.

Baldasarre, Mark. *A California State of Mind: The Conflicted Voter in a Changing World.* Berkeley: University of California Press, 2002.

Balderrama, Francisco E., and Raymond Rodriguez. *Decade of Betrayal: Mexican Repatriation in the 1930s.* Albuquerque: University of New Mexico Press, 1995.

Baldoz, Rick. *The Third Asiatic Invasion: Empire and Migration in Filipino America, 1898–1946.* New York: NYU Press, 2011.

Bardacke, Frank. *Trampling Out the Vintage: Cesar Chavez and the Two Souls of the United Farm Workers.* New York, NY: Verso, 2011.

Barnard, John. *American Vanguard: The United Auto Workers during the Reuther Years, 1935–1970.* Detroit, MI: Wayne State University Press, 2004.

Barreto, Matt A. *Ethnic Cues: The Role of Shared Ethnicity in Latino Political Participation.* Ann Arbor: University of Michigan Press, 2010.

Barvosa, Edwina. "Multiple Identity and Coalition Building: How Identity Differences within Us Enable Radical Alliances among Us." In *Forging Radical Alliances across Difference: Coalition Politics for the New Millennium,* edited by Jill M. Bystydzienski and Steven P. Schacht. Lanham, MD: Rowman and Littlefield, 2001.

Bauman, Robert. *Race and the War on Poverty: From Watts to East L.A.* Norman: University of Oklahoma Press, 2008.

Bauman, Robert. "Gender, Civil Rights Activism, and the War on Poverty in Los Angeles." In *The War on Poverty: A New Grassroots History, 1964–1980,* edited by Annelise Orleck and Lisa Gayle Hazirjian. Athens: University of Georgia Press, 2011.

Baxter, John O. "The Ignacio de Roybal House." *Bulletin of the Historic Santa Fe Foundation* 6, no. 1 (January 1980).

Becker, Lawrence C., Tyler Hughes, and Jason L. Morin. "The History, Development and Policy Influence of the California Latino Legislative Caucus." Center for Southern California Studies, CSU Northridge.

Bennett, Michael, and Cruz Reynoso. "California Rural Legal Assistance (CRLA): Survival of a Poverty Law Practice." *Chicana/o Latina/o Law Review* 1, no. 1 (1972).

Berman, Ari. *Give Us the Ballot: The Modern Struggle for Voting Rights in America.* New York, NY: Farrar, Straus and Giroux, 2015.

Berumen, Frank. *Edward R. Roybal: The Mexican American Struggle for Political Empowerment.* Los Angeles, CA: Crane Publishing Books, 2015.

Bingham, Clara. *Witness to the Revolution: Radicals, Resisters, Vets, Hippies and the Year America Lost its Mind and Found its Soul.* New York, NY: Random House, 2016.

Blingen, Steven. *Paramount: City of Dreams.* Guilford, CT: Taylor Trade Publishing, 2016.

Boatright, Robert G. *Getting Primaried: The Changing Politics of Congressional Primary Challenges.* Ann Arbor: University of Michigan Press, 2013.

Boyarsky, Bill. *Big Daddy: Jesse Unruh and the Art of Power Politics.* Berkeley: University of California Press, 2008.

Boyle, Kevin. *The UAW and the Heyday of American Liberalism, 1945–1968.* Ithaca, NY: Cornell University Press, 1995.

Briggs, Vernon. "American Unionism and U.S. Immigration Policy." Center for Immigration Studies (August 1, 2001), https://cis.org/American-Unionism-and-US-Immigration-Policy.

Brown, David S. *Moderates: The Vital Center of American Politics, From the Founding to Today.* Chapel Hill: University of North Carolina Press, 2017.

Brown, Willie. *Basic Brown: My Life and Our Times.* New York, NY: Simon & Schuster, 2008.

Buchanan, Patrick J. *The Death of the West: How Dying Populations and Immigrant Invasions Imperil Our Country and Civilization.* New York, NY: Thomas Dunne Books, 2007.

———. *State of Emergency: The Third World Invasion and Conquest of America.* New York, NY: Thomas Dunne Books, 2007.

Burt, Kenneth C. *The Search for a Civic Voice: California Latino Politics.* Claremont, CA: Regina Books, 2007.

Busch, Andrew E. *Horses in Midstream: U.S. Midterm Elections and Their Consequences.* Pittsburgh: University of Pittsburgh Press, 1999.

Buskopic, Joan. *Breaking In: The Rise of Sonia Sotomayor and the Politics of Justice.* New York, NY: Sarah Crichton Books, 2014.

Cain, Bruce, and Karin MacDonald. "Voting Rights Act Enforcement: Navigating between High and Low Expectations." In *The Future of the Voting Rights Act,* edited by David L. Epstein, et al. New York, NY: Russell Sage Foundation, 2006.

Chávez, Fray Angelico. "La Conquistadora is a Paisana," *El Palacio* 57, no. 10 (October 1950).

Chávez, John R. *Eastside Landmark: A History of the East Los Angeles Community Union, 1968–1993.* Stanford, CA: Stanford University Press, 1998.

Chavez, Leo R. *The Latino Threat: Constructing Immigrants, Citizens, and the Nation.* Stanford, CA: Stanford University Press, 2008.

Cheeseman Day, Jennifer. *Population Projections of the United States by Age, Sex, Race, and Hispanic Origin: 1992 to 2050.* U.S. Bureau of the Census, Current Population Reports, Series P-25, No. 1092. Government Printing Office, November 1993.

Citrin, Jack, and Isaac Martin, eds., *After the Tax Revolt: California's Proposition 13 Turns 30.* Berkeley, CA: Berkeley Public Policy Press, 2009.

Colker, Ruth. *Disabled Education: A Critical Analysis of the Individuals with Disabilities Act.* New York: NYU Press, 2013.

Cotera, Marta. "Chicana Conferences and Seminars, 1970–1975." In Garcia, *Chicana Feminist Thought,* 142–44.

Crouch, Dora P., and Alex I. Mundigo. "The City Planning Ordinances of the Laws of the Indies Revisited. Part II: Three American Cities," *The Town Planning Review* 48, no. 4 (October 1977): 409–17.

Davenport, David, and Gordon Lloyd. *The New Deal & Modern American Conservatism: A Defining Rivalry*. Stanford, CA: Hoover Institution Press, 2013.

————. *Rugged Individualism: Dead or Alive?* Stanford, CA: Hoover Institution Press, 2017.

Davidson, Chandler. *Minority Vote Dilution*. Washington, DC: Howard University Press, 1984.

Davis, Mike. *City of Quartz: Excavating the Future in Los Angeles*. New York, NY: Verso, 2006.

Davis Hansen, Victor. *Mexifornia: A State of Becoming*. San Francisco, CA: Encounter Books, 2003.

de Graaf, Lawrence B. "The Changing Face and Place of Race in Los Angeles City Government." In Rudd and Sitton, *The Development of Los Angeles City Government*, 729–93.

del Castillo, Adelaida R. "Comisión Femenil Mexicana Nacional." In *The Oxford Encyclopedia of Latinos and Latinas in the United States*, edited by Suzanne Oboler and Deena J. González. Oxford, UK: Oxford University Press, 2005.

del Olmo, Frank. "Hispanic, Latino or Chicano: A Historical Review." In *Latinos in the United States: A Resource Guide for Journalists*, National Association of Hispanic Journalists. San Jose, CA: Knight Ridder, 2002.

————. "Latino *Sí* – Hispanic, *No*." In Sotomayor and Beltrán-del Olmo, *Frank del Olmo*, 85–87.

Delgado, Richard, Juan F. Pera, and Jean Stefancic. *Latinos and the Law: Cases and Materials*. St. Paul, MN: West Academic Publishing, 2008.

Deverell, William. *The Whitewashed Adobe: The Rise of Los Angeles and the Remaking of its Mexican Past*. Berkeley: University of California Press, 2004.

Dewitt, Larry. "The Decision to Exclude Agricultural and Domestic Workers from the 1935 Social Security Act." *Social Security Bulletin* 70, no. 4 (November 2010).

di Stefano, Onofre. "'*Venimos a luchar*': A Brief History of *La Prensa*'s Founding." *Aztlán* 16, nos. 1–2 (1985): 95–118.

Donovan, Todd, Daniel A. Smith, Tracy Osborn, and Christopher Z Mooney. *State and Local Politics: Institutions and Reform*. 4th ed. Belmont, CA: Wadsworth Publishing, 2014.

Dyste, Connie. "Proposition 63: The California English Language Amendment." *Applied Linguistics* 10, no. 3 (September 1989): 313–30.

El Malcriado: The Official Voice of the United Farmworkers 2 (June 6, 1972), https://libraries.ucsd.edu/farmworkermovement/ufwarchives/elmalcriado/1972/June%206,%201972%20No%202_PDF.pdf.

Ennis, Sharon R., Merarys Ríos-Vargas, and Nora G. Albert. *The Hispanic Population: 2010*. 2010 Census Briefs, C2010BR-04 (May 2011).

Escobar, Edward J. "The Dialectics of Repression: The Los Angeles Police Department and the Chicano Movement, 1968–1971." *The Journal of American History* 49, no. 4 (March 1993): 1483–1514.

————. *Race, Police and the Making of a Political Identity: Mexican Americans and the Los Angeles Police Department, 1900–1945.* Berkeley: University of California Press, 1999.

Estrada, William David. *The Los Angeles Plaza: Sacred and Contested Space.* Austin: University of Texas Press, 2008.

Ethington, Philip J. "Segregated Diversity: Race-Ethnicity, Space, and Political Fragmentation in Los Angeles County, 1940–1994." Final Report to The John Randolf Haynes and Dora Haynes Foundation, Presentation to the USC Population Studies Lab, September 13, 2000, http://www-bcf.usc.edu/~philipje/Segregation/Haynes_Reports/FINAL_REPORT_20000719g.pdf.

————. "Spatial and Demographic Growth of Los Angeles." In Rudd and Sitton, *The Development of Los Angeles City Government*, 651–97.

Farrington, Joshua D. *Black Republicans and the Transformation of the GOP.* Philadelphia: University of Pennsylvania Press, 2016.

Fein, Seth. "Myths of Cultural Imperialism and Nationalism in Golden Age Mexican Cinema." In *Fragments of a Golden Age: The Politics of Culture in Mexico Since 1940*, edited by Gilbert M. Joseph, Anne Rubenstein, and Eric Zolob. Durham, NC: Duke University Press, 2001.

Fernandez, Edward W. "Comparisons of Persons of Spanish Surname and Persons of Spanish Origin in the United States." U.S. Bureau of the Census, Population Division Technical Paper No. 38 (June 1975).

Flores, Francisca. "Comisión Femenil Mexicana." In *García, Chicana Feminist Thought*, 150.

Fogelson, Robert M. *The Fragmented Metropolis: Los Angeles, 1850–1930.* Berkeley: University of California Press, 1967.

Fowler, Gene, and Bill Crawford. *Border Radio: Quacks, Yodelers, Pitchmen, Psychics, and Other Amazing Broadcasters of the American Airwaves.* Austin: University of Texas Press, 2002.

Frank, Larry, and Kent Wong. "Dynamic Political Mobilization: The Los Angeles County Federation of Labor." *WorkingUSA: The Journal of Labor and Society* 8 (December 2004): 155–81.

"From the Editors." *Boom: A Journal of California* 1, no. 1 (Spring 2011): iii-iv, http://boom.ucpress.edu/content/1/1/iii.

Fulton, William B. *The Reluctant Metropolis: The Politics of Urban Growth in Los Angeles.* Baltimore, MD: Johns Hopkins University Press, 1997, 2001.

Gabler, Neal. *An Empire of Their Own: How the Jews Invented Hollywood.* New York, NY: Anchor Books, 1988.

Ganz, Marshall. *Why David Sometimes Wins: Leadership, Organization and Strategy in the California Farm Worker Movement.* New York and Oxford: Oxford University Press, 2009.

García, Alma M., ed. *Chicana Feminist Thought: The Basic Historical Writings.* London and New York: Routledge, 1997.

Garcia, David G. "Remembering Chavez Ravine: Culture Clash and Critical Race Theater." *Chicana/o Latina/o Law Review* 26, no. 1 (2006): 111–30.

García, Ignacio M. *Viva Kennedy: Mexican Americans in Search of Camelot.* College Station: Texas A&M University Press, 2000.

García, Juan R. *Operation Wetback: The Mass Deportation of Mexican Undocumented Workers in 1954.* Westport, CT: Praeger, 1980.

García, Mario T. *The Chicano Generation: Testimonios of the Movement.* Oakland: University of California Press, 2015.

———, ed. *The Chicano Movement: Perspectives from the Twenty-First Century.* New York and London: Routledge, 2014.

———. *Memories of Chicano History: The Life and Narrative of Bert Corona.* Berkeley: University of California Press, 1994.

García, Mario T., and Sal Castro. *Blowout! Sal Castro and the Chicano Struggle for Educational Justice.* Chapel Hill: University of North Carolina Press, 2011.

Garcia, Matt. *A World of Its Own: Race, Labor and Citrus in the Making of Greater Los Angeles, 1900–1970.* Chapel Hill: University of North Carolina Press, 2001.

———. *From the Jaws of Victory: The Triumph and Tragedy of Cesar Chavez and the Farm Worker Movement.* Berkeley: University of California Press, 2012.

Garza, Melita M. *They Came to Toil: Newspaper Representations of Mexicans and Immigrants in the Great Depression.* Austin: University of Texas Press, 2018.

Gatewood, George. *A Monograph on Confidentiality and Privacy in the U.S. Census* (July 2001), https://www.census.gov/history/pdf/ConfidentialityMonograph.pdf.

Gerdes, Louise I., ed. *The 1992 Los Angeles Riots.* Farmington Hills, MI: Greenhaven Press, 2014.

Gerston, Larry N., and Terry Christensen. *Recall! California's Political Earthquake.* New York, NY: Routledge, 2004.

Gey, Fredric, Cecilia Jiang, Jon Stiles, and Ilona Einowski. "California Latino Demographic Databook, 3rd Edition: 2004." *California Policy Research Center* (November 2004), http://ucdata.berkeley.edu/pubs/Databook2004.pdf.

Gibbs, Jewelle Taylor, and Teiahsha Bankhead. *Preserving Privilege: California Politics, Propositions and People of Color.* Westport, CT: Praeger, 2001.

Gillette, Michael L. *Launching the War on Poverty: An Oral History.* 2nd ed. New York and Oxford: Oxford University Press, 2010.

Gomez, Fidel. "Peoples College of Law." *Crime and Social Justice* 20 (1983): 148–50.

Gómez-Quiñónez, Juan. *Mexican Students Por La Raza: The Chicano Student Movement in Southern California, 1967–1977.* Santa Barbara, CA: Editorial La Causa, 1978.

————. "*On Culture.*" *Revista Chicano-Riqueña* 5, no. 2 (*Spring, 1977*): 29–47.

González, Deena J. *Refusing the Favor: Spanish-Mexican Women of Santa Fe, 1820–1880.* New York and Oxford: Oxford University Press, 1999.

Gottlieb, Robert, and Irene Wolt. *Thinking Big: The Story of the Los Angeles Times, Its Publishers, and Their Influence on Southern California.* New York, NY: G. P. Putnam's Sons, 1977.

Gottlieb, Robert, Regina Freer, Mark Vallianatos, and Peter Dreier. *The Next Los Angeles: The Struggle for a Livable City.* Berkeley: University of California Press, 2005.

Graham, Wade. *Dream Cities: Seven Urban Ideas That Shape the World.* New York, NY: HarperCollins, 2016.

Gratton, Brian, and Emily Klancher Merchant. "*La Raza*: Mexicans in the United States Census." *The Journal of Policy History* 28, no. 4 (2016).

Griswold del Castillo, Richard, and Richard A. Garcia, *César Chávez: A Triumph of the Spirit.* Norman: University of Oklahoma Press, 1995.

Griswold del Castillo, Richard, Teresa McKenna, and Yvonne Yarbro-Bejarano, eds. *Chicano Art: Resistance and Affirmation, 1965–1985.* Los Angeles: Wight Art Gallery, 1991.

Guerin-Gonzalez, Camille. *Mexican Workers and the American Dream: Immigration, Repatriation, and California Farm Labor, 1900–1939.* New Brunswick, NJ: Rutgers University Press, 1994.

Gunckel, Colin. "The War of the Accents: Spanish Language Hollywood Films in Mexican Los Angeles." *Film History: An International Journal* 20, no. 3 (2008): 325–43.

————. *Mexico on Main Street: Transnational Film Culture in Los Angeles before World War II.* New Brunswick, NJ: Rutgers University Press, 2015.

Gutiérrez, David. "'Sin Fronteras?': Chicanos, Mexican Americans, and the Emergence of the Contemporary Mexican Immigration Debate, 1968–1978." *Journal of American Ethnic History* 10, no. 4 (Summer, 1991): 5–37.

————. *Walls and Mirrors: Mexican Americans, Mexican Immigrants and the Politics of Ethnicity.* Berkeley: University of California Press, 1995.

Gutiérrez, Elena R. *Fertile Matters: The Politics of Mexican-Origin Women's Reproduction.* Austin: University of Texas Press, 2008.

Gutiérrez, Félix, and Clint C. Wilson II. "The Demographic Dilemma: Is the *Los Angeles Times* Afraid to Expand Minority Coverage Because It Might Lose 'Upscale' White Readers?" *Columbia Journalism Review* (January 1, 1979): 53–55.

Hammerback, John C. "An Interview with Bert Corona." *Western Journal of Speech Communication* 44, no. 3 (Summer 1980): 214–20.

Hattam, Victoria. *In the Shadow of Race: Jews, Latinos, and Immigrant Politics in the United States.* Chicago, IL: University of Chicago Press, 2007.

Hayes-Bautista, David. *El Cinco de Mayo: An American Tradition.* Berkeley: University of California Press, 2012.

Hernández, Antonia. "Chicanas and the Issue of Involuntary Sterilization: Reforms Needed to Protect Informed Consent." *Chicana/o Latina/o Law Review* 3 (1976): 3–37.

Higham, John. *Strangers in the Land: Patterns of American Nativism, 1860–1925.* New Brunswick, NJ: Rutgers University Press, 1955.

Hochschild, Jennifer L., and Brenna M. Powell. "Racial Reorganization and the United States Census 1850–1930: Mulattoes, Half-Breeds, Mixed Parentage, Hindoos, and the Mexican Race." *Studies in American Political Development* 22, no. 1 (Spring 2008): 59–96.

Hoffman, Abraham. *Unwanted Mexican Americans in the Great Depression: Repatriation Pressures, 1929–1939.* Tucson: University of Arizona Press, 1974.

Hofstadter, Richard. *The American Political Tradition and the Men Who Made It.* New York, NY: Knopf, 1948.

Hogen-Esch, Tom. "Consolidation, Fragmentation and New Fiscal Federalism." In *A Companion to Los Angeles*, edited by William Deverell and Greg Hise. Malden, MA: Wiley-Blackwell, 2008.

Holliday, Peter J. *American Arcadia: California and the Classical Tradition.* New York and Oxford: Oxford University Press, 2016.

Horton, John. "A Contribution to the Critique of Academic Marxism: Or How the Intellectuals Liquidate Class Struggle." *Synthesis* 2, no. 1–2 (Summer-Fall 1977): 78–105.

Horwitt, Sanford. *Let Them Call Me Rebel: Saul Alinsky, His Life and Legacy.* New York, NY: Vintage Books: 1992.

Humel Montwieler, Nancy. *The Immigration Reform Law of 1986: Analysis, Text and Legislative History.* Washington, DC: Bureau of National Affairs, 1987.

Huntington, Samuel P. *Who Are We: The Challenges to America's National Identity.* New York, NY: Simon and Schuster, 2004.

Ides, Matthew Allan. *Cruising for Community: Youth Culture and Politics in Los Angeles, 1910–1970.* Ann Arbor: University of Michigan, 2009.

Ihn, Sarah. "The Long Road to Self-Determination: A Critique of Municipal Incorporation through the East Los Angeles Cityhood Movement." *Harvard Latino Law Review* 13 (Spring 2010): 67–90.

Jacobs, John. *A Rage for Justice: The Passion and Politics of Phillip Burton.* Berkeley: University of California Press, 1995.

Jensen, Richard J. "Cesar Chavez, 'Nomination Address for Governor Jerry Brown,' Democratic National Convention (July 14, 1976)." *Voices of Democracy* 6 (2011): 44–62, http://voicesofdemocracy.umd.edu/wp-content/uploads/2014/07/jensen-chavez1.pdf.

Kanellos, Nicolás. *A History of Hispanic Theater in the United States: Origins to 1940.* Austin: University of Texas Press, 1990.

———. *Hispanic Periodicals in the United States: Origins to 1960, A Brief History.* Houston, TX: Arte Público Press, 1999.

Kaplowitz, Craig Alan. *LULAC, Mexican Americans, and National Policy*. College Station: Texas A&M Press, 2005.

Kluger, Richard. *Simple Justice: The History of Brown v. Board of Education and Black America's Struggle for Equality*. New York, NY: Vintage Books, 2004.

Koegel, John. "Mexican Musical Theater and Movie Palaces in Downtown Los Angeles before 1950." In *The Tide Was Always High: The Music of Latin America in Los Angeles*, edited by Josh Kun. Oakland: University of California Press, 2017.

Kousser, J. Morgan. *Colorblind Justice: Minority Voting Rights and the Undoing of the Second Reconstruction*. Chapel Hill: University of North Carolina Press, 1999.

Kurashige, Scott. "Between 'White Spot' and 'World City': Racial Integration and the Roots of Multiculturalism." In *A Companion to Los Angeles*, edited by William Deverell and Greg Hise. Oxford, UK: Wiley-Blackwell, 2010.

Laslett, John H. M. *Shameful Victory: The Los Angeles Dodgers, the Red Scare, and the Hidden History of Chavez Ravine*. Tucson: University of Arizona Press, 2015.

————. *Sunshine Was Never Enough: Los Angeles Workers, 1880–2010*. Berkeley: University of California Press, 2012.

Lee, Eugene C., and Bruce E. Keith. *California Votes, 1960–1972*. Berkeley, CA: Institute of Governmental Studies, 1974.

Leggett, John C. *Mining the Fields: Farm Workers Fight Back*. Lanham, MD: Rowman and Littlefield, 1998.

Leonard, Kevin Allen. *The Battle for Los Angeles: Racial Ideology and World War II*. Albuquerque: University of New Mexico Press, 2006.

Lewis, Dan A., and Kathryn Nakagawa, *Race and Educational Reform in the American Metropolis*. Albany, NY: SUNY Press, 1995.

Lewthwaite, Stephanie. *Race, Place, and Reform in Mexican Los Angeles: A Transnational Perspective, 1890–1940*. Tucson: University of Arizona Press, 2009.

Levin-Waldman, Oren M. *The Political Economy of the Living Wage: A Study of Four Cities*. New York, NY: Taylor and Francis, 2005.

Levy, Jacques E. *Cesar Chavez: Autobiography of La Causa*. New York, NY: W. W. Norton & Company, 1975.

Linder, Marc. "Farm Workers and the Fair Labor Standards Act: Racial Discrimination in the New Deal." *Texas Law Review* 65, no. 7 (June 1987): 1353–80.

Lomelí, Francisco A. "Revisiting the Vision of Aztlán." In *Aztlán: Essays on the Chicano Homeland*, edited by Rudolfo Anaya, Francisco Lomelí, and Enrique R. Lamadrid. Albuquerque: University of New Mexico Press, 2017.

Lombardo, Paul A. *A Century of Eugenics in America: From the Indiana Experiment to the Human Genome Era*. Bloomington: Indiana University Press, 2011.

Luce, Stephanie. "Living Wages, Minimum Wages, and Low-Wage Workers." In *What Works for Workers?*, edited by Stephanie Luce, Jennifer Luff, Joseph A. McCartin, and Ruth Milkman. New York, NY: Russell Sage Foundation, 2014.

Lueders et al., "Providing Driver's Licenses to Unauthorized Immigrants in California Improves Traffic Safety." *PNAS* 114, no. 16 (April 18, 2017): 4111-4116.

Lustig, R. Jeffrey, ed., *Remaking California: Reclaiming the Public Good*. Berkeley, CA: Heyday Books, 2010.

Martin, Philip L. *Promise Unfulfilled: Unions, Immigration, and the Farm Workers*. Ithaca, NY: Cornell University Press, 2003.

Martinez, Al. *Rising Voices: Profiles in Leadership*. Glendale, CA: Nestle, 1993.

Martinez HoSang, Daniel. *Racial Propositions: Ballot Initiatives and the Making of Postwar California*. Berkeley: University of California Press, 2010.

Matthews, Jay. *Escalante: The Best Teacher in America*. New York, NY: Henry Holt, 1988.

Mathews, Joe, and Mark Paul. "How to Fix a Broken State." *Boom: A Journal of California* 1, no. 1 (Spring 2011): 25–35.

Matthiessen, Peter. *Sal Si Puedes (Escape if You Can): Cesar Chavez and the New American Revolution*. New York, NY: Random House, 1972.

McAndrews, Lawrence J. *The Era of Education: The Presidents and the Schools, 1965–2001*. Champaign: University of Illinois Press, 2006.

McWilliams, Carey. *Factories in the Field: The Story of Migratory Farm Labor in California*. Berkeley: University of California Press, 1939, 2000.

———. *North from Mexico: The Spanish-Speaking People of the United States*. Westport, CT: Greenwood Press 1948, 1975, 1990.

Medeiros, Francine. "*La Opinión*, A Mexican Exile Newspaper: A Content Analysis of Its First Years, 1926–1929." *Aztlán* 11, no. 1 (Spring 1980).

Mellow, Nicole. "The Democratic Fit: Party Reform, and the Eugenics Tool." In *The Progressives' Century: Political Reform, Constitutional Government, and the Modern American State*, edited by Stephen Skowronek, Stephen M. Engel, and Bruce Ackerman. New Haven, CT: Yale University Press, 2016.

Milkman, Ruth. *L.A. Story: Immigrant Workers and the Future of the U.S. Labor Movement*. New York, NY: Russell Sage Foundation, 2006.

———. "New Workers, New Labor, and the New Los Angeles." In *Unions in a Globalized Environment: Changing Borders, Organizational Boundaries and Social Roles*, edited by Bruce Nissen. New York, NY: Routledge, 2002.

Milkman, Ruth, and Kent Wong, "'Sí, Se Puede': Union Organizing Strategies and Immigrant Workers." In Milkman, ed. *L.A. Story*, 145–86.

Mora, Cristina G. *Making Hispanics: How Activists, Bureaucrats, and Media Constructed a New American*. Chicago, IL: University of Chicago Press, 2014.

Moynihan, Daniel P. *Maximum Feasible Misunderstanding: Community Action in the War on Poverty*. New York, NY: Free Press, 1969.

Mundigo Alex I., and Dora P. Crouch. "The City Planning Ordinances of the Laws of the Indies Revisited. Part I: Their Philosophy and Implications." *The Town Planning Review* 48, no. 3 (July 1977): 254–55.

Muñoz, Carlos, Jr. *Youth, Identity, Power: The Chicano Movement*. New York, NY: Verso, 2007.

Nava, Julian. *Julian Nava: My Mexican American Journey*. Houston, TX: Arte Público Press, 2002.

Navarro, Carlos, and Rodolfo Acuña. "In Search of Community: A Comparative Essay on Mexicans in Los Angeles and San Antonio." In *20th Century Los Angeles: Power, Promotion and Social Conflict*, edited by Norman M. Klein and Martin J. Schiesl. Claremont, CA: Regina Books, 1990.

Ness, Immanuel. "Labor Keeps the Democratic Party Accountable." *Working USA* 4 (2000): 127–35.

Nicolaides, Becky. "Survey LA: Latino Los Angeles Historic Context Statement." Los Angeles Department of City Planning, Office of Historic Resources (September 15, 2015), https://preservation.lacity.org/news/ohr-publishes-latino-los-angeles-historic-context-statement.

———. "'Where the Working Man is Welcomed': Working-Class Suburbs in Los Angeles, 1900–1940." *Pacific Historical Review* 68, no. 4 (November 1999): 517–59.

Nieto Gomez, Anna. "Chicana Service Action Center." In García, *Chicana Feminist Thought*, 148–50.

Noriega, Chon, et al., eds. *The Chicano Studies Reader: An Anthology of Aztlán*. Los Angeles: UCLA Chicano Studies Research Center Press, 2001, 2011, 2016.

North, David. "Immigration Reform in Its First Year." Center for Immigration Studies. CIS Paper #4 (November 1, 1987).

Ocampo, Anthony Christian. *The Latinos of Asia: How Filipino Americans Break the Rules of Race*. Stanford, CA: Stanford University Press, 2016.

O'Connor, Michan Andrew. "'Public Benefits from Public Choice': Producing Decentralization in Metropolitan Los Angeles, 1954–1973." *Journal of Urban History* 39, no. 1 (2013): 79–100.

———. "'These Communities Have the Most to Gain from Valley Cityhood': Color-Blind Rhetoric of Urban Secession in Los Angeles, 1996–2002." *Journal of Urban History* 40, no. 1 (2014): 48–64.

Office of the Historian, U.S. House of Representatives. *Hispanic Americans in Congress, 1822-2012*, 2nd Ed. Washington, DC: Government Printing Office, 2014.

Olivas, Michael A. "From a 'Legal Organization of Militants' Into a 'Law Firm for the Latino Community': MALDEF and the Purposive Cases of Keyes, Rodriguez and Plyler." *Denver University Law Review* 90, no. 5.

Oliveira, Annette. "Mexican American Defense and Educational Fund." In *Latinas in the United States: A Historical Encyclopedia*, edited by Vicki Ruiz and Virginia Sanchez Korrol. Bloomington: Indiana University Press, 2006.

Oropeza, Lorena. *¡Raza Sí! ¡Guerra No! Chicano Protest and Patriotism during the Vietnam War Era*. Berkeley: University of California Press, 2005.

Osuna, Juan P. "Amnesty in the Immigration Reform and Control Act of 1986." *American University International Law Review* 3, no. 1 (1988): 145–96.

Pardo, Mary. *Mexican American Women Activists*. Philadelphia, PA: Temple University Press, 1998.

Parker, Caitlin. "Hotel Workers Transform the Labor Movement." In *Nonviolence and Social Movements: The Teachings of Rev. James M. Lawson, Jr.*, edited by Kent Wong et al. Los Angeles, CA: UCLA Center for Labor Research and Education, 2016.

Pastor, Manuel. "Contemporary Voice: Contradictions, Coalitions and Common Ground." In *A Companion to Los Angeles*, edited by William Deverell and Greg Hise. Malden, MA: Wiley-Blackwell, 2010.

Pastor, Manuel, Chris Benner, and Martha Matsuoka. *This Could Be the Start of Something Big: How Social Movements for Regional Equity Are Reshaping Metropolitan America*. Ithaca, NY: Cornell University Press, 2009.

Pawel, Miriam. *The Crusades of Cesar Chavez: A Biography*. New York, NY: Bloomsbury Press, 2014.

———. *The Union of Their Dreams: Power, Hope and Struggle in Cesar Chavez's Farm Worker Movement*. New York, NY: Bloomsbury Press, 2009.

Payne, Gregory. "Shaping the Race Issue: A Special Kind of Journalism." *Political Communication* 5, no. 3: 145–60.

Payne, Gregory, and Scott C. Ratzan. *Tom Bradley: The Impossible Dream*. Santa Monica, CA: Roundtable Publishing, 1986.

Perea, Juan F. "The Black/White Binary Paradigm of Race: The Normal Science of American Racial Thought." *California Law Review* 85, no. 5 (October 1997): 1213.

———. "Death by English." In *The Latino/a Condition: A Critical Reader*, edited by Richard Delgado and Jean Stefancic. New York: NYU Press, 1998.

———. "The Echoes of Slavery: Recognizing the Racist Origins of the Agricultural and Domestic Worker Exclusion from the National Labor Relations Act." *Ohio State Law Journal* 71, no. 1 (2011): 95–138.

———. "Five Axioms in Search of Equality." *Harvard Latino Law Review* 231 (Fall 1997): 231–37.

———. "Los Olvidados: On the Making of Invisible People." *New York University Law Review* 70, no. 4 (October 1995): 965–77.

Perkins, R. Colby. "Evaluating the Passel-Word Spanish Surname List: 1990 Decennial Census Post Enumeration Survey Results." U.S. Bureau of the Census. Population Division Working Paper No. 4 (August 1993).

Phillips, Kevin P. *The Emerging Republican Majority*. New Rochelle, NY: Arlington House, 1969; Princeton, NJ: Princeton University Press, 2014.

Pitti, Stephen J. *The Devil in Silicon Valley: Northern California, Race, and Mexican Americans*. Princeton, NJ: Princeton University Press, 2003.

Podair, Jerald. *City of Dreams: Dodger Stadium and the Birth of Modern Los Angeles*. Princeton, NJ: Princeton University Press, 2017.

Prewitt, Kenneth. *What is "Your" Race? The Census and Our Flawed Efforts to Classify Americans*. Princeton and Oxford: Princeton University Press, 2013.

Pulido, Laura. *Black, Brown, Yellow, and Left: Radical Activism in Los Angeles*. Berkeley: University of California Press, 2006.

———. *Environmentalism and Economic Justice: Two Chicano Struggles in the Southwest*. Tucson: University of Arizona Press, 1996.

Putnam, Jackson K. "The Progressive Legacy in California: Fifty Years of Politics, 1917–1967." In *California Progressivism Revisited*, edited by William Deverell and Tom Sitton. Berkeley: University of California Press, 1994.

Pycior, Julie Leininger. *LBJ and Mexican Americans: The Paradox of Power*. Austin: University of Texas Press, 1997.

Quinn, T. Anthony. *Carving Up California: A History of Redistricting, 1951–1984*. Claremont McKenna College: Rose Institute of State and Local Government, 1988.

Ramos, George, and Frank Sotomayor. *Southern California's Latino Community: A Series of Articles Reprinted from the Los Angeles Times*. Los Angeles, CA: *Los Angeles Times*, 1983.

Rappaport, Julian. "In Praise of Paradox: A Social Policy of Empowerment Over Prevention." *American Journal of Community Psychology* 9, no. 1 (1981): 1–25.

Reps, John William. *The Making of Urban America: A History of City Planning in the United States*. Princeton, NJ: Princeton University Press, 1992.

Reeves, Richard. *President Nixon: Alone in the White House*. New York, NY: Simon & Schuster, 2001.

Richardson, James. *Willie Brown: A Biography*. Berkeley: University of California Press, 1996.

Richardson, Peter. *American Prophet: The Life and Work of Carey McWilliams*. Ann Arbor: University of Michigan Press, 2010.

Rieff, David. *Los Angeles: Capital of the Third World*. New York, NY: Touchstone, 1992.

Rivas-Rodriquez, Maggie. "The Mexican Exile Publisher Who Conquered San Antonio and Los Angeles." *American Journalism: A Journal of Media History* 21, no. 1 (Winter 2004): 75–89.

Rodriguez, David. *Latino National Political Coalitions: Struggles and Challenges*. New York, NY: Routledge, 2002.

Rodríguez Chávez, Marisela. "'We Have a Long, Beautiful History': Chicana Feminist Trajectories and Legacies." In *No Permanent Waves: Recasting*

Histories of U.S. Feminism, edited by Nancy A. Hewitt. New Brunswick, NJ: Rutgers University Press, 2010.

Romo, Ricardo. *East Los Angeles: History of a Barrio*. Austin: University of Texas Press, 1983.

Rothstein, Richard. *The Color of Law: A Forgotten History of How Our Government Segregated America*. New York, NY: Liveright Publishing, 2017.

Rudd, Hynda L., and Tom Sitton. *The Development of Los Angeles City Government: An Institutional History, 1850–2000*. Los Angeles, CA: Los Angeles City Historical Society, 2007.

Salazar, Ruben. *Border Correspondent: Selected Writings, 1955–1970*, edited and with introduction by Mario T. García. Berkeley: University of California Press, 1995.

Sanchez, Carlos. "The 'Golden Age' of Spanish-Language Theaters in Los Angeles: The Formation of a Transnational Cinema Audience." *Film Matters* 6, no. 1 (March 2015): 38–44.

Sanchez, George J. *Becoming Mexican American*. New York and Oxford: Oxford University Press, 1993.

———. "Disposable People, Expendable Neighborhoods." In *A Companion to Los Angeles*, edited by William Deverell and Greg Hise. West Sussex, UK: Wiley-Blackwell, 2010.

———. "Edward R. Roybal and the Politics of Multiracialism." *Southern California Quarterly* 92, no. 1 (Spring 2010): 51–73.

Sandoval, Gerardo. *Immigrants and the Revitalization of Los Angeles: Development and Change in MacArthur Park*. Amherst, NY: Cambria Press, 2010.

———. "Transforming Transit-Oriented Development Projects via Immigrant-Led Revitalization: The MacArthur Park Case." In *Immigration and Metropolitan Revitalization in the United States*, edited by Domenic Vitello and Thomas J. Sugrue. Philadelphia: University of Pennsylvania Press, 2017.

Schrag, Peter. *Not Fit for Our Society: Nativism and Immigration*. Berkeley: University of California Press, 2010.

———. *Paradise Lost: California's Experience, America's Future*. New York, NY: New Press, 1998.

Schwarzenegger, Arnold. *Total Recall: My Unbelievably True Life Story*. New York, NY: Simon & Schuster, 2013.

Schwendinger, Herman. "Editorial." *Crime and Social Justice: A Journal of Radical Criminology* 1 (Spring-Summer 1974), www.socialjusticejournal.org/SJEdits/01Edit.html.

Scott, William. *Troublemakers: Power, Representation, and the Fiction of the Mass Worker*. New Brunswick, NJ: Rutgers University Press, 2011.

Shafer, Byron E. *Quiet Revolution: The Struggle for the Democratic Party and the Shaping of Post-Reform Politics*. New York, NY: Russell Sage Foundation, 1983.

Sharma, Preeti. "The Philosophy of Nonviolence." In Wong et al., *Nonviolence and Social Movements*, 6–16.

Shaw, Randy. *Beyond the Fields: Cesar Chavez, the UFW, and the Struggle for Justice in the 21st Century.* Berkeley: University of California Press, 2008.

Skerry, Peter. *Mexican Americans: The Ambivalent Minority.* New York, NY: Free Press, 1993.

Skrentny, John D. *The Minority Rights Revolution.* Cambridge, MA: Harvard University Press, 2004.

Slessarev-Jamir, Helene. *Prophetic Activism: Progressive Religious Movements in Contemporary America.* New York: NYU Press, 2011.

Smith, Daniel A. "Direct Democracy and Candidate Elections." In *The Electoral Challenge: Theory Meets Practice*, edited by Stephen C. Craig and David B. Hill. Washington, DC: CQ Press, 2010.

Sonenshein, Raphael J. *Politics in Black and White: Race and Power in Los Angeles.* Princeton, NJ: Princeton University Press, 1993.

Sotomayor, Frank O. *The Pulitzer Long Shot: How Our 1983 Latino Stories for L.A. Times Won Journalism's Top Prize.* Frank O. Sotomayor, 2017, http://jourviz.com/long-shot/index.html.

———. "Foreword." Sotomayor and Beltrán-del Olmo, *Frank del Olmo*, 17–21.

Sotomayor, Frank, and Magdalena Beltrán-del Olmo, eds. *Frank del Olmo: Commentaries on His Times.* Los Angeles, CA: *Los Angeles Times*, 2004.

Spencer, Gregory. *Projections of the Population of the United States by Age, Sex and Race: 1983 to 2080.* U.S. Bureau of the Census, Current Population Reports, Series P-25, No. 952. Washington, DC: Government Printing Office, May 1984.

———. *Projections of the Hispanic Population: 1983 to 2080.* U.S. Bureau of the Census, Current Population Reports, Series P-25, No. 995. Washington, DC: Government Printing Office, November 1986.

Stansbury, Jeff. "L.A. Labor & the New Immigrants." *Labor Research Review* 1, no. 13 (April 1989), http://digitalcommons.ilr.cornell.edu/lrr/vol1/iss13/8.

Starr, Kevin. *California: A History.* New York, NY: Modern Library Chronicles, 2007.

———. *Embattled Dreams: California in War and Peace, 1940–1950.* New York and Oxford: Oxford University Press, 2002.

———. *Golden Dreams: California in an Age of Abundance, 1950–1963.* New York and Oxford: Oxford University Press, 2009.

———. *Inventing the Dream: California through the Progressive Era.* New York and Oxford: Oxford University Press, 1985.

———. *Material Dreams: Southern California through the 1920s.* New York and Oxford: Oxford University Press, 1990.

Stern, Alexandra Minna. *Eugenic Nation: Faults and Frontiers of Better Breeding in Modern America.* Oakland: University of California Press, 2015.

Strecker, David E. *Labor Law: A Basic Guide to the National Labor Relations Act.* Boca Raton, FL: CRC Press, 2011.

Strum, Philippa. *Mendez v. Westminster: School Desegregation and Mexican-American Rights.* Lawrence: University Press of Kansas, 2010.

Swatt, Steve. *Game Changers: Twelve Elections That Transformed California.* Berkeley, CA: California Historical Society, 2015.

Tajima-Peña, Renee. "'Más Bebés?': An Investigation of the Sterilization of Mexican-American Women at Los Angeles County-USC Medical Center During the 1960s and '70s." *The Scholar & Feminist Online* 11, no. 3 (Summer 2013), http://sfonline.barnard.edu/life-un-ltd-feminism-bioscience-race/mas-bebes-an-investigation-of-the-sterilization-of-mexican-american-women-at-los-angeles-county-usc-medical-center-during-the-1960s-and-70s/0/#.

Taylor, Dorceta. *The State of Diversity in Environmental Organizations* (Green 2.0, July 2014), http://www.diversegreen.org/wp-content/uploads/2015/10/FullReport_Green2.0_FINAL.pdf.

———. *Toxic Communities: Environmental Racism, Industrial Pollution and Residential Mobility.* New York: NYU Press, 2014.

Thompson, Gabriel. *America's Social Arsonist: Fred Ross and Grassroots Organizing in the Twentieth Century.* Oakland: University of California Press, 2016.

Tichenor, Daniel J. "Splitting the Coalition: The Political Perils and Opportunities of Immigration Reform." In *Building Coalitions, Making Policy: The Politics of the Clinton, Bush and Obama Presidencies*, edited by Martin A. Levin, Daniel DiSalvo, and Martin M. Shapiro. Baltimore, MD: Johns Hopkins University Press, 2012.

Tompkins, Adam. *Ghostworkers and Greens: The Cooperative Campaigns of Farmworkers and Environmentalists for Pesticide Reform.* Ithaca, NY: Cornell University Press, 2016.

Torres, Esteban E. "New Spirit in the Barrios." *Cry California* 8, no. 4 (Fall 1973). Reprinted in the *Congressional Record*, Proceedings and Debates of the 93rd Congress, First Session, Volume 119–Part 30, p. 39143.

Tushnet, Mark V. *The NAACP Legal Strategy against Segregated Education, 1925–1950.* Chapel Hill: University of North Carolina Press, 1987.

Tyson, Vanessa. *Twists of Fate: Multiracial Coalitions and Minority Representation in the US House of Representatives.* New York and Oxford: Oxford University Press, 2016.

Underwood, Katherine. "Pioneering Minority Representation: Edward Roybal and the Los Angeles City Council, 1949–1962." *Pacific Historical Review* 66, no. 3 (August 1997): 399–425.

US Bureau of the Census. "Persons of Spanish Surname." U.S. Census of the Population: 1950, Vol. IV Special Reports, Part 3, Chapter C. Washington, DC: Government Printing Office 1953.

Valencia, Richard R. *Chicano Students and the Courts: The Mexican American Legal Struggle for Educational Equality.* New York: NYU Press, 2008.

Vigil, James Diego. *Gang Redux: A Balanced Anti-Gang Strategy.* Long Grove, IL: Waveland Press, 2010.

———. *The Projects: Gang and Non-Gang Families in East Los Angeles.* Austin: University of Texas Press, 2007.

Voegeli, William. "Failed State." *Claremont Review of Books* 4, no. 4 (Fall 2009).

Wald, Sarah D. *The Nature of California: Race, Citizenship, and Farming since the Dust Bowl.* Seattle: University of Washington Press, 2016.

Waldinger, Roger, and Jennifer Lee. "New Immigrants in Urban America." In *Strangers at the Gates: New Immigrants in Urban America,* edited by Roger Waldinger. Berkeley: University of California Press, 2001.

Walker, Gordon. *Environmental Justice: Concepts, Evidence and Politics.* New York, NY: Routledge, 2012.

Weber, David J. "Spanish-Mexican Rim." In *The Oxford History of the American West,* edited by Clyde A. Milner II, Carol A. O'Connor, and Martha A. Sandweiss. New York and Oxford: Oxford University Press, 1994.

Welch, Susan, Albert K. Karnig, and Richard Eribes. "Changes in Hispanic Local Public Employment in the Southwest." *The Western Political Quarterly* 36, no. 4 (December 1983): 660–73.

West, Cornel. *Race Matters.* Boston, MA: Beacon Press, 2001.

Wilentz, Sean. *The Politicians and the Egalitarians: The Hidden History of American Politics.* New York, NY: W. W. Norton & Company, 2016.

Wilson, Karen S., ed. *Jews in the Los Angeles Mosaic.* Berkeley: University of California Press, 2013.

Wong, Kent. "Cultural Democracy and the Revitalization of the U.S. Labor Movement." In *Culture and Difference: Critical Perspectives on the Bicultural Experience in the United States,* edited by Antonia Darder. Westport, CT: Bergin & Garvey, 1995.

Wong, Kent, and Michael Viola, *Miguel Contreras: Legacy of a Labor Leader.* Los Angeles, CA: UCLA Center for Labor Research and Education, 2009.

Wong, Kent, Ana Luz González, and Rev. James M. Lawson Jr. et al. *Nonviolence and Social Movements: The Teachings of Rev. James M. Lawson Jr.* Los Angeles, CA: UCLA Center for Labor Research and Education, 2016.

Word, David L., and R. Colby Perkins, Jr. "Building a Spanish Surname List for the 1990s—A New Approach to an Old Problem." U.S. Bureau of the Census, Population Division Technical Working Paper No. 13 (March 1996).

Young, Julia G. "Making America 1920 Again? Nativism and US Immigration, Past and Present." *Journal on Migration and Human Security* 5, no. 1 (2017): 217–35, https://doi.org/10.14240/jmhs.v5i1.81.

———. *Mexican Exodus: Emigrants, Exiles, and Refugees of the Cristero War.* New York and Oxford: Oxford University Press, 2015.

Zacchino, Narda. *California Comeback: How a "Failed State" Became a Model for the Nation*. New York, NY: Thomas Dunne Books, 2016.

Dissertations and Theses

Espino, Virginia Rose. "Women Sterilized As They Give Birth: Population Control, Eugenics, and Social Protest in the Twentieth-Century United States." PhD diss., Arizona State University, 2007. University Microform Edition, 2008.

Leal, Jorge Nicolás. "Paving the Road to the White House or to La Panamericana? The Post-Electoral Hopes of the Southern California Viva Kennedy Clubs, 1960–1963." Masters thesis, California State University, Northridge, 2011.

Marín, Christine. "Always a Struggle: Mexican Americans in Miami, Arizona, 1909–1951." PhD diss., Arizona State University, 2005.

Rodríguez Chávez, Marisela. "Despierten Hermanas y Hermanos! Women, the Chicano Movement, and Chicana Feminisms in California, 1966-1981." PhD diss., Stanford University, 2004.

Sherman, Martin P. "Maximum Feasible Participation: The First Commandment of the War on Poverty." LL.M., University of Southern California, 1969. Hein's Legal Theses and Dissertations, 015–00080.

White, Joseph. "The Functions and Power of the House Appropriations Committee." PhD diss., University of California, Berkeley, 1989.

Films

Alfaro, Henry, dir. *Symbol of Heart: The Official Documentary of the East Los Angeles Classic*. Carmona Productions, 2003.

Goldfarb, Lyn, dir. *The New Los Angeles*. Los Angeles, CA: Lyn Goldfarb Productions, 2005.

Goldfarb, Lyn, dir., and Alison Sotomayor, prod. *Bridging the Divide: Tom Bradley and the Politics of Race*. Los Angeles, CA: Lyn Goldfarb Productions, 2015.

Gudiño, Roberto, dir. *Below the Fold: The Pulitzer That Defined Latino Journalism*. Gudino Productions; Working Title Films, 2007.

Rodriguez, Phillip, dir. *Ruben Salazar: Man in the Middle*. Los Angeles, CA: City Projects, LLC, 2014.

Snider, Cory, Eduard Grau, Josh Greenbaum, Nadav Schirman, Saar Klein, and Stevan Riley, dirs. *The Classic*. Los Angeles, CA: Delirio Films, 2017.

Tajima-Peña, Renee, dir. *No Más Bebés*. ITVS, 2015.

About the Authors

David R. Ayón, Senior Strategist and Advisor to Latino Decisions and Senior Fellow at the Center for the Study of Los Angeles, was born and raised in El Paso, Texas, and has been a student, teacher, and writer of the Latino political experience since the late 1970s. A graduate of Princeton University, his education includes doctoral studies at Stanford and graduate work at El Colegio de México. Ayón has taught Latino politics at California colleges and universities from Stanford to UC San Diego, as well as Occidental College, USC, and Loyola Marymount University in LA. His writings on Latino politics have appeared in *Los Angeles Times*, *La Opinión*, the Latin American edition of *Foreign Affairs*, *The American Prospect*, and in some 15 edited books and other publications in the United States and Mexico, including *The Oxford Encyclopedia of Latinos and Latinas in Contemporary Politics, Law and Social Movements*, and a regular political column for the Univision network news website (2014–15). A former Senior Advisor to the Mexico Institute of the Woodrow Wilson International Center for Scholars, Ayón was honored in 2012 as a White House "Champion of Change," served on the board of the U.S.-Mexico Foundation, co-chaired its Mexican American Leadership Initiative (MALI), and is a member of the Council on Foreign Relations and its term membership committee.

George L. Pla, Founder & CEO of Cordoba Corporation, is an entrepreneur and philanthropist dedicated to empowering Latino and underrepresented communities nationwide. Pla has worked throughout the California political landscape, from his start in grassroots community activism, to becoming one of the youngest officials in California Gov. Jerry Brown's first administration, to currently acting as advisor to officials in California and Washington, DC. He is Regent Emeritus at Loyola Marymount University, Presidential Associate at the University of Southern California, co-founder of the USC Latino Alumni Association, and a counselor to USC's Price School of Public Policy and UCLA's Luskin School of Public Affairs. For his support of educational institutions and public policy initiatives, Pla has received national recognition and numerous awards, including the Presidential Medallion from California State University, Los Angeles. Pla is an alumnus of East Los Angeles

Community College and California State University, Los Angeles, and holds a graduate degree in public administration from the Price School of Public Policy at the University of Southern California. Cordoba Corporation is a nationally ranked engineering and construction management firm whose business model can be found in a case study at the Harvard Business School.

Index